GW01373450

Applied Mysticism

Applied Mysticism
Studies of Meditation
and Psychedelics in Secular Contexts

RICHARD H. JONES

**SUNY
PRESS**

Published by State University of New York Press, Albany

© 2025 State University of New York

All rights reserved

Printed in the United States of America

No part of this book may be used or reproduced in any manner whatsoever without written permission. No part of this book may be stored in a retrieval system or transmitted in any form or by any means including electronic, electrostatic, magnetic tape, mechanical, photocopying, recording, or otherwise without the prior permission in writing of the publisher.

Links to third-party websites are provided as a convenience and for informational purposes only. They do not constitute an endorsement or an approval of any of the products, services, or opinions of the organization, companies, or individuals. SUNY Press bears no responsibility for the accuracy, legality, or content of a URL, the external website, or for that of subsequent websites.

EU GPSR Authorised Representative:
Logos Europe, 9 rue Nicolas Poussin, 17000, La Rochelle, France
contact@logoseurope.eu

For information, contact State University of New York Press, Albany, NY
www.sunypress.edu

Library of Congress Cataloging-in-Publication Data

Name: Jones, Richard H., 1951– author.
Title: Applied mysticism : studies of meditation and psychedelics in
    secular contexts / Richard H. Jones.
Description: Albany, NY : State University of New York Press, [2025] |
    Includes bibliographical references and index.
Identifiers: LCCN 2024039355 | ISBN 9798855801507 (hardcover : alk. paper) |
    ISBN 9798855801521 (ebook)
Subjects: LCSH: Meditation. | Hallucinogenic drugs. | Civilization, Secular.
Classification: LCC BL627 .J64 2025 | DDC 204/.22—dc23/eng/20241206
LC record available at https://lccn.loc.gov/2024039355

Contents

Acknowledgments		vii
Preface		ix
1	Mystical Experiences and the Neuroscientific Study of Meditators	1
2	Limitations on the Neuroscientific Study of Drug-Enabled Mystical Experiences	29
3	Pure Consciousness, Intentionality, Selflessness, and the Philosopher's Syndrome	69
4	Triggers of Altered States of Consciousness Experiences	89
5	Cognitive Bias in Mysticism and Its Study	103
6	Mystical Experiences, Consciousness, and Inverse Multiple Realization	117
7	The Role of Mystical Experiences in Psychedelic Therapy and Research	127
8	Secular Mysticism	159
9	Quantum Mysticism: Science Meets Mysticism in the New Age	189

10 Applying Mysticism to Social Action Today	227
Notes	259
References	287
Index	323

Acknowledgments

"Limitations on the Neuroscientific Study of Mystical Experiences," *Zygon: Journal of Science and Religion* 53 (4, December 2018): 992–1017.

"Limitations on the Scientific Study of Drug-Enabled Mystical Experiences," *Zygon: Journal of Science and Religion* 54 (3, September 2019): 756–92.

"Pure Consciousness, Intentionality, Selflessness, and Philosophers," *Journal of Consciousness Studies* 31 (3–4, 2024): 83–102.

"On the Role of Mysticism in Psychedelic Therapy and Research," *Journal of Psychedelic Psychiatry* 5 (2, June 2023): 26–47.

"Secular Mysticism," *Religions* 13 (7, July 2022): 650–77.

"Mysticism in the New Age: Are Mysticism and Science Converging?" in *Mysticism and Meaning*, ed. Alex S. Kohav, 249–77 (St. Petersburg, FL: Three Pines Press, 2019).

"The Lack of Social Action," in *Mysticism and Morality: A New Look at Old Questions*, by Richard H. Jones, 347–377 (Lanham, MD: Lexington Books, 2004).

All are published with the permission of the copyright owners and are revised and expanded.

Preface

Today is an exciting time for mystical studies. Scientists in the field of consciousness research are taking mystical experiences seriously (at least as mental events)—they are studying meditators and psychedelic subjects to gain knowledge of the brain and states of consciousness. Interest in such experiences is also ticking upward among academics, psychotherapists, the religious, and the spiritual among the unaffiliated (the "nones"). Mindfulness (broadly construed) is now a billion-dollar business worldwide.

This interest today often involves "applied mysticism." To be clear on terminology, "mystical experience" in this book does not denote all altered state of consciousness (ASC) experiences (e.g., visions or the sense of the presence of something distinct from oneself) but only short-term ASC episodes involving a direct (and hence "nondual") awareness of reality free of a sense of a discrete experiencing self or conceptualized differentiations. In some experiences, a sense of an experiencing self or of conceptual differentiations is only lessened and not completely eliminated. The paradigm of mystical experiences involves an inner awareness of a transcendent source of worldly phenomena (e.g., God or Brahman/Atman) or our true self/soul. But it should be noted that not all mystical experiences are tied to such alleged realities: mindfulness and nature mysticism involves only natural phenomena (and thus are "extrovertive"), but they are still genuinely mystical when "mystical" is defined in terms of experiences of selflessness (see R. Jones 2021a: 9–24 on types of mystical experiences). "Mystical states" will refer to more enduring selfless ASC states. Mystical altered state of consciousness experiences are what distinguishes mysticism from metaphysics and other forms of religiosity, but they are not the goal in traditional forms of mysticism—aligning one's life with what is deemed basically real is the goal, and the ASC experiences are only part of the process. Mystical experiences may or may not transform an experiencer's beliefs and outlook, their behavior, or their entire being. "Mystical enlightenment" is an enduring state of consciousness free of a sense of an encased phenomenal ego in which our conceptualizations are not seen as reflections of reality but only as our structuring. In mysticisms that value introvertive mystical experiences as epistemically central, enlightenment is seen as retaining contact with transcendent realities. "Mysticism" will be any encompassing system or way of life devoted to attaining enlightenment or at least a mystical state of consciousness (see R. Jones 2021a: 1–62). The adjective "mystical" will refer to the doctrines, codes of conduct, practices, rituals, institutions, and other sociocultural phenomena centered around a quest to end the sense of self and to end our conceptualizing mind from controlling our experience in order to bring oneself into a life in harmony with what is deemed fundamentally real.

"Applied mysticism" is not parapsychology or the techniques, disciplines, or practices of a mystical way of life. Nor should applied mysticism be confused with a common usage of the term "practical mysticism"—i.e., the "practical" side of mysticism (any actions by mystics or any practices utilized by mystics in their development [see, e.g., Zarrabi-Zadeh 2009; Gill and Clammer 2019]) or any nonmystical religious or spiritual motivation for social action (Gray and Lovat 2008). Rather, applied mysticism is taking mystical practices and experiences out of their traditional role in classical mysticism as a means for the total transformation of individual practitioners and applying them (often from a secular framework) to help other individuals with more limited problems of well-being in society, for general social change, or otherwise to deal with this-worldly matters. For example, meditators are letting neuroscientists examine their brain activity during meditations through neuroimaging to expand our knowledge of the workings of the brain. So too, Buddhist meditation is being taken out of its religious context as part of a way of life trying to end all of our existential suffering (*dukkha*) by ending our rebirths and is being adapted by psychotherapists to help with people's more limited problems, such as depression or addiction. These applications may lead some people to move in the direction of adopting a mystical way of life, but that is not their purpose. Rather, the intent is to provide only limited help to others that would make them more effective in some area of their daily life. Such applications of mysticism may or may not be of interest to traditional mystics.

Thus, the interest is in mystical experiences and practices as they may aid limited worldly issues, not interest in mystical doctrines or other aspect of mystical ways of life or in a transformation of all aspects of a person's inner life. The term first appeared in print in a letter from Aldous Huxley to Albert Hoffman (who first synthesized LSD) in February 1962:

> I have good hopes that this and similar work will result in the development of a real Natural History of visionary experience, in all its variations, determined by differences of physique, temperament and profession, and at the same time of a technique of Applied Mysticism—a technique for helping individuals to get the most out of their transcendental experience and to make use of the insights from the "Other World" in the affairs of "This World." Meister Eckhart wrote that "what is taken in by contemplation must be given out in love." Essentially this is what must be developed—the art of giving out in love and intelligence what is taken in from vision and the experience of self-transcendence and solidarity with the Universe.

Timothy Leary also was using the term in 1963. For Huxley, applied psychedelic mysticism was "to show how the inward power of these sacramental drugs could be used for the welfare of people living in a technological society hostile to mystical revelations" (A. Hoffman 1999 [1977]: iv). That is, applied mysticism is "a technique for helping individuals to get the most out of their transcendental experience and to make use of their insights from the 'other world' in the affairs of this world" (quoted in A. Hoffman 1999 [1977]: xv). Huxley's novel *Island* shows a society that utilizes psychedelics to design their industrialized culture.

Today this alternative to traditional mysticism is growing. Mystical experiences and states—especially the alleged state that is a selfless consciousness free of any differentiated content ("pure consciousness")—have become of great interest in the study of the brain and the nature of consciousness. Psychedelic-enabled mystical and other experiences and meditation (especially mindfulness broadly construed) are both hot topics in the neuroscientific study of the workings of the brain. Psychotherapists are exploring meditation and psychedelics as ways to help people who are resistant to traditional therapy. Michael Pollan has brought attention to psychedelic therapy in his bestseller *How to Change Your Mind* (2018). Also on the more popular front, New Age thinkers are extolling the alleged merger of post-Newtonian science (especially physics) with mysticism. New Age gurus are bringing "instant enlightenment" to bear on people's personal problems. Applied mysticism in the New Age movement ranges from neoshamanism to such things as "How to Set Prices Mystically."

The new field of "contemplative studies" is developing in universities (see Roth 2006, 2014; Gunnlaugson et al. 2014; Komjathy 2018), but this surge in interest is in the effects of meditation on for our psychological and physiological health rather than any deeper mystical goal. The traditional goal of meditation was a deep exploration of the mind to alter our very being, but today meditation is more often only for the pragmatic application for depression and so forth (Goleman and Davidson 2018: 2–3). Traditional meditative techniques may be adopted to calm the mind or to focus attention on the present moment in order to increase happiness or work efficiency, not for living in accordance with reality in the deepest way human beings are capable of. Some public schools, corporations, and MBA programs now have classes on mindfulness to aid in focusing attention, mental flexibility, efficiency, and decreasing absenteeism. Some medical schools are beginning to train physicians in meditation for clinical work in relieving patients' stress, anxiety, depression, and substance abuse and for pain management. Even the military now has meditation classes, and meditation is being "weaponized" as part of a program to produce "super soldiers" (Komjathy 2018: 194). Most of these objectives are not core goals of traditional forms of mysticism. Specific compassion meditations that are practiced in schools to help students become kinder to other students is the closest any programs come to traditional mysticism.

On the psychedelic front, many advocates see these drugs as having social repercussions: we can solve social problems by individuals having psychedelic-enabled experiences. The drug researcher Rick Doblin believes that mystical experiences can be a tool for political reconciliation—indeed, psychedelics can usher in a global *Pax Psychedelia* (Pace and Devenot 2021: 14). Mindfulness and psychedelics are seen as ushering in another "Great Awakening" that will have great positive social changes. In fact, meditation and psychedelics have been hyped as a cure-all for all social problems, although most researchers resist these grandiose claims.

Thus, applied mysticism differs from traditional mysticism in two ways: the focus is limited to particular worldly problems rather than a radical realignment of an individual's total life with what is deemed most fundamentally real and mystical insights and practices are applied toward helping others with such problems rather than primarily helping oneself. This does give the false impression that traditional mysticism was completely other-worldly and always self-centered. Mystical traditions differ in the degree of the ideal mystic's involvement in the world, but not all mystics are escapists or hermits or otherwise concerned only with themselves. (But neither were all classical mystics morally concerned with others.[1]) Daoism is the paradigm of a mystical tradition focused on this world, and the aspects of it that go beyond instructing how individuals should live in the world and venture into governing and warfare are cases of applied mysticism. But mystics throughout most of the history of the Abrahamic traditions also regularly engaged the world. Helping others with worldly needs (note Huxley's remark above from Eckhart) is a way of bridging the personal nature of mystical inner development with the social world. However, applied mysticism remains more worldly and limited in scope than most traditional mysticism. The psychologist and psychedelic researcher William Richards relates an instance that reflects the new attitude: a successful business leader had a spontaneous experience that met all of Richards's criteria for a genuine mystical consciousness, but the man's response to his experience was "That was nice. What is it good for?" (2016: 124). Looking for concrete help with particular problems in this world is the outlook of applied mysticism, not a quest to realign one's life with how reality truly is.

Applying mysticism to worldly problems makes having a positive impact on the world in general more central than individual enlightenment. It is not about leading others to enlightenment or keeping mystical insights to only a few committed disciples or only teaching a transcendent way to end all our problems, as in most traditional mysticism, but a matter of turning mystical insights into practical help for others with worldly problems. A mystical "insight" may be seen as involving transcendent realities, but for many today it is about simply calming and stabilizing the mind and seeing the interconnectedness of things in the world (both people with people and people with nature). Thereby, mysticism is brought to bear on making the world a better place and helping us feel at home in this world.

Ethics and psychotherapy are the two principal ways that mystical experiences and practices are applied to help others. It has been argued that psychedelic experiences may lead to a selflessness that enhances our cognitive capacity, empathy with others, altruism and service to others in general, and a greater sense of fairness (Ahlskog 2017; Tennison 2012). Virginia Ballesteros (2019) applies psychedelic-enabled mystical experiences toward improving our moral faculties and overcoming our "moral blindness" concerning our environmental and technological obligations. The political scientist Alexander Wendt applies "quantum mysticism" ideas to society and international relations (2015). The "political potential of mindfulness" is being discussed (Chari 2016). Much of the New Age spirituality and the human potential movement exemplified by the Esalen Institute in Big Sur, California, is applied mysticism. Psychedelics and mystical training can also help in other psychological areas—for example, with our creativity and imagination which may help scientists and others in their work and with general problem-solving.[2]

In sum, in the words of Gemini (Bard): "Applied mysticism is the practice of applying mystical insights and techniques to everyday life. It's about bringing the spiritual into the practical realm." That summary omits the central shift from traditional individual mystical concerns to this-worldly ways for helping others, but applied mysticism does, as it says, "seek to bring mystical insights and experiences into the everyday world" and "is not about withdrawing from the world or seeking an escape from reality." Classical mystics would reject characterizing mysticism as escapist rather than a way to get more in touch with a basic reality, but the new focus on helping others with limited worldly needs cannot be denied.

Whether this repurposing of mysticism for secular ends in exploring the nature of the mind and the workings of the brain, psychotherapy and well-being, and social and political action will last is an open question at present. Whether this trend may end up having a negative impact on traditional mysticism within different religious traditions is also an open question. So too, the scientific interest in mystical experiences and states (if not mystical claims about the world) may lead to a reevaluation of mysticism in our current society. But today mysticism outside its traditional settings is having an impact on society that most see as positive.

∽

Applied mysticism can be approached by different disciples in the sciences, social sciences, and humanities, but this book is a collection of essays limited to expounding the nature of applied mysticism and to examining their philosophical issues. The focus will be on some old and some new questions in philosophy of mysticism that the applied mysticism of meditation and psychedelics raises. This influences both philosophy of mysticism (Jones 2016) and the budding field of philosophy of psychedelics (Letheby 2021, forthcoming; Letheby and Mattu 2021; Hauskeller and Sjöstedt-Hughes 2022).

The first two essays discuss limitations in the foundational knowledge of applied mysticism today in the study of the brain and the mind: the neuroscientific study of meditation and psychedelics. Neuroscience has been chosen because that is the primary science studying mystical experiences today and to see, in an instance of applied mysticism, whether mystical experiences can expand our knowledge of how the brain works and the nature of consciousness. The third chapter more deeply explores whether mystical experience may add to our understanding of consciousness—meditation and psychedelics may give scientists access to consciousness in a way that other experiences cannot, but can there be a "pure" consciousness free of both all differentiated content and a sense of a "self" having an experience? The next three essays delve into aspects of the science of mystical experiences rather than deal directly with applied mysticism. The first deals with triggers of mystical experiences. The second deals with the dangers of expectancy bias and confirmation bias in both mystical experiences and in mysticism and its study. These are followed by an admittedly speculative essay on the possibility of the inverse of the issue of the possible "multiple realization" of mental events in different brain states—that different altered states of consciousness may be grounded in the same brain state. The seventh essay examines the role of mysticism in the psychedelic psychotherapy. Next is an essay on the new secular forms of mysticism: applying psychedelic and meditative practices and mystical experiences to gain well-being and a meaning to life within a naturalist framework void of transcendent realities and traditional religious goals. The last two essays show that mysticism can inspire applied mysticism both by mystics and also by those who have not had mystical experiences. First, the advocates of New Age thought attempt to use ideas from Buddhist and Daoist mystical metaphysics to aid science. This leads New Agers to the claim that modern science and ancient wisdom are merging. Finally, the challenges of applying the classical mysticisms from different traditions to social and political matters today are explored. The fact that this type of applied mysticism has been around for centuries is also noted.

Most of the essays here have been previously published, but those have been thoroughly revised here. Some repetitions have been deleted and cross-references supplied, but some duplications are retained so that each chapter remains a self-contained essay. Thus, each chapter can be read separately.

Chapter 1

Mystical Experiences and the Neuroscientific Study of Meditators

With advances in noninvasive brain-imaging technology, the last few decades have seen a marked increase in studies of the effects of meditation and other spiritual exercises (e.g., fasting, prayer, and liturgical practices) on brain activity and on other parts of the body. In particular, the examination of the neurological mechanisms and systems supporting mindfulness meditation has become a "hot topic" (Tang and Posner 2013: 1). The experiences have reproducible and measurable biological effects (Lutz et al. 2007: 257). Scanning subjects' brains during or immediately after meditation has become an important part of the budding field of cognitive neuroscience.[1] The effect of meditation on various physiological functions can be studied (e.g., changes in heart rate, skin resistance, breathing, or a general reduction of metabolic activity), as can changes in the autonomic nervous system and neurochemical activity in the brain. Behavioral changes are also studied to a lesser extent. Meditation's effect on such mental activity as attention, memory, perceptual sensitivity and processing, responses to stimuli, a sense of a "self," and the regulation of emotional states can also be studied. Meditative practices may also induce short- and long-term neural changes (Lutz et al. 2004; Lutz et al. 2015), both of which can be studied.

Brain-imaging technology is beginning to identify specific areas of the brain affected by meditation. Different areas and structures, such as the default mode network, are drawing attention. The left and right parietal lobes are responsible for maintaining both a sense of an experiencing self that is separate from the rest of the universe and a sense of one's body and orientation in space. Decreased activity there is associated with loss of a sense of self—"ego dissolution" to one degree or another, including a complete loss of a sense of self—and thus with an increased sense of "connectedness" or "oneness" with the rest of the universe. The thalamus processes sensory input and the communication between different parts of the brain. It also is important for alertness and consciousness in general. The limbic regions (including the amygdala) are associated with processing emotions. Mindfulness meditation decreases activity in these regions, while compassion meditation increases it. The hippocampus in the limbic system relates to long-term memory and spatial orientation. The right insula and caudate nucleus are associated with empathy and compassion. The frontal cortex relates to higher cognitive activity such as reasoning, analysis, and imagination. Initial meditative reflection may lead to an increase in activity there, leading to a sense of clarity; further meditation leads to decreasing activity, thereby permitting deeper parts of the brain to become more active in consciousness, and this may be connected to the sense of certainty in mystical experiences.[2] Lesions in the frontal and temporal brain regions also inhibit or disable mental executive functions and thereby enable mystical experiences to occur (Cristofori et al. 2016). Disabling some higher cortical functions may permit lower functions to become manifest, but that does not explain why mystical experiences involve simplicity (such as a sense of oneness) and calmness (as sense of peace).

Meditation encompasses any yogic or other attention-based technique for inner transformation that involves the mind or body undertaken to attain a mystical insight (Eifring 2016: 1). Mindfulness is the "awareness that arises through paying attention, on purpose, in the present moment, non-judgmentally" (Kabat-Zinn 2005: 4). Researchers tend to overextend the term "mindfulness" to sustained attention—i.e., to any practices concentrating one's focus—rather than restricting it to simply being mindful of one's mental or bodily states. But there are two different meditative tracks: the concentrative and the mindful. In Buddhism, the distinction is between tranquil concentration (*shamatha*) leading to deeper and deeper concentrative states (*jhanas/dhyanas*) and the more passive, open monitoring mindfulness (*smriti, vipassana*) that leads to the central insight (*prajna*) into the nature of phenomenal reality. The former focuses on a mental or sensory object (e.g., a flame, a crystal, a tradition's doctrine, a textual passage, or a visualized god), and attention is gently brought back to the object when the mind wanders. Thus, the mind is not empty of objects at the beginning of these practices, but one progressively withdraws attention from the focus on the object. Focusing the mind upon a single object calms and stabilizes consciousness and culminates in one-pointed attention (complete *samadhi*). It leads to states of feeling absorbed in the object of meditation, although mindfulness may also do the same. The second track is not about emptying the mind of content but about observing that content—one simply notes whatever floats into the mind. Mindfulness frees experience by removing conceptual encrustation in perception ending ultimately in a "pure awareness" or "effortless attention" that mirrors the flow of what is real as it is presented to the mind unmediated by conceptualizations and a sense of self. But both tracks can empty the mind of the sense of self and all conceptual divisions, leading to a "nondual" awareness that abolishes the distinctions of subject, object, and action. Consciousness seems "expanded" with the loss of a sense of a self-contained experiencer. Any loss of a sense of self will almost by definition be an altered state of consciousness (ASC) since a sense of self is integral to our ordinary modes of consciousness. So too with a loss of a conceptualizing framework for our perceptions. Practitioners can engage in both tracks and shift from one to the other, since mindfulness requires a degree of concentration and vice versa. Focusing on one's breathing is a way that many concentrative and mindfulness meditations start.

Some researchers in the field note that no general definition of "meditation" is utilized in neuroscience and that this leads to grouping all research on different types of meditation together, and that this in turn leads to inconsistent findings (Davanger 2013; Nash and Newberg 2013). Different techniques produce different effects (e.g., see Perlman et al. 2010), and this will be an issue when comparing data.[3] One may mistakenly assume that results from one meditative technique would be duplicated by other meditative techniques. Thus, rather than assuming that all meditative techniques must be alike in their neurological effects, scientists should specify the general features of whatever meditative techniques were involved in their experiment. Overall, scientists should be slow to speak of one generic "meditation effect."

Research results have garnered enthusiasm both from the religious who believe the results prove that mystical experiences are cognitive (e.g., Beauregard and O'Leary 2007) and thus prove some religious claim, and from materialists who believe that the results prove mystical experiences are only brain events and thus refute religious claims (e.g., Persinger 1987).[4] Many religious believers see the science as a validation of age-old wisdom (see Benson and Klipper 2000 [1975]: 75–78). But merely studying the neural bases of religious experiences does not transform neuroscience into a form of theology—"neurotheology" (Newberg 2018). Even if scientists invoke transcendent conceptions as part of an encompassing theory (as with Newberg and d'Aquili's model of an "Absolute Unitary Being"), this still does not make the science a form of *theology* unless the religious theory is actually utilized to *explain* neural events in the brain. And it must be noted that some experiencers today understand their mystical experiences in nonreligious and sometimes explicitly atheistic ways (see chapter 8; Newberg and Waldman 2016: 69–75). Nevertheless, even a critic of neurotheology can accept that "[t]he cognitive neurosciences have extremely rich potential for the study of consciousness, mental states, and senses of the self" (Geertz 2009: 319). But the nature of current neuroscience exposes limitations on what neuroscientists today can reveal about the nature of mystical experiences. Two of these problems are revealed by discussing one set of experiments (the Newberg-d'Aquili experiments) and one issue in the academic study of mystical experiences (constructivism).

Preliminary Points

But before addressing these problems, four preliminary points must be made. First, no one doubts that meditation has effects on the body. After all, meditation is an activity, and it is not surprising that it, like any bodily activity, has effects on brain activity. Calming the mind during meditation will at a minimum probably calm and stabilize some biological functions. There is no reason to deny that such effects may be measurable in different ways. Nor is there any reason to doubt that neuroscientists will eventually identify the exact parts of the brain that become more active or less active in different types of meditative experiences as indicated by electrical neurotransmitter activity measured in electroencephalograms (EEG), by the magnetic fields produced by electrochemical currents occurring in the brain during meditation measured in magnetoencephalograms (MEG), and by blood flow measured by functional magnetic resonance imaging (fMRI), positron emission tomography (PET), and single-photon emission computed tomography (SPECT). EEG and MEG currently are more fine-grained than the other procedures.

All cortical neurons are always active, communicating with each other through neurotransmitter molecules such as serotonin. The form of communication is chemical and also electrical; when groups of neurons in different parts of the brain are executing a particular function, the rate at which they exchange signals increases, while in other parts the rates of signaling remain the same or decrease; the difference in the rate of signaling in the areas executing a particular function is its activation pattern and the set of areas engaged is its functional network; when metabolic activity changes in the network, changes in blood flow can be measured (Papanicolaou 2021: 123).

Different neural and physiological bases and explanations are currently being proposed (for overviews, see Lutz et al. 2007; Schjoedt 2009; Yaden et al. 2017b). Meta-analyses of the models to date show that they are contradictory—even the collected data is not totally consistent (Lazar et al. 2000; Ospina et al. 2007; Sedlmeier et al. 2012; Clausen et al. 2014). There is also concern about trial design in psychedelic studies (and in medical research more generally) (Aday, Carhart-Harris, and Wooley 2023: 533). However, this does not rule out advances in the future and eventual consensus. But establishing a one-to-one correlation of conscious states with states of the brain would permit the stimulation of the mechanisms at work in the brain during particular mystical experiences, thereby enabling the experience. For a true correlation, there must be a one-to-one relation of changes in states of consciousness with changes in bodily states. All the varied phenomenological content of the experiences also must be accounted for.

Secondly, the religious may object that testing for mystical experiences is "putting God to the test," but neuroscientific studies of meditators does not reduce religion to something other than what it is or trivialize the transcendent aspects of religion: merely looking at the measurable bodily effects of mystical experiences does not make the effects a substitute for religion or otherwise reduce religion to something it is not. So too, letting themselves be studied does not reduce meditators to objects or otherwise dehumanize them or alter what they are doing—they are still focused on attaining the real, not conducting scientific experiments on their consciousness. The testing may well be irrelevant to the meditators themselves. Meditators also can acknowledge the biological effects while still maintaining that their objective in their practice is quite different than anything scientists measure to learn about how the brain works, just as they can agree that mystical experiences last a certain measurable amount of time even though they seem timeless to them.

Meditation for classical mystics is part of an encompassing way of life with a spiritual goal: mystics are not meditating only to explore various states of consciousness in an open-minded scientific manner as ends in themselves. Nor are they disinterestedly formulating and testing theories. They are trying to see "reality as it truly is" (as defined by their religious tradition) in order to align their lives with how things really are in order, for example, to end existential suffering or to attune their will to God's will. The popularity of meditation today may be because of its "secular" psychophysical effects, but these are at most secondary to the spiritual goals of classical mystics. Nor are these mystics interested in relaxation rather than greater awareness of true reality. Nor are they interested in the subjective experiences themselves: meditation is to stabilize their attention and to empty their mind of extraneous content in order to see reality clearly for their soteriological goals. For these test subjects, theirs is a traditional mysticism, despite it being applied mysticism for the researchers.

The third point is that it is hard to doubt that there must be a biological basis enabling mystical experiences to occur. These experiences, like all our experiences, are firmly embodied—these experiences are not disembodied transcendent events. That so many mystical techniques—fasting, asceticism, and so forth—speaks to the role of the body. Even all inner meditations affect the brain. Theists may argue that introvertive theistic mystical experiences involve a unique input from God alone. Nevertheless, there must be some basis in the human anatomy that permits God to enter our mind. The Fourteenth Dalai Lama suggests that there may be no neural basis for a transcendent "pure consciousness" (Gyatso and Goleman 2003: 42), but even if such consciousness exists independently of the brain, there still must be some basis in human beings permitting its appearance in us. That is, even if mystics realize a transcendent reality in certain experiences, there still must be some basis in our neurobiology for this to occur, and so mystical states of consciousness must somehow be mediated by the neurological processes in the brain, perhaps aided by the rest of the nervous system.

In sum, like all experiences, mystical experiences have neural substrates and a biochemical basis in our brain whether or not they are cognitive of a transcendent reality—i.e., some brain activity will be occurring when a mystical experience occurs. Mystical experiences do not differ from any other experience in this regard. As professor of behavioral medicine Richard Sloan says, "[T]here is nothing at all remarkable about reporting that ecstatic religious experiences are associated with a neurological substrate" since "all human conscious activity, religious or otherwise, has an underlying counterpart in the brain" (2006: 247, 249). Nor is there any reason to doubt that, like other experiences, scientists can study the brain as these experiences occur and that they may be able to identify their biological bases. Nor is there any reason to doubt that neuroscientists will ultimately be able to give as full an account of the brain mechanisms associated with these experiences—even if a transcendent reality is cognized—as any cognitive experience.

Thus, pointing out neurological bases in no way begs the question of mystical cognitivity: even if these experiences produce an insight, they need a biological basis to appear. For this reason, merely locating the neural basis for mystical experiences does not by itself establish grounds for reducing these experiences to mere subjective events generated by the brain alone—all that the sciences can establish is that certain brain states are associated with these experiences (see R. Jones 2016: chapter 4). As the clinical neurologist Andrew Papanicolaou concludes, nothing in the "activation pattern" of brain activity of any experiences determines their validity or invalidity: we must decide on grounds other than patterns of brain activation whether mystical experiences are veridical; indeed, even aberrations in brain activity are irrelevant until they are proven relevant on other grounds (2021: 122–26).[5]

The last point is this: whether mystical experiences are delusory or involve a genuine insight into the nature of reality, today it is becoming increasingly accepted that these experiences are associated with particular observable neurological events: mystical experiences are "real" and are distinct from other types of mental phenomena and are not merely products of the experiencer's imagination (Newberg et al. 2002: 7, 143). Much mental activity involves more than one area of the brain, and mystical experiences may too, but there is evidence of distinctive configurations of brain events being uniquely associated with different types of mystical experiences. According to Andrew Newberg, experiences of enlightenment "cause long-term changes that affect the emotional and cognitive centers of the brain" and "are real in that they are related to specific neurological events that can permanently change the structure and functioning of the brain" (Newberg and Waldman 2016: 42, 25). Thus, the experiencer's brain is neurologically transformed.

However, by "*real*," neuroscientists mean only that mystical experiences are *genuine neurological events* that can be observed and measured, rather than merely wishful thinking or only ordinary experiences interpreted as mystical, not that they must be *cognitively insightful*. Experiencers often believe that what they experienced was as real as, or even "more real" than, everyday reality and that this affects them powerfully and deeply, and this feeling often persists long after the mystical experiences are over, unlike with dreams. So too, the experiences are well-remembered afterward, unlike dimly remembered dreams. But most scientists are remaining neutral on whether these experiences are authentic realizations of a transcendent reality or are delusions (e.g., Newberg et al. 2002: 143, 178–79). Thus, two senses of *"genuine"* must be distinguished in these studies: establishing that mystical experiences are unique—genuine experiences distinct from other types of experiences—and establishing that the experiences convey a genuine insight into reality. Neuroscience can do the former but not the latter. In sum, "People may or may not actually be connecting to God or the supernatural, but ultimately there is something very powerful going on inside the brain" (Newberg and Waldman 2016: 25).

The Newberg-D'Aquili Experiments

In 1993, Andrew Newberg and Eugene d'Aquili (1999; Newberg et al. 2002) conducted experiments on experienced meditators—three Christian Franciscan nuns and eight Tibetan Buddhist monks—using SPECT neuroimaging to measure blood flow in different areas of the brain during or after meditative experiences. By observing the limbic system of the right temporal lobe, the thalamus, the prefrontal cortex, and the parietal lobes, they found that certain concentrative meditative techniques (which focus attention upon one object) led to the hyperactivation of the limbic system through the overload of sensory and kinesthetic stimulation, while certain "emptying" meditative techniques (which lead to mindful monitoring of mental activity without trying to control it) also led the hyperactivation of the limbic system through sensory deprivation (Newberg and d'Aquili 2002: 110–16). The decrease in neural activity in the frontal and parietal lobes can be sudden and dramatic; the decrease of activity in the frontal lobe leads from a sense of being in control to a sense of surrender (Newberg and Waldman 2016: 86).[6]

The researchers hypothesize that both the overload of sensory and kinesthetic stimulation and the deprivation of such stimulation lead to the partial or total elimination of neural signals to the orientation and association areas of the parietal lobes in the right and left hemispheres of the brain that are responsible for maintaining both a sense of a "self" separate from the rest of the universe and a sense of being bounded by one's body. Other researchers have found that mindfulness meditation can also dampen the activity in the brain that generates a "self-narrative" (Vago and Silbersweig 2012). The loss of these senses leads to the sense of one being boundless in space, which in turn leads to mystical experiences—i.e., a loss of any sense of an individual self with spatial boundaries produces a sense of selflessness. Neuroscientists deal with different senses of selflessness (Millière 2020).[7] Two philosophical issues here are (1) whether the "self" is a nonexistent artifice that when removed from our consciousness in mystical experiences gives a more insightful perception of the phenomenal world, or the experience is only a temporary loss of recognizing a real self, and (2) whether this experience should also change our beliefs, values, and behavior.

The decrease of activity in the parietal lobes was accompanied by an increase of activity in the prefrontal cortex in the right hemisphere related to attention, focusing, and concentration. Overall, all brain activity appears to be reduced in experienced meditators (Lazar et al. 2000). But this is distinct from drowsiness or simple relaxation: rhythmic alpha and theta waves decrease, but gamma waves (which are associated with awareness) grow stronger. Gamma waves also appear to remain strong in long-term meditators outside of the meditations in laboratories (Schwartz and Begley 2002). The more one meditates, the easier it is to make neurological changes. But the huge variation in participants' gamma readings may make these readings unreliable measures of meditative proficiency—when it comes to gamma waves, the resting state seems to be highly individual (Hinterberger 2014: 112). (It should be noted that, while scientists focus on specific areas of the brain during meditation, in any mental event the different areas of the brain still show a holistic coherence of activity.) When combined, these lead to a sense of being absorbed into an infinite spaceless and timeless void.[8] After a meditation session, activity increases once again in the frontal and parietal lobes, but some meditators can carry over the loss of a sense of self into their returning state of consciousness (see Berkovich-Ohana et al. 2024). The "enlightened" incorporate this sense of selflessness more permanently, thereby altering their postmeditation state of consciousness in a more lasting fashion.

Newberg and d'Aquili's experiments have drawn criticism. Edward Kelly and Michael Grosso slam their work as bad science unpublished in peer-reviewed publications and their theological model of an "Absolute Unitary Being" as "little more than a neurological fairy tale" (2007: 537–38). Richard Sloan also concludes that Newberg and d'Aquili speculate too broadly based on two small SPECT studies with a total of eleven subjects and no control group (2006: 247). More generally, the diverse methodologies and neuroscientific findings in all studies of meditators have been questioned (e.g., Cahn and Polich 1999; Azari 2006; Ratcliffe 2006). So too, Brian Lancaster (2005: 251) can reasonably ask if current neuroimaging technology shows only marginal changes in blood flow, whether that is sufficient to claim that there is "strong support" for the existence of a pure consciousness (Newberg and d'Aquili 1999: 118). As Newberg and Bruce Lee admit (2005: 477), it is not clear what degree of change in blood flow should be considered a relevant change—10 percent? 20 precent? What Fritz Staal noted in the 1970s is true today: we do not know what the significance of a change in, say, a brain's alpha-wave frequency is (1975: 109). Indeed, critics today dismiss the entire enterprise of trying to identify a locus in the brain of any behavior or complex mental event as "the new phrenology" (Uttal 2001).

Philosophical Issues

But let us assume that the Newberg-d'Aquili results will be replicated by others and that they hit upon something significant in the occurrence of mystical experiences. Any experiments are, of course, also limited by their focus. There are two classes of mystical experiences with several different types of experiences within each: "introvertive" and "extrovertive" (Stace 1960: 62–122), and there is empirical evidence suggesting that the brain functions differently during these two different classes of experiences (Hood 1997; Dunn et al. 1999). Consistent differences in neurological readings between different types of extrovertive and introvertive mystical experiences would strongly suggest a difference in the accompanying states of consciousness. So too, neuroscientists can distinguish concentrative and mindfulness meditation (Valentine and Sweet 1999; K. Fox 2016), and these may well generate substantively different neurological states because the former requires focusing on the mind on an object (leading to "one-pointedness" of mind) while the latter requires the opposite (letting the mind observe whatever comes to it in the flow of phenomena, leading to an "expansive" state of mind). And within the basic concentrative and emptying meditative tracks, there is also a plethora of techniques (see Andresen 2000; Shear 2006) that may also generate different neurological states. An example of other problems comes from a study of Japanese Buddhist monks. The researchers found that the monks' brain activity revealed by fMRI scans was different when chanting a mantra than when chanting a text (Shimomura et al. 2008). Thus, different activity is involved in merely repeating a short phrase than in chanting fuller content, even if one is not focusing on the meaning of the text.

The Newberg–d'Aquili subjects utilized introvertive concentrative techniques, and a basic philosophical question is whether there are different neural states for those introvertive mystical experiences with differentiated content and those without such content. There are several types of introvertive mystical experiences (see R. Jones 2016: 31–34 for a typology), and there is no reason in advance of research to believe that the neurophysiological bases are the same in every case. If so, different neurological explanations would be needed for each type of mystical experience. So too, can the *same* techniques lead to *different* brain states in different meditators? Or can *different* meditative techniques lead to the *same* states of the brain in all meditators? Mystical experiences in general are unexpected—experiencers are usually startled by their occurrence and usually also startled by their content—but scientists would also have to account for "spontaneous" mystical experiences that occur totally unexpectedly to persons with no meditative or other preparation. Scientists must explain what triggers such experiences and determine if the neural base is the same as experiences occurring in the lab.[9]

Moreover, one aspect of their experiments has been overlooked. The nuns and monks had different practices, but both meditative techniques were introvertive and concentrative in nature, and Newberg and d'Aquili got similar neurological readings for both groups. The different resulting experiences of "unity" affected the same areas in everyone's brain and produced similar neurological readings (Newberg and Waldman 2016: 91).[10] All subjects showed a slowing of activity in the posterior superior parietal lobes (Newberg et al. 2001: 4–5). Yet the Christians and Buddhists claimed to have had *radically different experiences of "unity"*: the Christians experienced being "united with God" and Buddhists experienced being "inextricably connected to all creation" (Newberg et al. 2001: 7, 2). If the descriptions are correct, the former experienced a transcendent reality while the latter experienced only the natural world. The former may have involved no differentiated content while the latter may have.

Newberg and d'Aquili report only "similar neurological readings" from their experiments with Christian nuns and Buddhist monks. Perhaps their data could be reexamined to see if there are in fact subtle differences between the two groups. Perhaps differing periods of time spent on various practices produced different brain states. Scientists monitor all brain activity, but the possibility that current neuroscience is focusing on the wrong aspects of the brain when it comes to mystical experiences cannot be ruled out. Most naturalists would assume that there must be unique neurological bases for each type of mystical experience, but current SPECT technology examining blood flow may not be finely grained enough to expose differences if there were any. Thus, if neuroscientists are currently measuring the correct neural basis, is the technology simply not yet fine-tuned enough to capture and measure the neurological differences? More precision may be necessary to reveal if there are more subtle differences in the Christian and Buddhist meditators' brain activity. Or perhaps an entirely new type of technology is needed to reveal the differences. Or perhaps other variables need to be measured.

But if objective evidence that nontheistic and theistic meditators produce the same brain activity during the two types of meditative experiences is produced, two important issues for the question of whether neuroscience provides any understanding of these experiences arise. First, did the nuns and monks have truly *different experiences*, or did they merely *interpret the same experiences* of a unified (differentiation-free) consciousness *differently* when they looked back on the experiences after they were over and they had returned to our baseline state of consciousness or another dualistic state? If the former, this would support constructivism: the conceptual framework of the nuns and monks shaped their experiences, and they had precisely the type of experiences that their religious traditions dictated. If the latter, this would be solid evidence against the constructivist explanation of mystical experiences: the nuns and monks applied their conceptual framework after the fact to experiences that were themselves free of such structuring. This would present a problem for first-person reporting: scientists would have to dismiss these accounts as what William James called "over-beliefs" and try to confine their attention only to the experiencers' more phenomenological descriptions of what the experience felt like. But the general reliability of the experiencers' accounts would be called into question if doctrinal interpretations are also inherent in their descriptions. Can subjects describe the felt phenomenology of their experiences in detail without framing it with a doctrinal understanding?

Second, if the nuns and monks had genuinely different experiences (one with a transcendent reality and one with only the natural realm, and perhaps one with differentiated content and one without), does this mean that the same neurological base was present for different states of consciousness? Can the same brain states have different states of consciousness associated with them? If so, it would be the inverse of the "multiple realization" question in philosophy of mind—i.e., exactly the *same set of neural events* would underlie two *significantly different mental events* (see chapter 6). There would be no one-to-one correlation of brain states and experiences: the same brain state may ground different experiences. Certain brain states may be necessary for an experience to appear but not necessary and sufficient as one-to-one correlations would require. (That the same experience is realizable with different brain states also cannot be ruled out in advance of study.) Those brain states may ground nonmystical altered state of consciousness experiences, or simply a state of deep relaxation. If so, how can we be certain that similar third-person data for different meditators means similar experiences?

If experiences that were radically different in nature did in fact occur in the Newberg-d'Aquili experiments, it would mean that genuinely different experiences can occur with the same neural base. Indeed, the subjects' entire ASC might have been quite different, not merely different experiences within the same state of consciousness.[11] This would undercut the idea that the brain and the mind are identical or that the brain causes mental states: each unique configuration of brain events would not have only one unique mental event associated with it—each experience would still have a corresponding brain state but not a unique one. Thus, neural states could not determine, or be identical to, mental states. Nor has a correlation been established between each type of mystical experience and specific configurations of brain events. A given meditative technique may have the same effect on the brain for each meditator, and so the brain conditions are the same, and yet different mystical or other ASC experiences occur.

In the future, more refined technology or scanning for other features may establish one-to-one correlations of meditative experiences and neurological states. Each meditative experience would then be associated with a unique state of the brain. But without such a correlation, a neuroscientific explanation of mystical experiences is not possible: all mystical experiences would be grounded in the body in some brain state, but simply identifying the brain state would not explain why a particular experience was realized in that brain state. Nor would an explanation rule out that that experience might be realized with another brain state.

Can Experiences Be Studied Scientifically?

If neuroscientists can study experiences themselves, the scientific study of meditators potentially would add a new way to study mystical experiences, not merely the brain during experiences. But inverse multiple realization, if established, would eliminate the possibility that neuroscience under its current approach could inform us in any way about the nature of mystical experiences—establishing the neural base of these experiences would not be able to tell us even what kind of experience is occurring since the same neural base would underlie different types of experiences, let alone anything about the nature of the experiences.

But even if we assume that solid scientific data exists or will be in the future that establishes one-to-one correlations of meditative and brain states, it would still be hard to argue that neuroscience studies mystical *experiences* at all. Establishing correlations or some grounding in the brain or some physiological effects is not studying the subjectivity or the experiences themselves even indirectly. It is not as if mystical experiences are observed by examining certain activity in the brain. All that is found is the brain activity accompanying the experiences. Are neuroscientific findings on brain activity simply irrelevant to questions of the nature of mystical experiences?

Consider first the well-known problem of a gap between brain conditions and consciousness (Chalmers 1995: 205; R. Jones 2013: 109–10): how do we get from the action of matter in the brain to something completely different, the felt experiences and other subjectivity of the mind? The gap is not just metaphysical but also methodological, explanatory, and conceptual.[12] No analysis of matter suggests the presence of phenomena of such a radically different nature as subjectivity or why it should appear or vice versa. Eliminationists in cognitive science simply deny subjectivity altogether. For them, studying the brain is all that is possible or needed. Reductionists reduce all mental phenomena to brain activity, and so studying the brain is studying conscious experiences (see R. Jones 2013: 98–102). But for the rest of us there is an issue here: can experiences themselves be studied scientifically?

This gap problem presents a very real issue of whether the subjectivity inherent in any experience can be studied scientifically at all. Even whether there are specific neural correlates and markers of consciousness and where they might be located is proving controversial at present (see Koch et al. 2016; Boly et al. 2017). There may not be any simple one-to-one matches between consciousness and neural correlates (Noë and Thompson 2004). A newer neuroscientific approach is not to look for correlates but to identify the overall brain functioning during conscious events—e.g., how the brain goes from receiving sensory input to producing structured perceptions (see Griffiths et al. 2008; Clark 2013).

But identifying what is going on in the brain when a mystical experience occurs is one thing; what meditators actually experience is quite another. To study the former events is not to study the "lived" experience itself—the felt sense of selflessness, unity, timelessness, or whatever. These felt aspects of sense experiences ("qualia") versus the physical activity in the brain occurring during the experiences present a problem in all consciousness studies (see R. Jones 2013: 106–9, 122–24). For most scientists, qualia remain distinct from brain mechanisms and cannot be explained away simply by identifying the base in the brain permitting them to occur—the first-person sensation of seeing the greenness of grass is not reducible to the sum of the physical events occurring when we look at grass. No third-person account of, for example, a broken leg can capture first-person experiences of the pain. So too, subjectivity has a point of view that objects do not (Nagel 1986).

In sum, subjectivity always has a private inner dimension that any corresponding neurological activity cannot have. For antireductionists, all our first-person experiences and mental activity share the same unbridgeable difference between the physical and subjectivity. Scientists may well be able to reduce some mental functions to the mechanical operation of physiological states, but subjectivity cannot be reduced to something objective. Indeed, subjectivity—what something seems like to an experiencer—cannot be studied at all by examining the electrochemical activity of the brain. Thus, the reductionists' method of explaining any *x* in terms of non-*x* will not work here precisely because what is to be explained is not something with physical properties, and physical properties can explain only other physical properties. In sum, first-person experiences are an irreducible field of reality, and therefore we cannot reduce the first-person ontology of consciousness to a third-person objective one.

In addition, meditation appears to be a case of the mind affecting matter: we can *rewire* the brain, and meditation is one way to do it. Meditation (and psychedelics) can bring about changes on the molecular, cellular, and network levels of the brain. Meditation can bring about functional and structural changes and increase the density of gray matter (Schwartz and Begley 2002; Lazar et al. 2005; Newberg and Waldman 2016: 41–63; Holzel et al. 2011; Kang et al. 2013; Clausen et al. 2014; Newberg and Waldman 2016). On the molecular level, dopamine and melatonin increase, serotonin activity is modulated, and cortisol and norepinephrine decrease (Esch 2014). Meditation may affect the activity of genes—e.g., stress-reducing practices may quiet genes that cause inflammation (Buric 2017). In sum, we cannot modify only our momentary mode of awareness but may be able to shape our brain and thus shape our enduring mind to the extent that it is dependent upon the brain. This apparent "downward" causation of the mind on the body presents a mind-body problem for materialists. Purely materialist explanations of mystical experiences will necessarily be faulty unless materialists can account for both functional and structural changes in the brain in terms of the brain rewiring itself internally without reference to experiences. So too, the experience's entire phenomenology requires explanation. If consciousness is a causal reality affecting the brain or other parts of the body, then neuroscience as practiced today is not merely incomplete but fundamentally misguided. Thus, research on meditation's effect on the brain may change science and thereby end up changing culture (Schmidt and Walach 2014: 5).

However, when neuroscientists speak today of a "science of consciousness," they are still referring to identifying the neural or other bodily basis of conscious events, not to studying the subjective side of these events such as the felt quality of qualia.[13] There currently is no direct science of consciousness itself, and to speak of one is misleading: identifying the basis in the body of particular conscious events (e.g., identifying the areas of the brain that are more active when we sense colors or when we make moral judgments) is not getting into the conscious events themselves. Most importantly, to date neuroscience cannot determine whether consciousness is identical to brain activity or is ontologically different (Overgaard 2017: 3). Merely identifying the neural activity tells us nothing about what consciousness is or its nature. Nor can it explain why consciousness exists. Nor does it determine whether changes in the neural base cause changes in consciousness or vice versa, or why conscious events are correlated with material events at all—indeed, a correlation of phenomena is not an explanation of anything but only an additional item that needs an explanation. Just because a brain state is *associated* with a mental event does not mean that it *causes* it (or vice versa) or that one is reducible to the other. And as the logical positivist A. J. Ayer pointed out, if a correlation of mind and brain is established, we would have as much reason to believe that the brain depends upon the mind as vice versa (1973: 130).

Most basically, there does not appear to be any way to study the subjectivity of a person's consciousness itself by objective, third-person means. Subjectivity is not phenomenal—i.e., it is not an object that can be presented for study. There simply is no way to present subjectivity itself for inspection or testing by others. This also complicates any "first-person science" (see Varela and Shear 1999; Shear 2014; Jinpa 2010: 880), "altered state sciences" (see Tart 1972, 1998), or "neurophenomenology" (see Varela 1996; Peters 2000; Petitmengin 2011) that would treat first-person states as irreducible and focus on those states directly, thereby supplementing the third-person approach of neuroscience. But a basic issue here is whether the very process of critically examining an ASC experience changes the *content* of an experience: Can we examine the *experience* without mentally distancing ourselves from the experience and making it into an *object*, thereby disrupting and ending a mystical ASC? Isn't what is observed not the lived experience itself? So too, can experiencers look back at their experiences objectively or only read them in light of their philosophical and religious beliefs? In the end, first-person introspection may help neuroscientists find a better map of the brain or how the brain works, but it would not overcome the limitations just discussed on neuroscience adding to our understanding of the nature of mystical experiences themselves. Rather, at most such an internal empiricism would be relevant at best only to the issue of what experiences relate to what brain states.

Religious practitioners with very similar backgrounds and amounts of meditative practice can produce very different EEG readings (Schmidt and Walach 2014: 3), but how could we utilize those readings to compare the practitioners' experiences? Moreover, no doubt scientists could conduct neuroimaging studies to demonstrate the differences in the activity of cerebral structures occurring while someone is listening to Beethoven or listening to white noise—but would this mean that this experience is exhaustively explained by the activity of a specific brain region and thus that this is all there is to it (Sloan 2006: 253)? Robert Ornstein likens EEG studies to placing a heat sensor on a computer and thereby attempting to determine the computer's program (1978: 124–25)—we can determine when the computer is on or off but nothing more. Would neuroscanning tell us anything about the content of the different experiences? Scientists can show that our conscious states are affected by changes in brain states, but this does not mean that studying those changes tells us anything about those states.

With their success in the study of brain activity, it is easy to see why neuroscientists may miss the philosophical issues and claim to be producing a "theory of consciousness." But as things stand, scientists are only studying something closely associated with the appearance of consciousness in us—its bodily underpinnings—and not consciousness itself. They study the state of the brain during an experience, not the experience itself or consciousness in general. In sum, as David Chalmers (1995) labeled the situation, neuroscientists study the relatively "easy problem" of identifying neural bases to types of mental activity (perception, memory, and so forth) and have not tackled the "hard problem" of consciousness itself—how and why conscious events accompany physical ones. Even if consciousness is a powerless epiphenomenon or an "illusion" in some sense, how is such a phenomenon possible in a material system?

In sum, any third-person experience of brains does not give us knowledge of anything but an object, and subjectivity cannot be made into an object: even if the mind and the brain are materially identical, there is an "inside" to experiences that cannot be studied from the "outside" by examining the brain. Neuroscanning can show what the brain is doing or not doing during an experience but not the experience itself. Even the emerging technology that "reads minds" reads only brain states, not experiences. No scientific account of the mechanisms active during sense experience or self-awareness can make us understand what it is like actually to experience those states. Indeed, from neuroscience alone we would not suspect that consciousness exists at all—no accounts of phenomena in purely third-person terms would ever even suggest the existence of, much less explain, the subjective qualities that constitute the bulk of our conscious life (Shear and Jevning 1999: 189). Even some neuroscientists see limits on what neuroscanning can accomplish concerning consciousness (e.g., Shulman 2013).

Can Mystical Experiences Be Studied Scientifically?

This general inability of one person to witness what another one experiences applies equally to meditative experiences. Mystical experiences share the consciousness gap with other conscious phenomena—even mystical "knowledge by participation" does not bridge the gap between the subjective felt experience and the objective brain events underlying the experiences. Again, this means that scientists do not study mystical experiences at all when they study the biological basis of an experience (also see R. Jones 1986: 219–22). A "science of meditative experiences" is not achieved by a science of a meditator's brain. Even if previous experiences can be reproduced by the meditators themselves during scientific experiments, the inability of others to see what is going on in the meditator's consciousness will always limit any science of meditation. Even when a neuroscientist who had mystical experiences—Mario Beauregard—speaks of a "new scientific frame of reference" that goes beyond materialism, he still ends up speaking only of the scientific investigation of the neural, physiological, psychological, and social conditions favoring the occurrence of mystical experiences (Beauregard and O'Leary 2007: 294–95), not the direct study of consciousness or mystical experiences. Similarly, measuring the spiritual or religious significance that an experiencer sees in these experiences after the experiences are over by assigning numbers to their answers to researchers' questions is not in any way measuring or quantifying the experiences themselves. So too, studying the frequency of certain words or phrases is not a study of the subjective experiences since respondents may be using only standardized cultural terminology that does not in fact actually reflect the subjective experience.

In addition, as of yet little is known about the neurobiological processes involved in meditation or about its possible long-term impact on the brain (Lutz et al. 2007: 500).[14] Even with more recent developments, the science of these states is in a very early stage. The biological studies of meditation to date have not produced anything dramatic about what is occurring during meditation but only about the effects on the brain and the body. The same holds today as Sloan said eighteen years ago: scientific studies reveal the "entirely unremarkable findings" that during meditation the areas of the brain associated with concentration and attention show increased activity compared to other regions (2006: 247–49).

The possible inverse multiple realization problem also must be mentioned again: apparently very different experiences can have the same biological bases. Herbert Benson found that there is a great variety of "subjective" (i.e., experiential) responses—including no change of consciousness at all—accompanying the same physiological changes produced by his simple relaxation techniques (Benson and Klipper 2000 [1975]: 130). Even if other meditators can duplicate the physical state of the brain of an enlightened mystic, how can we know that the subjective state of consciousness is also being duplicated? One's beliefs and expectations play a role in some experiences, but different states of mind apparently share the same bases in the brain. Thus, the explanation of the experiential level would still be missing from any neuroscientific account, as would why reality permits the higher-level events to occur at all.

All of this severely limits the value of neuroscience as currently constituted for mystical studies: it is not studying mystical experiences themselves at all. Even a complete neurological account of the brain during a mystical experience would miss the subjective side entirely and thus miss something of great value to the experiencers.

The Question of "Pure Consciousness Events"

Steven Katz (1978, 2014) made constructivism a major issue in philosophy of mysticism. The basic idea is that all of our experiences are structured by the concepts and other influences from an experiencer's cultural environment. That is, all mystical experiences must be mediated by religious and other cultural expectations: "*There are NO pure (i.e., unmediated) experiences*" (1978: 26, emphasis in the original). The focus here is not the biological mediation of experiences through brain activity but that *cultural forces* shape any experience.

Katz believes that there is no "substantive evidence to suggest that there is any pure consciousness" achieved by meditative practices (1978: 57). Robert Forman leads the "nonconstructivists" counterattack by presenting historical and contemporary examples to dispute this (1990, 1999). Nonconstructivists contend that meditation through a process of emptying the mind of all differentiated content can eliminate any basis or means for such expectations and predictions, leaving any experiential state bare of cultural structuring. Forman (1990) argues that at least some mystical experiences are not structured by any cultural beliefs (or any innate cross-cultural Kantian structuring). Forman argues that at least some mystical experiences are not structured by any cultural beliefs (or any innate cross-cultural Kantian structuring). That is, some mystical experiences are "wakeful contentless consciousness—direct and unmediated "pure consciousness events" (Forman 1990: 24). All experiences are "pure experiences" in one sense: even if they are culturally mediated, their content is purely subjective. But by "pure consciousness events," nonconstructivists are alleging that some mystical experiences are experiences free of any cultural elements. In extrovertive experiences, pure consciousness events are sensory experiences free of cultural structuring. Introvertive pure consciousness events are free of sensory input and of all internal differentiated content. No changes of content occur during these introvertive events. Nonconstructivists may argue that all types of mystical experiences are unconstructed, but it the allegedly empty "depth-mystical experience" or "pure consciousness event" that is the bone of contention. Indeed, many believe that this is the only type of mystical experience.

Nonconstructivists contend that mystics in different traditions interpret at least those mystical experiences that are empty of all differentiated content differently in light of their cultural beliefs *after the experience is over*, but this does not mean that the actual *phenomenology of their experiences* is different in different cultures. There may be no description that involves no interpretation whatsoever to some degree (Stace 1960: 203), but such descriptions may not be active during the experience itself. As Ralph Hood puts it, "Experience need not be socially constructed even though knowledge about it is" (2002: 10). Mystical knowledge is a "knowledge by participation" in which there is no distinction of the knower and the reality known, unlike ordinary "knowledge by acquaintance" in which construction by cultural phenomena is more easily possible. Something of the pure consciousness events is retained after the experience is over: the experiencer realizes that he or she had the experience (even if during the experience itself there is no sense of a subject or of ownership) and that the experience took time (even if during the experience there is no sense of time passing or of "before" and "after" during the experience and thus it is felt as "timeless" or an "eternal now").

Most importantly, something of the experience's content must be remembered—e.g., a general sense of fundamental reality, nondual consciousness, and profound importance—or there would be no grounds to advance a theory about what was experienced or to reject any other theory. Indeed, if the experiencer of a depth-mystical experience retained nothing, he or she would have to be said to be *unconscious* and not have had an *experience* at all. Thus, the experience is not literally "empty" but has some type of content: consciousness itself that is interpreted differently after the experience is over as the presence of God, Brahman, a soul, or some other transcendent reality, or as only natural consciousness. But the experience may have content that can be seen as such and discussed as such only once the experiencer returned to a dualistic (subject/object) state of consciousness.

Nonconstructivists contend that realizing these things after the experience is over does not mean that those concepts must have been present or active during the experience. Katz presents no scientific evidence showing that all experiences are culturally constructed—he admits it is only an *assumption* based on what sort of beings he takes humans to be (1978: 26). Constructivists could employ the recent "predictive processing" model in neuroscience to explain how such cultural structuring could occur: the brain generates expectations and predictions based on prior experiences and then interprets any new input accordingly; the brain also constantly compares its predictions with the input and can alter its expectations when a mismatch with predictions leads to errors (see Griffiths et al. 2008; Clark 2013; also see chapter 5). Or constructivists might try to ground this theory neurologically by invoking the neural plasticity of the brain: we can rewire the brain through mystical practices, and thus mystics in different cultures bring different culturally influenced neurological states to their resulting experiences that were shaped by their prior beliefs and training, and so their experiences must be different (Goldberg 2009: 329–30). Thus, no experience could be universal.

Nonconstructivists reply that if there is no differentiated content in introvertive pure consciousness events, then there is nothing in these experiences to be structured or to do any structuring. (This possibility is discussed in chapter 3.) Thus, whatever differences in the wiring of the brains that various mystics have in other regards, as long as they can have an experience that appears to them as empty of differentiated content, the experience must be the same for all experiencers in this respect (assuming we all are the same with regard to the neurobiological bases of these experiences) and thus must be universal. That is, the states of the brain would be invariant regardless of culture, and whether these states are either responsible for, or merely permit, such empty pure consciousness experiences, the experiences would be the same in all cultures in being empty of differentiated content.[15]

Most naturalists believe that there can be no consciousness without an object being present: consciousness is inherently intentional—when there is no object, there is no consciousness (Searle 1992: 84). But some neuroscientists and psychologists are quite conformable with accepting that experiences empty of all differentiated content can occur (e.g., Peters 1998: 13–16; Newberg and d'Aquili 1999; Hood 2006). Thus, if the depth-mystical experience is in fact empty of any differentiated content (leaving only consciousness itself to be experienced), and mystical knowledge participates in what is experienced, the experience would not have an object distinct from the experiencer or have any other differentiated content. In addition, there is evidence that some cognitive content of experiences may not be very susceptible to cultural influence (Nisbett et al. 2001: 305–6) and thus would be culturally invariant. Some mystical experiences may fall into that category. It must also be noted that the dogma in analytic philosophy that there is no nonconceptual content to ordinary perceptual states and knowledge is now being challenged (see Peacocke 1992, 2001; Van Cleve 2012; Bermudez 2015).

Personal reports also contradict constructivism for some mystical experiences. For example, the psychiatrist Philip Sullivan (1995) reported his own experience of an empty awareness of "something that was not nothing." It was an experience that was devoid of differentiated content, and yet he was not unconscious but aware—an awareness without any subject of awareness or sense of personal ownership and without any object of experience. Only the transitional states back to the ordinary baseline state of consciousness that were separate from this consciousness event had any informational content (Sullivan 1995: 53, 57). He relies on reports from the history of mysticism for corroboration (Sullivan 1995: 54–55). Constructivists might challenge that corroboration, but they are not in a position to challenge the phenomenology of Sullivan's own experience except by a dogmatic assertion of what must be the case. Ralph Hood (2006) also rejects the constructivist view of mystical experience and relies on interviews with persons who had mystical experience as evidence. And it may be that religious beliefs can affect the brain in such a way that there is no typical self-reference ("I," "me," "mine") pattern on the neural level (Han et al. 2008 [concerning Christians]; Wu et al. 2010 [concerning Buddhists]).

Neuroscience and the Pure Consciousness Event

Neuroscience would strike a conclusive blow against any thoroughgoing cultural construction of mystical experiences if it can establish a "pure consciousness."[16] Conversely, neuroscanning may not be able to distinguish one set of conceptual structuring from another (if all conceptualizing produces the same neurological effect on the brain), but perhaps it could show that the areas of the brain responsible for such structuring remain as active in all the mystical experiences that researchers have studied as they are in ordinary experiences—thus, all states are structured even if the exact structuring is irrelevant to the neural activity. But if there is no activity in the areas of the brain connected to conceptualizing occurring during certain mystical experiences or such activity is greatly diminished, there would be no way cultural concepts could affect the content of the experience and nothing for culture to affect. Do some types of meditation quiet the parts of the mind that process concepts, and can neuroscience find the basis of this in the brain?[17] Can neuroscience show that meditation completely stills the conceptualizing activity of the mind? That is, can it show us that the conceptual mind is completely or relatively inactive during certain mystical experiences? Or can it show that there is no differentiated content in certain states of consciousness?

In sum, the question is: can neuroscience establish that the areas of the brain that ground conceptual activity are active, or that they are partially or even completely inactive during certain mystical experiences?

The temporal lobe seems to be the locus of language, conceptualizing, and abstract thought, and this area does appear to have deceased activity altogether during mystical experiences (Newberg et al. 2002: 24–25), but some neural activity will remain present, and it may be that the areas of the brain grounding linguistic activity overlap the areas exhibiting increased activity during mystical experiences. But must we conclude that if there is some residual activity in that part of the brain that it must be affecting mystical experiences? We do not, and thus whether or not the experiences are culturally constructed could not be established by neuroscientists because the areas will be at least somewhat active for the mystical experience in either case. Moreover, there may be structuring of mental states that is nonlinguistic—e.g., dogs know their owners and babies in a prelinguistic state know their parents. No one suspects that animals and infants have a "pure consciousness" state of mind free of all structuring simply because they do not have any linguistic ability—they would not have the awareness that a meditator would. Experiences can be structured by symbols, images, or other nonlinguistic cultural influences. We all have had the experience of thinking "I have an idea" before we have actually put the idea into words. Indeed, Noam Chomsky (2006: 76) believes that it is obvious that we can think without language—the mind is still manipulating concepts before they are converted into linguistic terms.

Thus, neuroscience may not be able to reveal whether some mystical experiences are empty of all cultural structuring. However, nonconstructivists can still rightly ask why completely stilling the conceptual activity of the mind is not possible even if blood is flowing in the relevant parts of the brain, and how any cultural structuring could be occurring in those mystical experiences where the experiences are felt phenomenologically to be empty of all differentiated content—there would be no differentiated content for conceptual structuring to operate upon or any conceptual structuring present to do any structuring. Subconscious mental states may affect conscious states even if we are aware only of the latter, and neuroscientists may be able to detect subconscious or nonconscious processing occurring before or during alleged pure consciousness events. The issue then is whether the scientists can establish that these processes must be actively shaping the phenomenology of the experiences themselves. Peter Binns (1995) suggests that perhaps preconscious information processing of differentiated material somehow affects this experience—thus even bare awareness may be structured by cultural phenomena. Brian Lancaster (2005: 250) also believes that the fact that people claim to experience a contentless consciousness is an inadequate basis for presuming the reality of pure consciousness. But how any preconscious processing could change *the phenomenological character* of an "empty" experience free of differentiated content is not at all clear. If it cannot, that would eliminate neuroscience from informing us about the nature of mystical experiences on the issue of constructivism.

The Limitation of Neuroscience for Philosophy

All of the above discussion leads to the conclusion that there are major limitations on the significance that neuroscience can have for understanding the nature of mystical experiences. Beside the general problem of the subjectivity of experiences in general and that all consciousness events have some neural correlates, the possibility that the same neural base may ground different altered states of consciousness enabled through meditation further removes the possibility of a true "neuroscience of mystical consciousness." The discussion of constructivism also illustrates the limited utility of neuroscience for philosophical issues connected to mysticism. Neuroscientists may be able to establish that mystical experiences occur for persons with healthy brains and that mystical experiences are associated with unique configurations of neural activity, thereby suggesting that the experiences involve altered states of consciousness rather than merely being exotic interpretations of occurrences in ordinary dualistic states of consciousness. But that is the end of the relevance of neuroscience as currently constituted for experiences that are specifically mystical in nature.

Events in the brain may have a direct bearing on mental events, and to that extent studying the neural substrate of mystical experiences will help to explain aspects related to the presence of the experiences, but that would show only that the experiences are embodied. Nevertheless, the phenomenal characteristics of the content of the actual experiences will remain distinct. Thus, studying the neural base of events occurring in the mind will remain limited for our understanding of the felt sense of a mystical experience or what the proper understanding of the experience should be. How the brain influences the mind and vice versa may remain a "black box" for scientists—scientists can observe the input and output but may remain foreclosed from examining how exactly that output is produced.[18] Even a complete neurological account of what is occurring in the brain during a mystical experience does not rule out the possibility of mystical knowledge any more than a complete electrical engineering account of the events in a computer explains away the role of a software program.

Neuroscience may change, but for the foreseeable future neuroscientists will remain answering questions related to how mystical experiences are mediated by the brain—they will not be addressing the nature of mystical experiences. Learning how meditation or other mystical training affects the brain and the rest of the body is in the end irrelevant to those who are interested in the content of mystical experiences. In particular, there is no way to tell if brain activity causes mystical experiences or if meditation only sets up the necessary base conditions in the brain for receiving contact with a transcendent reality in some cases (see Fingelkurts and Fingelkurts 2009; R. Jones 2016: 151–59)—in short, does the brain *cause* mystical experiences or only *enable* them?

This also means that neuroscience does not offer evidence for or against the claim that mystical experiences are cognitive and thus veridical. That is, the neuroscience of mystical experiences cannot aid in determining whether the experiences reveal something about the nature of reality or that they are in fact no more than the product of chemical events in the brain that generate only groundless delusions. (If science established that only persons with *severely damaged brains* had mystical experiences, that would greatly tend to discredit mystical claims to insights. But scientists have found that people with totally normal brain have these experiences. Needing ASCs to have mystical insights does not mean someone's brain is "cracked" [see R. Jones 2020b: 265–66].) Does the decrease during mystical experiences in neural signals to the orientation and association areas of the parietal lobes that maintain a sense of a "self" separate from the rest of the universe mean that mystical experiences are not actually cognitive, or that the self is indeed unreal? Does dopamine explain away mystical bliss, or is the increase in its production the result of a mystical experience? By showing that forms of meditation that foster mystical experiences have unique neural bases the science may be seen as supporting religion, although it cannot prove religious understandings of these experiences; however, it may lead in the long run to the reduction of meditation to merely its effects in improving well-being and happiness without reference to any religious framework. At best, neuroscience as currently constituted may lead to new meditative techniques in light of findings on how meditation affects the brain. But neuroscience remains only about the working of the brain during mystical experiences, not about the experiences themselves.

The Value of Studying Mystical Experiences in Neuroscience

All of this limits the value of neuroscience to the philosophy of mysticism (also see R. Jones 2016: chapter 4). However, to end on a more positive note: even if neuroscience is not studying mystical experiences, meditative and mystical experiences constitute a range of experiences that is a potential source of new data for neuroscientists on how the brain works. Studying such experiences would be a case of applying mysticism to aid our understanding of the brain and mind. Perhaps, as many classical mystics claimed, there is a unique mental function at work in mystical experiences distinct from reasoning and other experiences—e.g., the "*nous*" of Neoplatonist mysticism and the "*buddhi*" of some Indian traditions, both of which are usually translated "intellect." Or meditation may aid in understanding consciousness itself by clearing away the noise in most conscious states, thereby leaving a "pure awareness," free of other activity. It may show that we are capable of controlling what were thought to be involuntary bodily processes or that we can train our awareness or our sense of compassion by using compassion as a meditative object.

Just as high-energy physics caused physicists to rethink aspects of Newtonian theory, so too developing "high-energy states of consciousness" may open neuroscientists to the need for new explanations (Wallace 2007: 167). This may lead neuroscientists to rethink the materialist framework adopted by most neuroscientists today that consciousness is simply an activity of matter or its product. Or perhaps not: merely because meditation may, for example, lower stress levels in the body does not mean that the mind is necessarily not a product of matter. Mystical experiences in themselves do not require that the mind or consciousness is unattached somehow to the brain—even if mystical experiences are cognitive, the mind may still simply be the product of (or identical to) the brain. So too, "pure consciousness" events may be explainable in a materialistic framework, even if this requires dismissing these experiences as a powerful feedback effect occurring when all sensory and other differentiated content is removed while one remains conscious. If so, mystical experiences are unusual but perfectly ordinary subjective events generated by the brain that mystics typically misinterpret. For example, theistic mystics understandably but mistakenly take these events to be profound and take the "bliss" as being loved by a transcendent reality when it is only the result of the mind remaining conscious when it is empty of anything to work with. Thus, reductionists and eliminationists will argue that no new theory is needed even for pure consciousness events.

Nevertheless, it may be that scientists cannot develop an adequate understanding of consciousness using only the instrumental/analytical functions of the mind and any nonanalytical functions currently recognized by scientists. Unless mystical experiences can be shown to be the result of mental malfunctioning, scientists cannot ignore them but must account for the receptive/contemplative modes of both the extrovertive and introvertive mystical experiences. If so, scientists would have to accept these experiences as new data on states of consciousness but not necessarily accept that mystical experiences provide insights into the nature of reality. So too, classical mystical analyses of various mental states, as in the Buddhist Abhidharma traditions, may also be helpful for devising new hypotheses about the mind (Lancaster 2005). If scientists revise their theories in light of mystical knowledge claims about consciousness or perception, this would be an instance of mysticism contributing to science (see Goleman and Thurman 1991; Austin 1998). Indeed, any role of mystical experiences for adding to our understanding of the mind and how the brain works would be a prime case of applied mysticism.

Chapter 2

Limitations on the Neuroscientific Study of Drug-Enabled Mystical Experiences

In his classic article from 1964, Huston Smith asked "Do drugs have religious import?" and concluded that psychedelic drugs regularly touch off experiences that give the users a sense of the sacred. Scientific interest in drug-enabled mystical experiences waned after the early 1960s, but interest has been renewed within the scientific community today with the study of the brain, and new findings warrant revisiting the issue. The most basic questions that mystical experiences occasioned by psychedelics raise are these: Do such drugs trigger genuine mystical experiences? Are drug-enabled mystical experiences the same in nature as naturally occurring ones? Do recent scientific findings provide grounds to support the cognitivity of mystical experiences or grounds to discredit such a claim? The issues also impinge on the larger issue of the nature of the human mind. Contemporary scientific studies do show that scientists can demonstrate that psychedelics in proper dosages can touch off genuine mystical experiences in a high percentage of cases, especially when administered in a supportive "set and setting," and that the brain's working during mystical experiences is distinguishable from that during more mundane experiences. Can science go beyond that and tell us about the nature or veridicality of mystical experiences?

Before addressing these issues, two preliminary points must be made. First, because psychedelics can "profoundly bend sensory processing, alter cognition," and enable "intense" experiences, these molecules "provide powerful tools for probing the human mind" (Kwan et al. 2022: 1407), but of interest here is only the scientific study of psychedelics as alleged triggers of mystical experiences.[1] The four classic psychedelics are mescaline (the active drug in peyote), LSD (derived from ergotamine found in ergot fungi), psilocybin (the active drug in "sacred mushrooms"), and DMT (the active drug in the ayahuasca vine). These in the proper dosages and setting touch off altered state of consciousness (ASC) experiences in a large percentage of users, especially in those disposed to having religious experiences. Two newer quasipsychedelic drugs, "ecstasy" (MDMA) and the anesthetic ketamine, touch off ASC experiences less frequently.[2] The term "entheogen" was coined in the 1970s (Ruck et al. 1979) for any substance that, when ingested, catalyzes or generates an ASC experience deemed to have spiritual significance. But the older term Humphrey Osmond coined in the 1950s in correspondence with Aldous Huxley, "psychedelic" (literally, "mind-opening" or "soul-revealing"), will be used here for the class of psychotropic chemicals, whether found in nature or artificially created, that allegedly enable mystical and other ASC experiences. This term fell into disrepute by 1980 because of its association with recreational use of such drugs, but it has regained scholarly respectability since the 1990s. It has the advantage of being more neutral than either "hallucinogenic" and "entheogenic," both of which carry baggage on the issue of whether mystical experiences are cognitive—the first con (i.e., "generating hallucinations") and the second pro (i.e., "generating God within").

Second, the term "mystical experience" is notoriously vague, and so what experiences will be included and excluded by the term must be specified. Here, the term "mystical experiences" will be restricted to the range of ASCs and experiences that involve emptying the mind of conceptual context and in particular a sense of a real experiencing phenomenal "self" (see R. Jones 2016: chapter 1).[3] This is a restrictive definition, but it includes more than the experience of "union with God"—different extrovertive and introvertive experiences fall within its range.[4] Extrovertive and some introvertive experiences retain differentiated content within the mind, but one type of introvertive experience is allegedly empty of all such content—the "depth-mystical experience." But mystical experiences as specified here differ from "religious experiences" in general such as praying, speaking in tongues, and so forth.[5] Mystical experiences involve a lessening or annihilation of a sense of otherness and allegedly involve contact between the experiencer and a reality. Thus, they can be distinguished from visions and auditory experiences of a person or other reality *set apart* from the experiencer.[6]

A Brief History of the Religious Use of Psychedelic Drugs

Psychedelic researchers are beginning to note the uses of indigenous psychedelics in different cultures (e.g., Barrett and Griffiths 2018: 395–400; Carhart-Harris et al. 2018: 725). Over one hundred natural psychedelic plants, fungi, and animals (e.g., the Colorado River toad) have been identified. The most familiar today are peyote (mescaline), certain mushrooms (psilocybin), cannabis, coca, opium poppies, and the ayahuasca vine (DMT) in the Amazon and Orinoco rainforests. Plants with DMT were once common throughout the Mediterranean region. Their mind-altering effects were probably discovered by accident in our early evolution (McKenna 1992; Damasio 2018; Arce and Winkelman 2021). All of these "flesh of the gods" or "sacred medicines" are found wild and do not require cultivation. They apparently became popular in agricultural societies beginning in the Paleolithic era (Devereux 1997; Guerra-Doce 2015). Evidence is found in early Mesoamerica, sub-Saharan and northern Africa (including Egypt), and from the Paleolithic era in territories from Europe to China. Some Neanderthal graves also contain plants with psychedelic properties. The fly-agaric mushroom was apparently used by shamans in Siberia; it was also used in the Baltics and Scandinavia. Germanic tribes apparently used opium poppies in rituals.

The experiences from psychedelic drugs may have had adaptive advantages for our early evolution (see Winkelman 2014; Arce and Winkelman 2021). It may be that the resulting experiences were a byproduct that led to evolutionary advantages at both the individual level (leading the experiencer to be more open and trusting of others within the group) and the social level (through the related rituals leading to more social cohesion). To have that wide effect, such plants would have to have been consumed by more than only a few shamans in each tribe. Use of psychedelics may account for some of the divergence between human and chimpanzee neurology, e.g., in the serotonergic system (Winkelman 2010).[7] Terence McKenna (1992) argues that psychedelic plants played an important role in stimulating the evolution of the modern human brain through mutations caused by the drugs, thereby altering our consciousness. Some scholars argue that drug-enabled brain states were catalysts for the development of our general cognitive abilities related to linguistic thinking, abstract thinking, and reasoning, as well as imagination, and integrating nonverbal corporeal, visual, and auditory information in visions (Weil 1986; Wasson et al. 1986; Winkelman 2013,

2017). Others argue that such drug-enabled visions explain why human beings have an ability to think symbolically that other primates do not have, and that from their use in the context of shamanic practices such drugs were the source of art and poetry (e.g., Lewis-Williams and Pearce 2005).

Neo-animists in anthropology see drug-enabled shamanic practices as the origin of religion, not social or material needs (e.g., see Forte 1997; Roberts 2001)—ecstasy-based shamanism was the Ur-religion from which all historical religions evolved. But religion involves much more than cultivating ASC experiences—it has social and other dimensions. Thus, advocates of psychedelics may want to revise their historical claim to the claim that drug-enabled shamanic ASC experiences were either the source or a major reinforcement of the ideas of a soul independent of the body, life after death, spirits, heaven and hell, grace, and forces behind nature. The nature of ASC experiences do suggest that these religious beliefs were formed in conjunction with these experiences and not from some prehistoric thinking alone. In any case, drug-enabled ASC experiences appear to have been part of religion since its earliest days (see Winkelman 1999, 2024). Indeed, shamanic practices constitute one of the oldest surviving forms of religiosity, and shamanic ASC experiences reinforced the idea of transcendent realities.

However, as societies became more complex, drug-facilitated states and ASC-oriented practices were dropped from the mainstream in the world's cultures in favor of more sedate practices. Nevertheless, references to their continued use have survived in early texts. In India, almost 12 percent of the hymns in the second-millennium BCE *Rig Veda* are devoted to *soma* (in the Zoroastrian *Avesta*, *haoma*), a now-unknown psychedelic concoction used in rituals; it is also referred to in many other hymns (see R. Jones 2014: 22–29, 170–71)—indeed, it permeates the *Rig Veda* and the Vedic central rituals. After Vedism, fewer references to psychedelic drug use are recorded in Hinduism—e.g., the god Shiva is often portrayed with a psychedelic datura flower in his hand. Buddhism condemned getting intoxicated as interfering with a mindful state, but Hindu and Buddhist Tantrics retained the use of psychedelics (Hajicek-Dobberstein 1995; Badiner and Grey 2015). (Psychedelics may have been seen as enabling visions, or as a way to clear the mind and thus enhancing mindfulness.) But the Tantric traditions are the last traditions within the world religions where psychedelic experiences are considered important.

In the West, vestiges of shamanic drug use are present in Greek mythology (Wasson et al. 1986). The Eleusinian Mysteries utilized a drink called "*kykeon*" whose central component may have had psychedelic properties similar to LSD's from a fungus ergot parasite in the rye that was a central component of the brew (Ruck 2006). The Delphi oracles may have uttered their prophecies under the influence of psychedelic ethylene vapors emanating from cracks in the earth. However, nonmystical forms of religion soon won out in Judaism, Christianity, and Islam. Nevertheless, some scholars have suggested that the story in the Bible of the forbidden fruit of the "tree of knowledge of good and evil" in the Garden of Eden may have evolved from tales of psychedelic herbs that were forbidden to the general population and that Moses's encounter with the burning bush that was not consumed but made his face shine brightly was a psychedelic-enabled vision (e.g., Shanon 2008). Other scholars have suggested that the frankincense given by the "wise men" (*magi*) to honor the birth of Jesus contained one or more psychedelic ingredients. Some have theorized that the original Eucharist was a psychedelic sacrament. There is also some evidence that these drugs played a role in the religious life of early Middle Eastern Christians and perhaps in the Islamic world (Ruck 2006; Shanon 2008). Medieval Jewish Kabbalah medical texts refer to the hidden powers of certain psychedelics such as mandrake. (Such theories are, of course, controversial—most Christians and Jews do not want even to consider the possibility that hearing the voice of God and so forth may be merely hallucinations occasioned by psychedelics.)

Psychedelics have remained outside the mainstream traditions of the Abrahamic religions for most of their history. However, the works of Aldous Huxley, Alan Watts, Timothy Leary, Richard Alpert (Ram Dass), and Ralph Metzner made psychedelics occasionally appear in religious circles in the 1960s (see Partridge 2018).[8] Many outside of the traditions also saw psychedelic experiences as having religious significance. Robert Masters and Jean Houston stated that from their research on LSD "authentic religious experiences may occur within the context of the psychedelic drug-state" (1966: 257). Timothy Leary said that the "deepest religious experience" of his life came from eating seven sacred mushrooms and that he had repeated the ritual "several hundred times" and almost every time he was "awed by religious revelations as shattering as the first experience," and in addition that over 75 percent of the several thousand participants in his research reported "intense mystico-religious responses" and well over half claimed that they had the deepest spiritual experience of their life (1968: 13–14). Elsewhere he stated that the data shows that if administered in a supportive but not spiritual setting, 40 to 75 percent of psychedelic subjects will report "intense life-changing philosophic-religious" experiences, and if the "set and setting" are supportive and spiritual, the numbers rise to 40 to 90 percent of the experiences being "revelatory and mystico-religious" (Leary 2001: 11–12).[9] Masters and Houston report similar numbers if the setting is supportive (1966: 255). That these are reports from the early 1960s, when psychedelics provoked general worry and distrust among the public, is significant. Usually, the general cultural opinion of psychedelics influences the expectations and preconceptions of individuals (Carhart-Harris et al. 2018: 726). Huston Smith, who took mescaline under Leary's supervision, said that "overnight" he became "a visionary—one who not merely believes in the existence of a more momentous world than this but one who has actually visited it" (2000: 15). He asked how something that felt like an "epochal change" in his life could be "crowded into a few hours and occasioned by a chemical" (Smith 2000: 15).

However, the cultural revolution envisioned by Leary and company in the early 1960s did not materialize—enthusiasm for psychedelics simply waned once the government declared these drugs illegal (Langlitz 2012: 13).[10] Even the political wing of the hippie movement disowned them. The association of psychedelics with the hippie culture led to regulation. By 1980, New Age gurus had begun to distance themselves from psychedelics and to focus more on meditation (Partridge 2005: 83)—if one could attain enlightenment in a pill, there was no need for gurus. But today some religious groups, including the Santo Daime tradition in Brazil (see Barnard 2014) and the Native American Church in North America, have made psychedelics a sacrament. DMT, psilocybin, and mescaline have become the drugs of choice in religious circles. Books are on the increase in theology and the anthropology of religions on psychedelic plants that play a central role in religious rituals—in particular, peyote of the American Plains Indians and brews from the ayahuasca vine containing DMT. Harvard Divinity School now has a chaplain of psychedelics. The Internet has also allowed the expansion of religious interest in psychedelics outside of religious institutions. Some advocates want to establish a new religion with psychedelics as the principal sacrament and educational tool, following Huxley's novel *Island* with its "moksha medicine."[11] Leary predicted that psychedelics would be the religion of the twenty-first century (he started the "League of Spiritual Discovery," with LSD as its sacrament).[12] Jack Kornfield is not alone in advocating psychedelics within Buddhist practice. But psychedelics have also pulled many seekers away from both Western and Eastern religious traditions to "neoshamanism" and "pagan" spiritualities thanks in large part to Carlos Castaneda, Terence McKenna, and Michael Harner.

However, the recreational use of major psychedelics has greatly declined since the mid-1970s and is not a matter of general public concern in the United States and Europe today (Langlitz 2012: 13). The quasipsychedelic MDMA has become more popular.[13] The West in the twentieth century also appears to be the first large culture in which these drugs were used mainly for mere recreation, even if some experiencers did end up attaching religious significance to their experiences. In prior cultures, use of psychedelics appears to have been confined principally to initiates in particular cults or to religious rituals involving specialists who administer the drug as medicine to members of the tribe. But now some people see psychedelics as a way to an "experimental mysticism."[14]

The late twentieth century also saw the first "secular mysticism" in which meditation is undertaken for merely psychological and physiological benefits and in which mystical experiences are understood as merely products of the brain having no cognitive significance (see chapter 8). In this context, psychedelics are seen as merely breaking the hold of our ego and letting material from our subconscious emerge into the conscious mind.[15] Inside and outside religious communities, a nagging doubt is expressed that if religious experiences come in a pill, psychedelic experiences cannot be cognitive of any reality but must be only purely subjective experiences generated by the brain. Many scientists studying psychedelics now understand both their effects on the brain and the accompanying experiences and their causes solely in natural terms. Thus, such metaphysical naturalists do not see the need to include any transcendent realities in the full explanation of mystical experiences and its effects.

The Scientific Study of Psychedelic Drugs and Mysticism Experiences

Psychedelics became an object of scientific investigation in the nineteenth century as Europeans and Americans observed their uses in other cultures. For example, the spreading use of peyote among Native Americans in the second half of the century led American and English researchers to study the effects of the cactus, and in 1897 through a series of self-experiments the German chemist Arthur Heffter identified and isolated mescaline as its pharmacologically active element (Langlitz 2012: 27). Scientific interest in such drugs entered the mainstream early in the twentieth century with William James's interest in conversion-experiences and his experimenting with nitrous oxide (1958 [1902]: 298). Interest lagged until Aldous Huxley's experiences of the "is-ness" of reality enabled by mescaline recounted in his *The Doors of Perception* (1954). In 1962, Walter Pahnke conducted the now famous "Good Friday" experiment in a chapel in which a group of Protestant theological students and their professors were given either psilocybin or a placebo after a religious service (Pahnke 1966; H. Smith 2000: 15–32), enabling experiences that they deemed mystical.[16] Masters and Houston (1966) also claimed to have duplicated through LSD all the phenomenological features of spontaneous and meditative mystical experiences, thereby making these experiences indistinguishable from, not merely something "similar" to, a natural mystical experience or a "partial" mystical experience.

In reaction to the recreational use of LSD and other drugs in the 1960s, the general use of psychedelics was declared illegal in the United States and most of Europe, and the scientific study of them ended. But clinical drug studies returned in the 1990s, first with DMT (Strassman 2001), as part of the "Decade of the Brain." Advocates of psychedelic research as a way to study the brain see these drugs as the "next big thing" in psychopharmacology (Carhart-Harris, Kaelen, and Nutt 2014: 662) since they affect the state of the brain as more exotic states of consciousness are occurring. But the attention paid to meditation, especially mindfulness, currently overshadows research on psychedelics, although the later is growing fast. Moreover, drug research still has not been endorsed by the psychological research community as a whole or by mainstream clinical psychiatrists. Government funding for experiments on therapeutic applications has occurred in some countries, but psychedelic researchers are still having difficulty gaining funding in the United States from the National Institutes of Health.

Nevertheless, the renewed investigation of psychedelics has significantly advanced neuroscientific knowledge (e.g., contributing to our understanding of cortical metabolism and the neurochemical substrates of psychotic processes), leading to new forms of psychotherapeutic treatment (Langlitz 2012: 240).[17] The effect of psychedelic molecules on the production of the neurotransmitter serotonin, which plays a role in regulating consciousness, has been of special interest because psychedelics inhibit prefrontal cortex activity. LSD apparently deactivates regions of the brain that integrate our senses and our sense of a "self," thereby permitting other areas of the brain to become more active. The self no longer feels confined to our body. Thus, psychedelics may expand the mind by (paradoxically) inhibiting certain brain activities (Cole-Turner 2014: 645–46; Halberstadt and Geyer 2015). In addition to more intense visual and auditory sensations, the extrovertive type of "mystical union" can lead to an extrovertive sense of being connected to others, the world, and the rest of the cosmos, and also to a better sense of what you are—in short, overcoming the sense of alienation and isolation in its various forms. But "cosmic consciousness" and LSD experiences in general may be qualitatively *different* states of consciousness (Smith and Tart 1998).

Along with disrupting cognitive and sensory systems, psychedelics have been found reliably to perturb self-consciousness and occasion ego-dissolution in steps in an orderly progressive dose-dependent manner (Nour and Carhart-Harris 2017: 178).[18] The sense of "self" that is disrupted or dissolved in mystical experiences is the coherent "narrative self" (ego-identity) built up by different neural networks; when this is dissolved, the "minimal self" of first-person subjective experiences, including a sense of unity, ownership of experience, and agency, still remains (Nour and Carhart-Harris 2017: 177; Lebedev et al. 2015). Psychedelics temporarily topple the brain's usual hierarchy—in the words of Robin Carhart-Harris, "All of a sudden, there is no big boss man in this brain governing the show" (quoted in Bean 2024: 4). Under normal conditions, communication between areas of the brain is organized into stable networks (Johnson et al. 2019: 47–51). One network is the background default mode network (DMN) that is involved in high-level psychological functions, including introspection and autobiographical memory (Johnson et al. 2019: 177). The DMN communicates less with itself and more with other areas of the brain (Bean 2024: 4). Recent MEG studies showed that the degree of ego-dissolution occasioned by psychedelics is correlated with increased whole-brain integration (by increasing the level of communication between normally unrelated brain networks) and inversely correlated with DMN network integrity (Johnson et al. 2019: 178; but see Lebedev et al. 2015: 10; Johnson et al. 2019: 48). A single dose of psilocybin "desynchronizes" brain activity across the brain but especially in the DMN (Siegel et al. 2024). Thereby, our baseline state of consciousness and our sense of self are disrupted. Changes in the activity, connectivity, and neural oscillatory processes in the DMN may ground dimensions of mystical experiences, especially the decreased self-referential processing and an altered sense of time and space (Barrett and Griffiths 2018: 414–21, 423–24). That is, there is an increase in global integration within the brain mediated by certain serotonin receptors on the membrane of brain cells and the thalamus but a decrease in the internal module integrity of the DMN network (Tagliazucchi et al. 2016: 1048). (Activation of one particular receptor—$5\text{-}HT_{2A}$—appears necessary for psychedelic-enabled experiences.)

Thus, ego-dissolution is dependent on changes in the whole brain, not just specific functional modules (Tagliazucchi et al. 2016: 1048). There may also be less interhemispheric connectivity than normal (Lebedev et al. 2015). Ego-dissolution is related to the increased feeling of connection to others and to one's surroundings (Nour and Carhart-Harris 2017: 178). It shares some phenomenological features with schizophrenia, but experiencers having mystical ASCs have a positive mental set producing a more stable and positive experience (Nour and Carhart-Harris 2017: 177–78). Long-lasting positive psychological effects of psilocybin, such as increased openness and creativity, are commonly reported (e.g., McCulloch et al. 2022). Thus, ego-dissolution is not necessarily an unpleasant or pathological experience (Lebedev et al. 2015).

On the negative side, these drugs can also enable disturbing and even terrifying experiences—visions of hells, not only heavens (Huxley 1955). "Bad trips" can deeply disturb a person's emotional balance (Newberg and Waldman 2016: 77, 79).[19] Meditation also may induce very negative experiences, but it appears to do so less often. In particular, the dissolution of a sense of an ego—the loss of all that makes our personality distinct—is an "experience of death." Destabilizing a sense of a self can be terrifying and dangerous for someone not prepared for it, even if one is psychologically healthy. It may exacerbate mental disorders and can lead to psychotic episodes. Introvertive experiences can lead to confusion, fear, panic, paranoia, and megalomania. One danger is "derealization"—i.e., confusion or uncertainty over what is real that lasts even months after the experience. In one study, 15 percent of the participants experienced derealization (Evans et al. 2023: 15).[20] In one drug study in which three-fifths of the participants had what the researchers considered "complete" mystical experiences, 44 percent of the volunteers reported at least some delusions or paranoid thinking. In a more rigorous double-blind randomized psilocybin study than Pahnke's 1962 experiment, a quarter of the subjects still reported that a significant portion of the session was characterized by anxiety, paranoia, and negative moods, and 31 percent experienced "significant" fear. The potential danger of psychedelics was played up in the 1960s and most of the substances were declared illegal.

Huston Smith refers to his visionary experiences as involving fear, awe, and fascination or even terror (2000: 12–13, 2005: 227). But unlike visions, mystical experiences do not typically involve an element of fearing what was experienced—the experiences may well have very negative elements, but the *reality allegedly experienced* is experienced as benign or loving. Smith also said that he had "very negative experiences" through psychedelics and that over time "the utility [of the experiences] seemed to go down quickly and the bummers increased" (2005: 227). He quoted Alan Watts: "When you get the message, hang up the phone" (1962: 26) and do not make any more calls. But he notes that "the Reality that trumps everything while it is in full view will fade into a memory" (2000: 131). In contrast, the continued recreational use or abuse of psychedelics (especially LSD) can lead to a postexperiential state with continuing distortions of perceptions—"Hallucinogen Persisting Perception Disorder" (or "flashbacks") may be so great that some people become impaired and require treatment (see Halpern, Lerner, and Passie 2018).

That negative experiences may be touched off by psychedelics has raised the question of whether making "positivity of mood" one criterion for a genuine mystical experience (Dax Oliver 2023).[21] Stressful environments and the lack of social support are associated with long-term negative responses to psychedelics (see Bremler 2023). Young age may be vulnerability factor (Bremler 2023). But it should be noted that some researchers and subjects felt that the negative experiences were simply "part of the process" leading to a valuable positive outcome (Evans et al. 2023: 18). Even the short-lived negative psychedelic experiences—or in therapeutic language, "acute challenging experiences"—may lead to *positive* cathartic effects later (Doblin 1991: 24; Schlag et al. 2022: 258; Yaden and Newberg 2022: 336). In one study 78.6 percent of participants who had negative experiences were still glad that they had taken the drug because ultimately there was a positive outcome (Schlag et al. 2022). In another study it was found that psychedelics may elicit psychosis-like symptoms during an immediate experience but improved psychological well-being in the mid- to long term by leaving a "loosened cognition" (Carhart-Harris et al. 2016).

But contemporary researchers have shown that with proper psychological screening, avoiding overdosing, and proper counseling during drug sessions, the risks are greatly reduced (e.g., Griffiths et al. 2006; Griffiths et al. 2008; Carhart-Harris et al. 2018; Barrett and Griffiths 2018). And if one is prepared psychologically (e.g., with a religious framework of beliefs), one can better handle the experiences associated with the changes in brain activity. Moreover, the negative effects, unlike the positive ones, do not usually last past the drug session (Griffiths et al. 2006; Griffiths et al. 2008).[22] Psychological turmoil may even trigger a mystical experience. Psychological turmoil may even trigger a mystical experience. Mystical experience enabled by psychedelics can lead to long-term spiritual growth (Schutt et al. 2024).

In one prominent study, one-third of the participants considered it the most significant spiritual experience of their lives, and for another quarter it was one of the top five, and that significance was still persisting when the participants were questioned fourteen months later (Griffiths et al. 2006; Griffiths et al. 2008; see Barrett and Griffiths 2018 for similar numbers). The researchers also found that the experiences occasioned by psilocybin induced persisting positive changes in attitudes, mood, life satisfaction, behavior, altruism/social activity, and social relationships with family and others.

A long-term study of Pahnke's experiment also showed that the drug-enabled mystical experiences had lasting positive effects for many participants on their attitude and behavior, and persisting negative effects only for a few (Doblin 1991). How they saw their experiences also changed slightly over time. The effects included recognizing the arbitrariness of ego boundaries, a deepening of religious faith, and a heightened sense of joy and beauty. Most of the psilocybin recipients had subsequent mystical experiences in dreams, during prayer, out in nature, or with other psychedelics. Significant differences between their nondrug and drug-enabled mystical experiences were reported, with the drug experiences reported as both more intense and composed of a wider emotional range; however, the nondrug mystical experiences were composed primarily of peaceful, beautiful moments, while the drug experiences had moments of great fear, agony, and self-doubt.[23] Feelings of unity led many of the subjects to identify with and feel compassion for minorities, women, and the environment. It also reduced their fear of death (also see Letheby 2024). But few reported completely positive experiences without significant psychological struggles such as paranoia, or fear they were going insane or dying. The researcher suspected that difficult moments were significantly underreported. For example, Pahnke did not mention that most who were given psilocybin in the "Good Friday" experiment experienced the fear that they were dying or "going crazy," or that one had to be restrained and given the antipsychotic Thorazine (Doblin 1991: 22).

One psilocybin study examined increases in well-being and the subjects' enduring traits in conjunction with ongoing daily meditation and spiritual practices (Griffiths et al. 2018). The study found that both the mystical experiences and spiritual practices contributed to positive outcomes, with mystical experience making a substantially greater contribution: "[M]ystical experience and/or its neurophysiological or other correlates are likely determinants of the enduring positive attitudinal, dispositional, and behavioral effects of psilocybin when administered under spiritually supported conditions" (Griffiths et al. 2018: 67). The analyses suggested that "the determinants of these effects were the intensity of the psilocybin-occasioned mystical experiences and the rates of engagement with meditation and other spiritual practices" (Griffiths et al. 2018: 68).

Science and Perennial Philosophy

Drug users often believe that they have attained the enlightening knowledge of all mystics, but three things must be pointed out. First, there are different types of mystical experiences—what any extrovertive experience allegedly involves is not the same as what different types of introvertive experiences allegedly do. Second, mystics have different understandings of what is allegedly experienced in mystical experiences—there is not one generic mystical enlightenment doctrine (see R. Jones 2021b). Third, there may be degrees or stages of enlightening knowledge after the initial cracking of the phenomenal ego. Since these experiences are not tied to any particular religious traditions, cross-cultural understandings of their significance such as "perennial philosophy" became popular in scientific circles, although few in the academic study of religion embrace it (see R. Jones 2021b). Concepts of transcendent realities from different traditions became interchangeable—as William Richards (2016: 211) says, one can say "God (or whatever your favorite noun for ultimate reality may be)."

Sharday Mosurinjohn, Leor Roseman, and Manesh Girn note that researchers in psychedelic studies have imported Christian perennialist metaphysical assumptions that limit the scope, nuance, and cross-cultural sensitivity of their investigations (2023: 2). Many in the field of the study of psychedelics are drawn to perennial philosophy (e.g., Richards 2016; Hood [2013: 301]; Grof 2009). That is not surprising because empirical psychologists focus only on the experiences themselves, since they want to advance "a scientific basis for exploring the immediate causes and consequences" of mystical experiences (Barrett and Griffiths 2018: 398), and thus they are not interested in matters of different doctrinal interpretations of mystical experiences. For their interests, mystical doctrines are not important. Saying "God (or whatever your favorite noun for ultimate reality may be)" is easier than studying the details of different doctrines in different mystical traditions. But they end up throwing together lists of unrelated concepts from different cultures. So too, they may mean only that all introvertive mystics have the same experiences or experience the same alleged reality and not intend the full metaphysics of perennial philosophy. Thus, the claim may not actually be about perennialism proper. But "perennial philosophy" is not simply shorthand for "All mystics have the same experiences and experience the same reality" but has a full emanationist metaphysics of reality (see R. Jones 2021b). It must also be remembered that classical mystics lived according to their tradition's specific doctrines—including their understanding of what transcendent reality was experienced in mystical experiences—not according to "whatever you want to call it."

In sum, the scientists may be too busy to read anything more than the snippets of mystics' doctrines in Walter Stace and William James, but they should realize that, while mystics who have had introvertive mystical experiences may well all have experienced *the same reality* or had *similar experiences* (within the different types), their full *understanding* of what is real is what guides their lives.

Set and Setting

Timothy Leary, G. H. Litwin, and Ralph Metzner (1963) popularized the importance of "set and setting" for the occurrence and nature of a mystical experience. That is, differences in a user's background beliefs, expectations, mood, mental attitude, and past experiences with psychedelics (one's mental "set") and the physical and social environment when a drug is ingested (the "setting") at least partially account for the great variation in the experiences, from deep mystical experiences to no ASC experiences at all. The experiencer's feeling safe and having trust and confidence in the guide is also important. General cultural and social elements may enter each experiencer's mental set. One's beliefs need not be tied to any particular religious tradition—any religious or nonreligious beliefs will do as long as they permit the experiencer to be open to experiences. The "setting" includes not only the physical environment and decorations but such things as lighting (Carhart-Harris et al. 2018: 726). The music chosen to be part of the setting may play a vital role (Leary, Metzner, and Alpert 1964: 11; Kaelen et al. 2018). Experiences within a group setting may differ from experiences occurring to a solitary experiencer.[24]

Set and setting have become accepted as of essential importance in the use of psychedelics in psychotherapy (Carhart-Harris et al. 2018), although the exact effect of settings on the experience has not been tested (Golden et al. 2022). People who are highly open to new experiences are more likely to have positive experiences, while people who are emotionally unstable or rigidly conventional in their views are likely to experience greater anxiety and confusion and have disturbing experiences (Studerus et al. 2012; but see Griffiths et al. 2018). Psilocybin users who are relatively unchurched are more likely to have mystical experiences than those who are deeply entrenched in traditional beliefs and practices (Newberg and Waldman 2016: 240, 247; Yaden et al. 2016: 249–50). When psychedelics are used recreationally, fewer mystical experiences occur (Newberg and Waldman 2016: 235–36). Ingesting the same psychedelic in the context of a religious ritual in a calming setting may produce a different experience than when the drug is ingested in a sterile lab. In one study, the researcher intentionally avoided anything that might be interpreted as a "religious setting" and yet 24 percent of the volunteers had a mystical or spiritual experience (see Partridge 2018: 24). With a secular set and setting, about a quarter to a third of the general population will nevertheless have a religious experience; when subjects have a religious proclivity in a more supportive environment, the figure jumps to three-quarters (H. Smith 2000: 20). Intentionally neglecting or even manipulating the setting in a negative way produces considerably less positive outcomes (Carhart-Harris et al. 2018: 726). But again, even in nonreligious settings, a significant percentage of the subjects may still report religious significance to their ASC experiences (Partridge 2005: 129).

Even a researcher calling the drug an "entheogen" rather than a "hallucinogen" affects the experiencer's mental set. One can use terms for mystical experiences that are less religious and encompass other types of experiences—e.g., "peak experiences," "self-transcending experiences," or "quantum change experiences." The experiments that Roland Griffiths's group at Johns Hopkins (Griffiths et al. 2006; Griffiths et al. 2008; Griffiths et al. 2011) conducted produced more mystical experiences than did those conducted by Robin Carhart-Harris's group at the Imperial College in London (Carhart-Harris 2012; Carhart-Harris, Kaelen, and Nutt 2014), perhaps in part because the former used terminology related to "mystical experience" while the latter used language related to "ego-death" and "psychosis-like states" (Cole-Turner 2014: 649–50). That is, the Johns Hopkins group was looking specifically for reports of mystical experiences, and this language helped to generate them, while the London group was looking for the neurological effects of psilocybin, not what they deemed "magical thinking," and thus employed less encouraging language and generated fewer mystical experiences. The Johns Hopkins group tried to provide "substantial controls" to counter expectancy bias, but Griffiths and colleagues (2006) conceded that the "setting" of the lab was "in many ways optimized to produce the kinds of experiences we are seeing." (He was accused of running his psychedelic studies "more like a 'new-age' retreat center" [quoted in Borrell 2024: 1].) But that group also used larger dosages of psilocybin.

The role of our mental set also raises the issue of whether members of different religions and nonbelievers have different experiences. Since each person has a unique background mental set, is each experience unique in a significant way, with the only exception being a mystical experience that is completely empty of any differentiated content (which would have no individualized content to be affected by differences in people's mental sets)? Psychedelics may set up the same neural base in the brain for mystical experiences as meditation does, but they more often facilitate a mystical experience only when the subject is prepared for one by pre-experience spiritual practices and beliefs and is in a religious or otherwise favorable setting, although the disruption of the baseline state of consciousness that is induced by the drugs (or other triggers) cannot guarantee a mystical experience will occur even then.[25] The drugs' disruptive effect may be universal due to our common physiology, but what subsequently fills our mind is not universal—from experiences with rich phenomenological content to experiences with no differentiated content to no changes in consciousness at all. Thus, psychedelics affect people in different ways even if the chemical reaction in their brains is the same.

In addition, volunteers for psychedelic studies who are spiritually inclined and seeking religious experiences are already predisposed to having such experiences. These persons may have a religious purpose and goal for volunteering.[26] Self-selected participants who are inclined toward having spiritual experiences would have the mental set conducive to having drug-enabled mystical experiences. If many or most participants to date are so inclined, scientists may not be getting a true cross-section of the population as a whole and these studies may be weighted toward producing mystical experiences. As a wider range of people participate, the picture may change. So too with lasting effects: if one is a seeker, one sees a significance in these experiences that reflects one's beliefs, and the effect of the experience may be transformative and have a lasting impact; but if one is not interested in religion, the experiences are less likely to have any lasting effect on how one sees the world. "Instant enlightenment" through drugs does not create any mystical wisdom in itself—one is simply "taking a trip" and returning home to one's old state of consciousness, either immediately or slowing over time, as the experience fades into a memory. The memory may affect one's beliefs and how one behaves, but for most experiencers their state of consciousness is once again ego-driven and dualistic.

Such experiences have led some drug users to adopt a mystical way of life. However, when a drug-facilitated experience does occur to someone already seeking a religious way of life, the experiencer may dismiss any sense of oneness or connectedness the next day as nothing more than a delusion produced by the chemical reaction in the brain, just as LSD's effects on perception are often dismissed. In general, isolated drug experiences do not usher in a permanent selfless enlightened state. Thus, psychedelics have not proven to be efficient in producing mystical lives. Hence, the mystical objection to psychedelics: mysticism is about aligning one's life with reality, not any momentary experience, no matter how interesting, and that requires a great amount of work outside of any psychedelic experience.

Psychedelic Drugs as Triggers

The effect of psychedelics usually occurs much faster than with other triggers. But calling psychedelics "triggers" is something of a misnomer since nothing can *force* a mystical experience to occur 100 percent of the time (see chapter 4). Even with a proper dosage and a supportive set and setting, mystical experiences or other ASC experiences are not guaranteed, although discussions of drugs as triggers often appear to presume that. With the proper set and setting and dosage, drugs induce a percentage of subjects—sometimes seventy-some percent—to have either extrovertive or introvertive mystical experiences or, more typically, visions of realities distinct from the experiencer. (LSD is especially connected to inducing visions.[27])

However, ingesting a psychedelic drug does not in fact assure *any* ASC experience or state. Sometimes no significant alteration of one's state of consciousness occurs at all. William Richards reports that a substantial number of people have ingested psychedelics on many occasions without experiencing any profound ASCs (Richards 2016: 15)—indeed, he notes that people can take psychoactive drugs hundreds of times without encountering anything deemed "sacred" (Richards 2014: 654). J. Harold Ellens found the same: many persons have taken psychedelics repeatedly and never come close to experiencing profound states of consciousness, spiritual or otherwise (2015: 22–23). (So too, many people meditate daily for decades without any ASC experiences occurring.) Sometimes mystical experiences or visions do not occur during drug-enabled states but precede or follow them (Richards 2016: 10). Charles Tart concurs and adds that once one has learned a response from a psychedelic one can ingest what one thinks is the drug (but is not) and the response will occur again; conversely, one can unknowingly ingest the active ingredient of a psychedelic without being aware of having done so, and no response occurs (1975: 152–53). This makes establishing a one-to-one correlation of experiential and brain states highly problematic. In any case, the process of attaining an experience is not mechanical but involves other elements than the trigger alone.

Thus, psychedelics apparently only break the hold that the ordinary ego-driven mind has on us by altering the chemistry of the brain in relevant areas—that breaks the hold of the dualism of a phenomenal experiencing self set off from multiple objects engrained in our ordinary state of mind, but what the mind finds after that depends on other factors. For this reason, it is not correct to refer to drugs as the *cause* of a mystical experience: the drug is part of a package of causes and conditions that can "enable," "facilitate," or "occasion" a mystical experience, but it is not a simple cause of any ASC experience.[28] Rather, a psychedelic drug is one way to arrange necessary conditions in the brain for a mystical experience to occur, but it is not sufficient to create any particular experience. The fact that some subjects who are given a placebo also have mystical experiences must also be explained. Another issue is the default mode network can be disrupted in other ways (e.g., by alcohol) without regularly enabling mystical or other ASC experiences. How do psychedelics differ from those? Another issue is that nonmystical states of consciousness may also result from disruption of the DMN. Thus, such disruption may be neither necessary nor sufficient for the appearance of mystical experiences.

It is also important to reiterate that psychedelics apparently enable a variety of experiences, including a variety of mystical ones—there is no one universal psychedelic ASC experience—even though researchers routinely refer to "*the* mystical experience" and "*the* psychedelic state" (e.g., Nour and Carhart-Harris 2017: 177).[29] Even if there is one distinctive brain state connected to all mystical experiences (or all psychedelic experiences), there is still a variety of subjective experiences, including no change of consciousness at all. That is, there is no one generic "psychedelic state of consciousness" following the ingestion of these drugs (Richards 2016: 16). Even during one session, there is a variety of states of consciousness during the actions of the entheogens (Richards 2016: 115).

Thus, as Huston Smith summed up, "there is no such thing as *the* drug experience per se—no experience that the drugs, as it were, secrete" (2000: 20). Psychedelics do not mechanically produce an experience even if the brain generates consciousness. That is, psychedelics have no inherent mystical or other experiential properties. Every experience results from a mixture of three ingredients—the drug, set, and setting (Richards 2016)—and perhaps other factors. The psychologist Stanislav Grof (2009) makes the point that LSD has no one invariant pharmacological effect, nor is there one inevitable experience associated with it—rather LSD, he believes, is a catalyzer that amplifies and exteriorizes dynamics within the experiencer's subconscious. Timothy Leary noted this when he first discussed set and setting: "Of course, the drug does not produce the transcendent experience. It merely acts as a chemical key—it opens the mind, frees the nervous system of its ordinary patterns and structures. The nature of the experience depends almost entirely on set and setting" (Leary, Metzner, and Alpert 1964: 11). So too, if one expects a life-changing experience, one will often get it, and if one does not, one will not.

Thus, brain activity may be altered by psychedelics, but whether consciousness is altered or what state of consciousness arises depends on other factors. If so, brain activity alone does not shape the full phenomenology of mystical experiences—indeed, perhaps brain activity does not shape any of the felt phenomenological content of these experiences at all. Even if people are all neurobiologically the same vis-à-vis mystical experiences and receive the same stimulants, people may still have different reactions to the drugs and have different experiences. Set and setting figure into this, but the diversity of psychedelic states connected to the same brain state remains. Transcendent factors also remain a possibility. Or if mystical experiences are totally subjective, with material merely coming from our subconscious, the issue of diverse states persists.

In addition, in these experiments some participants who were given only a placebo also had mystical experiences. Although mystical experiences occur with a higher frequency with a psychedelic than with a placebo in these experiments, some claim that psychedelics are high-voltage "active placebos" or catalysts (Olson et al. 2020): they do not merely block overactive neurotransmitters but also disrupt the neurobiology underlying our ego-driven baseline state of consciousness and make the experiencer more susceptible to the effects of set and setting; but in the case of visions and locutions, they do not set up any one altered state of consciousness—instead, our subconscious or other factors complete the experience. Indeed, they may be "active super-placebos" that do not merely break habitual constraints on sense perceptions but enhance the content of visions and locutions by increasing suggestibility and supplying symbols and other content from the experiencer's cultural worldview and social milieu (Dupuis and Veissiere 2022).

Thus, most researchers today agree that all the experiences are not products of simply the chemical changes alone—our underlying mental set and the setting are responsible for the differences in ASC experiences, not differences in the drugs or their effects on the brain. Psychedelics open healthy persons up to greater suggestibility (Carhart-Harris et al. 2015: 791) and magnify whatever meaning they bring to the experiences. This is why expectation and the rest of the set and setting are so important, and thus why studying those in connection with placebos may prove valuable (Hartogsohn 2016). The study of spontaneous mystical experiences (if possible) would also prove valuable in this regard.

Can Psychedelic Drugs Enable Genuine Mystical Experiences?

The current state of psychedelic research raises three philosophical issues concerning the alleged import of mystical experiences: Do psychedelics actually occasion "genuine" mystical experiences?[30] Are the drug-enabled mystical experiences the same in nature as those that occur spontaneously or through meditative preparation? Does the establishment of the brain chemistry associated with mystical experiences validate mystical cognitive claims or invalidate them?

As to the first question: the scientific evidence is that psychedelics can reliably occasion genuine mystical experiences under supportive conditions: the evidence from scanning indicates that the brain states of those having mystical experiences through meditation and those having experiences in drug sessions are relevantly similar. This suggests that the accompanying subjective ASCs may be the same. The firsthand phenomenological descriptions from both traditional mystics around the world and today's drug subjects also suggest that the experiences are in fact relevantly the same and are properly classified as "mystical." But it must be noted that establishing that *the configurations of brain events* occurring during ASC experiences are similar and differ from those occurring during ordinary sense experience or other mental events is the most that neuroscience as currently devised can do toward establishing similarities and differences in mental states and experiences. Science may change in the future, but without being able to examine the subjective states themselves, science cannot do more and thus is limited in definitively establishing differences in experiences. If different mystical experiences can accompany the same brain state, science is limited even more. The states enabled by psychedelics and meditation share phenomenological descriptions with classical mystics' accounts, and so, as Barrett and Griffiths state, "[I]t is tempting to interpret the neural correlates of hallucinogens and meditation as a model of the neural correlates of mystical experiences" (2018: 422–23).

It is also worth noting that psychedelics do not induce introvertive mystical experiences as readily as extrovertive ones, and the introvertive ones that are enabled are typically with differentiated content rather than the "empty" depth-mystical experience. "Unitive" experiences in which the sense of a distinct phenomenal self ceases are relatively rare in psychedelic studies compared to other types of ASC experiences (e.g., Strassman 2001; Griffiths et al. 2006; Griffiths et al. 2008). But some do occur. In extrovertive unitive experiences, the boundary between oneself and nature is dissolved. The world is no longer set up in a duality of a distinct ego set off from multiple material objects. One feels connected to the rest of reality, and the rest of reality is also seen as connected together.

But the felt *unified introvertive state of consciousness* must be distinguished from what mystics think is the proper ontological understanding of the experience. In introvertive experiences, the sense of the separation of one's self and a transcendent reality is overcome. In the West, this is most often seen as "union with God." Part of the reason for this may be that in Western cultures the religious see exotic experiences in terms of "union with God." But introvertive unitive states of consciousness with or without differentiated content are interpreted differently after the fact depending on one's tradition—e.g., as realizing a universal consciousness, connecting our soul with God, realizing a common transcendent reality underlying all phenomena (Brahman or the Dao), realizing our true self (the independent transcendent conscious souls of Samkhya-Yoga or Jainism), or only experiencing a unified state of natural consciousness free of differentiated content.

Thus, realizing an "empty" conscious state has not always led mystics to conclude that this consciousness is one universal reality or anything else transcending the experiencer. The unitive sense in the introvertive state of consciousness does not necessarily mean a "union" of all reality or of a self with God. Even among Abrahamic mystics who include a nonpersonal

Godhead in their ontology (such as Meister Eckhart), most affirm that the soul is in some sense separate from God even if God provides the soul's substance. Thus, the absence of a sense of "self" during the mystical experience is not always interpreted after the experience is over as a denial of the existence of a transcendent "self" or "soul." Rather, one is simply *unaware* of the sensing self during certain experiences, just as an experience that seems timeless does not negate the reality of time (at least in the phenomenal world)—the experiencer is merely blinded by the light of God, as it were, in the experience and does not see the soul. The sense of unity is then seen by theists as either a loving connection to God that overcomes a dualism to that extent or as only attaining the ground of one's own individual soul.

Thus, nondual unitive states of consciousness are not inherently *theistic*. William Richards prefers the terms "internal" and "external" unity (2016: 59–68). But "unity" is not the same in introvertive and extrovertive mysticism: inwardly, the unity is the absence of differentiations in the state of consciousness; outwardly, it is seeing the world free of being cut up into distinct entities and thus realizing that everything is connected. In outward unity, sensing discrete independent entities within the phenomenal world (especially a "self") is seen to be an illusion. The felt sense of unity in extrovertive mystical experiences from the loss of a sense of boundaries to the self may be seen as union with nature. Inward unity need not have any bearing on the ontic nature of external connectedness; at most, it may suggest only that everything may share the same beingness as does our consciousness. Roger Walsh notes that Westerners trained in shamanic practices may report unitive experiences, but they are experiences of union with the universe rather than with a deity (1990: 240). A "pronounced pantheistic tendency" is common in the history of entheogens (Partridge 2005: 127; also see Forte 1997), but pantheism is more impersonal than theism with its personal deity.[31] In introvertive experiences, the loss of a sense of self may be seen as union, but in drug experiences this tends to be seen in deistic terms or as realizing a universal and nonpersonal cosmic consciousness. Nor is it clear that those introvertive experiences that are taken to be theistic are actually constructed with cultural conceptions of a person or instead are seen as theistic only after the experiences are over (see R. Jones 2020a on constructivism).

In addition, a religious framework in one's mind that is prepared for or expecting not only a psychedelic experience but a religious one as well affects the content of an experience and also whether the experience has a continuing impact on the experiencer after it is over. The mystical experiences that psychedelics enable do not transform subjects' subsequent character as often as cultivated mystical experiences do, although some persons with only drug-enabled experiences do permanently change, and some become interested in a spiritual path. This suggests that a religious transformation is not from the drugs' effects on one's consciousness alone. Rather, if one has been engaged in a religious life and expects a mystical or other experience, one is more likely to see the experience as involving a reality beyond the natural mind, thus leading to a change in character or way of life, even if the phenomenological *content* of the experience ends up *not* being what one anticipated. Mystical experiences facilitated by drugs (especially from recreational use in a nonreligious setting by a person without religious beliefs) may seem to be more subjective even to the experiencer than "genuine" encounters with reality and thus may not have as great a lasting effect. But changes in one's *view of the world* brought about by drug experiences are more common among subjects with no religious aspirations (Newberg and Waldman 2016: 75–76). And as noted earlier, any lasting change of character may result more from an experiencer's beliefs and practices than the chemical effect of the psychedelic drug—perhaps the lasting change may occur even without the psychedelic experience.

None of the above alters the conclusion that psychedelics do disrupt our baseline state of consciousness and very often occasion experiences some of which are genuinely mystical in nature. But, as discussed above, the relation of the actions of the psychedelics on the content of the experiences and the continuing effect of the experience on the experiencer after the experience is over is not straightforward. Nor does the fact that the drugs may occasion mystical experiences mean that persons who have been engaged in mystical ways of life may not have deeper experiences than do nonpractitioners who have their first mystical experience enabled by taking drugs. So too, the drug-enabled experiences of those who have engaged long-term in advanced meditative practices or an ascetic disciplining of the body may be different from those of novices. The experiences of the nonpractitioners may seem superficial to the mystically engaged, however profound it seems to the experiencers themselves. And this leads to the next question.

Are Drug-Enabled Mystical Experiences the Same as Natural Ones?

Even if some experiences occasioned by psychedelics are mystical in nature, a recurring issue is whether the mystical experiences occasioned by the drugs are the *same in nature* as those occurring either spontaneously or through mystical practices or through the "grace of God." Are drug-enabled experiences in fact not duplicating the full phenomenology of a mystical experience occurring "naturally"? Or are some mystical experiences that are enabled "artificially" by psychedelics not merely *similar* to what theists deem "genuine" mystical experiences but the *same*?

The prevailing view in scientific discussions is that psychedelic-enabled mystical experiences are the same in nature as those facilitated by other means such as yoga or fasting—drugs produce the same effects in the brain as those activities do, and thus the resulting phenomenology of the experiences is the same.[32] As the philosopher Walter Stace said of chemically facilitated experiences, "It is not a matter of its being *similar* to mystical experience; it *is* mystical experience" (quoted in H. Smith 2000: 24). Huston Smith concurred: given the right set and setting, "drugs can induce religious experiences that are indistinguishable from such experiences that occur spontaneously" (2000: 20). That is, they are phenomenologically indistinguishable. Stace invoked what he called the "principle of causal indifference": if two experiences are phenomenologically indistinguishable, then one cannot be called a "genuine" mystical experience and the other not merely because they arise from dissimilar causal conditions (1960: 29–31).[33] Some base in brain activity may be necessary for a given type of mystical experience to occur, but whether that base is caused by a chemical reaction from a psychedelic, meditation, or some other trigger is irrelevant to the phenomenological content of the experience.

However, many theists object on theological grounds that drug-enabled experiences are not "genuine" mystical experiences but only pale copies—true mystical experiences are different in nature and content and come only from God. At most psychedelics clear the mind of its ordinary content. That in itself may produce an interesting experience, but for a genuine mystical experience God must enter choose to enter that cleared space. The Roman Catholic R. C. Zaehner was an early proponent of this view. He tried mescaline and ended up with only an upset stomach (1957: 212–26; also see Katz 2013: 3–4; and Horgan 2003: 44–45). This points again to the issue of a proper dosage and a supportive mental set and setting. Zaehner believed that the drug taker's consciousness bears only "a superficial resemblance to that of the religious mystic" (Zaehner 1957: xii). He did accept that "nature" and "monistic" mystical experiences may be enabled by drugs, but he insisted that "theistic" introvertive mystical experiences can be produced only by acts of grace from God (Zaehner 1957: 14–29). That is, no set of natural conditions such as ingesting a drug can *compel* God to act in any way or force God to be known against his will. To many theists, drug-enabled mystical experiences seem unearned and undeserved (see Pahnke 1966: 309–10)—a "cheap grace." So too, if genuine mystical experiences could occur without Christian faith, then grace would not be restricted to Christians. Mystical experiences may well be grounded in the brain, and theists could expect God to utilize our neural system to produce mystical experiences rather than somehow bypass it, but manipulating brain states with chemicals could not force God to enter our mind, since he chooses those whom he wants to know him.[34] Psychedelics merely fool users into thinking that they have experienced something more than brain events. In sum, God initiates all genuine theistic mystical experiences.

That comparatively few *theistic* mystical experiences occur through psychedelics also upsets some theists—as already noted, most drug-enabled introvertive mystical experiences do not involve any sense of connecting with a transcendent person or any reality personal in nature, nor do these drugs facilitate introvertive mystical experiences as readily as extrovertive ones and theistic visions. A higher percentage of non-psychedelic-enabled mystical experiences are seen as religious (Formoso 2023). It appears that psychedelics enable dualistic visions of realities distinct from the experiencer more often than mystical experiences, including theistic experiences of contact with God. For example, members of the Native American Church often have visions of Christ in their rituals with peyote as a sacrament (Masters and Houston 1966: 257). The psychedelic DMT apparently often touches off encounters with sentient beings seen as distinct from the experiencer (Strassman 2001; Davis et al. 2020). However, with the classical psychedelics some introvertive theistic experiences of a sense of being connected or "one'd" with a reality do occur, since mystical experiences break down barriers that our mind sets up between ourselves and the rest of reality. As also noted above, any sense of a transcendent reality is typically of a non-personal reality (a deistic source or encompassing transcendent consciousness), although after the experience theists often reinterpret their conception of "God" as nonpersonal (e.g., the ground of being) in order to fit the nonpersonal experience. Some theists have found their drug-enabled mystical experiences to be more intense than "natural" ones (Doblin 1991: 14; Yaden et al. 2017a), but drug-enabled experiences, especially those occurring outside of mystical training, apparently are not as full in diverse content as cultivated mystical experiences.[35] Thus, the quality may vary from "natural" mystical experiences, but not their general nature.

Nevertheless, many among the religious are enthusiastic about the results of these drug studies, claiming that psychedelics induce the same experiences facilitated by other means and that this proves mystical experiences are veridical. But theologians who do not attach importance to mystical experiences are inclined to dismiss drug experiences as delusions—they are no more indicative of reality than LSD effects on perceptions and a sense of time (but see Moen 2022)—and not the mystical "intoxication with God" through a direct encounter with a personal transcendent reality that is given by God's "grace." Theists may insist that the phenomenology of mystical experiences will in fact differ if God infuses the experiencer rather than if an experiencer simply has natural phenomena in his or her mind during the experience—the *content* of the experiences will differ in nature. But it is hard to see how theists could establish this: we obviously cannot get inside the mind of anyone else to see the experience from their point of view. Nor can we tell anything specific from canned cultural conceptions like "I was united to God." Hence the need for detailed and open-ended questions in psychological surveys and interviews on the phenomenology of persons' experiences. But even detailed questionnaires and interviews may not suffice, since how participants see their experiences would be influenced by their religious or nonreligious beliefs, and their answers would reflect those beliefs.

Nor can theists cite the impact of naturally triggered experiences to bolster their claim. In one study, religious, spiritual, and mystical experiences (RSMEs) that were induced with psychedelic substances were rated as "(a) being significantly more mystical, (b) having greater positive or existential impact (in terms of decreased fear of death and increased sense of purpose), and (c) increasing participants' spirituality more than did RSMEs triggered through other means" (Yaden et al. 2017a: 346–47). In short, "participants rated psychedelic-triggered RSMEs as more intensely mystical, more positive in impact, and more related to spiritual and existential outcomes" (Yaden et al. 2017a: 347).[36] "The theoretical literature on RSMEs typically casts psychedelically induced experiences as artificial. Thus, such experiences are viewed as reminiscent of, but not equal to, the 'real thing' (Walsh 2003). Additionally, psychedelically triggered experiences have often been assumed to be mere 'flashes in the pan' with little possibility for long-term positive outcomes (Zaehner 1972). Of course, many psychedelic experiences do not have religious or spiritual import. However, the data from this study cast doubt on the assumption that RSMEs induced through psychedelic substances are any less genuine, positive, or spiritually significant. The greatest difference between psychedelic and nonpsychedelic experiences concerned mystical experiences" (Yaden et al. 2017a: 347). "It may be the case that mystical experiences occasioned by psychedelic substances are rated as more mystical because of the degree of visceral subjective and sensory changes that psychedelics reliably produce" (Yaden et al. 2017a: 347). Positive mood and behavioral outcomes were also greater (Yaden et al. 2017a: 347). "The finding that psychedelic-induced experiences were rated as more spiritual than nonpsychedelic experiences was particularly surprising as psychedelic substances represent an obviously physical, rather than supernatural, causal trigger of the experience. However, as previous works on the topic have discussed at length, the psychedelic substance is often not considered the 'cause' but rather the 'occasion' of the experience (Griffiths et al. 2006; Hood 2014; Huxley 1958; H. Smith 1964). That is, psychedelic substances may provide a potent context for a genuinely spiritual experience, leading to enhanced feelings of spirituality" (Yaden et al. 2017a: 347). (This would be so even if it looks to theists like the natural trigger is compelling God to act.) Thus, this data provides evidence that the use of psychedelic substances is associated with RSMEs that are similar to, and may, on average, *surpass* in mystical quality RSMEs induced through other means (Yaden et al. 2017a: 347).

Theists will have to rely on establishing differences in the brain states associated with theistic and nontheistic experiences, which at present does not appear to be the case. Until theists can present actual evidence that the phenomenology of drug-facilitated experiences differs from that occurring in meditation or spontaneously from grace in some fundamental way, we must accept that the experiences are neutral with regard to the type of trigger associated with them, not that the neural basis of theistic introvertive mystical experiences must differ when drug-facilitated or God-given. (The great variety of ASC experiences complicates this issue.) In short, whatever is the source of the content in differentiated mystical experiences, there is no reason at present to suspect that natural and transcendent triggers would not cause the same effect. And the depth-mystical experience would remain empty of differentiated content regardless of the trigger.

An important subsidiary issue is whether the experiences occasioned by the drugs administered to people in scientific settings have the same type of content as natural mystical experiences. Does a laboratory setting or knowing that one is involved in a drug experiment by itself affect the felt content of the experience, since set and setting matter? As noted above, expectancy bias and even using the term "entheogen" or "hallucinogen" may affect what experience a subject has. Nevertheless, even if a scientific setting affects some of the content of those experiences, the experiments indicate that at least some of the experiences share the phenomenology of natural mystical experiences.

In fact, there is no empirical evidence to date suggesting that the base conditions in the brain are different when a drug or other artificial trigger is applied as opposed to meditative preparation or other natural triggers or experiences occurring spontaneously through "grace." All involved in the dispute also agree that the psychological disposition and beliefs of each person and the environment (the set and setting) and proper dosages are important in all drug-enabled experiences and that differences in these at least partially account for the great variation in the experiences. Differences in the set and setting would account for any differences in the phenomenology of drug-facilitated experiences for believers, seekers with no religious affiliation, and nonbelievers. That is, differences in the type of experiences and their intensity when enabled by psychedelics can be accounted for by purely natural circumstances. Theists have not advanced a better argument based on science and phenomenology to think that the ASCs of theists are different in fundamental nature. If so, drug experiences are not in a separate class but involve only another trigger disrupting our baseline brain conditions in the same way as other triggers.

It may be that there are no inherently theistic mystical experiences, but the differentiated content is neutral between theistic and nontheistic understandings of the experiences—it is a matter of attribution by the experiencer. Still, we cannot get into the subjective state of another, and perhaps different subjective ASC states are associated with the same base conditions in the brain (see chapter 6). But as things stand today, theists have only theological reasons to doubt the authenticity of psychedelic-assisted mystical experiences or their content—they have not presented any nontheological reason to suspect that the base conditions or basic features are different. Such experiences cannot be dismissed on empirical grounds as "inferior" or "unreal." Without more, it appears that genuine mystical experiences are as possible when drug-facilitated as when other means are employed.

Attribution Theory

A position touched upon earlier needs further consideration: the bearing of scientific findings on the claim that there are in fact no unique "mystical experiences,"—alleged mystical experiences are only quite ordinary experiences with no unique neural base. That is, some experiencers merely see some highly emotional experiences as "mystical." In other words, mystical experiences are ordinary states of mind seen mystically—it is this *attribution* to an experience that alone makes it mystical.

Attribution theorists in religious studies note the experiential nature of "mystical experiences," but they deny that the mystical overlay contributes anything cognitive—in particular, there is no cognition of transcendent realities. "Mystical" experiences are merely a matter of *emotion*, not *cognition*. Any theistic or nontheistic attribution is only subjective.[37] John Bowker (1973: 144–57) presented this theory, not to discredit the notion of genuine mystical experiences but to discredit the theory that the idea of God originated in psychedelic experiences. He argued that LSD does not induce experiences of a transcendent reality but only initiates a state of excitation that is labeled and interpreted from the available cues as "religious" by some experiencers, due to the setting and the experiencers' background. No drug introduces anything new into the mind but only accentuates or inhibits what is already there—i.e., psychedelics do not generate new ideas in an experiencer's mind but merely reinforce or confirm the conceptions that were already formed or were in the process of being formed (Bowker 1973: 153). The warrant for a particular label thus does not lie in the experience itself but in the conceptual background of the experiencer that created specific expectations and supplied the symbols to the structuring.

This idea can also be used to discredit any claim to knowledge of transcendent realities given in any mystical experiences. Wayne Proudfoot (1985) offers this "cognitive labeling" approach to deny the possibility of any transcendent input in any religious experience: experiencers unconsciously attribute religious significance to otherwise ordinary experiences. Religious experiences are simply general and diffuse patterns of agitation in states of our nervous system to which the religious give a label based on their prior religious beliefs in order to understand and explain the agitation. Any emotional state can be labeled "a religious experience" when an experiencer believes that the cause is a transcendent reality, but in fact all that is present are only cognitively empty feelings—bodily states agitated in purely natural ways. For Proudfoot, a transcendent reality is not even indirectly involved as the source of the agitation (1985: 154). He rules that out *a priori*: a transcendent reality, if any exist, by definition cannot be experienced. Ann Taves (2009) also groups all types of religious experiences together and concludes that no experience is "inherently religious." Rather, ordinary experiences are merely "deemed religious" by some people. Religious experiences are in fact only cognitively empty feelings structured by prior religious beliefs. That is, religious value or significance is given to unusual but otherwise ordinary experiences. "Religious experiences" are constituted solely by this-worldly elements and thus are exhaustively explainable in the same manner as any other experience.

This approach allows scholars to discount any role for "mystical experience" in the formation of religious doctrines or practices and instead to focus exclusively on religious texts to understand mystical beliefs—any religious significance seen in ordinary experiences arises from preexisting religious beliefs. Robin Carhart-Harris's group seems to agree: while conceding that some subjects of their psilocybin studies were "profoundly affected by such experiences (and often seemingly for the better)," they add that "some people celebrate and romanticize the psychedelic experience and even consider it 'sacred'" (Carhart-Harris et al. 2014: 12–13).

Attribution theory may well explain away many alleged mystical experiences: in many instances, people may be simply attributing greater significance to ordinary highly emotional situations. What one person sees as religious, another may see in secular terms. But the issue here is different from matters of *religious* attribution: is there a set of *inherently mystical experiences*, regardless of whether the understanding that a particular experiencer gives it is religious or secular? And as noted above, there is growing neuroscientific support for the claim that there are genuine mystical experiences—i.e., they have unique patterns of neural activity associated with them.[38] Thus, the data suggests that some experiences or ASCs are inherently mystical even if the experiences are understood nonreligiously by experiencers. That is, today mystical experiences are increasingly being accepted as being connected to unique, observable neural events: whether mystical experiences occasion insights into reality or not, they are "real" in that they are distinct from other types of mental phenomena and are not merely products of imagination (Newberg, d'Aquili, and Rause 2002: 7, 143). So too, neuroscientists are finding evidence that mystical experiences are not all of one type.

Thus, the religious may give a religious interpretation to virtually any experience, but there appears to be a class of a neurologically distinctive events or configurations of brain activity connected to mystical experiences. Mystical experiences are a matter of the ASCs associated with these unique patterns of neural firing regardless of whether they are seen as religious or not. If so, there is an experiential basis to mysticism that cannot be explained away as merely a mystical varnish given to ordinary sense experiences or emotions.

In short, religious experiences may not accompany unique brain states, but mystical experiences apparently do. If neuroscience can establish that unique configurations of brain activity ground different types of mystical experiences, mystical experiences are not merely ordinary mental events taken to be mystical. Thus, the attribution of being mystical would be hard to maintain concerning these experiences since such experiences apparently involve altered states of consciousness and unique neurological events. In sum, attribution theory may be applicable to the question of whether an experience is deemed religious but not to the issue of whether an experience is mystical.

Do the Drug Studies Validate or Invalidate Mystical Claims?

Arguing that drug-enabled mystical experiences are phenomenologically indistinguishable from those facilitated by other means or can be interpreted differently does not rule out the possibility that the drug-enabled experiences are cognitive—i.e., involve the experience of something real that produces some type of knowledge. A scientific finding that psychedelics can often enable mystical experiences does not require the natural explanation of these experiences as merely being caused by brain events: all the science shows is that the chemicals merely set up the conditions in the brain for a mystical experience—it cannot show whether or not a transcendent reality may still be involved in introvertive mystical experiences or whether or not extrovertive experiences give an insight into the beingness of the natural realm. The drug-enabled experiences may only be brain-generated events, or these drugs may "cleanse the doors of perception" and permit more reality to enter the mind. Advocates of mystical claims must accept that some grounding in the body is necessary for even an experience of a transcendent reality, and so they can accept neuroscientific findings as readily as naturalists who reduce the experience to nothing by a subjective product of brain activity (see R. Jones 2016: chapter 4).

Thus, the basic philosophical issue remains: psychedelics disrupt the state of the brain grounding our baseline state of consciousness that has evolved for our survival in the world, but does this disruption merely set up the brain conditions that permit various cognitive states of consciousness and experiences (including various mystical ones) to occur in some instances, or does the brain in conjunction with other personal elements totally cause the specific states of consciousness and types of experiences, and so the experiences are not cognitive?[39] Do the drugs in proper dosages *enable* a transcendent reality to enter the mind (or, in the case of extrovertive mystical experiences, an ASC perception), or is that mystical sense a delusion *caused* only by the brain?

However, as discussed in the last chapter, the study of the measurable objective features of the brain activity happening while the mystical experience is occurring cannot answer that basic question—science is addressing something external to the experience that does not bear on its possible cognitivity. In short, the neuroscience itself is *neutral* on the point of whether mystical experiences are cognitive of a reality beyond the individual's mind or are only brain-generated subject events. The one caveat is that if neuroscience could show that only persons with a defective brain had mystical experiences, then we could reasonably conclude that the experiences are probably not cognitive. But the recent studies of meditators and psychedelic users has put an end to that position. Neuroscience cannot establish or refute the epistemic validity of mystical experiences because the neurology would be the same in either case. Thus, neuroscience cannot contribute to the issue of cognitivity. All neuroscience can show is the association of particular types of mystical experiences with particular brain states, not the cause of this association or anything substantive about the nature of the experience itself.

This eliminates neuroscience as a means by itself of either confirming or disconfirming any mystical claims concerning the cause of mystical experiences or what is actually known in mystical experiences. Some researchers in psychedelic studies remain "metaphysically neutral" on whether the content of mystical experiences have a physical, idealist, or transcendent origin, while others are convinced of a strictly biological origin of mystical phenomena (Weiss 2024: 5), and yet others take a metaphysical stance. And, it should be added, even if science validated mystical experiences as veridical, it cannot confirm one belief about what is experienced in an introvertive mystical experience as valid or superior to alternative mystical explanations or the experience's general cognitive status, since the neural states would be the same regardless of the theories.

Thus, disputants over the cognitive status of mystical experiences will turn from science to the experiences themselves. For example, critics of mystical experiences will point to "bad trips" to conclude that no psychedelic experiences, including mystical experiences, can be insightful. All are only delusions, like the LSD distortions of sensory input. Or they may conclude the experiences involve only personal subconscious material welling up into consciousness when the ego-driven baseline consciousness is disrupted. Why should there be any bad trips and visions of hell at all if psychedelics open us up to an all-loving God or some benign transcendent reality? Why should we think pleasurable trips are any more insightful than the bad trips? Or do bad trips in fact also provide insights into reality? Or are all chemically enabled experiences, as Arthur Koestler put it, "confidence tricks played on one's own nervous system" (1968: 209–10)? The ability of psychedelics to solicit false beliefs is widely recognized (e.g., McGovern et al. 2023) raising the issue of whether psychedelics ever elicit cognitive insights.

Advocates of mystical claims assert that the chemistry is not the whole story and respond that the positive experiences feel "real" to the experiencers in the same way that once we wake up, the previous night's dreams no longer seem real, and that this effect often lasts a long time.[40] Experiencers often believe that what they experienced was *as real as or more real* than ordinary reality (Newberg and Waldman 2016: 61–62) and that they had a clarity and attention not experienced in ordinary perceptions. So too, experiencers distinguish the basic insight that there is more to reality than meets the naturalist eye from aspects that clearly conflict with what is established by ordinary experiences—experiencers can differentiate some obviously wrong beliefs (e.g., "The entire universe is pervaded by a strong odor of turpentine") that seemed certain at the time of the drug-enabled experience from other types of certainties (H. Smith 2000: 65).[41]

On pragmatic grounds, proponents will also point out that many experiencers enjoy a general enhancement of our sense of well-being, i.e., a sense of satisfaction with life or a purpose or meaning to life (see Hummel 2014). Psychedelic-enabled experiences can provide a sense of connection to others, nature, or the cosmos that can overcome a sense of meaninglessness or nihilism (see Plesa and Petranker 2023). The afterglow of the experience can linger for some time (see Evens et al. 2023). Critics, however, will reply that drug-enabled experiences are not uniformly beneficial—some lead to a mental breakdown—nor do the experiences always have a lasting positive effect once the initial glow has subsided. So too, psychedelic experiences can make hard-core materialists, positivists, skeptics, cynics, uncompromising atheists, and crusading antireligious Marxist philosophers suddenly become interested in a spiritual quest (Grof 2009: 97–98). But they can cause believers to abandon their faith (Newberg and Waldman 2016: 60). (For more on the issue of changes in metaphysical beliefs, see chapter 7.)

For skeptics, the experiences may be enjoyable but have no cognitive significance. The ASCs may come as a surprise and be interesting but not lead them to changes in beliefs. The sense of joy and happiness in itself is not indicative of a cognition or insight: one can be "blissed out" regardless of whether transcendent realities or delusions are involved in the introvertive experiences—the depth-mystical experience and the sense of bliss may only be the subjective result of the mind that keeps working even when it has no content to work with or there is a release of dopamine. So too, mystical experiences may have positive effects on our happiness even if no transcendent realities are involved, just as psychedelic therapy has helped to break the hold of depression and addictions and helped to comfort the dying by lessening their fear of death. Nor are the actions of those who have had mystical experiences uniformly moral, compassionate, or beneficial to others—a sense of disconnection from others was a top-five theme in one psychedelic study (Evans et al. 2023: 17).[42] So too, mindfulness meditation can have the effect of greater individualism and less generosity rather than prosocial action (see Poulin et al. 2021). This suggests that basic values and actions do not come from altered mental states but depend on factors outside of mystical experiences (see R. Jones 2004: chapter 13). And secular mysticism must be noted again: today not all mystical experiences are seen by the experiencers as cognitive of a reality or as having transcendent significance. And a "vivid" subjective sense that what is experienced is real is not the only criterion for what is objectively real, especially when there are other types of claims based on other types of experiences open to possible third-person checking.[43]

The dispute may come down to a conflict of basic metaphysics—i.e., one's intuitions of what is real. Part of this is another philosophical issue: the nature of the mind. Naturalist critics will invoke a naturalist view of the mind. Theological critics of mysticism may agree. Advocates of mystical claims may present a nonnaturalist theory of the mind. Theories in consciousness studies concerning the effect of psychedelics range from the theory that chemicals merely produce states of the brain that produce states of consciousness that distort what is real to theories, going back to F. W. H. Myers, William James, Henri Bergson, Charles D. Broad, and Aldous Huxley, that the brain is a "reducing valve" that lets in only enough of the "Mind at Large" that exists independent of our brains to allow us to function in the world without being overwhelmed and confused, and that the drugs loosen this value a little, thereby allowing more reality to pour into the brain (see Goodman 2002) to theories that human consciousness originally arose as what we now consider "altered" states of consciousness and that our "normal" state of consciousness evolved out of them to aid in our survival.

Limitations on the Philosophical Significance of Scientific Studies

In 2000, Huston Smith reflected back over the questions of psychedelics that had occupied him for forty years. His personal belief was "that when 'set and setting' are rightly aligned, the basic message of the entheogens—that there is another Reality that puts this one in the shade—is true" (2000: 133). But he also concluded that he was no closer to answering the central question: "[G]iven what we know about brain chemistry, can entheogenic visions be validated as true?" (Smith 2000: 127). The conclusions here do not offer encouragement that neuroscience will ever be able to answer that question. These conclusions are: (1) neuroscience shows that mystical experiences unique patterns of neural events, suggesting that the experiences are distinct from other types of experience; (2) it shows that psychedelics in proper dosages can touch off genuine mystical experiences in a high percentage of participants, especially when the set and setting are supportive; (3) the variety of subjective experiences and the role of "set and setting" strongly suggest that the drugs do not alter our state of consciousness but merely allow new states and experiences to appear by dislodging our ordinary state of consciousness; (4) there is to date no nontheological reason to suspect that drug-enabled mystical experiences are any different in nature from those occasioned by meditation or those occurring spontaneously; (5) mystical experiences are not the produce of a damaged brain but routinely occur to people with a healthy brain; and (6) science as currently constituted cannot answer the central questions of philosophical importance: studying the effects of psychedelics on our neural circuitry can tell us nothing about the nature, significance, or veridicality of mystical experiences.

Scientists studying psychedelics usually believe that they are studying *mystical experiences* by studying the *brain states* associated with them. For example, Frederick Barrett and Roland Griffiths state: "The use of classic hallucinogens makes the study of mystical experiences more tractable because hallucinogens can be administered under double-blind conditions and can occasion mystical experiences with high probability" (2018: 395). But merely being able to produce or predict the occurrence of an experience with some regularity is not studying the experience itself or its content. And as noted in the last chapter, whether studying neural conditions or anything else material is studying *experiences* in general is hard to maintain. Barrett and Griffiths rightly note that scientific explanations of the content of consciousness do not completely explain consciousness itself, and similarly "explanations of the individual neural elements of mystical experiences may not provide a complete account of a mystical experience" (Barrett and Griffiths 2018: 413). But it is not merely not a "complete account" of the experience: it is only an account of the neural bases, and unless eliminationists in the philosophy of mind are correct, there is more to account for—the subjective "felt" side of the experience is not touched at all. Neuroscience at present remains a matter of studying the states of the brain, not the accompanying states of mind or their relation to states of the brain.

However, as Barrett and Griffiths add, identifying and understanding the neural and psychological processes that relate to mystical experiences is still valuable for the study of the brain: "[T]he study of the neural correlates of mystical experiences may lead to a better understanding of the possible brain mechanisms underlying self-referential, spatial, and temporal processing, as well as complex emotions such as reverence and sacredness" (Barrett and Griffiths 2018: 413–14). More is being learned about the neural mechanics of the effects of psychedelics on the brain every year. Neuroimaging studies of the neurobiological mechanisms of psychedelics have broadened our understanding of the brain, the serotonin system, and the neurobiological bases underlying consciousness (Johnson et al. 2019: 3). It is a major instance of applied mysticism for the benefit of science.

But studying the brain states existing during any experience tells us nothing about the nature of that experience or its phenomenological content—the subjectivity of any experience remains a distinct matter. At present neuroscientists are studying only the neural bases and mechanisms connected to consciousness, and psychedelics remain part of the chemistry operating in the brain during these experiences, not part of the felt mystical experiences. Studying the neurobiological effects of psychedelics is not like studying an unobservable physical object indirectly through its effects on other objects—experiences have a subjective element that is not addressed at all by studying the activity of physical objects.

That limits the ability of these studies to tell us anything substantive about the nature of these experiences or their relation to the brain. Most basically, current neuroscience cannot establish whether the chemicals merely enable these experiences or substantively create them. The effect of psychedelics on our state of consciousness does establish that the brain and the mind are associated, but one's answer to the question of whether the brain causes mental events or whether mental events remain distinct and are received by the brain currently rests on a matter of metaphysics.[44] The alternatives are not yet testable in neuroscience and may never be. Nor, as discussed, do the scientific findings per se dictate what the significance of mystical experiences must be, including the basic issue of the truth or falsity of any mystical cognitive claims or a philosophical reduction of mystical experiences, let alone anything concerning the specific doctrines of any particular mystical tradition. Such questions must be answered on other grounds.

Overall, as neuroscience is currently constituted, neuroscientists may be able to use psychedelics to generate and even control what types of experiences occur (although set and setting figure in). But until neuroscience can delve into the subjective aspects of experiences, it will be limited in what it can tell us about the experiences themselves. Until then, the "neurobiology of consciousness" (Carhart, Kaelen, and Nutt 2014: 664) remains the science of something consciousness-adjacent and not a science of consciousness or of mystical experiences.

A Word of Caution from Huston Smith

One final point should be made. Drug enthusiasts want to integrate psychedelics into the religious life or otherwise view psychedelic experiences from a religious point of view (e.g., Richards 2016), but they tend to make religion only about attaining ASC experiences and not about a full way of life. For example, for Thomas Roberts (2013), religion is only about cultivating mystical experiences: rituals and beliefs are no more than ways to induce mystical experiences, not ways to incorporate mystical insights into one's life—"word-based" religion is only a recipe, while mystical experiences are actually tasting the food. However, as Huston Smith said, "[R]eligion is more than a string of experiences" (2000: 30).[45] The goal of religion "is not religious experiences but a religious life" (Smith 2000: 80). Psychedelics are effective in inducing the former but not the latter—indeed, "chemically occasioned 'theophanies' can abort a quest as readily as they can further it" (Smith 2000: 80). To quote Smith once again: "Drugs appear able to induce religious experiences; it is less evident that they can produce religious lives"

(Smith 2000: 30). That the psychedelic experiences come more easily and change consciousness for only a relatively short time compared to experiences enabled by meditative and other religious practices may account for the drugs' relative ineffectiveness in inducing a religious life.

Smith's point also holds for mysticism: the goal is a life aligned with reality, not a string of exotic experiences. The objective is not altered states of consciousness per se but sustained altered personality traits (H. Smith 2000: 153). Mystical experiences are the way to gain insight into the nature of reality, but a mystical experience gives only a glimpse of the reality that mystics want to incorporate into their lives in order to align their life with "reality as it truly is" (as defined by their tradition). The final objective is to transform the flash of light into an abiding light—to live in conformity with God's will or otherwise to align one's life with how a mystic sees reality.

Smith rightly points out the difference between merely having a mystical experience and the difficulty of attaining an enlightened mystical way of life. Enlightenment involves incorporating the sense of selflessness from a mystical experience into one's continuing state of consciousness after the experience is over—most drug users (and meditators) return to our ordinary baseline state of consciousness after their mystical experiences, not to a state altered by the loss of the sense of a self. The loss of what is often taken to be the most meaningful experience in one's life can lead to a sense of failure, depression, and hopelessness—integrating the insight into one's life may be long and difficult. As Smith adds, enlightenment is not easy but requires hard work, nor are the experiences always pleasurable—in short, "ecstasy" is not fun (2000: 27, 130).

Even if psychedelics can occasion glimpses of alleged transcendent realities in introvertive mystical experiences and can break the cycle of attachments at least momentarily, they are not as effective in integrating these insights into a person's life. If one has already been devoting all of one's life to the cultivation of a mystical way of life, a drug-enabled mystical experience is more likely to initiate a truly selfless enlightened life. These experiences can show us that we are not identical to a phenomenal ego, but the ego can return quickly. Breaking attachments and addictions may lead to a life of mystical detachment, or one may return to a life in which these attachments resurface and new ones may form. Thus, any short-term effects of psychedelics should not be confused with any lasting change of a person. And Smith also appears correct when he states: "[I]t is indeed possible for chemicals to enhance the religious life, but only when they are set within the context of faith (conviction that what they disclose is true) and discipline (exercise of the will toward fulfilling what the disclosures ask of us)" (2000: 31). This is why many who are led by their drug experiences to adopt a mystical way of life give up the drugs once they are engaging in that way of life.

Chapter 3

Pure Consciousness, Intentionality, Selflessness, and the Philosopher's Syndrome

Experiences enabled by meditation and psychedelics lead to applied mysticism in the field of our understanding of the nature of consciousness. The type of mystical experience of particular interest is the one that involves an altered state of consciousness (ASC) that is free of all differentiated content, all intentionality, and any sense of a self having the experience, or ownership of the experience, leaving nothing but a clear "pure" consciousness. Some take the introvertive experiences free of differentiated content in a naturalist fashion to be an awareness only of consciousness itself rather than a direct awareness of some transcendent reality such as God, Brahman, or our true self. But philosophers have raised arguments that such experiencers must be wrong—they argue that no such experiences of a pure intentionless, selfless awareness can in fact be possible.

Let's examine the parts of the alleged phenomenology of these mystical experiences in question to see if those philosophers' arguments are warranted: can a sense of pure consciousness, experiences free of intentionality, and experiences free of a sense of an experiencing self or ownership of the experience be ruled out? If mystical experiences could establish that such a state exists, it would be a prime instance of applying mysticism outside the search for enlightenment to a general understanding of consciousness.

What Is "Pure" Consciousness?

A "pure" extrovertive state would have differentiated sensory content, but that content would be unmediated, altered, or constrained by any conceptualizations that our mind might supply. There would be a loss of all sense of discrete entities (including a distinct experiencer) and of any limited being. There would be sensory input that is not structured into perceptions. Such a state of consciousness would be like seeing Gestalt figures as simply lines or patches of black and white with no structure (including any sense of "lines" or "patches").

But the focus of most discussions of "pure consciousness" is usually an introvertive state of consciousness: the state that is allegedly empty of all differentiated content leaving only consciousness itself. Only a "pure" introvertive state would be an experience of "consciousness *per se*" or "consciousness alone." It is simple, without actions or variations, and without parts. Naturalist philosophers generally reject the idea of an unstructured introvertive pure consciousness. They tend to believe that there can be no consciousness *without an object being present*: when there is no object, there is no consciousness. Thus, consciousness is not a searchlight that is on even when there are no objects to illuminate. Hence, some content more than consciousness itself must be present in any state of consciousness, and therefore consciousness is never "pure" in that sense but has some additional content. So too, consciousness is always from particular perspective, as Thomas Nagel (1986) emphasized, and so is never disembodied.

But the introvertive depth-mystical experience in which it seems that consciousness is free of all differentiated content presents a problem with this position. During the experience, experiencers are not conscious of what the experience involves because it is not observed as an object distinct from the experiencer (hence the name "nondual")—making the experience an object of attention would destroy it. But after the experience is over, the experiencers do retain something of what was experienced—e.g., a general sense of realizing a fundamental reality, nondual consciousness, peacefulness, and profound importance. Thus, experiences of pure consciousness would still have a minimal phenomenology even if the experiencer cannot label the consciousness at the time of the experience since there is no mental distance between it and the experiencer.[1] Pure consciousness seems disembodied in a way that ordinary experience is not.[2]

But if that experience is remembered, it must have had content—if experiencers remembered nothing, they would have to be said to be *unconscious* during the event. After the experience, experiencers realize that they had an experience (even if during the experience itself there is no sense of a subject or of ownership of the experience) and that the experience took time (even if during the experience there was no sense of time passing or of "before" and "after" since there was no differentiated content that changes, and thus it is "timeless" or an "eternal now"). So too, something of the experience's content is remembered, as evidenced by mystics' later claims. If nothing is retained, mystics would have no basis to advance some claims or to reject others based on this experience. Thus, although that experience is often characterized as an experience of "emptiness," the experience is not literally "empty" but has content: since the experiencer is aware, at least consciousness itself can be called the experience's content.

Thus, this "empty" introvertive experience is seen as an experience with phenomenology only after the experience is over and the experiencer has returned to some dualistic (subject/object) state of consciousness. The experience then becomes an object of thought. Only then can one ask "What is the experience of?" Minimally, the experience is consciousness itself devoid of any object of consciousness. Whether it is *more than that*—e.g., an experience of a transcendent reality such as a self or soul, Brahman, or God—is a matter of metaphysical considerations that arise after the experience is over, but the phenomenology of the experience itself is empty of differentiations. That is, the mystical state becomes an object of consciousness only after it is over and the experiencer has returned to a state of consciousness permitting differentiations. So too, accepting the experience as cognitive is a decision made outside the experience based on other considerations.

But the important point here is that realizing these things *after* the experience is over does not mean that those concepts must have been present *during* the experience itself shaping the felt phenomenology of the experience. Critics of the possibility of pure consciousness find this point problematic. For example, Rocco Gennaro, who is committed to the theory that all consciousness must have high-order thought, says: "[I]t seems to me that anyone having a truly introvertive experience must be consciously employing the I-concept" during the experience (2008: 107).

Let me relate a personal experience: the only truly terrifying experience I ever had was coming out of full anesthesia after an operation. There was no one around when I was coming to. I didn't know what was happening, where I was, who I was, or what I was. I think the experience lasted less than half a minute and then it faded and I realized "You're a person named Richard Jones, you're in such and such hospital, and you just had an operation." I have to describe it in terms of "I" and "my" experience, but there was no sense of self in that experience. I can look back on it and remember my state, but I can't reenter that state because of my perspective with an implicit sense of "I" blocks that—it is now just an object of reflection. But merely because I have a latent sense of "I" when remembering the experience does not mean that sense was in any way present in that experience.

The postexperiential sense of personal possession of an earlier mystical experience is no different: a mystic can later look back on a mystical experience and say "I had an experience that was empty of differentiated content" without that thought or a sense of "I" being present in the experience in any way—simply because the mystic in a dualistic state of consciousness after the mystical state of consciousness has abated has a sense that the experience occurred to himself or herself is not a reason to assume a sense of "I" must have been present in the mystical experience itself. Moreover, mystics also report experiences that at the time did not seem to belong to them or to be individualized at all.

Constructivists in mystical studies, however, take up the cause of philosophers who deny that there can be either an introvertive or extrovertive experience free of specific content. Constructivists insist that because of the nature of human beings, all of our experiences have differentiated content and that this content is influenced by the mystic's cultural phenomena. Thus, there is no introvertive experience empty of everything but a pure consciousness since both some cultural structuring and some content to structure are always present. Nor can there be any extrovertive experience free of cultural content and structuring. As Stephen Katz puts it:

> [L]et me state the single epistemological assumption that has exercised my thinking and which has forced me to undertake the present investigation: *There are NO pure (i.e., unmediated) experiences*. Neither mystical experiences nor more ordinary forms of experience give any indication, or any grounds for believing, that they are unmediated. That is to say, all experience is processed through, organized by, and makes itself available to us in extremely complex epistemological ways. The notion of unmediated experience appears, if not self-contradictory, at best empty. This epistemological fact seems to me to be true because of the sort of beings we are, even with regard to experiences of those ultimate objects of concern with which mystics have intercourse, e.g., God, Being, *nirvana*, etc. This "mediated" aspect of all our experience seems an inescapable feature of any epistemological inquiry, including the inquiry into mysticism, which has to be properly acknowledged if our investigation experience, including

mystical experience, is to get very far. (1978: 26, emphasis in the original)

"As a result of his process of intellectual acculturation in its broadest sense, the mystic brings to his experience a world of concepts, images, symbols, and values which shape as well as colour the experience he eventually and actually has" (Katz 1978: 46). All "givens" are "the product of the processes of 'choosing,' 'shaping,' and 'receiving'" (Katz 1978: 59). As Hans Penner put the verdict of constructivism succinctly, the idea of a structure-free "pure" consciousness is an "illusion" (1983: 89).

Nonconstructivists in mystical studies disagree: there are introvertive experiences that are totally free of any content to structure, and sensory extrovertive experiences free of cultural content. Robert Forman (1993) sees this event as immediate, nonlinguistic, nonconceptual, and nonintentional. General meditation involves "forgetting" and "unknowing" all differentiated mental content, not a new form of enculturation or reconditioning of our mental content, as Katz alleges (i.e., a substitution of one form of conditioned consciousness for another [1978: 57]). Extrovertive meditation is a deconditioning of the senses and our way of knowing, while introvertive meditation is an emptying of the mind that in the end allows no content upon which construction could operate.[3] It removes the social dimension to a person and perhaps also the personal.[4] In addition, it may be that any two experiences with differentiated content are never exactly the same, but if a truly pure introvertive consciousness event devoid of all diverse content does occur, then logically all such experiences must be phenomenally identical, at least with regard to the issue of content: these must be the same in this respect for all experiencers regardless of their culture and historical era (assuming the mind is the same in all people in this regard) since there could be no content to distinguish them. Within the other categories of mystical experiences, mystics may not have identical experience, but a state devoid of differentiated content would be only one introvertive state of consciousness. That is, all the pure consciousness experiences would be the same in having no diffuse content and nothing to structure. Different people could, of course, have different degrees of intensity and alertness in their experiences, but all would have experiences free of anything to construct.

Personal firsthand reports of experiences of apparent pure consciousness have occurred across the world in culturally unrelated societies in diverse historical eras (see Forman 1990, 1999 for examples). This makes it difficult to see the descriptions as merely the product of some particular culture. Such experiences continue to occur in the West today. For example, the psychiatrist Philip Sullivan (1995) reported his own experience of an empty awareness of "something that was not nothing." It was an experience that was devoid of content, and yet he was not unconscious but aware—an awareness without any subject of awareness or sense of personal ownership and without any object of experience. Only the transitional states back to the ordinary baseline state of consciousness that were separate from the pure consciousness event had any informational content (Sullivan 1995: 53, 57).

Naturalists can accept that there are such introvertive pure consciousness experiences without being committed to anything transcendent: such a state may be merely the monitoring activity of the mind continuing in the absence of any representational processing; thus, when the mind is emptied of all sensory, conceptual, and ideational content, a lucid conscious state of the natural mind results (Peters 2000). And it must be admitted that the philosophers' case against pure consciousness is weak. Constructivists merely assume that those who have actually had certain mystical experiences must be wrong when they assert things that indicate that certain mystical experiences are different in nature from other types of experiences. But constructivists must present arguments for why those mystics who have had these experiences must in fact be mistaken about the phenomenology of their own experiences—an argument that must go beyond baldly assuming a priori how all human experience must be (see R. Jones 2020a).

Critics of mysticism can attack many aspects of mystics' beliefs—e.g., what mystics claim is the explanation of why the experience occurred. But no one is in a position to attack the *phenomenology* of the experiencer given by the experiencers—i.e., what the experience felt like to the experiencer. This is true of any experience—if you think you have a headache, you have a headache, and that is the end of the matter. People can question what reality if any mystics claim to be experiencing, but they cannot question what the experience felt like to the experiencer. Experiencers are in a privileged position on that issue. Thus, if someone claims to have experienced a state free of all differentiated content, the most that opponents of the possibility of a pure experience can argue is that experiencers are merely engaging in a kind of expectancy bias: they have heard that mystics in the past have had "empty" pure experiences and think that they are now having the same experiences those mystics had, and so the experiences they are now having must be described as empty despite the true phenomenology of what they actually felt (see chapter 5). But if the experiencers are aware of that issue and still persist in claiming a "pure" awareness, we have to accept it and deny it on metaphysical grounds.

Can Neurological Research Establish or Rule Out Pure Consciousness?

Philosophers, especially naturalists, may turn to science to bolster their case. But it may surprise naturalists that, despite the prevailing philosophical position, neuroscientists today are coming to accept the idea that experiencing an introvertive pure consciousness state can occur—a "nondual awareness," "consciousness-as-such," or "consciousness *per se*" (e.g., Newberg, d'Aquili, and Rause 2002). The empirical case for the existence of such experiences is made both from the study of meditators by empirical psychologists focusing on the phenomenology of the experiences through surveys and interviews, and from third-person research by neuroscientists through neuroimaging brain scans as they look for neural correlates and configurations of neural activity during meditative and psychedelic experiences. Neuroscientists do not study mystical states directly, but they can at least show that different configurations of brain activity are active when experiencers report mystical experiences. That is as far as neuroscience can go in suggesting different states of the mind. The focus of study is usually extrovertive experiences of pure consciousness, i.e., experiences in which there is still sensory phenomena that is experienced free of a sense of self or conceptualized divisions (e.g., Gamma and Metzinger 2021; Costines, Borghardi, and Wittman 2021).

The terminology in "contemplative neuroscience" (Winter et al. 2020: 1) is not yet standardized, and different concepts are often conflated (Josipovic and Miskovic 2020: 2). Introvertive and extrovertive experiences are not always distinguished, and this hurts the strength of a neuroscientist's conclusion. "Minimal" emptiness is considered extrovertive, while the label "absolute" emptiness is reserved for the introvertive experience of pure consciousness (Costines, Borghardi, and Wittman 2021). The introvertive pure consciousness experience is considered to have no phenomenology (which was disputed above), and the phenomenology of the extrovertive experience is considered a pure sensory awareness. A pure state of consciousness could be a state underlying all conscious events, or the introvertive and extrovertive states of pure consciousness may simply be two more states in the spectrum of conscious states. But researchers typically treat it as a nondual level of consciousness that is always present (e.g., Travis and Pearson

2000: 77; Josipovic 2019: 292) even though experiencers are not usually aware of it because our ordinary dualistic state of consciousness overrides it. The extrovertive state may involve a mindfulness free of any conceptual structuring, sometimes integrating an introvertive pure consciousness into a state of consciousness in which sensory experiences are present.[5] The latter state may become an enduring or permanent state in which an introvertive event is an ingrained mental trait informing an extrovertive state that has consciousness with conceptual structuring (although the structuring is seen for what is it—our addition to what is there). For mystics, this is an enlightened state of consciousness.[6]

The issue of pure consciousness has become an important topic for consciousness studies. Neuroscience could strike a conclusive blow against any thoroughgoing cultural constructivism if it can establish a "pure consciousness." However, it is currently difficult to differentiate the neural signature of nondual awareness from the neural signatures of meditative states surrounding it (Josipovic 2019: 283). Perhaps neuroimaging could show that the areas of the brain responsible for conceptualizing are still very active in all the cases of mystical experiences that researchers have studied, even though neuroimaging would not be able to distinguish one set of conceptual structuring from another (assuming all conceptualizing produces the same brain activity). That would favor constructivism. However, if no activity or a marked decrease in activity is occurring in those areas during certain mystical experiences, then how cultural influences could affect the content of the experience is not clear, and that would favor nonconstructivism.

But can neuroscience show that meditation completely stills the conceptualizing activity of the mind, leaving a pure consciousness? That is, can it show that the conceptual mind is inactive during certain mystical experiences? Do some types of meditation quiet the parts of the mind that process concepts, and does neuroscience find this occurring in the brain? Or can neuroscience show that there is no differentiated content present in certain states of consciousness? Conversely, can it tell us whether cultural concepts permeate experiences? If neuroscientists could at least establish that the areas of the brain that ground conceptual activity are partially or completely inactive during certain mystical experiences, that would make the idea that cultural phenomena affect these experiences difficult to maintain and would leave a pure consciousness as a genuine possibility.

The temporal lobe appears to be the locus of language, conceptualizing, and abstract thought, and this area does appear to have dramatically deceased activity during mystical experiences (Newberg and Waldman 2016: 24–25). Newberg and d'Aquili place the neural grounding of mystical experiences in the general area of the brain that also is related to thought and language (the prefrontal cortex), but they accept the possibility of a pure state of consciousness free of those activities. However, some neural activity will remain present in all areas of the brain. Moreover, it may be that the areas of the brain grounding linguistic activity overlap the areas exhibiting increased activity during mystical experiences. If so, whether or not the experiences are culturally constructed may not be answerable by neuroscientific research since the relevant areas will have at least some residual activity during the mystical experience in either case. In addition, there may be structuring of mental states that is nonlinguistic—e.g., dogs know their owners, and babies in a prelinguistic state know their parents, despite having no linguistic abilities. But no one suspects that animals and infants are in a pure state of consciousness simply because they have no linguistic ability. Experiences can be structured by symbols, images, or other nonlinguistic cultural phenomena.

Thus, neuroscience may not be able to reveal whether some introvertive mystical experiences are empty of all structuring. However, scientists in the field tend to endorse a cross-cultural common phenomenological core to the introvertive pure consciousness of a depth-mystical experiences that occurs across all religious and cultural traditions (e.g., Hood 2006, 2016). And we can still rightly ask why any residual activity in the areas of the brain that underlie conceptualizing means that some mental conceptualizing is active in these experiences or must be affecting the phenomenology of all experiences, or why completely stilling the conceptualizing could not be possible. Subconscious and nonconscious mental processing may affect conscious states even if we learn of it only later. Experiencers would be unaware of such processing going on in their brain during the experiences, and they may regard their experiences differently when they reflect upon their meditative and psychedelic experiences afterward while in a dualistic state of consciousness. Neuroscientists may be able to detect the brain processes occurring before or during alleged pure consciousness events, but the issue then is whether the scientists can establish that these processes are actively shaping the phenomenology of those introvertive experiences that seem to the experiencers themselves to be empty of differentiated content. How any nonconscious processing could change the *phenomenological character* of a state of consciousness that is felt to be without differentiated content is not clear since it would have no content to work upon.

If neuroscientists cannot conduct experiments on this issue, this limits what neuroscience can tell us about the possibility of a state of pure consciousness or about the nature of mystical experiences more generally (see chapters 1 and 2).

Do Mystical Experiences Involve Intentionality?

Following the nineteenth-century philosopher/psychologist Franz Brentano, analytic philosophers today generally accept that consciousness is inherently intentional: when there is no object of attention, there is no consciousness.[7] That is, states of consciousness are always awareness by an experiencer *of* some material or mental object that is in some way distinct from the experiencer. Some philosophers contend that we cannot consider certain states of consciousness as intentional—e.g., sensing a state of the body (such having a headache) does not involve sensing something distinct from the mind as an intentional object—but mainstream naturalist philosophers still believe that there can be no consciousness without some content being present to the subject as an object (see Crane 2003). As John Searle puts it: "Conscious states always have a content. One can never just be conscious, rather when one is conscious, there must be an answer to the question, 'What is one conscious of?'" (1992: 84). Intentionality does not require that the experiences are conceptualized, but a pure conscious state would be empty of any object (conceptualized or not) to intend.

But some neuroscientists and psychologists today are quite comfortable accepting a pre-reflective, pure consciousness free of all intentional objects (e.g., Hood 2001). If they are correct, then some experiences are not experiences *of* anything and thus have no intentional objects. If the depth-mystical experience is in fact empty of all content but consciousness itself, the experience would not have an object distinct from the experiencer or any differentiated content in the mind toward which to direct attention, and thus the experience could not be accurately described as intentional. The experiencer can ask "What is it an experience of?" only after the experiencer is over. If this is so, then not all human experiences would have distinct objects or involve intentionality or a sense of an experiencing self. In particular, any depth-mystical experience free of any content but consciousness would not be an experience of any object but is still a state of awareness, one that mystics take to be the realization of a reality.

A state of pure consciousness would be nonintentional since there would be no mental object involved but only our consciousness—there would be only awareness. It could also be called "pure experience" because nothing else occupies the mind but the experience itself. Philosophical and theological judgments of what reality is really experienced in the experience do not makes those alleged realities part of the phenomenology of the experience. Normal "knowledge by acquaintance" or "knowledge of factual claims" has a threefold structure: a subject, an object of consciousness, and the consciousness connecting the two. But in mystical experiences, there a "knowledge by participation" or "knowledge by identity" that binds the three components in a way that removes the threefold structure and makes the state of consciousness seem connected to both the subject and object in one reality: one is "absorbed" in the experience with no differentiated subject or object. Such knowledge by participation could not have a separate intentional object of attention. Thus, any mystical awareness would be nonintentional since it would involve the mind's direct participation in what is experienced, and this would preclude any distinct intentional object.

Because of the nondual experience's lack of intentionality, some scholars in mystical studies prefer to avoid the word "experience" here since the term connotes a dualism of an *experiencer* experiencing a separate physical or mental *object*. Bernard McGinn prefers simply "consciousness" (1994: xviii) or "awareness" (2006: xv–xvi). But most philosophers today argue that "consciousness" and "awareness" are also inherently intentional—a subject is conscious or aware *of* something—and thus necessarily dualistic. McGinn also uses "presence of God" for the history of Christianity (1994: xvii), a phrase common in theistic mysticism, but it too suggests a dualism: the presence of something *to* the experiencer that is distinct from the experiencer (as in a vision)—in short, a dualistic state of consciousness of an encounter of two things. So too, one can have a "sense of presence" of an object in an ordinary state of consciousness. It also would not apply to experiences of something that is always present in us, like Brahman or the Dao, even though we are unaware of that reality because a dualistic state of consciousness currently prevails in us. Robert Forman prefers the term "event" (1990: 8) for the awareness of pure consciousness, but that term does not capture the experiential nature or the felt sense of the occurrence.

We unfortunately, however, do not have any experiential terms that do not connote a separation of subject and object, since that is how the terms would have arisen in all cultures. Even "realization" is realization *of* something. So too with "apprehension" or "awareness." Duality and intentionality seem inherent in any of our experiential terms. Thus, those who experience something nondualistically have a terrible time with language: they have to use the terminology from ordinary experiences that presumes dualistic experiences, but they then assert that the terms do not apply since no separation of subject and object is present in a mystical experience or state. More generally, language is a matter of making distinctions, and thus it is hard to express what is without distinctions in any language.

But a state of knowledge by participation in a pure consciousness would still have content (as discussed above) even without an intentional object. After the experience, pure consciousness can become an object of thought. But if one is aware of one's consciousness *as an object of attention*, it would not be a case of pure consciousness but a state of dualistic consciousness. Since an object is involved in the experience, the experience would not be a pure awareness of a reality but an experience involving our conceptual mind. So too, if the experience itself felt like an experience of "emptiness": distinctions would be in the mind during that experience, and thus it would not "pure." Similarly with experiences of bliss or feeling loved: the mind is not truly empty but has content other than awareness itself. Thinking *of* awareness makes pure consciousness into an object of analytical thought, and thus this experience has an intentional object. Thus, the intentional awareness is not the same as pure consciousness that is its object: the thought of pure consciousness becomes the content of an analytical state of consciousness. Thinking or speaking of pure consciousness also bestows a grammatical object onto it, and this makes it into something it isn't—an object. It is ineffable in the sense that to express it one must drop out of it and make it something it is not: a mental object. Hence the problem of talking about it. But this linguistic problem does not preclude the possibility of such a nonintentional experience, even though descendants of the 1950s linguistic philosophy may reject the possibility solely of the grounds of the grammar of language.

Is an Experience with No Sense of Self Possible?

Those philosophers who deny the very possibility of a pure, nonintentional consciousness would no doubt deny that there can be an experience free of any sense of the experiencer—a truly "selfless" experience. This raises both ontological and phenomenological questions.

The ontological question is whether a sensing self must exist in any experience. Since David Hume, some philosophers (such as Daniel Dennett and Derek Parfit) have questioned whether there is a "self" either in the "*narrative*" sense (a self with beliefs, emotional traits, and so forth) that would provide personal identity over time or in the more minimal sense of a self as a "*subject*" (some distinct ontological entity that has experiences). But most philosophers ask how could there be an experience without the subject of that experience? How could there be a state of consciousness without an individual having that state? Mustn't either a phenomenal or transcendent self be present to have an experience? Does it even make sense to speak of "experiences" without some subject who "*has*" those experiences? Doesn't the fact that experiencers remember an allegedly "selfless" experience prove that a self exists? Raphaël Millière dubs this the "self-awareness principle": "[N]ecessarily, whenever one is in a conscious state, one is minimally self-aware" (2017: 14). Thomas Metzinger asks if any experiencer's report of a selfless state is an "inherent logical fallacy" and a "performative self-contradiction"—"How can you coherently report about a selfless state of consciousness from your own, autobiographical memory?" (2004: 566; see Metzinger 2024).

But some neuroscientists do not see a need even for the minimal concept of a "self." Eugene d'Aquili and Andrew Newberg suggest that scientific research supports "the possibility that a mind can exist without an ego, that awareness can exist without self" (Newberg, d'Aquili, and Rause 2002: 126). Of course, simply because a sense of "self" is not present in an experience does not mean that no self exists—the experience merely obliterates awareness of the self temporally—but it does raise the possibility that there is in fact no self. The idea of a "self" may have simply arisen from the fact of "self-awareness"—i.e., becoming aware of our awareness—but this awareness does not necessarily come from a separate sensing entity (a "self") but may be merely yet another mental function of the mind that our brain generates.

Early Indian Buddhism also advanced a selfless ontology: we never experience an unchanging ontological "essence"—a "self" (*atman*)—to a person in any sense in our everyday and meditative experiences but only impermanent phenomena. Although we have a deep-seated prejudice in favor of a self, no permanent self underlying our transient experiences is actually ever found in our experience. Nothing observed in the mind remains invariant in all circumstances. Under this approach, when we examine our experiences all we observe are the constantly changing material forms, feelings, perceptions, dispositions, and consciousness (the five aggregates [*skandhas*]) that we associate with a "person," but we never experience a permanent, unchanging observer. All we are is a series of impermanent and temporary states of consciousness with no "subject" self that does the experiencing—there is seeing but no "seer," actions but not "actor," knowing but no "knower." Any awareness of being conscious ("self-awareness") is only just another conscious state and not evidence of a distinct ontological entity behind the experience that does the observing. There is still consciousness and the other subjective components of the mind even if there is no "self," but consciousness is only a series of individual, independent events, not some continuous reality. Thus, these Buddhists see no reason to posit a permanent and unaffectable core—a "self" that has the experiences or does the experiencing.[8] Rather than a self, there is only a connected stream of transitory and conditioned elements (*dharmas*) in the continuous cycling of rebirths. For convenience, we may speak conventionally of a "person" who has consciousness, but in the ultimate analysis there is no such entity. We are a stable functioning whole made of changing parts like a car: the parts are real but impermanent, and there is no "car" in addition to the parts. Thus, the denial of a "self" does not mean that we do not exist but only that there is no permanent "subject" self or other entity that exists in addition to the flux of elements that has experiences. In short, mental events occur, just without a central monitor or actor. Thus, we exist but not in the way we normally suppose.

This leads to the question of the phenomenological sense of selflessness: even if we assume there must be an entity that has the experiences, can there still be experiences that leave no trace of the experiencer and lead experiencers mistakenly to believe there is no self? Can there be an experience truly void of any direct or indirect sense of "self" or ownership of the experience? But research in psychology has shown that a sense of "self" is in fact not necessary for consciousness (Millière 2020).[9]

Nevertheless, for most philosophers there must be a self, and so it must be at least latent in all human experiences. These philosophers believe that awareness has always a sense of ownership—whether it is ordinary sense-perception, self-awareness, or an ASC experience, it is always I who have my experiences and not someone else, and this constitutes part of the experience. Our experiences seem attached to our body in some sense, and thus a sense of "I" must be part of the phenomenology of any experience. That is, this sense of ownership is part of ordinary experiences, and thus these philosophers reject the very possibility of any "selfless" awareness or consciousness. For them, there is always a sense of ownership of any experience—even the pure consciousness of depth-mystical awareness, like all awareness, has a sense that it belongs to the experiencer. The "self of ownership" of the experience is ever present in any state of consciousness. That self does not dissolve, and the boundaries between that and the world remain intact for any experience—it is always "I" who has the experience, and we are aware of that fact in any experience. Even if consciousness is not generated by the person but is a "transpersonal" or "nonpersonal" reality, and even if in a mystical experience the consciousness does not seem to come from the experiencer, there is always an individual subject who has the experience of consciousness, and that sense is part of the experience. So too, there is always a perspective in any experience, and so there is always a "subject" self, and this personal perspective is also part of any experience. Thus, in all cases there is still a particular person who is having the conscious experience, and according to most philosophers the sense of that experiencing person cannot be eradicated.

Enter once again mystical experiences. A core feature of the phenomenology of extrovertive and introvertive experiences is a lack of a sensing self. So too, a sense of an independent, self-contained "subject" self within the phenomenal world is absent. (This does not require rejecting a belief in a transcendent self or soul, as noted below.) The mystic has no sense of owning the consciousness in the experience or that it is individual to him or her. The pure consciousness experience seems to be happening *to them*, not arising *from them*.[10] There are no features of an individual personality in this experience. Nor is there an experience from "my point of view" or seeing things in terms of what might be valuable or desirable to the experiencer. Nor is there any intentionality, since there is no individual in the experience to intend something and no separate object of attention.

Phenomenological selflessness is not merely not being aware of a subject sensing something during an experience (most experiences are like that), but that during the experience or looking back after the experience the experience seems to lack ownership or being attached to the person. But this is not a loss of subjectivity: there is still the consciousness but no discrete entity that "has" it or produces it. The Theravada Buddhist no-self model does not deny subjectivity or a subjective point of view but only that there is a substantive "experiencer" of our experiences that exists in addition to the components of the mind and body. That is, there is no discrete ontological entity in the phenomenal realm that "has" experiences, but there is still an impermanent and conditioned configuration of sensing, feeling, and thinking. Similarly, for advanced mindfulness in general, there is no subject as a separate reality or a dualism of subject and object, but subjectivity need not be denied.

Other classical mystical traditions can affirm a selfless state of consciousness in mystical experiences while still affirming the ontological reality of a transcendent self. In Advaita Vedanta, a worldly individual self (*jiva*) is denied—realizing that Brahman/Atman is our only reality removes all sense of an individual or personal features of our mind, leaving only the transcendent consciousness.[11] All individuality is lost in the pure consciousness that is Brahman/Atman.[12] Vedantic theists still see some individuality and distinction somehow remaining while aware of God (see R. Jones 2024: 236–38). Theists, that is, do assert the existence of a transcendent "soul" even though any awareness of it is absent in introvertive theistic mystical experiences: the brightness of God blots out the awareness of anything else, including oneself. In medieval Christianity, Bernard of Clairvaux used such common images as a drop of water seeming to disappear in a vat of wine, but he added: "No doubt, the substance [of the soul] remains though under another form, another glory, another power" (McGinn 2006: 436). Only our *will* is melted with God's will (McGinn 2006: 436). Thus, Bernard did not believe that persons lost their identity in this union with God, and he used the marriage imagery from the biblical "Song of Songs" for the relation of the soul to God in mystical experiences, as did other Christian mystics. The "glue of love" joins two substances (God and the soul) tightly into an "indivisible unity" but not unified into one substance. Such "love" mysticism was also prominent in Islam and Hinduism (see R. Jones 2024: chapters 6–7). After death, the individuality of different "selves" is retained, unlike in Advaita, in which all individuality vanishes and only a personless consciousness exists. In this way, the loss of any sense of self in mystical states of awareness is reconciled with the ontological affirmation of individual souls.

Today there is a debate in psychedelic studies on whether a sense of "self" is necessarily part of all human experiences. Some contend that a first-person point of view is necessary to any experience and that denying this is a contradiction in terms (see Millière and Metzinger 2020; Sebastián 2020; Fink 2020). But some research suggests that a sense of "self" is not in fact necessary for consciousness (e.g., Millière 2020; Millière and Newen 2024). Chris Letheby (2021; Letheby and Mattu 2021) also defends the possibility of a truly selfless awareness in psychedelic experiences against the claim that all awareness must seem during the experience to belong to someone—a sense of ownership or "for-me-ness" to all experiences—and thus there must be an experiencing "self." And as pointed out earlier, simply because when we look back on an experience after it is over and we once again have the sense of ownership does not mean that that sense was part of the phenomenology of the experience itself—*remembering* that an experience is one's own experience after the event does not mean that a sense of self was *present in the experience itself*. Nor is it a contradiction to say that the felt content of a "selfless" experience is free of any sense of ownership even though looking back on it after it is over from a dualistic state of consciousness—in which a sense of "I" may be inherent—we are aware that it was our experience and not others'. So too, if there is an "expansion of consciousness" beyond any sense of consciousness being confined to oneself, then there is no sense of "self-awareness" in any meaningful sense (contra Fink 2020). The sense of ownership is not in a special class of content in this regard.

If so, the *subjectivity* necessary for any experience may not carry within it a sense of an experiencer—a "*self*"—or any type of a sense of ownership (the sense of being the subject having an experience) or agency (the sense of being the agent producing the experience). Nor is there necessarily a separate ontological entity called the "self," as the Buddhist analysis demonstrates. The sense of "self" may simply be an illusion. It appears that psychedelics disrupt the neural underpinnings of our sense of "self" (Letheby 2021), and mystical experiences that deconstruct the sense of an isolated "self" leaving a selfless experience are one type of experience that may replace that sense of self. Thus, the experiences of selflessness may provide experiential input not only for the phenomenological issue of whether all experiences imply that there must always be some self-awareness but also for the ontological question of whether there is a phenomenal "self." It is a case of applying mysticism to issues of interest to nonmystics.

Thus, it appears that unbinding a sense of self through mystical experiences sometimes introduces states of consciousness with the phenomenology of only a pure consciousness devoid of intentionality and a sense of ownership. Of course, in a trivial sense calling this a "subjectless consciousness" is a misnomer or at least ambiguous, since, regardless of one's ultimate metaphysics, there indeed is what we conventionally call a particular *"person"* having that experience even if one is not aware of it at the time. Even if consciousness is not generated by our brain or by anything else that is natural, pure consciousness experiences are still manifested only in certain persons, not in everyone—there are still separate persons who are recipients of the transcendent consciousness and have separate streams of consciousness.[13]

But that is a matter of metaphysics, not of the phenomenology of an experience. The important point for the issue at hand is that there is no sense in the experience of an experiencing self, of intentionality, or of consciousness arising from the experiencer. In addition, there is still the problem of the expressing such an experience: experiencers must still use the only language we have—the conventional dualistic/intentional language of "I was conscious of . . ."—since we have no other way of expressing an experience when the consciousness is felt not to be originated by, arising from, or confined to the individual experiencer. But the felt phenomenology of an experience may not mirror the particular ontology one accepts after the experience—phenomenology does not follow from ontology. Thus, a philosophical position on the self cannot rule out what may be the content of an experience.

The Danger of the Philosopher's Syndrome

Some philosophers may have no trouble with the idea of a pure consciousness lacking differentiated content, intentionality, and a sense of self, but many no doubt will continue to reject the idea out of hand. This response is epitomized by the quotation above from John Searle and the constructivists' letting ordinary experiences dictate the nature of all experiences.

However, one cannot help but notice that the denial of the very possibility of a pure nonintentional consciousness or a selfless state comes from applying concepts concerning ordinary states of consciousness to extraordinary states through an assumption based only on our ordinary experiences and states of consciousness. That is, experiences of pure, nonintentional, and selfless consciousness are deemed impossible because of the meaning of the words in ordinary discourse devised for the dualistic situations from which the terms "consciousness," "experience," and "self" arose. Our terminology was devised for dualistic (subject/object) experiences, but experiences of pure consciousness are nondual in nature. Thus, such experiences provide a different context from that in which the terms "consciousness" and "self" arose. But can our words and ordinary experiences put limits on what human experiences are actually possible? Can our understanding of mystics' experiences be limited in that way? As the philosopher Donald Evans (1989) asked concerning constructivists, are nonmystics in a position to deny that pure consciousness free of a sense of self is even possible? Can philosophers legislate what is possible? Again, it is the phenomenology of these experiences, not their explanations, that is being challenged. Also remember that philosophers develop their ideas of "experience," "consciousness," and "intentionality" without considering mystical states of consciousness (Bernhardt 1990: 232–33), and we should have no qualms about expanding their meaning of "consciousness" and "experience" and denying the necessity of "intentionality" once other states of consciousness and experiences are considered simply as states of consciousness and experiences. The counterposition must assert more than "Well, ordinary experiences are not like that, and so no other types of human experiences are possible." It should be noted that the dogma in analytic philosophy that is being relied upon—that there is no nonconceptual content to ordinary perceptual states and knowledge—is now being challenged (see Peacocke 1992, 2001; Van Cleve 2012; Bermudez 2015). So too, it is difficult to see sensations, pains, and pleasures as intentional objects of consciousness rather than simply as states of consciousness without a subject/object relation.

The philosopher Daniel Dennett speaks of the "Philosopher's Syndrome": "mistaking a failure of imagination for an insight into necessity" (1991: 401).[14] Many philosophers do not even see their assumptions but treat them as obvious facts. Or they reason in effect "I can't accept the claim that there is a conscious state not framed by a sense of self, so there cannot be states of consciousness without a sense of self." So too with nonintentionality and a pure consciousness. It is an example of bad reasoning substituting for experience. And it is no more convincing that arguing that life is "meaningless" because only words have meaning and life is not a word. Such philosophers simply ignore those who have had such an experience or believe those experiencers must be misinterpreting what happened—it must be that way because the only experiences that they are familiar with dictate that a sense of self is necessary to any state of consciousness, as are diffuse content and intentionality, and so no altered state of consciousness experience qualifies as being selfless, nonintentional, and pure.

But even if mystical experiences are dismissed as noncognitive hallucinations, they still are states of consciousness, and the possibility that some are events with the phenomenology of pure consciousness free of any sense of ownership cannot be ruled out a priori by philosophers. Nor is any person in a position to deny the felt phenomenological content of another person's experience. The burden is on philosophers who categorically deny the possibility of a selfless pure consciousness to present substantive arguments and explain how so many experiencers could be mistaken about the phenomenology of their own experiences. This is especially so since descriptions of pure consciousness have occurred around the world in culturally unrelated societies for millennia. Philosophers should begin with the empirical evidence, not dictate what is possible. They should not rule out some empirical evidence as necessarily mistaken simply because in ordinary experiences and states of consciousness there is differentiated content, intentionality, and at least a tacit sense of self. Or perhaps they should even undertake the procedures that may induce one of the relevant experiences.

Chapter 4

Triggers of Altered States of Consciousness Experiences

Many events and substances affect certain serotonin receptors in the brain, thereby triggering various types of experiences in altered states of consciousness (ASCs). Well-known triggers from the study of tribal societies and the history of religion include different types of meditation; some types of prayers; fasting; contemplating the beauty of nature or art; intense physical dangers; silence; ritualized chanting (constant repetition of short phrases); rhythmic drumming; rituals and other group activities; rhythmic rocking and dancing; sensory overload; overstimulation through music and singing (although sensory overload through people creating a general dissonant noise is not as effective); sensory deprivation (e.g., in the darkness of caves); strenuous physical exertion (including recreation and athletics) leading to exhaustion; stilling the rational activities of the mind by depriving it of new input (e.g., endlessly working on a riddle); staying awake during long vigils and other types of sleep deprivation; social isolation; enduring extreme pain; physical and verbal punishment; stress (especially among the young); despair; psychological trauma; illness; near-death experiences; hyperventilation; sex or celibacy; and giving birth. Lesions on the inferior parietal lobe can also trigger ASC experiences (Yaden and Newberg 2022: 242–43). In short, anything that disrupts our baseline state of consciousness can sometimes enable extrovertive or introvertive mystical and other ASC experiences.[1] But whether the trigger is active or passive, the resulting state of mind is relaxed and receptive, what William James characterized as "passive" (1958 [1902]: 293). Each type of trigger may affect different people differently.

The different types of triggers may also not all have any shared common characteristics (see Yaden and Newberg 2022: 115).

In scientific experiments, scientists can focus attention on only one trigger and thus may limit the issue of "compound triggers" that arise in tribal and religious settings (e.g., using both psychedelic drugs and drumming in a ritual). Today one traditional trigger is getting special attention because of the study of its widespread historical use and its resurrection in scientific research: psychedelic drugs.[2] Psychedelics routinely touch off ASC experiences in a large percentage of users. Their effects usually arise much faster than with the other triggers. Over a hundred natural psychedelic plants, fungi, and animals have been identified. The most familiar triggering psychedelics today are psilocybin (in certain mushrooms), DMT (in the ayahuasca brew from the Amazon and Orinoco rainforests), mescaline (the active ingredient in peyote), LSD, and cannabis. Psychedelic mushrooms were especially important historically and were common throughout temperate regions (Winkelman 2019). They were used as medicine or in carefully crafted rituals. All of these "flesh of the gods" and "sacred medicines" are found wild and do not require cultivation. They apparently became popular in agricultural societies of the Paleolithic era. In fact, there is evidence that psychedelics were among the first plants that human beings domesticated—indeed, perhaps the first—rather than foodstuffs (Rudgley 1999: 140–41).

Scientific questions concern what are triggers and their effects on the brain. What things are triggers? What areas of the brain are affected by each type of trigger? How do triggers work in enabling ASC experiences? How does a sense of connectedness or transcendence of the sense of self actually arise? What actually triggers a change in the state of consciousness or generates the changes in the sense of meaning and significance after the experience? Do all psychedelics affect the same part of the brain? Do different psychedelics affect different parts of the brain and yet induce the same experiences? Why do meditation (an action of the mind) and psychedelics (a chemical action on the brain) appear to affect the brain the same way, i.e., affecting the same areas and producing similar neurological readings? And why do they enable the same type of experiences? Do all triggers (including different psychedelics and different types of meditation) have the same effect on the brain and create the same brain conditions? Why do the same triggers have different effects on different people, if for example psychedelic drugs have the same chemical reaction in the brain of each person? Can triggers help identify what conditions in the brain are necessary for mystical experiences? Why do different triggers occasion different specific experiences (e.g., LSD induces more visions than introvertive mystical experiences free of differentiations and nonpsychedelic ketamine more easily facilitates near-death experiences)? Why can one or a few brief experiences trigger lifelong changes in a person? Do the chemical effects produce the changes, or do the experiences open up the neuroplasticity of the brain? How do chemical triggers interact with an experiencer's "set and setting"? What do spontaneous mystical experiences mean for the issue of triggers and about the conditions set up in the brain by triggers? Do any ASC experiences occur without a trigger? Conversely, why do amphetamines, alcohol, and drug addiction disrupt connectivity in the default mode network but do *not* typically lead to ego-dissolution or psychedelic experiences (Shinozuka et al. 2024: 12)?

The relation of ASC experiences to the brain complicates the matter of triggers. How do brain events trigger any experience or state of consciousness? One issue is that the default mode network operating in the brain can be disrupted in other ways (e.g., by alcohol) without regularly enabling mystical or other ASC experiences. Why are psychedelics triggers and alcohol usually not triggers? How do psychedelics differ from other disrupting substances? So too, nonmystical states of consciousness may also result from disruption of the default mode network in brain activity. Thus, such disruption may be neither necessary nor sufficient for the appearance of mystical experiences. The relation of triggers to mystical experience therefore becomes complicated. Scientists studying psychedelics usually write as if they are studying ASC states when they are only studying the brain states associated with them—the subjective "felt" side of the experience is not touched at all. Neuroscience at present remains a matter of studying the states of the brain, not the accompanying states of mind or their relation to states of the brain. It remains a matter of understanding the neural processes that correlate only with mystical and other ASC experiences.

The Nature of "Triggers"

Different triggers have different degrees of effectiveness in enabling mystical experiences, but none approach producing mystical experiences 100 percent of the time. For example, direct neurostimulation of the brain by Michael Persinger's "God helmet" (1987) enables experiences only about 40 percent of the time (Horgan 2003: 92) (and his results are disputed [Yaden and Newberg 2022: 114–15]), and these experiences are mostly dualistic visions and voices rather than mystical experiences. With a naturalist set and setting, about a quarter or a third of the general population who take a psychedelic drug will have a religious experience (H. Smith 2000: 20). With conducive mental sets and physical and social settings, seventy-some percent of subjects who take a psychedelic drug have a mystical experience (H. Smith 2000: 1–7). But the number of experiencers never reaches 100 percent for any trigger.

Thus, calling these things "*triggers*" is somewhat of a misnomer since none can *force* a mystical or other ASC experience to occur every time, even when the experiencer's mental "set" (beliefs, expectations, mood, and so forth) and the physical and social "setting" (a "sacred" location or a room decorated by religious symbols rather than being symbolically sterile) are supportive for inducing mystical experiences.[3] That is, a user's background beliefs, preparation, expectations, disposition, propensity for ASCs, personality traits, mood, and past experiences with drugs and the physical and social environment in which a drug is ingested cannot guarantee that an ASC experience will occur. Set and setting also apply to meditation. For example, the experiences may differ and the effects of meditation on the brain may differ if the meditator's intention is to strive for a spiritual goal rather than merely to relieve stress or some other limited health-related goal. So too, a spiritual framework for understanding meditation may be more effective in reducing stress and increasing tolerance to pain than secular meditation (see Wachholtz and Pargament 2005). One issue in this regard is whether the experiences occasioned by the drugs administered to people in scientific settings have the same content as mystical experiences occurring outside that setting. Since set and setting matter, does a lab setting or knowing that one is involved in a drug experiment by itself affect the felt phenomenological content of the experience or even the possibility of having an ASC experience?

Thus, every triggered experience involves a mixture of at least three ingredients: the trigger, one's mental set, and the social and physical setting. Differences in personality types may be a factor (Yaden and Newberg 2022: 96–99). Genetics may be a factor, even if there is no specific "God gene" (Yaden and Newberg 2022: 99–100). So too, different areas of the brain are affected by triggers—there is no one "God spot" (Yaden and Newberg 2022: 84). Moreover, different triggers have varying effects on different parts of the brain (Yaden and Newberg 2022: 84). Different psychedelics appear to act differently—LSD and psilocybin have different effects on serotonin receptors, and LSD mystical experiences seem less intense than psilocybin-enabled ones (Winkelman 2017: 3). A frame of mind prepared for or expecting some religious experience to arise or accepting the possibility of a mystical experience occurring in a religiously inspiring physical and social environment increases the likelihood of such an experience, although the resulting visionary or mystical experience may not be what the experiencer expected and may surprise the experiencer because of his or her prior beliefs.[4] As discussed above, a variety of ASC experiences are possible. So too, there is no one-to-one relation of different triggers and different types of mystical and other ASC experiences. But based on the phenomenological accounts of mystics and experimental subjects, different psychedelics, meditation, and other natural (and perhaps nonnatural) triggers can produce some experiences that are phenomenologically indistinguishable.

In sum, the same trigger may occasion different experiences, and the same experiences may come from different triggers. Thus, different triggers do not each enable a unique type of experience. The same trigger (e.g., psilocybin) may enable different mystical and also nonmystical experiences. Thus, ASC experiences should not be put into separate categories according to the trigger involved. In particular, drug-enabled experiences are not in a special class but simply another way to disrupt our baseline state of consciousness. This also means that the trigger does not affect the specific content of the experiences. That is, the triggers do not appear to be part of the experience—it is not as if different triggers "enter" the experiences and produce experiences unique to that trigger. Nor is the experience "in" the trigger, as it were. Thus, the trigger and the phenomena triggered must be distinguished, and the trigger does not shed light on the phenomenological content of any given ASC experience. Scientists therefore should not focus on the triggers or any one specific trigger when looking for explanations of the *content* of a given mystical or nonmystical experience. (Theists' objections will be discussed below.)

The role of different factors and the resulting diversity of ASC experiences eliminate any simplistic reduction of ASC experiences to a mechanical effect of the triggers. For example, drugs disrupt the neural events grounding our normal state of consciousness and bring about other configurations of brain activity, but what experience occurs depends on other factors. For example, people who are highly open to new experiences are more likely to have positive experiences, while people who are emotionally unstable or rigidly conventional in their views are likely to experience greater anxiety and confusion and have disturbing experiences. Psilocybin users who are relatively unchurched are more likely to have mystical experiences than those who are deeply entrenched in traditional beliefs and practices (Newberg and Waldman 2016: 240, 247). When drugs are used recreationally, fewer mystical experiences occur (Newberg and Waldman 2016: 235–36).

According to scientific reports, psychedelics enable visions of realities appearing distinct from the experiencer more often than mystical experiences that negate boundaries. Nor do psychedelics enable introvertive mystical experiences without differentiated content as readily as extrovertive ones and introvertive experiences with such content. Why don't psychedelics set up the chemical base in the brain for the tranquility of depth-mystical experiences as readily as other mystical and visionary experiences? Do psychedelics stimulate portions of the mind that interfere with an experience empty of differentiated content while inhibiting metabolism in other portions? Do depth-mystical experiences emerge from a deeper part of the brain that psychedelics do not readily affect? Are depth-mystical experiences not connected to the brain in the way visions and differentiated mystical experiences are? Are they more extreme than other types of mystical experiences? Do they require more training? Do different psychedelics and different doses each adjust our brain chemistry in a unique way to more readily produce a specific type of ASC experience? Or do psychedelics do no more than merely disrupt our baseline state of consciousness, thereby permitting different types of ASC experiences to occur in the mind, and the exact type of mystical experience that does occur depends on other factors, with more people expecting differentiated content in mystical experiences?

Psychedelics may increase mindfulness (Radakovic et al. 2022). However, the mystical experiences that psychedelics enable do not transform subjects into an enduring selfless enlightened state of consciousness as often as do those cultivated in mystical ways of life with meditation and other religious practices. When there is a sense of a transcendent reality, it is typically nonpersonal, and after the experience theists sometimes reinterpret their conception of "God" as something without personal traits in order to fit the experience (e.g., a nonpersonal deistic reality or a nonpersonal transcendent consciousness or ground of being). For example, Roger Walsh notes that Westerners trained in shamanic practices may report unitive experiences, but they are experiences of union with the universe rather than with a transcendent deity (1990: 240). But introvertive theistic experiences of a sense of communing with a divinity who is personal in nature do occur.

It must also be reiterated that ingesting drugs or utilizing other triggers does not guarantee that an ASC experience will occur. William Richards reports that a substantial number of people have ingested psychedelics on many occasions without experiencing any profound ASCs, spiritual or otherwise (Richards 2016: 15). J. Harold Ellens found the same: many persons also have taken psychedelics repeatedly and never come close to experiencing profound states of consciousness, spiritual or otherwise (Ellens 2015: 22–23). Sometimes there is no change of the state of consciousness at all. So too, many people meditate daily for decades without any mystical experiences occurring.

The placebo effect also apparently holds for psychedelic drugs: once we learn a response, we can be given what we think is the drug (when in fact it is a placebo) and an ASC will occur; conversely, we can unknowingly ingest the active psychedelic ingredient and no change in consciousness occurs (Tart 1975: 152–53). This effect makes it harder to correlate states of consciousness with brain states and to determine if the psychedelic is a causal trigger. Mystical experiences also occur spontaneously, i.e., with no preparation, intent, or anticipation and with no chemical or other administered trigger (Yaden and Newberg 2022: 95–96), and so these seem to have no trigger. Spontaneous mystical experiences may be the most common—respondents in one study revealed that they accounted for 68 percent of their experiences (Yaden and Newberg 2022: 95)—but studying the brain states of someone underlying a spontaneous experience may prove impossible. In any case, spontaneous mystical ASC experiences have not gained much attention in scientific circles. The differences between those and psychedelic-enabled mystical experiences are not well described (James et al. 2020).

Of course, spontaneous ASC experiences may in fact result from triggers (e.g., the fatigue of long-distance running) that have a similar effect on the brain that psychedelics have, but that would have to be established empirically. However, the issue of whether mystical experiences are responsible for the brain configurations or vice versa is especially clear with spontaneous mystical experiences. This also complicates the question of whether brain events alone are the cause of ASC experiences and how one can initiate such experiences. So too, if placebos can touch off mystical experience, the entire issue of triggers and a necessary chemical base in the brain for these experiences is called into question. The experiential mechanism involved in psychedelic therapy may be complex: it may be that the ego-dissolution that lasts only a short period of the psychedelic experience is not the direct cause of the lasting mental changes but rather the cause is the resulting sense of connectedness to other things cultivated through meditation (see Kałużna et al. 2022) or other religious practices. This would remove the triggers two steps from the resulting states of consciousness, further complicating the role of triggers in enabling ASC experiences.

Thus, triggers alone apparently do not cause ASC experiences but only open the mind to the possibility of experiences in an ASC by their chemical action on the brain. Triggers break the hold of the ordinary ego-driven subject/object mode of mind by altering brain activity in relevant areas that disrupts the configuration of brain events grounding our ordinary dualistic states of consciousness. But as just noted, not all disruptions of baseline brain activity lead to ASC experiences. So, what occurs in the mind after our baseline consciousness is disrupted depends on factors such as the experiencer's mental makeup and the setting but not the brain's chemistry. As things currently stand, nothing in the brain activity can be said to trigger one state or experience rather than another. For this reason, it is not correct to refer to triggers as *the cause* of a mystical experience: they are part of a package of causes and conditions that can enable a mystical experience by disrupting a sense of self, but there is no simple mechanical causal trigger of any ASC experience. In sum, triggers arrange necessary conditions in the brain for a mystical or other ASC experience to occur, but they are not sufficient to create any particular experience.

Natural and Transcendent Triggers

Can natural triggers enable experiences of transcendent realities (if introvertive mystical experiences in fact do that)? Must a reality greater than the natural brain/mind be involved to trigger the rise of a sense of transcendence and infinity? One prominent philosophical issue is theologically based: Do natural causes enable substantively different experiences than does a trigger from a transcendent reality (i.e., a reality transcending or encompassing the natural world and thereby not open to scientific scrutiny)? That is, are mystical experiences occasioned by drugs or other "artificial" triggers the *same in nature* as those occurring (either spontaneously or through ongoing mystical practices) that the experiencers' take to be triggered by the "grace" of God? Are naturally triggered experiences even with a positive religious set and setting in fact not duplicating the full phenomenology of a mystical experience initiated by God? Are chemical triggers "artificial," and thus are the enabled experiences are also "artificial"?

As discussed in chapter 2, the experimental reports indicate that at least some of the ASC experiences enabled by drugs share the full phenomenology of spontaneous and cultivated mystical experiences and so cannot be dismissed as "mere drug experiences." As also discussed, theists to date have not produced scientific or phenomenological evidence that naturally triggered mystical experiences are different in nature from allegedly God-triggered ones. In fact, there is no empirical evidence to date that the brain states of participants in psychedelic and meditation studies undergoing ASC experiences differ materially according to the trigger. However, ASC experiences that theists deem "genuine" may well be grounded in the brain—the experiences are not unconnected to the experiencer. Theists may well accept that God would utilize our neural system to produce mystical experiences rather than somehow bypass it, but they would still insist that manipulating brain states with natural triggers could not force God to enter our mind, since God chooses those to whom he reveals himself. The natural triggers may well set up conditions in the brain for God to enter, but only when God chooses is there a resulting genuine mystical experience. Thus, theists need not insist that the neural basis of theistic introvertive mystical experiences must differ when drug-facilitated or when God-given: experiences not initiated by God will not be genuine experiences of God despite having the same neural base. But if the configuration of brain activity for a naturally triggered ASC experience and one initiated by God are the same, theists would not be able to distinguish the "genuine" experiences from the "artificial" ones by the scanned activity of the brain.

Thus, this eliminates current science as a means to distinguish "genuine" and "artificial" mystical experiences. And without some adequate explanation, there is no reason currently to think that the ASCs of theists are different in fundamental nature. Members of different religions, seekers with no religious affiliation, and atheists may have different experiences due to their differing mental sets, but differences in the set and setting or dosages in the case of psychedelics may be all that is needed to account for any differences in the phenomenology of the experiences. If so, differences in the type of experiences and their intensity when enabled by psychedelics or other triggers may be accounted for by purely natural reasons. And until theists can present actual evidence that the brain state or the phenomenology of naturally facilitated experiences must differ from that in experiences occurring spontaneously from "grace," we should accept that the experiences are neutral with regard to the type of trigger associated with them.

In sum, based on the hardware (the brain activity) and the software (factors such as set and setting), the experiences appear to be phenomenologically indistinguishable regardless of whether the trigger is natural or transcendent—there is no evidence to date from these experiments for a theist's claim of a separate class of experiences triggered by "grace." The finding mentioned earlier that some experiences naturally triggered by psychedelics are more intense, more positive in their impact, and more related to spiritual and existential outcomes than mystical experiences enabled by other means (Doblin 1991: 14; Yaden et al. 2017a) also hurts the theists' case—such experiences may be even more "genuine" or "authentic" than mystical experiences allegedly occasioned by "grace."

As things stand today, the neurochemical condition of the brain is the same in the cases of alleged transcendent triggers and natural ones, and theists have not presented a nontheological reason to suspect that the phenomenology or base conditions are different. But that drugs or other natural triggers cannot force or guarantee a mystical experience means that more than a trigger's neural effects is always involved. As noted above, it may be that all triggers do is open the mind to having possible mystical or other ASC experiences, and what occurs then depends on other factors in the experiencer's mental makeup.

Do Brain States Cause ASC Experiences or Only Enable Them?

As noted in chapter 1, theists should not object in general to the scientific study of the brain of persons undergoing mystical experiences: even if a transcendent cause is at work, theists should accept that experience must somehow be grounded in the brain for the experience to occur for a person, and all that scientists are doing is merely identifying the areas of the brain affected in such an experience—the science does not require *rejecting* that a transcendent cause as a trigger may be at work.

But the science does lead to the major philosophical issue discussed in chapters 1 and 2. Triggers reconfigure activity in the brain, but does the reconfiguration cause the experience so that the experience is nothing but a brain-generated event? The triggering is not the occasioned mystical experience, but can it give an insight into that experience? Do triggers set up conditions in the brain that produce mystical and other ASC experiences, or do they merely set up conditions for the mind to receive some input from sources not confined to the brain? That is, do triggers in conjunction with other bodily conditions *cause* mystical experiences, or do they merely *enable or permit* them to occur? If the former, it is hard to see ASC experiences as cognitive of anything outside the individual's mind, and thus mystical cognitive claims concerning the nature of reality or transcendent realities can be rejected. If the latter, the brain is like a radio receiver, and all triggers do is set up conditions in the brain to receive a signal from reality (natural or transcendent) that is not clearly received in other mental states. Thus, if the latter, triggers only work on establishing base conditions in the brain for genuine cognitive events to occur but are not the cause of the experience in any meaningful sense. This is true even if only nontranscendent natural factors are involved in mystical experiences.

A common philosophical reaction to triggers is illustrated by pathological states as triggers. Epileptic microseizures in the left temporal lobe are a popular explanation (e.g., Persinger 1987). However, only very rarely (in 1 to 2 percent of patients) are positive ecstatic experiences of well-being, self-transcendence, and certainty triggered by these epileptic seizures (Devinsky and Lai 2008; also see Greyson et al. 2015). Such triggering may be significantly less common than triggering of mystical experiences in the general population. Nor are all mystical experiences "ecstatic" in the emotional sense: ecstasy is only one type of emotional response to mystical experiences—serenity and calm characterize many such experiences. In addition, the epileptic experiences usually last only a few seconds out of a larger episode and usually are not a matter of joy but of fear and anxiety (Kelly and Grosso 2007: 531–34). If seizures were the cause, why the vast majority of patients do not have mystical experiences would have to be explained. So too, this pathology does not explain why people with healthy brains also have mystical experiences.

Moreover, mystical experiences have a different phenomenological content from the content of epileptic seizures overall (Greyson et al. 2015). Studies aligned with the temporolimbic model truncate and misrepresent the experiential phenomenological features of mystical experiences (Bradford 2013: 113). These models also make emotion, rather than cognition, the central feature of mystical experiences, but this does not jibe with the historical record (Bradford 2013: 113): emotion typically does not precede and initiate perceptual and cognitive changes—the emotional response is triggered by the mystical experience, not vice versa. And again, not all mystical experiences involve ecstatic outbursts. So too, mystical experiences more often have a positive impact on the life of an experiencer than do pathological experiences. The loss of a sense of self outside of the latter experiences is associated with maladaptive outcomes such as a sense of disconnection from other people and a loss of empathy, but mystical experiences more often are correlated with positive changes in family life, reduced fear of death, better health, and a greater sense of purpose, although some patients do require therapeutic care (Yaden et al. 2017b: 59), and with healthy indices of personality and adjustment (Hood and Byrom 2010).

As the scientific study of the brain has expanded more recently, relatively simple explanatory models of triggering (such as epileptic seizures) have declined in influence; current explanations of religious experiences are relatively complex, integrating structures and systems outside the area of the brain affected by epileptic seizures (Bradford 2013: 103). It appears that scientists who jump to a pathology as a ready explanation of mystical experiences have not studied the scientific findings or the philosophical issues thoroughly and are already prejudiced against finding any possible value of such experiences.

When the philosophical issues are examined, the science here appears neutral (R. Jones 2016: 121–70; here, chapters 1 and 2): all scientists can do is examine the brain and determine the brain activity that is present during an ASC experience. Thus, science itself, as currently constituted, cannot in principle determine an answer to philosophical issues—the correlates that scientists identify in brain activity of ASC mental events may constitute the real substance of the experiences, or brain states may only be a platform for something more to occur. Thus, in our epistemic situation our decision on the basic philosophical question here comes down to our position on metaphysical issues related to the fundamental of reality and the nature of the mind. To those materialists and other naturalists who reduce mystical and other ASC experiences to the brain activity or the natural mind, ASC visions may churn up material in our subconscious, and mystical experiences at best may reveal something of the natural mind, but that is all—the experiences are merely hallucinations, and thinking otherwise is a delusion. With other metaphysics, one at least may accept the possibility that something more is involved in these experiences, and thus the science of brain states does not explain away ASC experiences. But the science of the triggering of these experiences itself remains neutral.

Conclusion

For the matters at hand, all that can be said about triggers is that in our current state of knowledge their role also remains neutral. That mystical or other ASC states can be reliably triggered does not prove that the states must be generated by brain or a natural mind rather than prove that triggering establishes conditions for another event. But naturalists take the high percentages of subjects who have mystical experiences under natural triggers as demonstrating that scientists can safely and reliably induce mystical experiences and so only natural causes are actually involved in mystical experiences, not any nonnatural realities. Naturalists would also point out that spontaneous mystical experiences do not prove that some nonnatural reality must be the initiating cause of mystical experiences: purely natural but currently unidentified mechanisms may still be all that is at work.

But in any case, the fact that the same trigger enables different ASC experiences means that natural triggers are at most only proximate causes—the ultimate causes of each particular type of experience currently remain unknown. It must also be remembered that we do not understand how exactly triggering events in the brain enable experiences—these triggers remain part of the "black box" mysteries surrounding the brain and consciousness.

This examination of triggers leads to the conclusion that triggers play an important role in the appearance of ASC experiences, but they do not determine their content or cognitive status. Experiences allegedly triggered by a transcendent cause are not necessarily different from those triggered by natural means. Again, that ASC experiences can be reliably triggered by "artificial" means does not indicate that such experiences are only products of the brain. Triggers arrange the necessary conditions in the brain for a mystical or other ASC experience to occur, but they are not sufficient to create any particular experience—the triggered brain conditions break the hold of ordinary state of consciousness, but what occurs after that is not determined by the trigger. And whether what happens after that is caused merely by the brain or natural mind or is something more cannot be answered by the science of triggers. All of this limits what the science of triggers can tell us about the nature of mystical experiences or other ASC experiences or more generally about consciousness. In the end, triggers trigger only brain activity—they do not trigger mystical experiences or other conscious events.

Chapter 5

Cognitive Bias in Mysticism and Its Study

A well-known danger in psychology is the cognitive bias of researchers affecting their findings. It can affect how researchers interpret their data and can inadvertently affect the persons being studied who pick up on the researchers' biases. Double-blind studies were instituted to help overcome this problem. But the danger occurs outside psychology in other disciplines and also in everyday life. And it can help us understand mysticism and its study.

There are two closely related types of cognitive bias. First, confirmation bias is "a well-established tendency to store, recall, and interpret information in a way that confirms one's preexisting beliefs or hypothesis" (Sebastián 2020: 18). It is a matter of "seeking or interpreting of evidence in ways that are partial to existing beliefs, expectations, or a hypothesis in hand" (Nickerson 1998: 175). This bias leads us to look for, and give greater weight to, information that confirms or supports our existing beliefs while ignoring or missing conflicting information. So too, we tend to interpret ambiguous data as supporting our beliefs. In looking for explanations, merely antidotal evidence can lead us to seeing causation between types of events where there is none. We also tend to remember confirming facts and ignore contradicting ones and to look for confirmations of our beliefs rather than conflicting facts. We tend to stop looking once we find what reassures us and not look for anything that would challenge our beliefs. So too, confirmation bias could have a "looping effect": we take the experiences as objectively establishing a theory when the result was in fact precisely what was hoped for and indeed expected all along. This only strengthens our beliefs, leading to explaining away any data that might conflict with those beliefs or dismissing such data without even examining it. Because of the power of mystical experiences, this may be greater in mysticism than in most areas of life. Such bias is not absolute and can be overcome, but it is often very hard to see.

This bias occurs in everyday life and is a well-known problem in science. Thomas Gilovich suggests that the most likely reason for the excessive influence of confirmatory information is that it is easier to deal with cognitively (Gilovich 1993; also see Nickerson 1998: 197–205). That is, it is easier for us to see a piece of information as supporting our position than to see how it might conflict with it. Seeing cases as conflicting requires even more intellectual effort than to see them as negative or to consider them as significant. It has led to conservatism among scientists concerning existing theories and empirical findings, and thus the persistence of outdated theories, and to overconfidence in one's own findings and theories (Nickerson 1998: 194–97). Thus, novel theories meet more resistance than if data were greeted more openly, and this can lead to suppression of innovations (Horrobin 1990). Such bias can lead to skewing data or to designing experiments in ways that would lead only to finding data that supports one's views (Koehler 1993), thus leading to unsound science. Confirmation bias can also control what gets published: research reports that agree with mainstream scientists' prior beliefs are judged to be of higher quality than those that disagree; the effect is larger for general evaluative judgments (e.g., relevance, methodological quality, or results clarity) than for more limited analytical judgments (e.g., adequacy of randomization procedures) (Koehler 1993: 28). Academic psychologists show a tendency to rate the quality and appropriateness of scientific studies more favorably when results and conclusions conform to their own prior expectations (Hergovich, Schott, and Burger 2010). Skeptics invoke the alleged confirmation bias of researchers as the reason to dismiss any seemingly positive outcomes from experiments in parapsychology.

In short, confirmation bias is related to looking for and finding evidence that confirms one's theory and ignoring possible counterevidence. It is a matter of looking back and reflecting on mystical experiences. This involves understanding and interpreting the experiences after they are over. The second type of cognitive bias relates more directly to one's own *experiences and observations*: expectancy bias. That is, we tend to accept experiences to be of what is expected and ignore other possibilities. This may *shape* experiences themselves. Such biases exist in endeavors other than science, including law, medicine, journalism, and politics (Nickerson 1998; Sutherland 2013

[1992]: 98–103). An often-cited example involves pilots landing planes: they tend to focus on what would indicate a safe landing and ignore hazards.

What is of interest here is that these biases can occur both to persons having a *mystical experience* and among scholars *studying mysticism*. Let's start by discussing the issue of experiential bias. The prospective of expectancy bias shaping mystical experiences, as constructivists in mystical studies may argue, will not be addressed here (see R. Jones 2020a), but that that bias may affect how mystics understand and interpret their own experiences will be. That it also affects scholars' study of mysticism will be discussed below.

Expectancy Bias and Mystical Experiences

Under the emerging "predictive coding" model of the brain, the brain operates as a prediction machine that constantly generates predictions about the world based on prior knowledge and sensory input; when predictions match sensory data, there is minimal prediction error, leading to a feeling of coherence and confirmation; but when there is a mismatch, the brain updates its predictions, resulting in a sensation of surprise (Holas and Kamińska 2023: 8). Meditation may reduce prediction errors by focusing on the present and thus minimizing the brain's forecasting; and psychedelics too may temporarily disrupt the usual predictive processes (Holas and Kamińska 2023: 8–9). However, the role of beliefs in most, if not all, mystical experiences complicates the issue, but the danger of expectancy bias among those who have had mystical experiences is that any mystical experiences would naturally be taken as conforming to the experiencer's own previous beliefs.

The importance of an experiencer's "set and setting" has been discussed in previous chapters. An austere setting may lead experiencers not to expect a mystical experience, and thus fewer mystical experiences are reported in that setting. A religious setting has the opposite effect. An experiencer's mental set of beliefs and expectations can affect what they take their experience to involve and can even affect what type of experience they have. Not just their teacher's doctrines but a researcher's beliefs can have that effect. Even a psychedelic drug researcher calling the drug a "hallucinogen" rather than an "entheogen" affects the experiencer's mental set. So too, the hype surrounding the effectiveness of psychedelics may introduce an expectancy bias, producing more positive therapeutic outcomes, regardless of the chemical effects of the psychedelic (Butler, Jelen, and Rucker 2022: 3048). Such bias may help to explain positive effects of placebos (Butler, Jelen, and Rucker

2022: 3052; also see Hartogsohn 2016). Indeed, expectancy effects may be an inextricable part of many types of drug treatments, although the effect can be mitigated somewhat (Butler, Jelen, and Rucker 2022: 3052–53). The Johns Hopkins group tried to provide "substantial controls" to counter "expectancy bias," but Roland Griffiths and colleagues (2006) conceded that the "setting" of the lab was "in many ways optimized to produce the kinds of experiences we are seeing." But that group also used larger dosages of psilocybin.

It should be pointed out that traditional mystics do not take their experiences as *confirming* their basic texts and doctrines. That is, classical mystics did not take their own experiences as an empirical verification or proof of their tradition's doctrines or as authority for those doctrines. That is a modern idea arising from religion's encounter with modern science. Rather, for classical mystics the *reverse* is true: they appeal to their tradition's authorities, doctrines, and texts to establish the correct understanding of their experiences. For them, their tradition's fundamental doctrines do not need any empirical proof or testing, and experiences are not needed to convince mystics of the texts' truth. For example, Shankara appeals to the Vedas, not experience (*anubhava*), for justification of his doctrines.[1] In this way, mystics take whatever their experiences are as conforming to the basic doctrines.

Thus, mystics typically see their experiences in terms of what they had expected prior to having the experiences from their tradition's doctrines. This can shape not only the postexperience understanding but also the experiences themselves (with a depth-mystical experience free of any differentiated content being a possible exception). Despite the overwhelming power of mystical experiences, expectancy bias may actually be greater here than with scientific observations due to the lack of controls.

Confirmation Bias in Mysticism

This does not mean that expectancy bias absolutely controls a mystic's understanding of what was experienced: an experience may so defy experiencers' expectations that they radically change their beliefs (e.g., going from belief in a personal god to belief in nonpersonal deistic reality or transcendent consciousness). But mystics will try to conform their understanding of the experience to their tradition's doctrines. The felt sense of certitude and profundity given in the experiences is usually transferred to the doctrines of a mystic's tradition. But mystics have also sometimes challenged their tradition and revised their doctrines. For example, Shankara insisted that even his ultimate authority (the Vedic Upanishads) needs *interpretation* when the literal meaning of passages do not conform to his nondualism. The Vedantins Ramanuja and Madhva give different interpretations to the same passages to fit their own metaphysics that conflict with Shankara's and each other's. Each of these Vedantins is an instance of mystics who sometimes twist the plain meaning of passages in their basic religious texts to make the texts say what they want them to say. In effect, in a circular manner the mystic's own metaphysics dictates the meaning of the basic scripture, which in turns validates their metaphysics.

But even if some mystics must interpret their scriptures to fit their ideas, nevertheless they see their scriptures (properly interpreted) as the source of knowledge and confirmation of the proper understanding of their experiences. For example, Meister Eckhart applied a Neoplatonism to his understanding of God and made the distinction between the personal God (*Gott*) who creates, acts, and has attributes and the "God beyond God"—the still, inactive Godhead (*Gottheit*), the source of all being including God's (Eckhart 2009: 293–94). This nearly got him excommunicated, but he still took the Bible (as interpreted by him) as the ultimate authority. Thus, for Eckhart any experience of God or of the Godhead would confirm the church's doctrines (as interpreted by his metaphysics).

A more recent example of how a mystical tradition can alter and control a mystic's postexperiential understanding comes from Martin Buber. He had an "unforgettable experience" from which he knew "well that there is a state in which the bonds of the personal nature of life seem to have fallen away from us and we experience an undivided unity" (Buber 1947: 24). However, he added:

> But I do not know—what the soul willingly imagines and indeed is bound to imagine (mine too once did it)—that in this I had attained to a union with the primal being or the godhead. That is an exaggeration no longer permitted to the responsible understanding. Responsibly—i.e., as a man holding his ground before reality—I can elicit from those experiences only that in them I reached an undifferentiated unity of myself without form or content. . . . In the honest and sober account of the responsible understanding this unity is nothing but the unity of this soul of mine, whose "ground" I have reached. (Buber 1947: 24–25)

He initially interpreted his felt sense of "undivided unity" to be unity with the Godhead, but his "responsible understanding" was that what he actually experienced was the unity of his soul. The latter understanding was dictated by his Jewish background in which the gulf between God and creature is unbridgeable.[2]

But notice that while Buber's religious beliefs may have controlled his *understanding*, they did not enter his *experience* itself or control its actual felt content: his change in understanding came only later and did not affect his sense of the character of the experience itself in which he felt an "undivided unity." Expectancy bias was at work: it did not affect the content of the experience, but his understanding of the nature and significance of the experience was conformed to his understanding of his tradition's basic scriptures. His understanding of what was experienced also changed over time. The process may become circular: the texts confirm the mystics' understanding of the nature and significance of their experiences, which in turn increase their conviction of the truth of the texts. Traditional mystics did not rest with their experiences being in discord with their faith—the experiences were not seen as challenging their conviction but as reassuring it.

Aldous Huxley is an example of this reinterpretation process occurring outside of traditional religions. He changed his mind on the nature of his mescaline experience: he initially considered it an experience of the bare "is-ness" of reality, but in 1955 he wrote to Humphry Osmond, the psychiatrist who had supplied him with the mescaline (and who invented the word "psychedelic"), that his feeling of being "cut off from the human world" was false—"the things which had entirely occupied my attention on that first occasion I now perceived to be temptations to escape from the central reality into false, or at least imperfect and partial Nirvanas of beauty and mere knowledge" (Huxley 1999 [1977]: 81). He later came to believe that the drug supplied a "sacramental vision of reality . . . of Love as the primary and fundamental cosmic fact," and that its message is that one never loves enough. Before his mescaline trip, he wanted "to know, and constantly be, in the state of love," and after his experience he (somewhat later) concluded that his experience confirmed that love is "the primary and fundamental cosmic fact" (Huxley 1999 [1977]: 769). Morgan Shipley says that Huxley's later interpretation, "occurring with greater distance from his first moment and supplemented by more experiences and efforts to understand the meaning of the heightened awareness made possible by psychedelics . . . is strictly religious" and connected to his belief in perennial philosophy as, in Huxley's words, "a Highest Common Factor, present in all the major religions of the world" (2015: 76–77).

In sum, cognitive bias may or may not affect the content of a mystical experience, but it affects the understanding given to the experience after it is over, and in the end, one's beliefs are confirmed. Cognitive bias has a conservative effect, but, as with expectancy bias, cognitive bias is not absolute—some experiencers do change even their most profound beliefs after mystical experiences (e.g., Timmermann et al. 2021; Nayak and Griffiths 2022). The experiences are not always controlled by confirmation bias. Under the proposed REBUS (RElaxed Beliefs under pSychedelics) model (Carhart-Harris and Friston 2019), psychedelics weaken the control of one's beliefs, thereby permitting more influence from experiential input and making experiencers more flexible in their resulting beliefs. It is true that psychedelics do not necessarily make an atheist into a theist (Glausser 2021), but there may be a "significant decreases in identification as atheist and agnostic and significant increases in belief in ultimate reality, higher power, God, or universal divinity" (Davis et al. 2020: 1018; also see Letheby 2022). This may suggest that mystical experiences in general are not controlled by the experiencers' prior beliefs but open experiencers to the possibility that there is more to reality that they had previously thought. However, psychedelics also open healthy volunteers up to greater *suggestibility* (Carhart-Harris et al. 2015: 791; Gandy 2022: 32), and here one's prior beliefs may affect the understanding given the experiences: experiencers naturally tend to accept their prior doctrines in these matters even if those doctrines have to be adjusted. (But increased suggestibility also opens the experiencer to the stated or implied beliefs of a researcher or therapist.) Indeed, the experiences may be so powerful as to adjust one's basic beliefs.

Cognitive bias also has an impact on the philosophical issue of whether mystical experiences are grounds for knowledge. Mystical experiences can be taken as supporting whatever beliefs one already holds, even though mystics of different traditions have the same confidence in their beliefs despite the fact that knowledge claims from different mystical traditions often genuinely conflict over basic beliefs. Classical mystics do not typically consider the possibility of the limitations of mystical knowledge due to the presence of multiple interpretations of the nature and significance of mystical experiences in the religious traditions of the world that conflict (see R. Jones 2016: 71–120). It is understandable that mystics do not usually engage in philosophical analysis: like most people, they may well simply accept the doctrines of their own religious tradition as the means for the proper understanding of all of their experiences and focus on practices. As discussed, mystical experiences may cause mystics to adjust their religious beliefs. But even if mystics were aware of other mystical traditions and conflicting mystical understandings of relevantly similar mystical experiences, cognitive bias would tend to keep them from seeing any reason to question their own understanding. Nor is it obvious that there can be any meaningful peer review across traditions to limit the force of such bias.

Cognitive bias has not happened only in the past. It can occur today even among the philosophically sophisticated. Huston Smith believed that in his first psychedelic drug-enabled experience in 1961 he was "experiencing the metaphysical theory known as emanationism" that was part of the perennial philosophy he had been espousing for years; he was now *seeing* what previously had only been conceptual theories for him; his experience "supported the truth of emanationists of the past" (2000: 11). Bergson's view of the brain as a reducing value also now struck him as true (2000: 11). The experience was a matter of "empirical metaphysics" (2000: 11) He could say "I had no doubt that my experience was valid, because it was retracing exactly what I was convinced was the nature of reality" (2005: 227)—"the substances simply poured experience into the molds of my existing worldview" (2005: 235). The experience "experientially validated my world-view that was already in place" (2005: 227), and he felt "incomparably fortunate to have that validation" (2005: 234). However, he also believed that in his psychedelic experiences he had experienced only the penultimate level, not "the infinite, the Absolute" (2005: 227) that is also part of perennial philosophy. But the important point is that he believed that he was being shown what he already believed to be true.[3] He was certainly well aware of the diversity of conflicting mystical claims from his years of studying and teaching world religions, and yet he saw his experiences as confirming his prior beliefs. He did not see the experiences as being in a more ambiguous position that would undercut their support for only one interpretation. So too, classical mystics would see their experiences in terms only of their own tradition and not a cross-cultural perennialism that he espoused (see R. Jones 2021b).

Confirmation Bias in the Study of Mysticism

Confirmation bias can also occur among scientists studying people who have had mystical experiences and among scholars studying mystical traditions.

It has also been employed to explain away accounts by mystics of their experiences that conflict with a theorist's theory. Here are four examples—a philosopher of mind, a constructivist in mystical studies, a secularist, and a perennialist historian.

First the philosopher. Miguel Ángel Sebastián believes that a total lack of a sense of self is impossible, and thus he dismisses reports by mystics that their experiences did indeed involve a radical disruption of self-awareness as most probably due to a cognitive bias derived from the expectations and the cosmological and metaphysical views of the experiencers; thus, this bias is good reason for mistrusting the reports (Sebastián 2020: 1). He gives the example of the concentrative state of *samadhi* in Buddhism and Hinduism that is often described as a selfless experience. He accepts that advanced meditators undergo experiences whose phenomenology is in fact different from that of ordinary waking experiences and that their experiences differ from less-experienced meditators, as their reports and neuroimaging suggest (Sebastián 2020: 18). His claim "is rather that there are good reasons to think that the information stored and recalled from their experiences as well as the interpretation of these memories as reflected in their reports is likely to be influenced by their beliefs. A control for cognitive bias in the experiments is required" (Sebastián 2020: 18). A mystic's expectancy bias is a concern: prior writings in Buddhism and Hinduism of others allegedly having selfless experience cause new experiencers to see their own experiences that way because they believe previous experiencers had their experience even though the experiences are not truly selfless.

However, Sebastián does not consider that in a case of confirmation bias his own prior beliefs about the nature of consciousness cause him to dismiss the Buddhist and Hindu reports out of hand. Mystics may be subject to confirmation bias, but so may scholars: Sebastián's own prior studies from which he concluded complete ego-loss is impossible would influence his understanding of mystics' reports and incline him to reject them in advance of actually studying them. Meditative practices or other triggers may enable a state of consciousness that Sebastián had not encountered before and that he did not consider seriously since he believed that he already knew its nature based on his prior study of other states of consciousness. Sebastián does not address whether he is being open to changing his own prior beliefs. He does recommend future tests that try to control confirmation bias among experiencers, but such tests must allow experiencers options that he himself would reject, and Sebastián must be open in his own beliefs. (The possibility of a selfless experience was addressed in chapter 3.)

For similar reasons, it can also be argued that confirmation bias operates in the prevailing model of mystical experiences in mystical studies today: constructivism (see R. Jones 2020a). Constructivists argue that no experience is possible that is truly empty of all diverse content, even though some accounts by mystics suggest that. Rather, all human experience must be structured by cultural phenomena. This is based on the theory in philosophy of mind that sense experience is never free of some cultural structuring (although this theory is being questioned in philosophy today). So too for a sense of self and other inner conscious activity. Thus, constructivists deny the validity of reports of "empty" mystical experiences before even studying them. Steven Katz admits that the belief that there can be no pure (i.e., unmediated) experiences is an epistemological assumption (1978: 26), but constructivists apply this assumption to their historical research, and it requires them to reject much of what mystics actually say in advance of studying their remarks. With this strategy in place, nothing mystics could say could provide counterevidence to constructivism even in principle since whatever mystics say after their experiences will reflect their tradition's doctrines and constructivists will automatically take this as evidence for their position on what occurs in the experiences—but that conclusion that was already predetermined by their prior assumption. Constructivists claim to be empirical (e.g., Katz 1988: 752), but they argue that certain mystical reports must be false merely on the grounds of their assumed theory that no human experience can be free of mediation by cultural structuring. Hence, no actual historical data would lead them to rejecting their assumption: mystical accounts will always be immediately interpreted to fit their theory, and so it is unfalsifiable in principle. Only a rejection of the theory would permit adopting another theory that might be falsifiable by the study of mystics. In sum, the constructivists' confirmation bias may be determining their understanding in advance of actually studying mystical writings.

There is another danger of confirmation bias in mystical studies in this regard: having a mystical experience may give you a general sense that there is more to reality than you previously believed, but it may also lead you to believing that you now know what all mystics in all cultures and eras know. To give instance of this: Frances Vaughan said of her mystical experience: "The perennial philosophy and the esoteric teaching of all time suddenly made sense. . . . My understanding of mystical teaching, both Eastern and Western, Hindu, Buddhist, Christian, Sufi alike, took a quantum leap. I became aware of all great religions, and understood for the first time the meaning of ecstatic states" (quoted in Shipley 2015: 10). Thus, one does not have to study the actual teachings of mystics to know what they really mean.

However, that position also is based on the very questionable assumptions: that all mystics had the same experience you had, and that all mystics in all cultures and eras hold the same doctrine. First, there are *different types of mystical experiences* (see R. Jones 2021a: 9–24)—simply because you have had one of them (or a vision) does not mean that you have experienced what all mystics have experienced or gained all the insights that mystics are alleged to have gained. For example, a theistic differentiated introvertive experience is not the depth-mystical experience of Eckhart's or Advaita Vedantins' discussions. (Smith conceded that he had only experienced the penultimate level, not "the infinite, the Absolute" [2005: 227].) Nor does an introvertive mystical experience convey the Buddha's extrovertive enlightening insight into the ultimate impermanent nature of the natural realm. You cannot consciously or unconsciously assume that all mystics must have had that particular variety of mystical experience. Second, if the history of mysticism is actually examined, it is blatantly obvious that this is not true (see R. Jones 2024). Just because you see your experience as bringing your own beliefs to life, it does not mean that any other mystics—let alone all of them—hold your beliefs. That is, any type of mystical experience may give you the sense that there is more to reality than you previously believed, but you cannot assume that all mystics would endorse your particular understanding of the experience or of reality. In addition, having a mystical experience most assuredly does not by itself lead to understanding, say, the medieval Christian Meister Eckhart's doctrines of the Godhead, being, and the "birth of the son" in the soul. Even if you could say "Now I know what Eckhart was talking about," you still could not say "Now I understand Eckhart's Neoplatonist metaphysics" without actually studying Eckhart's works. There is no reason to believe that mystical experiences grant a person an instant understanding of all mystics' specific teachings.

In sum, we cannot conclude that simply because we have had a mystical experience that Eckhart, the Buddha, and so forth must all have had the same experience and espoused the same beliefs about reality and that those beliefs are the ones an experiencer endorses. Nevertheless, the powerful effect of a mystical experience may lead easily—indeed, almost inevitably—to the error of assuming that all mystical experiences are of one type and thus that all mystics have the same experience one had oneself. And this may well lead to imposing one's own understanding of one's experience on all mystical doctrines—the sense of profundity and certainty given in a mystical experience may easily lead the experiencer to believe that all mystics must hold the same beliefs that the experiencer holds. But with this variety of confirmation bias one's understanding of one's own mystical experience controls the meaning of all mystical texts, and this can easily lead to *distorting* mystics' teachings, including those of one's own religious tradition—one may easily believe that all mystics endorse one's beliefs, and so one's own beliefs supply the proper understanding of all mystics' teachings as easily as believing all mystics had the same type of experience as one's own.

Consider the nature-mystical experience that the author Mark Waldman had in which the trees, fence, and weeds outside his office window all seemed "perfect" and in which he felt a "pure bliss." The first thing he remembered thinking was "Oh! This is what those Buddhists and Hindus were writing about when they described enlightenment" (Newberg and Waldman 2016: 190). Actually, that is *not* what the Buddhists and Hindus traditionally claim: the Buddhist enlightenment experience is about seeing the impermanence and conditionality of all phenomena, not their "perfection," and the Hindu ideas of enlightenment involve something both interior to our being and transcending the natural world, not something observed in the natural realm. In addition, his beliefs suddenly and radically changed at the moment of his experience: he "knew" (his quotation marks) that there was no heaven or hell or God and that when he died that would be his end (Newberg and Waldman 2016: 190). This, of course, is not what Buddhists and Hindus conclude in their mysticisms. After several months, Waldman's feeling subsided and feelings of doubt arose. Then one day a small voice whispered to him: "Mark, you don't know a damned thing about religion" (Newberg and Waldman 2016: 190–91). He then started to study the works of mystics.

Another example is the perennialist Swami Abhyananda, whose experience of a "unitive vision" led him to adopt perennial philosophy. He wrote a history of mysticism along those lines (Abhyananda 2012). For him, the "unchanging testament" of mysticism includes not just all classical mystics but all of religion—e.g., ancient Egyptian religion. He believes that all of religion can be interpreted in terms of an eternal Absolute consciousness that emits a primal male and female pair. He reads all myths and religious texts through this prism. He also concludes that all religious texts encode the same mystical experience that he had. In his history, he often had to disregard what mystics actually wrote and instead told us what the mystics really meant. This perspective permeates down to creating very misleading translations of key terms in order to make all mystical ideas seem the same—e.g., translating disparate concepts all as "consciousness" or "Self" without looking at their contexts. (To perennialists, there is no need to examine their cultural contexts because perennial philosophy is their true context.) But by imposing a metaphysics of beliefs Abhyananda thinks all true mystics hold, he badly distorted the doctrines of the different religions of the world. Perennial philosophers in general do the same (see R. Jones 2021a).

It should also be pointed out that the fields of meditation and psychedelics have been accused of being "marked by strong bias effects" (Holas and Kamińska 2023: 10). Roland Griffiths was accused of running his psychedelic studies "more like a 'new-age' retreat center" (quoted in Borrell 2024: 1), which may lead to a higher percentage of participants having mystical experiences. Of course, critics' possible prejudice *against* psychedelics must also be considered in *their* findings. The danger of the "illusion" of knowing more about how psychedelics work than scientists actually do (Ona, Maja, and Bouso 2022) may easily lead to seeing mystical experiences as confirming one's own theory, whatever it is.

Michiel van Elk and David Bryce Yaden raise a word of caution about the current state of the fields of psychedelic research and therapy: many of the findings that they reviewed are still preliminary, and the field as a whole "is still in its infancy; and so far much of the field has not yet jumped on the bandwagon of using open science practices" (van Elk and Yaden 2022: 12). Here "there is a potential of researcher bias, especially because many people doing research in this field are psychedelic enthusiasts" (van Elk and Yaden 2022: 12).

Conclusion

The conclusion of this discussion is that cognitive biases appear to be present both in mysticism and in mystical studies. Ironically, there is actually a danger for the study of mysticism in having a mystical experience. Common sense would suggest that having a mystical experience would help to understand better the mystical traditions of the world. Indeed, one can argue that having such an experience is even necessary for such study (e.g., Staal 1975). But the dangers in having a mystical experience of distorting others' mystical experiences and mystical doctrines were discussed above. Cognitive bias may well be especially strong when it comes to our most deeply entrenched beliefs: we would normally see only things that confirm our basic way of looking at the world and not look for evidence that would uproot it. And when it comes to mystical experiences, the bias may be especially great for experiencers, since in experiments a majority of participants rate their mystical experiences *the* most meaningful ones in their life or among the top five; this impact occurs immediately after the experience (Griffiths et al. 2006: 274) and is long-lasting (Griffiths et al. 2008: 624; Aday et al. 2020).

In science, cognitive bias can be lessened, if not eliminated, by experiments devised by multiple scientists with different points of view and utilizing double-blind setups. More generally, the bias can be lessened by education in different points of view and with training in critical thinking. But doing this with respect to powerful altered state of consciousness experiences may be difficult. People do not naturally seek out data contrary to their beliefs. Thus, many would not study mystical traditions other than the one that they adopt that might show the variety of mystical experiences and mystical doctrines. Moreover, that each type of mystical experience is open to different basic interpretations eliminates new experiences as means to empirically test one's own understanding. But as Raymond Nickerson warns: "If one were to attempt to identify a single problematic aspect of human reasoning that deserves attention above all others, the confirmation bias would have to be among the candidates for consideration" (1998: 175). Being open-minded and impartial is another state of mind that is difficult to achieve.

Chapter 6

Mystical Experiences, Consciousness, and Inverse Multiple Realization

Differences in neuroscans of the brain are the closest that scientists can suggest differences in "subjective" mental states. That is, if two persons have exactly the same brain state, then most people would assume the two have the same mental state, and if the scans are different, then so are the mental states. Physicalists (materialists) are vested in there being a one-to-one correlation of brain states and mental states in order to see the mind as material or as a product of the brain. That is, many different experiences may involve the same general neural activity, but even two similar sense perceptions would not have exactly the same neural states—each mental event would have a unique neural configuration. But a well-known problem in philosophy of mind involves the issue of "multiple realization": can the *same* mental events and states be realized by *different* neural configurations (see R. Jones 2013: 38–39, 47–48; Polger and Shapiro 2016)?[1] However, current research on persons undergoing mystical experiences enabled by psychedelic drugs or meditation presents a different challenge: the possibility of the inverse multiple realization (IMR). That is, although the effect of the same drug or meditative technique on the brain can be assumed to be uniform in all relevant respects for all subjects until there is reason to believe otherwise, different states of consciousness and experiences result from the same trigger. For example, if psilocybin affects the brain of all people in the same general way and the same general configuration of brain activity results, physicalists would have to explain why the subjects have significantly different types of experiences—even the same experiencer may have quite different experiences on different occasions or even during the same experimental session. In addition, some persons have no change in their state of consciousness at all. Thus, it appears that the *same brain state* (the pattern or configuration of neural activity) underlies *different mental states*. If so, IMR enters the picture, and this presents a problem for physicalists.

Most people assume that two similar visual sense perceptions do not have exactly the same neural activity. For example, a switch in perception of a Gestalt figure (e.g., going from seeing the duck to seeing the rabbit) is accompanied by some slight change in brain activity. The brain events would differ on some level. But different sense perceptions would involve the same general pattern of neural activity—they occur in the same general *state of consciousness*. That is, each of these mental events would have a unique neural configuration, unless they are multiply realizable, but the experiences would occur in our baseline state of consciousness and thus are uniform in nature in that regard.

The problem that mysticism presents is that psychedelics and meditation appear to disrupt our baseline state of consciousness, thereby permitting other states to operate, and many fundamentally different types of experiences occur in those altered states of consciousness (ASCs). ASCs involve, in Charles Tart's words, a qualitative shift in the stabilized pattern of mental functioning from our baseline state (1969: 1). Common altered states are dreaming, daydreaming, and being drunk. ASCs of interest in mystical studies include those states in which nondual introvertive and extrovertive mystical experiences occur—i.e., experiences in which a sense of self and conceptualized differentiation in our mental input are lessened or eliminated, unlike with visions and locutions, where the dualism of a subject and object is retained. It is hard to say that all of these experiences are merely different experiences in the same state of consciousness, like different sense perceptions in our baseline state of consciousness.[2]

Different triggers may have effects on the brain that result in differences in the enabled ASCs and experiences—e.g., LSD occasions more visions while psilocybin occasions more nonvisual experiences.[3] However, based on the phenomenological accounts of experimental subjects, different psychedelics, meditation, and other natural (and perhaps nonnatural) triggers produce some experiences that are phenomenologically indistinguishable. There is no one-to-one relation of different triggers and different types of experiences: the same trigger may produce different experiences, and the same experiences may come from different triggers. Nor do triggers "enter" the experiences to produce the felt phenomenological content.

But if substantively different types of experience are associated with the same neural state, the IMR issue arises. It currently appears that exactly the same set of neural configurations underlie two significantly different types of mystical mental events. Thus, we cannot be certain that similar third-person data for different meditators means that the experiences they are having are similar in nature (Schmidt and Walach 2014: 3). Do advanced meditators have quite different ASCs or experiences than do novices utilizing the same meditative techniques even though they share the same neural signature? If other meditators can duplicate the physical state of the brain of an enlightened mystic, how can we know that the subjective state of consciousness is also being duplicated?

Psychedelic-Enabled Experiences

Consider first mystical and other ASC experiences enabled by psychedelics. The problem arises from the fact, noted earlier, that there is no one universal psychedelic ASC or experience. That is, there is no one generic "psychedelic state of consciousness" following the ingestion of these drugs (Richards 2016: 16). Even during one session, there is a variety of states of consciousness during the actions of the entheogens (Richards 2016: 115). Thus, psychedelics apparently enable a variety of experiences, including a variety of mystical ones. Thus, there is no one universal psychedelic ASC experience, even though researchers routinely refer to "*the* psychedelic state" or to "*the* mystical experience" (e.g., Nour and Carhart-Harris 2017: 177). In fact, there are significantly different types of mystical experiences (see R. Jones 2021a: chapter 2), let alone all ASC experiences.

Moreover, as also discussed, ingesting a psychedelic drug does not in fact assure *any* ASC experience or state—sometimes no major alteration of one's state of consciousness occurs at all (Richards 2016: 15; Ellens 2015: 22–23; Tart 1975: 152–53). Sometimes mystical experiences or visions do not occur during drug-enabled states but precede or follow them (Richards 2016: 10). So too, many people meditate daily for decades without any ASC experiences occurring. The process of attaining an experience is not mechanical but involves other elements than the trigger.

Thus, as Huston Smith summed up, "there is no such thing as *the* drug experience per se—no experience that the drugs, as it were, secrete" (2000: 20). The psychologist Stanislav Grof (2009) makes the point that

LSD has no one invariant pharmacological effect, nor is there one inevitable experience associated with it—rather, he believes that LSD is a catalyzer that amplifies and exteriorizes dynamics within the person's subconscious. Timothy Leary suggested this possibility when he first discussed set and setting: "Of course, the drug does not produce the transcendent experience. It merely acts as a chemical key—it opens the mind, frees the nervous system of its ordinary patterns and structures. The nature of the experience depends almost entirely on set and setting" (Leary, Metzner, and Alpert 1964: 11).

It is often the case that people react differently to the same drug—aspirin does not help everyone. But among those who do react to psychedelics, the resulting experiences are quite diverse and no one-to-one correlation of experiences and brain states appears possible. If the experiences were a product of the drug, one would expect them to be more uniform. Also note that in these experiments, some recipients who received the *placebo* also had mystical experiences: there would be no change in the brain state (or the mind alters the brain) and yet changes in the mental state. This would lead to further questioning of the tie of mind to body.

The variety of states of consciousness and experiences connected to one state of brain conditions triggered by a given psychedelic presents the IMR issue. We have no reason to suppose that these drugs have different chemical effects on different brains. How could a given psychedelic drug have the same chemical effect on all brains and yet enable different experiences? Brain activity is altered by the drug, but apparently whether consciousness is altered or what state of consciousness arises depends on the other factors. If so, brain activity alone does not account for the phenomenology of mystical experiences—indeed, perhaps brain activity does not shape any of the any of the felt phenomenological content of these experiences at all. That is, even if we are all neurologically the same with regard to mystical experiences and we receive the same stimulants and appropriate dosages, we may have significantly different experiences. Differences in the "set and setting" of each individual experiencer figures in this, but these are not related to the chemistry of the brain. Thus, unless set and setting can be shown to be in fact physical properties, invoking set and setting only reinstates the problem. Factors transcending the entire natural realm are another possibility, but even if the material shaping the experiences is coming from our subconscious, the issue persists.

In sum, even if these experiences are totally subjective, the diversity of mystical and other ASC psychedelic states associated with the same brain states remains.

Meditative Experiences

The great variety of "subjective" (i.e., experiential) responses—including no change of consciousness at all—also accompany the same physiological changes produced by meditative techniques (e.g., Benson and Klipper 2000 [1975]: 130). The question here, as with the psychedelic experiences, is whether there must be different neural states for introvertive and extrovertive mystical experiences and for introvertive experiences with differentiated content and those without such content. If so, different neurological explanations would be needed for each case. So too, can the *same* techniques lead to *different* brain states in different meditators? Or can *different* meditative techniques lead to the *same* states of the brain in all meditators? Or, the question of particular interest here: can the *same* neural state underlie radically *different* meditative experiences?

As discussed in chapter 1, Andrew Newberg and Eugene d'Aquili (1999; Newberg, d'Aquili, and Rause 2002) conducted experiments on three Christian Franciscan nuns and eight Tibetan Buddhist monks who were experienced meditators using SPECT neuroimaging during their meditation or shortly afterward. The subjects utilized their tradition's concentrative meditative techniques. What is interesting about the experiments for the IMR issue is that Newberg and d'Aquili got similar neurological readings for both groups concerning the slowing of activity in the area of the brain connected to the orientation and association of a person in space and with phenomena, and yet the Christians and Buddhists claimed to have had *radically different experiences of "unity"*: the Christians experienced being "united with God" (an introvertive experience with differentiations), while Buddhists experienced being "inextricably connected to all of creation" (an experience of feeling connected to external phenomena with no personal elements in which oneself feels "endless and intimately interwoven with everyone and everything [that] the mind senses") (Newberg, d'Aquili, and Rause 2002: 7, 2, 6). The two groups had different practices, but the different experiences of "unity" affected the same areas of the brain in each participant's brain (Newberg and Waldman 2016: 91). All subjects showed a slowing of activity in the posterior superior parietal lobes (Newberg, d'Aquili, and Rause 2002: 4–5).

Newberg and d'Aquili reported only "similar" neurological readings (Newberg, d'Aquili, and Rause 2002: 7) from the Christian nuns and Buddhist monks. Perhaps their data could be reexamined to see if there are in fact subtle differences between the two groups. The scientists monitored all brain activity, but the possibility that current neuroscience is focusing on the wrong aspects of the brain when it comes to mystical experiences cannot be ruled out. Perhaps differing periods of time spent on various practices produced different brain states. Perhaps current SPECT technology examining blood flow may not be exact enough to expose differences if there were any. Newberg concedes that the SPECT imaging technology used in their experiment "is known for its somewhat poor spatial resolution, meaning that the areas of the activation in the brain that were measured are rather large and non-specific" (Yaden and Newberg 2022: 242).[4] Thus, if neuroscientists are currently measuring the correct neural basis for these experiences, is the technology simply not yet refined enough to detect the neurological differences? More precision may be necessary to reveal if there are more subtle differences in the Christian and Buddhist meditators' brain activity. Or perhaps other variables need to be measured. Or perhaps an entirely new type of technology is needed to reveal the differences. But if the Newberg-d'Aquili results are replicated by independent researchers, there would be objective evidence that these nontheistic and theistic meditators produced the same brain activity during the two different types of experiences, and it would be difficult to maintain that they occurred in one state of consciousness, since one is introvertive and without differentiated content while the other has differentiated content.

One caveat is to ask whether the nuns and monks had radically different experiences at all or merely interpreted the same experiences of a unified consciousness differently when they looked back on the experiences after they were over. Nonconstructivists in mystical studies would argue the latter. Overall, there are three possibilities. First, both the nuns and monks had the same contentless experience (e.g., free of all differentiated content but only consciousness) that was only interpreted differently after the experience. Once the nuns and monks returned to a more dualistic state of consciousness, they applied the conceptual framework of understanding that their tradition's doctrines prescribed to experiences, but this was only *after* the fact—the experiences themselves were free of such structuring. The terms they used may be radically different, but the experiences were the same. Second, they had the same type of experiences with the same type differentiated content, but they again interpreted them differently after the experiences were over. The exact content and structuring supplied by the meditator's culture may be irrelevant to the brain state, and so the different experiences would be neurologically similar and may well be occurring in the same ASC. Third, they had significantly different experiences: the

Buddhists' experiences were not empty of differentiated content and structure, but the nuns' experiences were. If the Buddhists' experiences involved sense-experiences (and thus were extrovertive) while the nuns' did not, the difference in ASCs would be greater. The nuns' experiences had personal content while the Buddhists' had only nonpersonal content. "Set and setting" would explain what type of experience occurred.

The third possibility implicates IMR. If such different experiences in fact did occur in the Newberg-d'Aquili experiments, it would mean that radically different experiences can occur with the same neural base if the Christians and Buddhists had radically different experiences—one with differentiated content and one without. Indeed, their underlying altered states of consciousness might have been quite different, not merely different experiences occurring within the same state. It is not like the slight differences in two different ordinary sense perceptions.

Such a finding would wreak havoc with the idea that the brain and mind are identical or that the brain causes mental states: each unique configuration of brain events would not have only one unique mental event associated with it. Each experience would still have a corresponding brain state but not a unique one. Thus, neural states could not determine, or be identical to, mental states. The meditative technique, like each psychedelic, may have the same basic effect on the brain for each meditator, at least in producing the same general neural configuration of events. If so, the brain conditions are the same. And yet different mystical or other ASC experiences occur, experiences that are different enough to raise the prospect that different states of consciousness are involved. No one-to-one correlation of brain and mental states could occur if either multiple realization or IMR is the case.

In the future, more refined technology or scanning for other features may establish one-to-one correlations of meditative experiences and neurological states. Each meditative experience and mental state would then be associated with a unique state of the brain. But without such a correlation, no naturalist reduction of mystical experiences to brain events could be possible: all mystical experiences would be grounded in the body in some brain state, but simply identifying the brain state could not explain why more than one ASC experience is grounded in the same state or why a given experience was realized in that brain state. Nor would the possibility be rule out that that experience might be realized with another brain state.

Thus, IMR, if established, would eliminate the possibility that neuroscience in its current state could tell us what type of experience is occurring, let alone anything about its nature: establishing the neural base by establishing one-to-one correlations of meditative and brain states would not tell us anything about what experience is occurring, since different experiences would be correlated with the same brain state.

The Physicalists' Fallback Positions

At present, there appears the real possibility that substantively different states of the mind may have the same biological bases—i.e., the same set of neural events underlie fundamentally different mental events or states. If data suggesting IMR is replicated by other researchers or IMR is confirmed by other research, physicalists have some serious work to do to maintain their theories of the relation of the mind to the body.

However, the above discussion touches upon what would be the physicalists' fallback positions to preserve materialism. First, perhaps the brain states underlying different mystical and other ASC experiences are really different—neuroscientists simply have not yet devised equipment to identify the differences. The Newberg-d'Aquili experiment does not really address the issue. The differences in patterns of brain activity are too subtle for current technology—greater resolution, as it were, is needed to catch the differences or a different kind of technology is needed. Perhaps some as yet unthought of but more sophisticated means will establish one-to-one correlations of brain state and each type of ASC experience. After all, current technology is not designed to pick up different perceptions but only the general state of the brain. Or it could be that statistical averaging simply hides the highly individual nature of brain patterns. That is, statistical analysis washes out the "uniqueness of individual patterns and single events" during meditative sessions (Hinterberger 2014: 96). If so, each experience may have a unique brain state underlying it. A second fallback mentioned above is that, as non-constructivists argue, each experiencer actually has the same experience but only interprets it differently, in terms of their personal beliefs, after it is over. A third position is that, like two sense perceptions, an experience empty of differentiated content and one with differentiated content and an introvertive and an extrovertive mystical experiences are all really the same type of experience despite phenomenological differences occurring in the same state of consciousness—it is not as if the same brain states have different states of consciousness associated with them or the same set of neural events underlie two fundamentally different mental events.[5] There are no "altered states of consciousness" at all, or at most only one. A fourth response is that the psychedelic drugs, meditative techniques, or other natural triggers have different effects on different brains in different persons, thereby producing different types of ASCs, although why the chemical effect of the drugs in these cases should be different would have to be explained. A fifth position is that other areas of the brain that are not currently being studied with regard to these experiences are responsible for the experiences. Once those regions or the entire brain rather than only selected regions are focused upon for these experiences through neuroimaging and electrophysiological recordings during these experiences the different brain states will become apparent. Another position is that it is something in the brain other than the neurological level of activity that is responsible for differences in experiences.

In the end, physicalists may merely throw up their hands and admit they do not know if there is a one-to-one correlation but exclaim "Of course, there's a one-to-one correlation—there must be because materialism requires it! Our contemporary technology is simply not sensitive enough to detect the differences in what appears to be the same neurological state for different experiences. It's no big deal. It only shows that science is in an early state in this field. The experiments speak only to the general areas of the brain at work and do not have any bearing on whether there is a one-to-one correlation of brain and mental events." But this response is just an admission of dogma: these physicalists are not following the best scientific evidence of the day but refusing to question what their metaphysics demands.

Conclusion

If nothing else, the possibility of IMR shows that there are problems that have not yet been addressed in the science of meditators and psychedelic users. If physicalists do not even admit the possibility of IMR, it is an admission that they do not accept what state-of-the-art science today is saying—if someone offers another metaphysical view, physicalists could not reply that at least they are committed to the best science of the day. They do not know in advance what science will find, but they must admit that their philosophical assumptions are not dictated by science. In this way, the dilemma presented by IMR becomes a litmus test for physicalists and other naturalists: is their philosophical commitment really to what *science says is real* or to *materialism*?

But if physicalists cannot come up with some strategy that is convincing, and if various mystical experiences and other ASC experiences are substantively different, IMR would show a disconnect between brain states and mental states. The difference in positions on the issue may come down to whether one accepts that the differences in ASC experiences are not simply like different sense-experiences occurring in ordinary consciousness. But IMR would move neuroscience another step away from informing us about the nature of any mystical experience. (In chapters 1 and 2, it was argued that neuroscientific findings on brain activity would be simply irrelevant to questions of the nature of mystical experiences.) More generally, it would untether consciousness from the body: consciousness would be independent of the brain rather than produced by it or otherwise tied to it. The explanation of the presence of any experiential level would be missing from any neuroscientific account, as would why reality permits the higher-level events to occur at all.

Chapter 7

The Role of Mystical Experiences in Psychedelic Therapy and Research

Since the "psychedelic renaissance" that began in the 1990s, psychedelics have been hyped as not only a quick fix for all mental disorders but a panacea for all our social ills—wars, climate change, and so forth. That is, they will bring about a utopia by making us nicer people and better citizens: by transforming individuals through psychedelics, society as a whole will become more liberal and progressive. However, the drugs do not necessarily produce liberal or progressive changes or actions for someone not previously so inclined. In fact, psychedelics have been touted by authoritarian right-wing groups, including neo-Nazis today (Pace and Devenot 2021). It appears that the suggestibility caused by psychedelics leads to *amplifying* whatever values one already has (Pace and Devenot 2021). Reaction to the hype has also caused some researchers to focus on the negative effects (some long-term in a small percentage of subjects) of psychedelic use (Bremler et al. 2023; Evans et al. 2023). Some young researchers have left the field of psychedelic studies disillusioned because the drugs have turned out not to be a wonder drug cure-all; nor have the drugs revealed the nature of consciousness (see Langlitz 2012: 233–39).

However, for many patients there is at least a modest but measurable benefit from psychedelic therapy in cases of, for example, depression, anxiety, and addiction for those who are resistant to more traditional therapies (Roseman, Nutt, and Carhart-Harris 2018). Perhaps when psychedelics disrupt the sense of self, they disrupt a patient's connection to the pathology. The effects also begin more quickly than with other therapies. The beneficial therapeutic effects of classic serotonergic psychedelics (psilocybin, LSD,

DMT) has been generally accepted (Andersen et al. 2021). These benefits may have been hyped in this early stage of study—a significant percentage of patients have not been helped at all, and the studies usually involve only a small number of participants. Nevertheless, some have even claimed that the benefits result exclusively from the drugs and not the psychotherapy (Goodwin et al. 2024: 23).

Psychedelic therapy has also gained popular attention since Michael Pollan's *How to Change Your Mind* (2018). But unlike other psychotropic drugs, psychedelics may have a drastic effect on the phenomenology of a subject's consciousness. And this leads to the issue of whether the cause of the long-lasting psychophysical benefits is the *chemical effect* of the psychedelic molecules alone or the principal cause is the enabled *mystical experience* of a loss of a sense of self.

A number of articles appeared a few years ago on whether research on the therapeutic effects of psychedelics should exclude all references to mysticism in order to gain more scientific respectability. One camp (D. Olson 2020; Johnson 2021; Sanders and Zijlmans 2021) argues that the positive therapeutic effects result only from the direct pharmacological actions of the drugs on the brain. Thus, the subjective experiences that are sometimes enabled by the drugs are only a therapeutically unimportant byproduct of the chemical reactions. Use of "a mysticism framework creates a 'black box' mentality in which researchers are content to treat certain aspects of the psychedelic state as beyond the scope of scientific inquiry" (Sanders and Zijlmans 2021: 1253). Thus, since mystical experiences actually play no role in psychedelic therapies, talk of the experiences should be eliminated from psychedelic therapy and from any scientific research on psychedelics. The opposing camp (Yaden and Griffiths 2021; Jylkkä 2021; Breeksema and van Elk 2021; Gandy 2022; also see Roseman, Nutt, and Carhart-Harris 2018; Lyon and Farennikova 2022; Weiss 2024; and Yaden et al. 2024) argues that the experiences are in fact essential to any positive (or at least the best) psychological results and hence should remain part of psychedelic therapy. Thus, for this camp talk of any altered state of consciousness (ASC) experiences enabled by the drugs should be included in psychedelic therapy and also in broader research. This dispute affects not only psychotherapy but also neuroscience and pharmacology.

Two points will be argued here. First, unless the effects of these drugs can be shown to be strictly chemical, which to date is not the case, the discussion of the experiential dimension in psychedelic therapy remains necessary and thus cannot be expunged. It is premature to consider dismissing the experiential component until more is known about how psychedelics work. Second, the language of mysticism best captures the experiential dimension for some types of psychedelic-enabled experiences, even if such language disquiets many naturalists. These positions also affect broader scientific research on psychedelics and models of consciousness.

The Dispute

The starting point for the dispute is that the therapeutic use of some well-known psychedelics (in particular, psilocybin) has proven that at certain doses these drugs have long-term benefits for patients dealing with depression, anxiety, post-traumatic stress disorder, end-of-life distress, cancer, and drug or alcohol addiction.[1] Mystical type experiences have been found to be associated with improvements in well-being, psychological insights, and emotional breakthroughs (Kangaslampi 2023). The beneficial changes in well-being and quality of life typically last for months and may last for years (e.g., Aday et al. 2020). Negative symptoms are reduced, and positive traits connected to well-being and optimism are increased after one or a few sessions. There are indications that the positive effects are greater with psychedelics than with other drugs or traditional talk therapies (Hearn 2021: 180). But it widely accepted that "no psychedelic substance is a 'magic bullet' that will permanently cure any condition" (Richards 2016: 143).

How the drugs affect the brain is currently not known—indeed, the scientific study of psychedelics and consciousness is still nascent (Yaden et al. 2021: 620). So too, psychological knowledge of ASC experiences is still in its infancy (Gandy 2022: 39). But psychedelics change how neurons communicate with each other, and they also increase communication between areas of the brain that normally are not connected. Current theories of how the drugs effect change in the brain include disrupting specific serotonin receptors in the brain, disrupting the default mode network (DMN) underlying our ordinary states of consciousness, or having broader network effects (Johnson 2021: 579). That creates more chaos in the brain. The disruption allows other types or levels of consciousness to be manifested in our waking consciousness. Disruption of the DMN alone may break the hold of depression brought on by relentless self-critical and other negative thoughts regardless of any resulting states of consciousness.

Proponents of disengaging mystical language from psychedelic therapies argue that at best the subjective experiences are irrelevant to the drugs' effectiveness and at worst the experiences are dangerous—powerful negative experiences are very possible.[2] Negative experiences also affect the issues of whether experiences are a result of chemical effects on the brain alone—if the experiences were the product of the chemicals, the experiences should be uniform—and thus of whether the chemical effects alone are responsible for therapeutic outcomes. Thus, psychedelic therapy should be "demystified": reference to experiences should be ended altogether. It is only the chemical effects on the brain of these psychoactive drugs that bring about the positive changes. Psychedelics are psychoplastogens that alter neural structure over time—they "rewire" the brain leading to changes in brain activity and to greater structural connectedness—and this chemical effect by itself accounts for the long-lasting beneficial psychological effects, and so only references to the chemical effects should be made in therapy or research or discussed with patients. David Olson (2020: 564–65) points out that the quasipsychedelic MDMA promotes structural and functional neural plasticity that brings about long-lasting changes in most subjects, but only a small percentage of subjects have even extremely mild perceptual alterations.

The effects of the drugs as rewiring catalysts that effect the growth of key neurons in the prefrontal cortex (increasing the number of dendrites, dendritic spines, and synapses) would explain the beneficial changes in a person's behavior long after the compounds have cleared the body (D. Olson 2022). The positive effects last after the experiences have faded and in fact sometimes grow. Thus, even a sense of well-being or of the significance of the universe's being must be only a powerless byproduct of the chemical effect, not an actual cause of the psychological transformation. Correlation of a greater intensity of an experience with better results (e.g., Davis et al. 2021: 486–87; Ko et al. 2022) does not mean that the experiences were the causes but only that the drugs had a greater effect on the patient's well-being and also produced a more intense byproduct.[3] This camp can also point to the fact that even the short-lived negative "bad trip" psychedelic experiences—or in therapeutic language, "acute challenging experiences"—may lead to positive cathartic effects later (Doblin 1991: 24; Schlag et al. 2022: 258; Yaden and Newberg 2022: 336) as suggesting that only the chemical effects are really what produce the positive results rather than the subjective experience during the drug session.[4]

All of this leads these researchers to conclude that the experiences associated with the biological effects are only epiphenomena of the neurobiological mechanisms and have no causal power—these particular experiences have an interesting phenomenology but do no work. Different patients may subjectively respond differently to the same drug or the same patients may respond differently at different times, but only the drugs' chemical effects on the body matter. Thus, they argue that the actual science of psychedelics should be disentangled from all talk of mysticism so that the focus is on brain chemistry alone.

On the other side, those who consider experiences to be part of psychedelic therapy readily acknowledge that a reorganization of brain activity is produced by the chemical effect of the drugs on areas of the brain connected to a sense of "self," a sense of boundaries, and a sense of emotional importance, and that this rewiring is part of the causes of positive therapeutic effects; but they also affirm a mediating role for the experiential effects (Yaden and Griffiths 2021: 568). In fact, it may be the mystical experiences that are responsible for the structural changes in the brain (Yaden and Newberg 2022: 243–44). These proponents also point out that analyses suggest that mystical-type experiences play an important role apart from the overall intensity of the drug's chemical effect (Yaden and Griffiths 2021: 570). This may well be more than only an indicator of greater chemical effects. Indeed, it may be that the *intensity* of the experiences accounts for their potential transformative effect (Hearn 2021: 189). One meta-analysis found that "mystical-type experiences" are associated with positive long-term psychological changes in subjects after the drug sessions and that these changes are not just the result of the chemical action of the drugs but from causation by the experiences (Fuentes et al. 2020). Even when there is not a full dissolution of the sense of self as in mystical experiences, the psychedelic-enabled experience may still be therapeutically effective (S. Hoffman 2022: 6). In anecdotal accounts of psychedelic treatments, meaningful insights and belief changes are also frequently cited by patients as fundamentally important to enduring positive outcomes (Yaden and Griffiths 2021: 570). The negative experiences were simply "part of the process" leading to a valuable positive outcome (Evans et al. 2023: 18). Negative experiences need not mean that only chemical effects matter. In one study, 78.6 percent of participants who had negative experiences were glad they took the drug because ultimately there was a positive outcome (Evans et al. 2023: 18).

Critics of a role for mystical experiences in therapy must account for the therapeutic benefits that persist long after the chemical effects have ended. Advocates of the role of experiences in these therapies believe that the case is "compelling" for "the subjective effects playing a major role in the enduring beneficial effects" (Yaden and Griffiths 2021: 570) or "a profound, potentially transformative psychological experience is critical to the treatment's efficacy" (Roseman, Nutt, and Carhart-Harris 2018: 2), even though the proponents disagree on exactly *how* the experiential component may aid in therapy (see Lyon and Farennikova 2022). They argue that having mystical-type ASC experiences in therapy sessions is not only a "reliable predictor" but a "key determinant" of long-term positive psychological changes (Gandy 2022: 32). Rosalind Watts (2022) believes that psychedelics are only a catalyst that "opens the door" by deactivating the defenses of the ego, but the patient letting go and surrendering to the deepest levels of long-suppressed feelings is (along with the aid of therapists or guides) what brings about the therapeutic healing. Proponents of decoupling talk of mysticism rightly point out that the experiences being indicators or predictors of therapeutic change does not mean that the experiences are necessarily a *cause* in the process—they still might powerless byproducts. But the fact that these drugs, unlike other psychoactive ones, enable *experiences* may indicate an important role for them. And the correlation of high results with the presence of ASC experiences should not be dismissed out of hand (Roseman, Nutt, and Carhart-Harris 2018). The philosopher Chris Letheby (2021: chapter 4) argues that the central mechanism in psychedelic therapy is a psychological factor, not the chemical stimulation of the brain, and this factor correlates with an ASC experience. And at least one vocal advocate of decoupling talk of mysticism in therapy, David Olson (2020: 565), is willing to accept that the experiences may be needed to achieve the maximal efficacy of the psychedelics.

Thus, advocates for retaining a role of experience argue that, unlike for most drugs, it may be the case that with psychedelics it is the experiences and not the chemical changes in the brain that are most important for producing the psychological benefits and for those benefits to be lasting. It would be a case of applying mysticism in therapy. The experiences often lead experiencers to see the world and their lives as more satisfying, purposeful, and meaningful, even if no exact meaning of life is given. Participants often rate their experiences *the* most meaningful ones in their life or among the top five (e.g., Griffiths et al. 2006; Griffiths et al. 2008; Aday et al. 2020). In one study (Griffiths et al. 2006), two-thirds of the participants valued their experience in that way, and they stated that its impact was equivalent to the impact of such events as the birth of a child or death of a parent. It may be this profound impact, not only the chemical effects of the drug, that is the source of the therapeutic change. The experiential mechanism may be complex: it may be that the ego-dissolution that lasts only for the short period of the psychedelic experience is not the direct cause of the therapeutic benefits but rather that the resulting sense of connectedness to other people and the rest of reality cultivated through meditation is the cause of lasting benefits (Griffiths et al. 2018; Kałużna et al. 2022). The triggering of changes in brain activity caused by ingesting psychedelics would then be two steps removed from the psychological changes involving a loss of the sense of a self.

In addition, as discussed in the first chapter, the neuroscientific community today studying the bases of ASC experiences in brain activity is coming to accept that mystical experiences are not merely products of our imagination or emotional embellishments of ordinary experiences but instead are distinctive experiences based in distinctive patterns of neurological activity (e.g., Hood et al. 2001; Yaden et al. 2017a: 60). If these ASC experiences have causal power, these experiences may be able to produce enhanced effects for a person's well-being. If so, the experiences may hold the key to the most effective therapies.

Testing the Competing Positions

The question then is this: are ASC experiences the *cause* of the positive (or at least the best) changes, or are they only an expendable *side effect* of the chemical actions that actually produce those changes? That the experiences sometimes last long after the drugs have left the body is interpreted by proponents of decoupling to mean that the drugs had rewired the brain, while proponents of retaining talk of mystical ASC experiences interpret this to mean that, while the drugs may both rewire the brain and enable the experiences, the ASC experiences are also a causal factor in the enduring positive therapeutic results. Both camps can cite data favoring their side, but both sides concede that more research is needed on the issue.

Can the two options be directly tested empirically? One possible way is to produce nonpsychedelic analogs that have the same beneficial therapeutic effects but not the "hallucinogenic" effects. This would radically change the nature of therapies: without psychedelic side effects, such analogs could, like aspirin, be self-administered at home without the presence (or expense) of a therapist—it is the psychedelic experiential effects lasting up to six hours that require the guidance of therapists before, during, and after the drug is administered.[5] David Olson (2020: 565) believes that the "hallucinogenic" and psychoplastogenic effects can be decoupled through careful design, but that work still needs to be done to determine if positive therapeutic responses can be produced without inducing behavioral effects characteristic of classic psychedelics. And several companies in the United States funded by the government have begun to alter the psychedelics or develop new drugs that they hope will produce the beneficial effects on depression without the mind-altered subjective experiences (Cao 2022; Kaplan et al. 2022).[6] Analogs may target serotonin receptors related to depression without targeting the receptors associated with psychedelic experiences. Current analogs produce behavior in mice associated with antidepression without producing "hallucinogenic" behavior even when the same serotonin receptors that LSD and psilocybin affect are triggered, with effects lasting up to two weeks. However, whether this will have the same effect in human beings has not yet been tested (Carhart-Harris 2023). Nor does it answer the question of whether the psychedelic-enabled experiences may lead to greater and longer-lasting beneficial effects and thus that the psychedelics are still needed for the best results.

Researchers are now also experimenting with low doses of drugs—"microdoses" of perhaps 10 percent of a normal dose taken several times a week—that produce no psychedelic experiences to see if they still have a transformative impact on a sense of well-being. Microdosing can touch off some experiences that are connected to mysticism—increased awareness and sensations and mindfulness—but not the more robust experiences (Wit et al. 2022). In one study, the microdosing did not produce experiences that affected the emotion-related symptoms or processing of the patients (Marschall et al. 2022; see also Griffiths et al. 2016). One study found that microdosing produced some subjective experiences, but there was no evidence of enhanced well-being, creativity, or cognitive functioning (Cavanna et al. 2022). This suggests that those experiences are not causal elements in therapy. At best, microdoses appear no more effective than a placebo (D. Olson 2020). But this does not affect the claim of proponents of decoupling that in the proper doses, psychedelics' chemical effect is all that matters. However, such proponents still have the problem noted below that placebos can enable some therapeutic-level ASC experiences.

But the power of a subjective element that is in dispute makes testing the alternative positions extremely difficult. David Yaden and Roland Griffiths (2021: 570) propose a test to determine the relevance of subjective effects. They claim that the only definitive study that could disprove the importance of the subjective effects would be one in which a psychedelic is administered to individuals who are fully unconscious at the time (e.g., via deep anesthesia) and who subsequently report no memory of psychedelic experiences and yet have the positive psychological effects. They suggest that positive psychological effects will not occur in such an experiment (Yaden and Griffiths 2021: 568). Letheby concurs: "[A]lmost all relevant clinical trial evidence suggests that a full-blown psychedelic experience is necessary for a complete therapeutic response" (2022: 70). Advocates of decoupling would predict that the benefits would accrue even to unconscious patients. Thus, if no changes occur to these patients or only relatively minor changes occur and the patients affirm that no experiences occurred, the case for decoupling mysticism and psychedelic therapy is damaged. However, if no changes occur, proponents of decoupling may contend that such a test shows only that psychedelics affect the brain differently when subjects are *awake* than when they are *asleep*. (This would suggest a role for consciousness and an interaction of consciousness and the brain.) They would then have to find independent evidence establishing that. Other responses are also possible—e.g., that the anesthetic may suppress all the core action of the psychedelic drug (see Weiss 2024: 3). Or perhaps psychedelics cause *different* neurochemical reactions in the brain when no experiences occur than when experiences do result.

Also note that this dispute over the role of ASC experiences need not be seen as a broad dispute on the nature of the mind between materialism and nonmaterialism. Materialists do not want the subjective as part of the picture, but proponents of decoupling need not deny that consciousness has causal powers—they may merely treat *consciousness as physical* in nature and treat mental causation as actually material in nature. These proponents may not dismiss all experiences as having causal powers but see only psychedelic-enabled ASC experiences as a type of experience that has no causal power and thus treat these specific experiences as extraneous and useless epiphenomena that can be ignored. For these proponents, psychedelics are like any medication in which the mental state of the patient is irrelevant. The burden then is on such theorists to make a compelling case that these particular experiences play no causal role. Such a case cannot be limited to results of studying the hardware of the brain: all neuroimaging can show is what the brain is doing or not doing while an experience is occurring—it cannot examine the ASC experiences themselves and thus cannot tell us anything of their role or nature.

However, materialists who treat consciousness as nonmaterial and also deny any mental causation in favor of the causal closure of the material realm have a further problem. When all we have are the reports of material activity in the brain during these experiences, what could neuroscientists who adopt a materialist metaphysics take as evidence even in principle of an ASC experience being a cause of brain activity? Their metaphysics would preclude the very possibility of finding any evidence that consciousness is a separate causal power from the psychedelic's chemical effects. All data would be interpreted to fit the metaphysics. But if finding empirical evidence for something is precluded in advance, then *not* finding evidence cannot be evidence against its existence. Thus, as neuroscience is currently designed, no experiment could rule out a conscious event, such as an ASC experience, as a cause guiding the course of neural activity in the brain. Consciousness may be like software guiding the course of events in the hardware (the brain), but all we can see in any experiment is the activity of the hardware. The problem, then, is how to devise an experiment in which consciousness events might or might not be a cause.

Thus, at present those denying ASC experiences as a cause of positive therapeutic outcomes are not in a position to prove that ASC experiences are not causes in the brain events, and until then, proponents of decoupling cannot rule out ASC experiences as possible causes of therapeutic results for experiment-based reasons. But until these proponents have made the special case for the exclusion of psychedelic-enabled ASC experiences as causes, treating them as causes is warranted. Why is this preferable to simply ignoring the experiences? First, these drugs, unlike most drugs, enable experiences, and those experiences are mostly beneficial and so should be included until discredited, despite the potential for negative experiences (some of which, as discussed, lead to positive effects). Indeed, mystical experiences are the strongest indicator of a helpful outcome (Gandy 2022) even if they are not the cause. Second, considering that neuroscientists currently do not have a complete knowledge of the workings of the brain or how psychedelics affect the brain or the basic nature of consciousness, common sense suggests that the safer course at present is still to include ASC experiences in psychedelic therapies, especially since the decouplers' objection is based on a disputed metaphysics. So too, our knowledge of the mind is still in the beginning stage of investigation. Third, at present patients themselves attach great significance to the experiences. Thus, therapists should not ignore, dismiss, or downplay the experiences—an explicit or implicit denial by a therapist may negatively affect the effectiveness of the therapy. That conclusion is, no pun intended, a no-brainer.

In such circumstances, as things stand today, nonpharmacological experiential factors appear essential to a positive therapeutic outcome. Thus, the best course of action at present is, as Joost Breeksema and Michiel van Elk suggest, "acknowledging the varieties and weirdness of psychedelic experiences should be at the heart of any research program on the topic" (2021: 1471). The experiences should not be eliminated simply by invoking disputed metaphysics (as discussed below). Proponents of decoupling psychedelic therapy and mysticism must make their case based on empirical evidence and not simply on the basis of a contentious assumption that only the chemical effects can possibly have effects. All naturalists should remain neutral and open-minded until convincing empirical evidence against the role of experiences is presented. (As noted below, a positive naturalist interpretation of mystical experiences is also possible.) The inclusion of ASC experiences as an essential part of psychedelic therapy by itself also makes such experiences an important topic within the scientific study of psychedelics.

The Variety of Subjective Responses

Proponents of retaining talk of mysticism may prefer that there is only one type of ASC experience with one uniform therapeutic effect. But one problem for proponents of ASC causation is that there is no *one* universal psychedelic ASC or experience. That is, there is no generic "psychedelic state of consciousness" following the ingestion of these drugs (Richards 2016: 16). The research shows that psychedelic drugs apparently enable a variety of experiences and states, including a variety of mystical ones, even though researchers routinely refer in the singular to "*the* psychedelic state" and "*the* mystical experience" (e.g., Nour and Carhart-Harris 2017: 177), as if all mystical experiences were the same in nature and in their therapeutic effect. The psychologist Stanislav Grof (2009) also makes the point that LSD has no one invariant pharmacological effect, nor is there one inevitable experience associated with it—rather, he asserts, LSD is a catalyzer that amplifies and brings into consciousness dynamics that are within the person's subconscious. In addition, as noted in the chapter 2, no alteration of consciousness at all may occur.

Contemporary researchers have found a great variety of ASC experiences enabled by psychedelics that are nonmystical (i.e., experiences still involving a subject/object duality). These include visual, auditory, and tactile experiences; kaleidoscopic and fractal visions; seeing two-dimensional pictures as three-dimensional and animated; synesthesia; and alterations of the perception of time and of the body. So too, there is no one mystical experience but significantly different types of mystical experiences (see R. Jones 2021a: chapter 2). Different psychedelics have different effects on brain activity—e.g., LSD appears to enable more visions than does psilocybin. Different dosages of a given drug may also produce different neurochemical states that ground different experiences. Moreover, the same person may have both psychedelic-enabled experiences that fit the characterization of "mystical" given below and some that do not.[7] Even during one session, there is a variety of states of consciousness under the chemical actions of the psychedelics (Richards 2016: 115).

Differences in therapeutic benefits for those with different experiences or no experiences would be significant for the question of whether the chemical effects of the drugs are all that matters. But if the same benefits accrue despite differences in experiences, this presents a problem for advocates of the retention of a role for ASC experiences. Thus, this offers an empirically testable issue: if different experiences give rise to different positive therapeutic outcomes or if some have no effect, this suggests that some ASC experiences play a role in the outcome; but if all ASC experiences or no changes in consciousness have the same effect, this suggests that the chemical effect of the psychedelic is all that matters.

Outside of the dispute at hand, researchers today generally agree that all psychedelic experiences are not simply products of the chemical changes alone. As discussed in chapter 2, an experiencer's mental "set" (i.e., background beliefs, preparation, expectations, disposition, propensity for altered states of consciousness, personality traits, mood, and past experiences with drugs) and the "setting" (i.e., the social and physical environment) when a drug is ingested both matter (see Gandy 2022: 33–34).[8] For example, a subject's disposition of a "willingness to surrender" is associated with "stronger" mystical experiences (Carhart-Harris et al. 2018; Gandy 2022: 36), and meditation prior to a psilocybin experience can yield beneficial results (Gandy 2022: 37). These are important to whether psychedelic experiences occur at all and to what type of experience occurs. Their differences at least partially account for the great variation in the experiences enabled by the drug. As discussed below, a frame of mind that is prepared for, or expecting, some religious experience to occur or for the possibility of a mystical experience occurring combined with a religiously inspiring physical and social environment enhances the likelihood of such an experience, even if the resulting visionary or mystical ASC experience is not what the experiencer anticipated (see Letherby, Mattu, and Hochstein 2024). A laboratory setting may negatively affect both the possibility of having a mystical experience and its phenomenological content. Experiences in a forest may lead to a greater sense of connection to nature (see Ruffell et al. 2024). A group setting may enhance a sense of well-being and social connectedness (Kettner 2021), whether all are ingesting psychedelics or not. Even a researcher calling the drug an "entheogen" ("generating God within") or a "hallucinogen" ("generating hallucinations") can affect the experiencer's mental set one way or the other through an expectancy bias. So too, researchers must inform participating subjects that they may receive a mind-altering drug, and that may affect the experiences that result. Thus, every psychedelic experience appears to result from a mixture of at least three ingredients—the drug, set, and setting. The particular dosage is also an important factor in the mix (Fuentes et al. 2020: 10). Genetics, race, and demographics (Preller and Vollenweider 2018) and the propensity to become completely absorbed in an experience (Gandy 2022: 35) are among other possible factors.

In addition, although mystical experiences occur with a higher frequency with a psychedelic than with a placebo in the controlled experiments cited here, some participants who were given only a placebo also had mystical experiences. In one study of placebos, 61 percent of the participants reported some effect from the placebo—some effects having magnitudes typically associated with moderate or high doses of psilocybin (Olson et al. 2020.) The drugs may be "active super-placebos" that increase suggestibility and the influence of nonpharmacological factors (Dupuis and Veissière 2022). The drugs disrupt the neurobiology underlying our baseline state of consciousness and make the experiencer more susceptible to the effects of set and setting but do not set up any one ASC or experience—instead, our subconscious or other factors are involved in the experience.

Thus, our underlying mental set may be responsible for the differences in experiences in a person's ASC, not a drug's chemical effects on the brain. For example, if one expects a life-changing experience, one will often get it; if one does not, one will not. Proponents of decoupling must explain the placebo effect here if the chemical effect of psychedelics is all that matters. Even if the placebo effect is explained through a participant's expectations, these proponents would still have to explain this when there is an apparent lack of a prior chemical alteration in the brain.[9] This raises the issues of whether a trigger is in fact needed and whether there is a necessary chemical base in the brain for these experiences. Psychedelics may occasion strong but short-term and reversible disruptions of self-consciousness; but the long-lasting effects on well-being do not appear to be necessarily mediated by intense experiences but rather by the training of different cognitive mechanisms through meditation (Millière et al. 2018: 21, 20). In this way, the two approaches may be synergistic: the psychedelics may enable the initial disruption of our sense of self, and meditation is needed to ingrain the insight into a patient's consciousness; psychedelics may subsequently deepen the meditative practices (Holas and Kamińska 2023). It is a common claim that those who have had a psychedelic-enabled experience require further guidance and training to make the insight last (e.g., Sotillos 2024: 47).

One problem with determining long-term effects of psychedelics (and meditation) would arise if most subjects in these studies were self-selected participants who were members of particular religious traditions or unaffiliated "seekers" already desiring a religious experience. This would predispose the participants toward a religious understanding and a lasting religious impact. If so, it is difficult to determine if any changes in values or ways of living are the results of chemically induced neural changes or of the participants' prior disposition and religious beliefs or continuing training—do the lasting effects result from new brain conditioning alone or from a mixture of a memory of the experience and the subject's prior intentions? Participants in drug studies also may adjust their impressions of the realness of spiritual experiences over time (Yaden et al. 2017a). Thus, the long-lasting effects of these experiences on one's character may result not from rewiring the brain but from the impact of an experience on how the experiencer decides to live. So too with the waning of the psychological effects. That is, even if there may be some lingering chemical effect of the drugs on the brain, changes in character as a result of the experience and perhaps other factors not related to the chemical actions account for the increase in positive effects over time.

All of this complicates the picture for those who believe psychedelic-enabled experiences matter: does the variety of subjective responses to psychedelics mean that those responses are irrelevant, or does it mean that the chemical reaction of the drugs is irrelevant and the particular psychedelic response that a particular subject experiences is all that matters? Or is there a combination of the two? If there is no therapeutic benefit from ASC experiences arising from a placebo, that would point to the importance of the chemical effect of the psychedelics. But the picture is complicated further if some participants in a study who are given a placebo also end up with life-changing transformations or a new sense of meaning. If psychological benefits also accrue from experiences occurring when placebos are given or when ASC experiences occur through meditation or spontaneously (i.e., without any preparation or expectation), then the impact of the chemical effects of psychedelics on the brain falls into question—there is an apparent disconnect of the experience from chemical changes in the brain that proponents of decoupling must explain.[10]

It may be that no one mechanism accounts for the therapeutic efficacy of psychedelics and that a pluralistic approach to analysis and explanation may be needed (van Elk and Yaden 2022: 10–11). But it does appear that the drugs in certain doses open up the mind to different states of consciousness by disrupting the everyday state of mind that sets up a subject/object duality and conceptualizes multiple objects. Different psychedelics may disrupt different brain networks, thus tending to facilitate different types of ASC experiences, but they all have the same disrupting effect on all subjects' neural configurations. However, what happens after our baseline state is disrupted depends not on the drugs but on other factors.

In sum, psychedelics enable various ASC experiences to occur but do not mechanically produce, induce, or trigger any particular experience or determine an experience's significance for the experiencer or an experiencer's sense of meaning that alters his or her life, and it may be those experiences that matter at least as much as the neural changes in any therapeutic outcome.

Characterizing ASC Experiences as Mystical

The last section brought up some ASC experiences that researchers label "mystical," and this leads to the second issue: if it is accepted that psychedelic-enabled experiences play a necessary role in psychedelic therapy, should at least some of these ASC experiences be characterized as *mystical*? James Sanders and Josjan Zijlmans argue that talk of "mystical experience" is too inexact to be scientific and that use of that language biases the reports that patients give of their experiences; also the unwarranted and risky "blend of mysticism and science risks damaging the credibility and potential of psychedelic science" and may lead to misinterpreting the findings of psychedelic research or to being seen as asserting a role for a transcendent reality in these experiences (Sanders and Zijlmans 2021: 1254–55). In addition, patients who need help may avoid getting treatment because of the stigma attached to mysticism in the general populace. On the other side, Joost Breeksema and Michiel van Elk (2021: 1471) argue that (1) critics have an incomplete understanding of mystical experiences as a scientifically validated and rigorously studied domain of human experience; (2) experiences that are specially mystical in nature are clinically and scientifically highly relevant; (3) good methodological tools are available for studying these experiences; and thus (4) the scientific community ought to embrace these "weird" experiences and that in fact it would be unscientific to ignore mystical frameworks and language simply because they supposedly are incompatible with the metaphysics of naturalism, since the participants themselves take mystical frameworks seriously; thus, experiences that are in fact mystical in nature are part of the therapy and their effects must be accounted for.

Critics are correct about the vagueness of the words "mystical" and "mysticism." Moreover, the term "mysticism" also has negative connotations in our culture today. This has led to the term being used for a wide range of phenomena that are generally looked down upon, and academics today apply the term generally to anything deemed flaky. Even those who advocate a role for experiences in psychedelic therapy and research dance around the term "mystical"—they use "mystical-*like*" or "mystical-*type*" experiences or phenomena "*related*" to mysticism (e.g., Yaden and Griffiths 2021) rather than accept that the experiences in fact *are* mystical. At best, "mystical experiences" are treated as only a subcategory of positive "self-transcending" experiences (Yaden et al. 2017b).

Unfortunately, researchers in the dispute do not usually give a precise definition to the term "mystical." It often means any ASC experience or only an experience deemed "union with God." So too, the experiences enabled by psychedelics often seem to the experiencers themselves to involve this-worldly matters related to mental well-being and not to involve alleged other-worldly realities. But even a fairly tight definition of "mystical experience" can be seen as applicable to some of the psychedelic-enabled ASC experiences that appear to have a positive effect in psychedelic therapy—i.e., experiences involving a *loss of a sense of a distinct "self"* (LOSS) separate from the rest of reality and a resulting sense of *connection* to something deemed more real; our *conceptual distinctions* are also loosened (see R. Jones 2021a: chapters 1–3). Ego-dissolution is central to any mystical experience. Researchers in psychedelic studies often focus on this and not other aspects of mystical experiences and treat it as not a "mystical experience." It should also be noted that psychedelics disrupt more than a sense of self—representations related to the world—and these other disruptions may also figure in the therapeutic effects (Van Eyghen 2023). An extrovertive LOSS state of consciousness loses the duality of an experiencing subject distinct from a multiplicity of objects. Thus, the category encompasses more introvertive experiences than a sense of connection or union with a transcendent reality.

The category includes other introvertive experiences free of a sense of self and also extrovertive experiences lacking a sense of boundaries between the experiencer and objects and between objects in the phenomenal world (i.e., mindfulness and nature mysticism).

Any LOSS in "ego-dissolution" would necessarily disrupt our ego-driven baseline state of consciousness, thereby producing an altered state of consciousness. There are different phenomenological features for different types of states labeled "loss of a sense of self" (see Millière et al. 2018; Millière 2020). No sense of "I" or self-consciousness seems connected to the experiences. LOSS experiences may lead to the best long-term therapeutic results, but the dissolution of a sense of self is often dreaded by patients. Western psychotherapists also typically attempt to strengthen the self and integrate it into our place in the world, not dissolve it in an experience of the rest of the world. Indeed, from a psychological point of view, there is little reason to suspect that a LOSS would be anything but negative—even terrifying—and yet LOSS in psychedelic-enabled experiences is often reported to be "profoundly positive" (Yaden et al. 2017b: 11). At most, mainstream therapists and researchers may accept LOSS mystical experiences as of some value in accessing consciousness more directly but not as indicating that there is no phenomenal self.

In mysticism, LOSS is not a matter of merely not being aware of a subject sensing something in the moment (most experiences are like that), but that during the experience (or looking back at it later) it seemed to lack ownership or being attached to the person. Sometimes LOSS results in a state of consciousness that does not seem personal or temporal and may lead the experiencer to believe there is no personal or individual survival of death. But it is not a loss of subjectivity. In Theravada Buddhism, the no-self (*anatta*) doctrine does not mean that there are no subjective experiences but only that there is no discrete experiencing entity in the phenomenal realm—there is still an impermanent and conditioned configuration of sensing, feeling, and thinking even though no separate sensing "self" is ever observed or otherwise found in the mix in any of our experiences. That is, only the reality of a substantive "experiencer" in addition to our actual mental activity is denied, not subjectivity or a subjective point of view. Similarly, in advanced states of mindfulness in general, there is no "subject" as a separate reality or a dualism of subject and object, but a subjective element need not be denied.

The space created by a LOSS may be filled by ASC visions, locutions, and other such phenomena. Broader definitions of "mystical experience" would include such experiences as visions and voices that involve a sense of a duality of subject and object. But losing a sense of a phenomenal self is also central to mystical experiences in classical religious traditions. (It should be noted that there is evidence that a mystical LOSS can lead to positive changes in our sense of well-being, but *visual or auditory experiences* do not [Kangaslampi 2023: 23].) In addition, participants' self-reported phenomenological accounts in research studies—i.e., firsthand accounts of the felt content of the experience with little or no interpretation of what was experienced—often contain language that is central to any narrow definition of "mystical experience." The LOSS does not necessarily result in a sense of "union with God" or anything else transcendent—LOSS may lead only to a sense of connection to other people or to the rest of the phenomenal world (i.e., nature mysticism).

Researchers have been following or elaborating on Walter Stace's summary of the defining characteristics of mystical experiences (1960: 131–32) to characterize "mystical-type" experiences: feelings of unity, transcendence of space and time, a noetic quality,[11] ineffability,[12] paradox, and sacredness, as well as positive feelings of bliss, joy, wonder and awe and a sense of ego-dissolution and an enhanced perception of emotions (e.g., van Elk and Yaden 2022: 7). Awareness becomes more vivid and stable. There is a sense of a loss of boundaries to the self and a resulting sense of connectedness (to others, nature, or the cosmos), "absorption," emotional acceptance (rather than avoidance) (e.g., Watts et al. 2017). Often a sense of empathy, compassion, or love results. A sense of overall well-being in this life may result. In a recent review of the reports on meditative experiences, researchers have found that experiencers of "pure consciousness" (i.e., a state of awareness empty of all thoughts, images, concepts, perceptions, and feelings) retained some content after the experience: an inner stillness, silence, simplicity, naturalness, calm, relaxation, rest, bliss/joy, a sense of knowing, freedom, wholeness, security, unity, depth, or profundity (Woods, Windt, and Carter 2022: 41). A sense of "oceanic boundlessness," a term derived from Freud (see R. Jones 2021a: 98–99), when the ego is dissolved is also gaining use.

Those who equate "mystical experience" with "union with God" will not want to label such a loss and an extrovertive connection as a "mystical experience." However, the basic problem in the rejection of mystical language may be only a discomfort with the term "mystical experience," not a denial that a LOSS may result in a mystical experience. Some types of mystical experiences appear to be more easily facilitated by psychedelics than others. Introvertive experiences that are free of all differentiated content are less common with psychedelics than other introvertive or extrovertive mystical experiences and visions and voices (e.g., Griffiths et al. 2006; Griffiths et al. 2008). A resulting increase in mindfulness has also been associated with ingesting psychedelics (Søndergaard 2022; Radakovic et al. 2022). Researchers in psychedelic studies will have to examine the different types of mystical experiences as related by experiencers for their therapeutic impact, if any. If the different types of mystical experiences may have different impacts, this would point to the issue noted above of whether the uniform changes in the brain produced by the chemicals are the sole source of the psychological effects.

Researchers who reject any role for ASC experiences in psychedelic therapy or in research on consciousness of course want to disavow any connection to mysticism, but that does not mean that the term "mystical experience" is not appropriate for some of the experiences enabled by psychedelics in therapy sessions (but not all). "ASC experiences," "peak experiences," "spiritual experiences," and "awakening experiences" are broader categories that cover more than only mystical experiences, as is simply a generic "therapeutic experience" (Beswerchij and Sisti 2022). But if those experiences that are specifically mystical in nature cause particular therapeutic effects, then using the term is not overreliance on the mysterious but something that needs to be retained. The term "mysticism" has fallen out of fashion in our culture at large, and researchers may seek to use another term without its allegedly negative connotations—terms such as "transpersonal experience," "spiritually transformative experience," or a "quantum change experience" (e.g., James et al. 2020). Dissolving a sense of a phenomenal self is central to any experience properly labeled "mystical," and the term "self-transcending experience" is gaining popularity (e.g., Yaden and Newberg 2022: 99–100). The term "selfless experience" is also problematic. But using the phrase "self-transcendent experiences" may be confusing to those with a philosophical background, it sounds as if the experience transcends itself rather than referring to experiences that transcend a sense of self. Perhaps a new term derived from Greek or Latin may be invented to avoid the unwanted connotations, but the phenomena covered by that term will nevertheless still be covered by standard definitions of the word "mystical."

A simpler route would be to retain the term "mystical" but advance an exact stipulated working definition of the term for psychedelic studies. Some of the psychedelic-enabled ASCs would still be properly labeled "mystical," and these experiences of ego-dissolution and connectedness are related to the positive long-term benefits of psychedelic therapy. Researchers could devise a typology of mystical and nonmystical psychedelic-enabled ASC experiences and their effects in therapy. The interdisciplinary study of mysticism may inform better research in this regard (see Mosurinjohn, Roseman, and Girn 2023). The term could then be utilized in scientific research for the limited range of phenomena that is covered by that term. As research advances, the term may be eliminatable in the future.

Nor should the negative attitude of the general public be a deterrence. After all, the general public has a generally negative attitude toward the term "psychedelics" because of its history, and yet the term has gained respectability in scientific circles. And, it should be noted, notions of "naturalizing" mystical experiences and of a "secular mysticism" that removes alleged transcendent implications are taking root in our culture today (see chapter 8). Mystical experiences transcend a sense of "self," but they are not inherently tied to a belief in realities transcending the natural realm, and experiencers of the mystical experiences enabled by psychedelics may not take them to be religious in nature. Thus, this removes some of the religious and transcendent overtones of "mysticism" that secularists want to overcome. Overall, even if the term "mysticism" is out of fashion in our culture, it would not be too surprising if the term "mystical experience" becomes common in psychedelic research (Yaden and Newberg 2022: 396).

The Problem of Employing Mystical and Antimystical Language

If therapists and researchers accept psychedelic-enabled experiences as part of therapy and that mystical language is appropriate, how should the experiential component be presented in therapy and research? The wording of questionnaires given to subjects in therapy and in broader research on psychedelic-enabled ASC experiences should be scrutinized to avoid prejudicing for or against mysticism (see Earleywine, Low, and De Leojdeleo 2021; McCulloch et al. 2022). Researchers may be interested more in the experiences themselves than in their therapeutic value, but they may advance questions related to specific metaphysical beliefs and not to the phenomenological content of the experiences themselves. Instead, questions related to the phenomenological content alone should be included and should be first. But when it comes to therapy, patients may see these experiences as provoking the "big questions" of philosophy and science concerning what is real and what is meaningful in life, and then questions about what the experiencers believe they experienced must also be included (Johnson 2021: 580). Psychedelics may indirectly lead the participants to being more open to such questions because of the shock of the unexpected in ASC experiences or the temporary disruption of their normal state of mind. Moreover, experiencers may not clearly distinguish the experience and what they think was experienced—their description of the former may be in terms of the latter.

Questions cannot be limited to only those that naturalists think are appropriate and thus are expressed in naturalist terms. Questions should be phrased in such a way that they do not limit the opportunity of respondents to express themselves in their own terms, which are often in terms of their religious tradition's transcendent realities, in order to let participants have a wide latitude of responses. Experiencers also often modify their beliefs about transcendent realities and express them in more abstract terms, not in terms of a theistic personal god and doctrines of the respondent's culture and tradition. The beliefs may still be religious even if they do not reflect the doctrines of a specific tradition. Scientists are not constrained by the participants' responses in the *explanations* that they give mystical experiences, but participants should be given the opportunity to express their understanding and description of the experiences and of what was allegedly experienced in an open-ended form in order to let the participants feel free to express themselves and thereby to gain the fullest accounts of the alleged content of these experiences—not accounts within the confines of the therapist's metaphysical framework. The experiencers' beliefs about what is allegedly experienced and not merely the phenomenology of the experiences matter, but scientists can discuss mystical states of consciousness and their impact on experiencers without being committed to the existence of any alleged transcendent realities.

Thus, questionnaires should be phrased as neutrally as possible and not predispose respondents toward either transcendent or natural realities. They should give respondents the opportunity to describe the *phenomenology* of the felt aspects of an experience without reference to what supposedly was experienced, but in addition they also should permit experiencers to express their beliefs about what was experienced without leading questions. Researchers may later set aside the experiencers' explanations, but they must pay attention to the phenomenology of the experiences, and experiencers may express this in terms of their beliefs. Having a strictly secular questionnaire can be seen as neutral when the researcher is looking only at the phenomenology of the experiences, but when looking for the *impact* of the experiences on the respondents a thoroughly secular set and setting is not neutral. However, the risk of *monotheistic bias* is particularly great when it comes to transcendent realities—nonpersonal and deistic realities as well as naturalist alternatives should also be options. So too, questions in terms only of what happens to the self without reference to more encompassing transcendent realities should be included. But religious language can be used without tending to elicit a particular response if it is used in conjunction with other options. Thus, mystical terminology should not be ruled out by fiat.

A related problem is the physical setting of therapy sessions and research labs. Different types of settings may be seen as suggesting either a transcendent mystical experience or a naturalist understanding. A purely secular setting is not "neutral" or "more scientific" (contra D. Olson 2020). A religiously sterile room may bias participants against where their own mental framework would otherwise lead them. So too for settings that intentionally point in the direction of a general spirituality or transcendent realities. A therapist should not inadvertently advocate or discourage any type of experience or any understanding of the significance of the experiences. The setting should be neutral between interpretations to the extent that that is possible in terms of decor, lighting, music, and so on so as not to interfere with the experiential process and its aftermath. The goal of therapy is to help the patient, and thus, as Matthew Johnson (2021: 580) states, "[t]he goal of a clinician should be to create an open and supportive environment where the patient can make her or his own meaning, if any, from such experiences"—and "open" does not mean religiously sterile.

Finding a truly open setting may prove difficult—a hodgepodge of multiple religious and secular elements may not be best for removing any anxiety a participant may have or for setting a mood that is open to having a mystical experience. It may offend or alienate the nonreligious and even members of a Western religion who think they are being indoctrinated into an Asian religion or some formless "*philosophia perennis.*" But the object of therapy is to help people, and there is some evidence that a purely secular standpoint diminishes the effectiveness of psychedelic therapy and is ill-suited to help people process the ontological shock that may be associated with psychedelic-enabled experiences (see Gandy 2022: 32–33).[13] Arguably, the secular approach is actually harmful to the religious (since it may create a conflict in their mind) rather than helpful. But the problems just noted show how difficult it may be to determine the best setting.

Both the participant's and the therapist's mental framework can affect what occurs in the ASC experiences themselves and how a participant later reacts to the experiences. Psychedelics open healthy volunteers up to greater suggestibility (Carhart-Harris et al. 2015: 791; Gandy 2022: 32) and magnify whatever meaning they bring to the experiences. The volunteer is now more susceptible to the therapist's influence, and thus the danger of the therapist's beliefs affecting the experience is very real. After the experience, the experiencer's own postexperiential understanding of what was experienced may also be influenced by the therapist's beliefs. The state of mind during an experience can be distinguished from the experiencer's postexperiential understanding (constructivists disagree), even though both are "subjective" (i.e., internal and experiential) and may not seem distinct to experiencers but two phases of the same event. So too, any questionnaires should reflect this distinction.

All of this points to the need for sensitivity in how mystical language and religious symbols are handled in psychedelic therapy and research. If mishandled, the resulting experience or lack thereof may be misconstrued as evidence for the researcher's own position on the issue of mysticism in psychedelic research. A setting that makes the participant comfortable, including symbols from his or her religious tradition, may lead to more mystical experiences, while a setting void of religious symbols may lead to fewer mystical experiences. But this neither proves that mystical or other psychedelic-enabled experiences are purely hallucinatory nor that the chemical effects of the drugs alone have impact—it only points to the importance of the role of one's mental set and the setting in these experiences.

Psychedelic Experiences and Metaphysics

In sum, a mental framework preconditions experiencers to follow a certain mental track and may predispose them to certain understandings. For example, theistic beliefs of a totally transcendent god may direct experiencers to interpret the felt sense of nonduality or pure consciousness (i.e., a state of consciousness empty of differentiated content) to be the ground of only the soul or to be merely a powerful hallucination and not indicate any actual unity to a "wholly other" creator god who is by definition unexperienceable or to any other transcendent reality. Or theists' expectancy bias may direct experiencers to take any psychedelic experience to be a "glimpse" of God or a "taste" of transcendent knowledge. The philosophical issue of whether mystical experiences are in fact cognitive of a reality (see R. Jones 2016: chapter 3) can be ignored for the question of therapeutic benefit, but another issue does arise: if the patient believes the psychedelic-enabled experience is cognitive, is the therapeutic effect different than for a patient who does not believe that?

It may be that the beliefs one holds at the time of the experience are not the base for a transformative effect—the experience may lead to changing one's beliefs later, but a more general ASC insight into oneself rather than any specific doctrines that one holds at the time of the experience itself may be the basis for any change (Nygart et al. 2022: 933). That is, any new beliefs are not psychological factors in the therapeutic effects related to the experiential dissolution of a sense of self (Letheby 2022: 87–88). Thus, it may be a psychological insight into oneself by itself, not the updating of one's beliefs, that brings the therapeutic benefits (Acevedo et al. 2024). But being able to successfully incorporate the insight into one's religious and metaphysical beliefs may be necessary for long-term psychological benefits. Thus, any changes in metaphysical beliefs are a occur *after* the acute experiences are over. They would be a consequence of the mystical experience, not a cause of it. And changing the beliefs would not necessarily involve being in an altered state of consciousness.

It may be that ASC experiences do not introduce new beliefs but only alter a person's existing beliefs and their impact (McGovern et al. 2021). Under the proposed REBUS (RElaxed Beliefs under pSychedelics) model (Carhart-Harris and Friston 2019), psychedelics weaken the control of one's beliefs, thereby permitting more influence from experiential input and making experiencers more flexible in their resulting beliefs. In one study, 87 percent of the participants reported that the experience changed their fundamental conception of reality (Nayak and Griffiths 2022). Psychedelics do not necessarily make an atheist into a theist (Glausser 2021; Nayak et al. 2023b), as is often claimed, but there may be "significant decreases in identification as atheist and agnostic and significant increases in belief in ultimate reality, higher power, God, or universal divinity" (Davis et al. 2020: 1018; also see Letheby 2022). In one study, the percentage of individuals who believed in an ultimate reality, higher power, or a god jumped from 29 to 59 percent, especially if the participant had a mystical experience (Nayak and Griffiths 2022). Thus, it does appear that psychedelic-enabled experiences tend to cause a shift in the experiencers' metaphysics away from "hard" materialism or to accepting transcendent realities (Timmermann et al. 2021; Letheby 2021: 206).[14] Part of the issue is how "atheism" is defined and its contrast to traditional Western monotheism (see Letheby 2022: 73–79), but psychedelics do appear to have a "robust tendency to make users believe in some other (non-physical) Reality that puts this one in the shade" (Letheby 2022: 78). Theists may also change their beliefs to embrace a panpsychism, cosmopsychism, or a transcendent consciousness or a nonpersonal "Ultimate Reality" that is the ground of the natural universe. A single psychedelic experience may also have a lasting effect on how the person views consciousness (Nayak and Griffiths 2022). Such effects on beliefs are correlated with positive mental health changes and a sense of well-being, and the metaphysical changes may be long-lasting (Timmermann et al. 2021).

Imposing Naturalism

As discussed above, it is important to realize the influence of expectations, dominant discourses, and social and cultural beliefs in both the set and setting of psychedelic-enabled experiences and in the postexperiential understandings. But it must not be assumed that only the religious have a mental set that affects their experiences and their postexperiential understanding. Naturalists routinely recognize the danger in scientists and clinicians unconsciously imposing their personal religious or spiritual beliefs in the practice of psychedelic medicine and condemn introducing their own "nonempirically supported beliefs" (Johnson 2021: 579–80). Clinicians without an explicit endorsement of supernatural beliefs may still implicitly impose them (Johnson 2022: 4) when gaining a rapport with the participants. But the reciprocal danger that *naturalists* themselves may unknowingly impose their own unacknowledged *naturalist beliefs* also must be recognized: in accounts of mystical experiences in natural terms, naturalist therapists and research may well give the impression that the experience must have only natural features. The framework that therapists employ may affect not only how participants *describe* their experiences but the *experiences themselves* (Letheby, Mattu, and Hochstein 2024: 131).

Naturalists are free to reject experiencers' accounts in their explanation, but the descriptions should reflect the experiencers' version of the events—when experiencers are recounting what occurred, they should not be told what really occurred according to the naturalists. Patients and research subjects should not be led to believe the experiences can be explained purely in natural terms if that is not how they felt the experiences to be: if the participants in therapy feel restricted in this regard, the experiences they have may not be as beneficial as they would be if the experiencers had free rein; in research, participants may mischaracterize how their experiences felt in light of the researchers' questions—indeed, they may not even have had an ASC experience and yet characterize it as such because of the researcher's questions. (Brain scans can at least indicate whether a participant's brain activity was unusual or not during an alleged ASC experience.)

Naturalists believe their account is "neutral" in the way that religious accounts are not. Arguably, a scientific account would be neutral, and naturalists believe their accounts are dictated by science and therefore in a privileged position. Thus, they believe that imposing their beliefs is permissible. But naturalism is *not science*. Nonreligious, antireligious, and agnostic naturalists are in the same boat as those who are not naturalists: the naturalists' position is as *metaphysical* as the ones they reject. Metaphysics is about the basic nature of things, and how things hang together. It need not entail any transcendent realities. Naturalism is a worldview based on taking science alone as answering the fundamental questions on the nature of the world, but science itself does not require that only what is revealed by science is real and thus does not require naturalism. In naturalism, all that exists is open to scientific examination, and thus all that is real is the natural world (with the possible exception of mathematical entities). But this is a matter of metaphysics and cannot be equated with science or deduced from scientific findings. Thus, a naturalist position is not neutral for therapy concerning either set or setting. So too, a naturalist setting or instructions to the participants in a postexperiential session or questionnaire risks biasing participants as much as a religious presentation does—participants may be led to believe that a clinician's presentation in naturalist terms is proven scientific fact. This raises ethical as well as therapeutic issues.

As Adam Greif and Martin Šurkala (2020) argue, naturalism remains a controversial position in metaphysics and should not be imposed in therapy or medical practice more generally. The danger of suggestibility applies to naturalism as much as anything else. This leads to the question of what role metaphysics should play in the therapy sessions and research (see Sjöstedt-Hughes 2023; Gladziejewski 2023; Cheung and Yaden 2024). Sandeep Nayak and Matthew Johnson (2021: 167) have the goal of providing a "common conceptual vocabulary" for psychedelic therapy and find it in a "secular framework" of only naturalist terms (Johnson 2021: 580; also see Earleywine, Low, and De Leojdeleo 2021). Naturalists believe that having only an "unambiguously secular" framework will enable researchers to describe and explain psychedelic-enabled experiences without seeming to connect science with transcendent realities (Sanders and Zijlmans 2021: 1254). This may seem "more scientific" to a naturalist. However, a framework is not neutral that does not give the experiencers' own views an *equal status*. Imposing such a framework seems to be a reasonable course of action only to one already denying any nonnatural options. But a purely naturalist framework is one-sided and can distort the experiencers' own view of their ASC experiences or even hamper their having ASC experiences: providing questionnaires that are devoid of transcendent terms may be taken by experiencers to mean that the experience cannot be of anything but the natural world—after their experience, experiencers may reconceptualize their experiences in the preferred terminology of the naturalist therapist even if the experiences did not feel that way. These problems are lessened in research when the focus is only on the felt phenomenological content of the experiences alone, but in therapy this is a problem: the clinician's naturalism may diminish the effectiveness of the psychedelic therapy (Gandy 2022: 33). So too, it may result in the experiences not being integrated into the patient's life (Gandy 2022: 33). Thus, therapists should be as metaphysically neutral as possible. This involves at least not making a philosophical judgment of the content of the psychedelic-enabled under the guise of being "scientific." An "epistemic pluralism" may be more advisable (Zeller 2024). Thus, religious and related points of view and not just naturalism may have to be integrated into psychedelic-assisted therapy (Palitsky et al. 2023).

Many naturalists disparage the term "mystical" because "it suggests associations with the supernatural that may be obstructive or even antithetical to scientific method and progress" (Roseman, Nutt, and Carhart-Harris 2018: 2). But no experiences per se conflict with science—only possible *understandings* of their nature and significance may conflict. Indeed, some prominent naturalists—e.g., the philosopher Bertrand Russell and the physicist Alan Lightman—have had mystical experiences without giving up their naturalism or agnosticism. And naturalists can give a naturalist interpretation of mystical experiences in which the experiences are taken seriously as more than hallucinations or the product of a defective brain. Naturalist understandings of mystical experiences as *cognitive* have been advanced and not dismissed as hallucinations (Angel 2002; Harris 2014; Jylkkä 2021; Letheby 2021; Letheby and Mattu 2021).[15] For example, the sense of oneness is explained in terms of the natural mind simply being empty of content and experiencing pure consciousness or the beingness of the natural world. A sense of connection is explained in terms of the experiencer overcoming a sense of existing independently of the rest of the natural world—all that happens during a mystical experience is that the area of the brain responsible for a sense of a boundary between the sense of a "self" and the rest of the universe receives less input and the area attaching importance to events is more active, and so mystics quite understandably feel themselves to be without a separate "self" and feel more connected to the universe, which in naturalist metaphysics we in fact are: everything on earth—including ourselves—is a product of the stardust of an ancient supernova. Broader metaphysical explanations can also be given.

For example, Jussi Jylkkä (2021: 1469) proposes a naturalist panpsychism to explain the claim that we are merely "waves on a sea of consciousness" that gives consciousness and naturalized mystical experiences fundamental roles in our understanding of the universe.

In his philosophy of psychedelics, Chris Letheby (2017) presents a "naturalized spirituality" supported by a neurocognitive theory that can account for transcendence of the sense of a discrete experiencing "self" (i.e., a theory in which a "self" does not exist but is only a mental construct), feeling connected to others and the world, heightened emotions and awareness, and in which psychedelic-enabled experiences have a transformative impact. This spirituality also presents a meaning of life, all within a "disenchanted" naturalist worldview in harmony with science. Thus, psychedelic-enabled experiences may give genuine insights into reality that transform the experiencer (Letheby 2021: 220). Letheby believes that this will explain why these experiences are the key causal factor in psychedelic therapies that gives rise to the sense of well-being and the other psychological benefits. It can also get around the "comforting delusion" stance that clinicians may utilize "metaphysical hallucinations" in a therapy session despite believing them to be wrong if the "hallucinogens" have pragmatic value (Flanagan and Graham 2017; see Greif and Šurkala 2020).

Thus, a secular approach changes the understanding of mystical experiences, but it can still support the idea of "mystical insights" as genuine and experiential—even if no transcendent realities are involved—rather than as spurious insights fabricated under the influence of hallucinogens. This may also lead to the general acceptance that the term "mysticism" need not carry nonnaturalist connotations. Naturalists rightly point out that mystical experiences are open to the same type of examination as any experience—their religious impact does not make them off-limits—and that it is epistemologically legitimate for scientists to advance explanations of the mechanics of the brain during the experience that differ in type from metaphysical explanations of the source and significance of the experiences proffered by the experiencers themselves or by other researchers. In short, mystical and other ASC experiences are as open to scientific explanations as any other experiences. In principle, neuroscience can give as complete an account of what is occurring in the brain during an ASC experience or state as it can for any conscious event even if a transcendent consciousness or other realty is involved. Thus, there is no "psychedelic exceptionalism" in consciousness research (Sanders and Zijlmans 2021: 1253). But when it comes to presentations to patients and participants in psychedelic studies, there also is no "naturalism exceptionalism."

The Contribution of Mystical Experiences to the Science of Psychedelics and the Science of Consciousness

Despite the rise of such positive naturalist understandings of mystical experiences, most naturalists may still wish to exclude mystical experiences from consciousness studies. Mystical experiences for many are simply "metaphysical hallucinations" (Flanagan and Graham 2017)—experiences that are perhaps psychologically convincing to the experiencers themselves but of no more interest to scientists than other hallucinations. But naturalist therapists might embrace "mystical fictionalism" (Garb and Earleywine 2022) in applying mysticism as long as positive results arise (Flanagan and Graham 2017; Greif and Šurkala 2017). But can the study of mystical experiences add more to general psychedelic and consciousness research?

Mystical experiences are more limited in what they can contribute to psychedelic research and to the study of consciousness than many advocates of psychedelics claim. In particular, these experiences do not help with the most basic problems: they do not explain the relation of the mind to the body, show the true nature of consciousness, or overcome the "hard problem" of why subjectivity is attached to some physical events. Antoine Lutz and Evan Thompson realized in 2003 that neurophenomenology also has not yet bridged the gap between the material brain and immaterial consciousness (2003: 47), and the situation has not changed since. In one study, David Yaden and his collaborators (2021) concluded that psychedelics are unlikely to provide information relevant to the hard problem. Mystical experiences are exotic cases that add to the pool of data on consciousness to be studied, but they remain merely another type of experience or state even if they are open to interpretations in terms of transcendent realities. So too, mystical experiences in which consciousness seems disembodied and not belonging to the experiencer do not prove that consciousness is independent of matter as long as a naturalist explanation of these experiences in which consciousness is either identical to the brain or is a naturally emerging property remains a viable alternative (see Angel 2002; Letheby 2021). And as Matthew Johnson (2021: 579) also concludes, to date psychedelic science has not provided a substantial advancement in our understanding of either the easy or the hard problems related to consciousness. Yaden and his collaborators called for "epistemic humility" on this topic in psychedelic studies (2021: 621). Neuroscientists generally adopt a "methodological materialism" in which they tend simply to ignore the hard problem and use the term "consciousness" to refer to a wide array of the contents of the mind in general (e.g., perception, thoughts, and emotions) (Yaden et al. 2021: 617).

But mystical experiences can contribute to the study of consciousness in a number of ways. Most importantly, the different types of mystical ASC experiences and states of consciousness add to the spectrum of consciousness and to neuroscience, since unique configurations of brain activity ground the experiences in the body. They too must be accounted for in developing models of consciousness or models of how the brain works in underlying subjectivity, whether mystical experiences are cognitive or not. Even if they have no causal properties, their presence must be taken into consideration and accounted for. These experiences may be like the high-energy physics that caused physicists to revise Newtonian physics (Wallace 2003: 167).

The mainstream position in philosophy is that all consciousness involves a sense of "self" in one degree or another—a sense of self is somehow neurologically tied to any human experience. But in psychedelics studies today, there is a debate on whether a sense of self is necessarily part of all human experiences (see Millière and Metzinger 2020; Sebastián 2020). Some research suggests that a sense of "self" is not in fact necessary for consciousness (e.g., Millière 2020). Chris Letheby also defends the possibility of a truly selfless awareness against the claim that all awareness must be to someone—a sense of ownership or "for-me-ness" to all experiences—and thus there must be an experiencing "self" (2021; Letheby and Mattu 2021). That is, *subjectivity* is necessary for any experience but not necessarily a separate ontological entity called the "*self*" (see chapter 3). This too may lead to revising our view of the nature of consciousness or how consciousness works.

There may also be a state of consciousness devoid of all content except consciousness itself—a "pure" consciousness with no separate object to be aware of. Whether a state of consciousness truly empty of all diverse content is in fact possible is a matter of debate in philosophy (see R. Jones 2020a), and the study of "pure" consciousness or awareness has become an increasingly important subject of empirical and philosophical research on consciousness (Gamma and Metzinger 2021: 2). Whether such a consciousness is a core consciousness that is present in all states of consciousness or is only one state of consciousness would be an issue, but in either case studying a state of consciousness free of the usual content may prove of value for understanding the nature of consciousness.

Mystical experiences can also contribute to science in other ways. First, the brain states underlying extrovertive and introvertive mystical experiences with diverse content may contribute to scientists' understanding of the supposedly "easy" problems of consciousness such as vision (through the vividness of these experiences), how information is integrated, how some cognitions are impaired, or the sense of unity to consciousness (e.g., Bayne and Carter 2018). Second, the experiences may expose something of the subconscious layers of consciousness. Mystical experiences may also help the study of the hardware of the brain. For example, studies show that psychedelic drugs can produce rapid changes in the brain's plasticity on the molecular and cellular levels (e.g., Vos, Mason, and Kuypers 2021), but the experiences (and not just the chemical effects of the psychedelic drugs) may also add to the study of neural plasticity (see, e.g., Doss et al. 2021) and neurotransmitters.

All of this touches upon the broader issue of the nature of consciousness. Mystical and other psychedelic-enabled states and experiences may require some remodeling of the mind, even though it appears that to date these states and experiences have done less than many advocates of them claim. Indeed, in the end these experiences and states may actually only increase the mystery of consciousness.

Situating Mysticism in Psychedelic Therapy and Research

To sum up: proponents of disengaging mysticism from psychedelic therapy have not yet made their case, and as long as psychedelic-enabled experiences appear to be part of the beneficial effects of psychedelic therapies, experiences appropriately labeled "mystical" are part of the therapeutic picture and the explanations of the effects. Suppressing or ignoring the subjective experiential component at present will hurt the positive and meaningful therapeutic effects. Thus, keeping mystical and the other ASC experiences as part of the therapy while some researchers try to develop drugs that have the positive therapeutic effects of psychedelic drugs but without the ASC experiences should not be controversial. And it must also be remembered that our knowledge of how psychedelics bring about therapeutic benefits is still limited (see Aday et al. 2024; Beans 2024), and psychedelics still remain part of the "black box" mysteries surrounding the brain and consciousness and more broadly what constitutes a human being.

Thus, mystical experiences should not be expunged from broader psychedelic research at this relatively early stage of research of how psychedelics affect the brain. Scientists can accomplish their explanatory task without mysticism introducing a collision of science and religion or surreptitiously smuggling nonnatural transcendent realities into scientific explanations. Mystical concepts may need to be clarified for purposes of psychedelic science, but mystical experiences do not per se conflict with science. Mystical experiences are open to naturalist understandings, but as long as consciousness is part of the picture in psychedelic studies it is not obvious that these experiences must be seen only in naturalist terms. However, research on psychedelic-enabled experiences and the applied mysticism of psychedelic therapy have less potential in addressing the fundamental issues of consciousness and the mind than many enthusiastic advocates of psychedelics currently assert—mystical experiences is a subset of the general problems of consciousness, not their solution. Nevertheless, if a "new paradigm" in therapy that treats psychedelic-enabled experiences as causal does become mainstream, the study of mysticism (including its practices, rituals, teachings, and values) should become part of the training of clinicians and researchers in psychedelics studies.[16] The current use of mysticism in psychedelic research has been rightly described as "fraught with limitations and intrinsic [historical and cultural] biases that are seldom acknowledged" (Mosurinjohn, Roseman, and Girn 2023: 1).

Chapter 8

Secular Mysticism

Religious authority has declined in the West on both the societal and individual levels (Ecklund and Long 2011: 253), but Western society today is not so much secularized as pluralistic—i.e., a common religious legitimation to society has been lost, and so people now have a number of live options regarding religion to choose from (Berger 2014). The variety is manifested in mysticism too: the religious and nonreligious today have a variety of options—meditation (especially mindfulness taken out of its original Buddhist context), psychedelic drugs, and New Age religiosity. One viable option in today's chaotic cultural mix is the rejection of any religious affiliation or a traditional religious framework involving transcendent realities at all: a purely secular form of mysticism. Almost 30 percent of Americans today are not affiliated with any religious tradition (Pew Research Center 2024). The well-publicized atheism of the two best-known scientists of the last fifty years—Stephen Hawking and Carl Sagan—gave rejecting theism a boost in our culture. But not all of the "nones" are unspiritual or antireligious. Many still seek an all-encompassing meaning to life, but they now seek meaning within a purely secular and naturalist framework. So too, many are interested in meditation and in psychedelic-enabled altered states of consciousness (ASC) for nonreligious reasons.

Thus, it is not surprising that in our culture's new open atmosphere a new phenomenon has appeared in the last few decades: the total separation of mystical practices and experiences from any theistic or other nonnaturalist religious interest. The new approach applies mystical experiences and practices to deal with worldly problems. In addition, there is now also a more full-blown "secular mysticism"—i.e., a "naturalized" mysticism that rejects any framework with transcendent realities but retains a spiritual interest.[1] The latter is a spirituality that is mystical and yet grounded in a metaphysics of naturalism. In sum, it is both a mystical type of naturalism and a naturalist type of mysticism.

Naturalism

Ontological naturalism can best be defined by what it denies: no realities, either personal or nonpersonal in nature, exist that transcend the range of scientific examination. So too, there is no transcendent purpose or meaning to the natural realm. Hence, only the "natural" realm exists, not gods or nonnatural selves, or life after death in another realm. As Carl Sagan famously said: "The Cosmos is all that is or ever was or ever will be" (1985: 1). To put the metaphysics another way, naturalists believe that if the natural cosmos somehow completely went out of existence, nothing would be left, while nonnaturalists believe that something real would remain—nonnatural realities that transcend the natural realm in the sense of not being open to scientific scrutiny. Prominent possible nonnatural realities are a theistic god, the Neoplatonist One, Brahman in Hinduism, an eternal soul, and the transcendent self of Jainism and Samkhya-Yoga. Methodological naturalists remain agnostic about whether there are nonnatural realities, but like ontological naturalists, they too accept that the natural realm is closed: no transcendent nonnatural realities, if they exist, are active in the natural realm (including in human beings), either through causation or some informational input or in any other way. At best, the only realities transcending the natural cosmos that naturalists accept are mathematical entities needed in order to make science work. But only science, albeit fallible and changing, provides authoritative knowledge of the nature of reality. And for mainstream naturalists, in the end only in our ordinary base-line state of consciousness we can attain scientific knowledge.

Many naturalists show little interest in the Big Questions of why the natural realm exists or where it came from, but they do deny that a god or other supernatural reality is responsible for it. So too, human beings are purely natural: persons have no nonnatural transcendent dimension, and no part of us survives death in a nonnatural realm. But naturalists need not be physicalists (materialists) who reduce the mind to brain activity or its product. Some naturalists accept that consciousness is a purely natural but nonmaterial phenomenon that is not reducible to matter, although how such a reality fits into the scientific picture is problematic. But in whatever form, naturalism appears to be the mainstream position with analytic philosophy today. It is based on the success of science, but naturalists go further and claim that only their metaphysics truly reflects the practice of science (see De Caro and Macarthur 2004).

Mysticism

The term "mysticism" is problematic, and any proposed definition is in part stipulative. Here the term "mystical experiences" will mean an allegedly direct awareness of fundamental realities in short-term ASC episodes that are free of a sense of a discrete self and of the conceptual divisions that normally structure our mental life. Emotions such as joy and empathy often accompany the experiences but need not—serenity is sometimes the immediate result of a mystical experience. Mystical experiences give the feeling that everything is meaningful (even if no specific meaning is given). There are various extrovertive and introvertive types of mystical experiences.[2] Extrovertive mystical experiences involve sense perceptions, but they are different from other ASC experiences that involve a dualism of experiencer and what is experienced, as in visions and locutions. Here "mystical states" will denote more enduring states of such consciousness than transient experiences. "Mysticism" will refer to the cultural phenomena—teachings, texts, practices, social institutions, and so forth—centered around an interior quest to turn off the sense of self and to end our conceptualizing mind from controlling our experience in order to bring oneself into alignment with what one deems ultimately real. Thus, mysticism is more encompassing than simply having a mystical experience. For someone on a quest for such experiences, it involves, not merely a web of phenomena but also a comprehensive way of life having practices, codes of conduct, rituals, and a specific goal, with doctrines about the nature of what is deemed real as its philosophical spine. Other nonordinary phenomena such as paranormal powers and visions may or may not occur in such ways of life.

How can mysticism fit into a naturalist picture? Naturalists first separate the experiences from the nonnaturalist beliefs and practices permeating traditional mysticism. They reject all nonnatural realities or explanations since by definition these would be untestable by scientists in any fashion and hence are rejected. But they need not deny that genuine introvertive and extrovertive mystical experiences occur (including the depth-mystical experience empty of differentiated content) or that they occur to healthy persons with properly functioning brains. Rather, naturalists simply deny that these experiences are cognitive of nonnatural realities or that nonnatural realities initiate or participate in these experiences. The experiences and states themselves can be accepted as unusual but perfectly natural experiences and states of the brain. Indeed, surveys show that mystical experiences are actually far more common than generally believed (e.g., Hardy 1983; Hay 1994; Hood 2005).[3] Naturalists can also accept any verified physiological or psychological benefits of meditative practices or psychedelic therapy as more than merely a placebo effect. So too, even if the same meditative manipulations of the mind or the same drugs were to induce the same experiences in people regardless of culture or era, this does not mean that these experiences must be cognitive of nonnatural realities—it only means that we all share a common neurophysiology.

Undergoing a mystical experience is not tied to holding any specific metaphysical belief or to belonging to a religious tradition. Being struck by the wonder of the night sky or the intricate organization of things has led many persons to become scientists, and it can also lead to mystical experiences. In fact, naturalists themselves, including a number of prominent atheists and agnostics, have had mystical experiences.[4] The experiences for naturalists are usually of the nature-mystical variety—e.g., the experiencer's sense of self dissolves while contemplating the night sky and the vastness of things. Friedrich Nietzsche wrote of experiences of ecstasy in which the reality of everything was affirmed in their "eternal return"—everything is of value, and the eternal return of everything counters their deterioration in value through time. The experiences may lead naturalists to give up their metaphysics and embrace theism or deism or another nonnaturalist option, but these experiences may have only the effect that a near-death experience had on the atheist A. J. Ayer (1990): it "slightly weakened" his conviction that his death would be his end but did not cause him to give up that belief. The experiences' impact may be great, but it may affect only the emotions. It would then not upset the naturalist's basic metaphysical beliefs. Bertrand Russell had a mystical experience in 1901 induced by seeing the suffering of a friend dying from cancer. The experience transformed him into a more loving person and to opposing war—it dramatically affected his values and emotions but not his agnosticism concerning possible nonnatural realities. The philosopher John McTaggart had a mystical experience that he took as revealing the universe to be a system of immortal loving souls, but he did not give up his disbelief in God. The physicist Alan Lightman's nature mystical experience in which he dissolved into the infinity of the universe did not cause him to give up his naturalism, but he thereafter saw the structures of nature as sacred. Naturalists can refer to the existence of the natural realm *in toto* as "the All" or "being itself" without transcending the natural realm even though science has nothing to say about the sheer being or "that-ness" of the universe. Michael Pollan's *How to Change Your Mind* (2018) popularized the idea that psychedelic-enabled experiences need not lead one to belief in God.

Notice that mystical experiences may have a *negative effect* on one's prior religious beliefs. Mystical experiences in the past were typically associated with religion: anything powerful was assumed to have religious significance, and this of course included mystical experiences. But mystical experiences need not be connected to nonnatural realities or a quest for meaning. In fact, while mystical experiences normally have a positive effect on one's religiosity, these experiences can lead to becoming convinced that there is no god or life after death and to abandoning religion entirely (Newberg and Waldman 2016: 60, 67–81). The French philosopher Pierre Hadot had mystical experiences in which he felt his self melt into the vastness of the universe but which also revealed that there is no god. This led him to abandon Christianity. Moreover, any emphasis on gaining mystical experiences alone can lead away from religion as a means to foster these experiences or as providing a framework for understanding them. And some experiencers today understand their mystical experiences in nonreligious and sometimes explicitly atheistic ways (e.g., Newberg and Waldman 2016: 69–75).

Naturalists explain these experiences only in terms of the workings of the brain, although some may become less certain of their metaphysical assumptions. Their explanations keep all introvertive and extrovertive mystical experiences within the natural universe. Extrovertive experiences may be considered more important than introvertive ones because the natural world is all that is real in naturalist metaphysics. Naturalists may deny that introvertive mystical experiences empty of all differentiated content can occur, arguing that all experiences are intentional, and thus the conscious mind is never truly empty of all diverse content. (Constructivism is discussed below.) Or if they admit such an experience, they will insist that it is either the result of the brain malfunctioning, or only a feedback effect of the monitoring activity of the natural mind that continues despite being deprived of any content to process, or at most an awareness of a purely natural consciousness in its bare state. That is, consciousness arose and evolved through natural forces, and an "empty" introvertive mystical experience at best is the experience of that natural consciousness.

Thus, they conclude that these experiences at best show that the purely natural mind has a greater depth and complexity than normally accepted—there is no nonnatural consciousness. That is, in these experiences they gain direct experiential knowledge of themselves or the being of the world. So too, the experienced sense of bliss results only from the calm resulting from the purposeless spinning of mental wheels when there is no mental content to work on or there is a release of dopamine—that mystics take the bliss as indicating an experience of being loved or the presence of something transcending the natural realm shows only that they misinterpret the experience. Theists erroneously attach more significance to any experiences of light or warmth as "the presence of God" only because of the strangeness of the states of consciousness, their prior belief in a supreme nonnatural reality, and their belief that others had experiences of God and so these experiences must be that (see chapter 5 on expectancy bias). That is, the religious are expecting to experience God, and so they naturally interpret mystical experiences that way, even though the experiences in fact have no nonnatural input. Even if there were an encompassing nonnatural reality that is immanent in the natural world and thus in the brain, naturalists contend that none of our experiences realize that reality, nor does that reality play any part in mystical experiences that it does not play in all our experiences.[5]

To naturalists, introvertive mystical experiences with differentiated content are merely cases of some subconscious content of our mind welling up into consciousness. Mindfulness is only a relaxed but focused attention on the beingness of things in the world. In a mindful state, one's awareness is broadened as the conceptual constrictions that the mind normally applies in our sensing are loosened or totally eliminated. One may become totally absorbed in the present and lose any sense of time or of a discrete sensing entity—the "self." But mindfulness merely switches our mental focus from differentiations to the "that-ness" of things and thus reveals nothing new about what is or is not real. Experiences of beingness are treated as not more cognitive than our ordinary structured perceptions of the differentiated parts—the divided parts and their interactions remain real, distinct, and valuable even if when we focus on the uniform beingness the conceptualized boundaries disappear. All that happens during a mystical experience is that the area of the brain responsible for a sense of a boundary between a "self" and the rest of the universe is less active and the area attaching importance to events is more active, and so mystics quite naturally feel more connected to the universe, which in naturalist metaphysics we in fact are: we are evolved products of stardust with nothing dividing us into ontologically disconnected realities. Our connection with everything else extends beyond our planet to the rest of the solar systems and extends in other ways to the rest of the galaxy and the rest of the universe. No mystical experiences are needed to realize that everything is changing and that there are no hard-and-fast boundaries between things. (Buddhists would concur with the impermanence and connectedness.) Moreover, living in the "now" without concerns for the future would certainly bring a sense of peacefulness, but this does not negate anything about the complexity of reality or life—such an escape eases stress, but our life will be short if we ignore the difficulties that await us. But the transcendence of a sense of "self" valued in spirituality can thereby be achieved without transcending the natural realm—the loss of a sense of self can lead to no more than feeling connected to a social group or to the rest of the natural realm. The very distinction of a separate "self" from objects may disappear. It is a "horizontal" transcendence within the natural realm rather than a "vertical" one reaching a nonnatural realm (Goodenough 1998), but it satisfies any human need to transcend a sense of an isolated "self" and to feel connected to what is real.

By focusing on the present, naturalists may have a naturalist type of "everyday mysticism" in which the ordinary is seen as extraordinary. Gratitude for existing and for the world is a common emotional response. Naturalists can treat nature mystical experiences (with their sense of a glow to the world) as only caused by the brain. If nature mystical experiences transition into cosmic consciousness (with the felt experience of something more than the natural world), the felt sense of something transcending natural world is dismissed as delusional. To naturalists, that experience can no more be insightful concerning the nature of reality than the interesting but cognitively empty effects of psychedelic drugs such as LSD that distort our perceptions and sense of time. The sense of selflessness can be explained away as merely our being momentarily unaware of the self in an overwhelming experience or it involves an experience without a personal perspective. Or this sense may be treated as empirical support for naturalist theories such as Daniel Dennett's that the sense of "I" is ultimately an illusion (1991: 412–31): there are only various brain monitoring activities without any one unified center and thus no distinct reality commanding or controlling all the activities. The "self" is only a useful construct that the brain spins out of these monitoring activities to simplify things. So too, everything that makes us human is tied to a sense of the reality of a phenomenal self even if we deny the existence of an ontologically discrete entity called the "self."

Spirituality

Spirituality concerns a search for the meaning of life, personal growth and fulfillment, connections to each other and to nature, personal values, what is fundamentally real and important, and the Big Questions of philosophy and science (see Sheldrake 2014). Spirituality need not involve God or other transcendent realities. Scholars who speak of "spirituality" rather than "religion" typically focus on an individual's personal development, a sense of well-being, a sense of connectedness to the rest of reality, and a practical sense of purpose or meaning that makes life seem worth living rather than religious institutions or traditional religious doctrines. A naturalist who is "spiritual" may be interested in the "sacred" in the sense of something of overriding significance (Stone 2012: 493), even if the object is not transcendent, and regardless of whether he or she is affiliated with a religious tradition. But the term "God" becomes used less often because of its nonnaturalist connotations. A naturalist can become interested in personal growth and experiences of the sacred, but any sense of transcendence would remain within the natural realm.[6]

Mysticism is typically a form of spirituality, but spirituality encompasses more than mysticism and is in fact not necessarily connected to mysticism. Thus, the terms should be distinguished. Spirituality has been slowly severing its ties to mysticism since the 1950s, and today spirituality is replacing mysticism (with its ties to premodern cultures and otherworldliness) in the cultural marketplace (Carrette and King 2005). Indeed, some in the field believe that the past focus on interiority in spirituality was a mistake (Thomas 2000). A complete "privatization" of spirituality leaves it without a doctrinal content or social focus (Carrette and King 2005: 68–69). In such circumstances, any sense of self-transcendence may well remain a matter of our ordinary state of consciousness. Enlarging one's perspective to encompass more than oneself may well influence our lives in how we deal with others and see ourselves. It may lead to the belief that there is no entity—a "self"—separate from the rest of reality. But unless this sense alters our baseline state of consciousness into an ASC, it is not properly seen as mystical.

Because of variations in naturalist beliefs and values, there is a variety of secular mysticisms. For example, today both inside and outside of the Abrahamic traditions there now are "religious naturalists" who reinterpret monotheistic language into naturalist terms—e.g., "God" becomes merely the creative laws of nature. (Some but not all "secular humanists" are religious naturalists.) In a kind of secularized re-enchantment of the world and our place in it, these naturalists highlight awe and wonder at the majesty of nature, but they may be atheists or agnostics (see Goodenough 1998; Solomon 2002; Crosby 2008; Ecklund and Long 2011: 265–67; Stone 2012; Crosby and Stone 2020; Swimme 2019). However, mystical and psychedelic-enabled experiences do not appear to play a major role in this religiosity, not even a mysticism of everyday life.[7] Indeed, religious naturalists tend to avoid the word "mysticism." The Routledge handbook on religious naturalism (Crosby and Stone 2020) mentions mysticism only once. When mystical experiences are acknowledged, they are given a naturalist interpretation as showing only the depth and mystery of the natural world (Wildman 2011: 244–66). Wesley Wildman believes that as the knowledge of the brain events occurring during mystical experiences increases, the transcendent options for explaining mystical events will fade away and the claim of cognitivity, moral value, and existential authenticity of these experiences will become limited to the natural realm (Wildman 2011: 241).[8] However, as Eric Steinhart (2018) points out, religious naturalism will remain merely an "intellectual exercise" unless these naturalists come to utilize the "technologies" of psychedelics and meditation for generating experiences and also organize ceremonies and celebrations of all of the natural world.

The Scientific Study of Mystical Experiences

Studying the effects of meditation and psychedelics on people has been a prominent part of the resurgence in the interest in consciousness and the workings of the brain since the 1990s. Theories have been advanced on the neurology underlying mystical experiences (see, e.g., Lutz, Dunne, and Davidson 2007; Barrett and Griffiths 2018; Schmidt and Walach 2014; Tang, Hölzel, and Posner 2015). For example, neuroscanning of brain activity shows how meditation and drugs disrupt the neural mechanisms underpinning our sense of a "self" distinct from the rest of reality, permitting a different level or type of consciousness to emerge. Triggers of mystical experiences besides meditation and psychedelics are also being studied. Many naturalists may not be particularly interested in these studies since they already assume that the experiences and states of consciousness are purely natural, and so discovering the actual mechanics underlying them need not concern them—even if none are found, this would not upset their assumption but only show the limits of science. However, the studies do show how mystical experiences can fit into the naturalist picture of a person.

Whether mystical experiences involve real insights into the nature of reality or are delusional, today it is increasingly becoming apparent that the experiences themselves are real and their occurrence can be observed and measured through the accompanying neural activity (e.g., Yaden et al. 2017b: 60). There may be no one area of the brain devoted to mystical experiences, but there is evidence of distinctive configurations of brain activity uniquely associated with each category of mystical experiences—scans indicate that electrochemical activity increases or decreases in certain areas when a mystical or another ASC experience is occurring even if the experience is not produced by the brain. So too, scientists have found different neurophysiological effects from extrovertive and introvertive meditation (Hood 2001: 32–47; Dunn, Hartigan, and Mikulas 1999) and can distinguish the neurological effects of concentrative and mindfulness meditation (Valentine and Sweet 1999). So too, neuroscience suggests that "cosmic consciousness" is a different state of consciousness than the state of LSD-enabled visions (Smith and Tart 1998).

However, by "*real*" neuroscientists mean only that mystical experiences relate to distinct neurological events—i.e., they are not products of imagination or simply interpretations of ordinary experiences in the baseline state of consciousness or necessarily the product of a damaged brain. Rather, they involve unique configurations of neural activity of healthy brains functioning properly. This is as far as neuroscience can go toward establishing that distinctive mystical experiences occur. Meditation and psychedelic drugs enable different types of mystical experiences. Scientists may remain neutral on whether some mystical experiences are authentic encounters with a nonnatural reality, insights into the natural world or oneself, or are delusions. Only what is going on in the brain is of interest to neuroscientists qua scientists. So too with mindfulness: scientists may confirm that, say, Buddhist meditative techniques calm the mind and quell desires, but this does not confirm Buddhism's theories of rebirth and liberation. Learning more about the necessary neural or physiological bases to these experiences may help in reproducing them, but that does not relate to the doctrines that mystics espouse.[9]

In addition to aiding in establishing the uniqueness of mystical experiences, the beneficial effects of meditation and psychedelics such as psilocybin and LSD in aiding such psychological problems as depression and addiction are now being demonstrated (see chapter 7). The reported benefits from meditation to date have been small but measurable. Thus, neuroscience appears to validate the positive effects of meditation and psychedelic therapy on our well-being. All of this leads many people to the belief that science is now giving credence to mystical experiences. But again, it is now a secular understanding of the nature of mystical experiences and natural effects that is gaining attention. It is simply applying mysticism to our everyday well-being, not traditional religious goals.

To naturalists, the studies to date are taken only as reinforcing the view that the only value in mystical experiences is in their effect on the body. The experiences are "real" neurologically, and to naturalists the significance and value of the experiences are exhaustively explained by scientific accounts. Any nonnatural explanation is obsolete and superfluous and in the future will become seen to be a fantasy and a delusion. The possibility that the brain states that scientists observe are merely the base conditions that permit nonnatural input into our mind may not even be seen as an issue. If mystical experiences are considered cognitive, they are given naturalist understandings; otherwise, the alleged insights into transcendent realities are dismissed entirely on naturalist grounds. Only the effect on the body matters: if drugs could be devised that had the beneficial psychophysiological effects without any mystical experiences, secularists would be content since this would show that the experiences are only epiphenomenal side effects. So too, if these results can be shown to be achievable by means other than hours of meditation, interest in meditation may fade quickly. In short, to naturalists mystical experiences are merely events produced by the brain even if they have positive effects on our health and well-being, and that is the only value that the experiences and practices have.

Forms of Secular Mysticism

Of course, scientific interest in mystical experiences and states of mind is not itself a form of mysticism. So too if one is interested only in the experiences themselves or what they may tell us about our mind, not in transforming one's character in a fundamental way. Similarly, if one participates in meditation or psychedelic therapy only for their limited psychophysiological effects, it is hard to consider this mysticism. But if the resulting mystical experiences affect one's life more generally, then this is mysticism—a "secular mysticism" integrating mystical experiences into one's life in a naturalist framework.[10] Such a secular mysticism need not be a full-blown secular religion with rituals and doctrines built around naturalism and mystical experiences to be rightfully called "mysticism."[11] Nor need practices such as meditation and drug sessions approach the more extreme and arduous training of classical mystical traditions. The secular emphasis is usually in immediate results rather than long-term changes. But if mystical experiences or practices profoundly alter how one lives, this is a form of mystical spirituality.

Mystical experiences enabled through psychedelics or meditation or occurring spontaneously disrupt the mechanisms in brain activity underlying a sense of a self-contained "self" separate from the rest of the natural realm and make one feel connected to others and the rest of the world, and secularists see this in terms of the natural world alone. The effect of mystical experiences on beliefs may last for years and can lead to lasting increases in altruistic and prosocial behavior (Griffiths et al. 2006, 2008, 2011), all without transcendent beliefs. This natural spirituality appears more tied to mystical experiences than to other types of psychedelic-enabled ASC experiences (Letheby 2021: 200). It is not a matter of "cosmic consciousness" or anything leading to a belief in nonnatural realities, or of aesthetic experiences as possible triggers of mystical experiences. Since naturalists see mystical experiences only in terms of a natural consciousness and nothing transcendent, secular mystical accounts may in general be less "ramified" with theoretical terms since naturalism's ontology is simpler than nonnaturalist ones. In addition, naturalists may be less interested in ontological accounts of these experiences. Some philosophers today, however, are speculating on the relation of consciousness to matter. Naturalists could endorse a panpsychism in which consciousness is as fundamental a property of matter as physical properties such as mass and electromagnetism (see Skrbina 2017). Panpsychism is a naturalist philosophy that attempts to overcome the problem of how something subjective in nature (consciousness) could arise from something not conscious in any sense (matter). Sarah Lane Ritchie (2021) connects panpsychism to psychedelic states and spiritual flourishing. It does not involve a nonnatural "Mind at Large" or consciousness as an emergent property of matter but treats consciousness as purely natural. Naturalists could also accept a cosmopsychism that makes consciousness to be more fundamental than matter.

Naturalists may be hesitant to use the term "mystical" or even the more general "spiritual." Mystical experiences involve altered states of consciousness, but the postexperiential state of consciousness may or may not be altered. However, when a mystical experience has a transformative effect on one's inner life and how one lives and acts toward others, it is a mystically informed life and thus use of the term "mystical" is appropriate. Mystical experiences engage spirituality if they are attached to seeking a meaning or purpose to one's life. The sense of "self" may persist in one's consciousness, but it may now be seen to be merely a useful fiction that our brain devised for its evolutionary benefit and that in fact has no basis in reality. The nonexistence of an enclosed entity is realized directly in an experience. Emotions may change, with increases in joy at just being alive; awe and wonder at the vastness, intricacy, and beauty of the world; and empathy with others, even though naturalists do not take the experiences as "seeing the face of God." Indeed, the secularists' lives are transformed without their adopting a belief in God neutralizes a changed life as evidence of the existence of God.

But this mysticism may affect naturalists' beliefs and attitudes. It may be that the experiences do not introduce new beliefs but only alter a person's existing beliefs and their impact (McGovern et al. 2021). Under the recently proposed REBUS (RElaxed Beliefs under pSychedelics) model (Carhart-Harris and Friston 2019), psychedelics weaken the control of one's beliefs, thereby permitting more influence from experiential input and making experiencers more flexible in their resulting beliefs. Psychedelics do not necessarily make an atheist into a theist (Glausser 2021), but there may be "significant decreases in identification as atheist and agnostic and significant increases in belief in ultimate reality, higher power, God, or universal divinity" (Davis et al. 2020: 1018). It does appear that psychedelic experiences tend to cause a shift in the experiencers' metaphysics away from "hard" materialism to panpsychism or to accepting nonnatural realities (Timmermann et al. 2021; Letheby 2021: 206; but see Nayak et al. 2024). One may become more open about the nature of consciousness and accept that it exists independently of the brain. A single psychedelic experience may have an effect on how the person views the basic nature of consciousness that lasts for years (Nayak and Griffiths 2022). Meditation too may have an "implicit spiritual nature" even if not all participants in an experiment have spiritual experiences or see the spiritual effects in nonnaturalist terms

(Wachholtz and Pargament 2005: 382).[12] Strong but short-term and reversible disruptions of self-consciousness can be occasioned by psychedelics, but any long-lasting effects of meditation on well-being appear to be mediated not necessarily by intense experiences but by training of different cognitive mechanisms (Millière et al. 2017: 20–21). Such effects on beliefs are correlated with positive mental health changes and a sense of well-being, and the metaphysical changes may be long-lasting (Timmermann et al. 2021).

Thus, a reductive materialism may be rejected—an expanded framework that is still naturalist may be adopted. In any case, a secularized understanding of mystical experiences has been adopted by many today, including some who endorse mystical experiences for our worldly well-being (e.g., Kornfield 2001; Forman 2011; Harris 2014; also see Langlitz 2012 on "mystic materialism"). The value of mystical experiences thus is cut off from traditional mysticism. Consciousness or the natural universe is taken to be the fundamental reality that is experienced. Transcending our baseline state of consciousness in experiences still attracts many, even when the resulting experiences are not deemed cognitive of a nonnatural reality. There is a loss of a sense of a "self" even though it is not taken to be exposure to a nonnatural reality but instead to be an expanded natural consciousness only—self-transcendence remains naturalized. A sense of selflessness may lessen desires and fears (including fear of death) and self-centered concerns, and increase a sense of being connected to others and to nature, but it is not taken as indicating a reality transcending the natural world or as having any further ontological significance. Moreover, the negative mystical experiences—the proverbial "bad trips" (see Schlag et al. 2022: 5)—are readily explained as cases of disturbing subconscious traits entering consciousness when the destabilization of the baseline state of consciousness permits such psychological conditions to manifest themselves.[13]

Nature plays a major role in secular mysticism, as it also does for nonmystical religious naturalists. The metaphysical oneness of the common being of the natural realm, the connection of things, and the unifying lawful order of things become important. In extrovertive mystical experiences, nature may seem alive or to have a consciousness. But nature is not "re-enchanted" as the creation or body of a god—nature remains "profane" in not having a relation to a nonnatural reality, but the world can be treated, along with human beings, as "sacred" since it is all that actually exists and deserves reverence. Scientific research into the features and structures of reality takes on a spiritual significance.[14] But many naturalists, even spiritual ones, may simply accept the idea that there is anything rather than nothing and why the universe has the particular basic structures it has as mysteries that we are incapable of answering with our evolved cognitive skills. Natural suffering is accepted as what it is: there is no need for a theodicy to explain suffering since it is simply a natural result of what is real—the works of nature are, in the words of Charles Darwin, "clumsy, wasteful, blundering low and horridly cruel." So too, life and consciousness are naturally evolved, and for naturalists such evolution is unguided by a higher hand. Naturalists need not feel compelled to support neo-Darwinism in which the evolution of life is unguided. They could endorse evolutionary, emergent, or biological principles that lead to greater complexity that may guide the course of life and even nonorganic evolution. But for naturalists, such laws would be as natural as gravity and electromagnetism—no guidance by a nonnatural reality would be necessary. No all-powerful nonnatural reality creates or controls nature, but we are to trust nature and its laws in a way that theists are to trust the will of God. Mindfulness and psychedelics may expand some people's moral concern to all human beings and also to animals if one already has a moral concern for others. A moral concern for all living things can also lead to a concern for the environment, not only to preserve human life, but because the natural realm is all that is real. Ursula Goodenough (1998) suggests that life should be greeted with gratitude and reverence and that the natural order and the epic of evolution may be reworked into a naturalist analog to the biblical creation story.[15]

Meditation is removed from any religious setting and "naturalized": it is repurposed in secular forms for limited worldly psychophysiological benefits rather than transforming one's character for a transcendent goal.[16] Books on how to lead a mindful secular life are becoming popular (e.g., Tart 1994). The means for facilitating mystical experiences have also been secularized (see Heller 2015)—in particular, psychedelics, mindfulness, and some concentrative meditation for focusing attention upon one object. Susan Blackmore (2009) and Sam Harris (2014) advocate jettisoning traditional Buddhist transcendent elements (beliefs in afterlife, rebirth, and nonnatural realities) while still retaining Buddhist meditative practices for purposes other than cultivating insight (also see Batchelor 2015 on "secular Buddhism"). Yoga becomes a matter of enhancing only psychophysiological well-being. Indeed, in the West, yoga is often reduced to a stretching exercise for physical fitness, but even that may relieve stress. Herbert Benson's concentrative "relaxation response" (Benson and Klipper 2000 [1975]) and Jon Kabat-Zinn's (2005) mindfulness-based stress reduction program (MBSR) are popular. Meditation helps with psychological and physiological problems whether one's understanding of it is secular or religious. Today the government, corporations, hospitals, prisons, and schools are experimenting with secular forms of mindfulness meditation that were adapted from modern versions of Buddhism to see if attentiveness and positive psychophysiological effects accrue (see Csikszentmihalyi 1990). Compassion meditation is also beginning to be practiced in schools. But meditation also is being "weaponized" as part of a program to produce "super soldiers" (Komjathy 2018: 194), without the spiritual dimension of classical samurai training.

Secularists may accept religious texts as useful today for outlining practices and delineating states of consciousness, but eventually these texts will be discarded as no more helpful here than in astronomy.[17] Traditional religious metaphysics and postmortem goals will become ignored as anachronisms even as the experiences have a profound personal impact. The goal of a total inner transformation is not needed for secular spirituality to be mystical, but an inner change is necessary. Thus, meditation guides are still necessary, but teachers of metaphysical doctrines are no longer needed, nor is adherence to difficult monastic labor and conduct. Meditating for overall well-being means well-being within a naturalist framework—improved moods, higher self-esteem, and the overall satisfaction with one's life. Naturalists may see mysticism not in terms of cognition but in terms of emotion, as Bertrand Russell did (1918: 11), and still conclude it is valuable. Russell believed that there is "an element of wisdom to be learned from the mystical way of feeling, which does not seem to be attainable in any other manner" and thus that mysticism can be "commended as an attitude towards life" but not as a "creed about the world" because "this emotion, as colouring and informing all other thoughts and feelings, is the inspirer of whatever is best in Man" and even science "may be fostered and nourished by that very spirit of reverence in which mysticism lives and moves" (Russell 1918: 11–12).

However, mystical experiences and their cultivation have been absorbed into modern culture without much interest in understanding what has been experienced. With the loss of interest in classical mystical ways of life, any claim that mystical experiences provide possible cognitive insights into a nonnatural reality is not so much denied as simply ignored or not even noticed. Any cognitive component to mystical experiences is reduced to an awareness of aspects of the natural realm. All that matters is the natural realm—here, the psychophysiological well-being that mystical experiences, meditation, or psychedelics may foster. One need not consider a nonnaturalist worldview to provide an explanation when neurological theories of the brain explain all that is of value. That is, when the only interest is a pragmatic one of whether meditation or psychedelics work for better psychophysiological conditions, doctrines on the relation between the states of consciousness attained and reality or whether one gains an insight into reality or participates in a nonnatural reality do not matter. Only such practical worldly effects of a mystical experience are of interest. William Richards tells of a successful business leader who had a spontaneous experience that met all the criteria of mystical consciousness—the man's reaction was "That was nice. What is it good for?" (2016: 124). And mystical experiences may be generally useful for (or at least a useful indicator of) increases in a sense of well-being: one study of a decade and a half of research reported that increased well-being "is one of the most reliable psychological changes following a psychedelic experience" (Peill et al. 2022: 12).

Since for naturalists only the natural world matters, mystical experiences in a naturalist framework can still be seen as aligning experiencers with how things really are if they enable experiencers to have greater personal well-being and to function better in the world. Consciousness can be seen as a purely evolved natural phenomenon. Losing a sense of a "self" is consistent with naturalism (e.g., Austin 1998). Even if the sense of a "self" evolved because it has advantages for survival, it appears that it can be overcome in the "pure consciousness" type of mystical experience. And incorporating such selflessness into one's life makes one a mystic. This is consistent with the causal closure of the natural realm and the completeness of physical causes if consciousness is treated as a powerless epiphenomenon that we can bring into our direct awareness (Angel 2002, 2004).

Thus, mystical experiences can be taken as making us more at home here: with no nonnatural realities such as a "soul" to worry about, such experiences make us feel more connected to reality (as defined by naturalists) and thus help us overcome any emotional alienation from the natural world and from other people that our false sense of a separate "self" has generated. Secularists do not believe that they are being deluded by the material world and are out of step with reality—it is the traditional mystics with ideas of two realms who are deluded and need their beliefs corrected. This is our home—we are not "strangers in a strange land" exiled from our true home.

Is Secular "Mysticism" a Legitimate Mysticism?

Secularizing mysticism may seem to remove the aura of specialness to mystical experiences and mysticism. Secular mysticism also raises four questions for the philosophy of mysticism. The first is raised by the claim that there are mystical experiences and yet no nonnatural realities such as god, no nonpersonal reality such as Brahman, or no personal nonnatural soul. Can introvertive mystical experiences actually not involve nonnatural realities? Are naturalists simply deluding themselves that the experiences are purely natural? That is, is something that transcends the natural realm really present in these experiences despite the fact that secularists do not believe so? In short, is a truly secular mysticism actually a distortion of what is occurring in mystical experiences and thus is not a legitimate mysticism?

However, what realities are actually involved in introvertive mystical experiences is impossible to determine by a scientific experiment. There is no test to determine if the experiences are purely natural or involve some nonnatural element: all scientists have are the reports of brain activity during these events. It is like the problem of detecting consciousness: if we look at neuroscientific reports, there is no evidence of consciousness at all—all there is is the activity of the material brain. From neuroscience alone, there is no reason to believe that there is consciousness. And the same problem arises for nonnatural realities that might be involved in mystical experiences enabled by either meditation or psychedelics. Naturalists may be right that the experiences do not involve nonnatural realities. Even depth-mystical experiences do not prove that consciousness is independent of the body and transcends the natural cosmos—the experiences are possible even if consciousness is an emergent property, a reducible property, or a panpsychic property. The phenomenology of the experience of the "empty" state of pure consciousness would be the same whether a nonnatural reality is present or not. The experiences may have the same base in the brain whether there are nonnatural realities involved or not. Theists and other nonnaturalists cannot show that the experiences must be neurologically different if no nonnatural realities are involved.[18] Nonnaturalists cannot demonstrate that experiences cannot be purely natural, nor can naturalists demonstrate that they are. Both parties are rational in accepting their position, at least as far as what science can demonstrate, and scientific results are all that naturalists will recognize as legitimate reasons.

Thus, we are in a position that naturalists may rationally accept that mystical experiences are purely natural events generated by the brain. From the science alone, nonnaturalists cannot demonstrate that naturalists are necessarily wrong or showing bad faith. Nonnaturalist metaphysics are not required to understand the nature and significance of these experiences, and nonnaturalists cannot demonstrate that mystical experiences are impossible without nonnatural realities. And thus, naturalists are within their epistemic rights (at least as far as science goes) to accept a secular mysticism. So too, they can treat mysticism spiritually within that framework, since for them the natural realm is the only reality or at least the only reality that we are aware of.

In sum, a secular life incorporating these experiences of selflessness constitutes a legitimate mysticism. There are a few secular humanist organizations that may or may not include secular mystics. Overall, secular mysticism may remain an individualist phenomenon—indeed, a self-centered phenomenon—with individuals unconnected to mystical traditions or other groups in their selection of beliefs and practices. However, the lack of an organized community does not make secular mysticism less spiritual or mystical.

Must Mystical Experiences Be Cognitive of Nonnatural Realities?

The second philosophical impact that secular mysticism has is on the epistemological question of whether mystical experiences give any insight into reality or other knowledge. Since William James, the claim that mystical experiences have a "noetic" quality (1958 [1902]: 293) has been a central issue in the philosophy of mysticism—i.e., the experiences allegedly give us direct insights into some aspect of reality.[19] Both extrovertive and introvertive experiences are traditionally deemed to be cognitive, offering direct and unmediated insights into the natural world in extrovertive experiences or nonnatural realities in introvertive experiences. However, if naturalists can have mystical experiences that do not even appear to the experiencers to give any insights into nonnatural realities but have only affective elements or at best give them nothing more than mundane insights into something that is only natural—either the being of the natural universe or the nature of the natural mind—we have to ask whether mystics' nonnaturalist knowledge claims come only from the teaching of their traditions rather than from mystical experiences and to ask what role, if any, these experiences actually play in the beliefs that mystics hold.

To naturalists, any mystical knowledge can involve only the natural realm. Loosening a sense of a "self" and the conceptual framework in our perceptions may lead to extrovertive mystical experiences that lead to awe, wonder, and a sense of connection to others and nature, but this does not mean that they offer insights we cannot attain through other means. At best, the experiences show us nature more intensely or highlight the natural connection ("oneness") of all things in the universe as products of the Big Bang. Introvertive experiences at best show us only aspects of our mind or new functions of naturally evolved consciousness. We cannot simply assume that introvertive experiences must be of a nonnatural god, soul, or other reality even though theists routinely do. Claiming that God was experienced is the automatic go-to position in Western cultures for any overwhelming experience, but naturalists have now offered a reasonable alternative of what the experiences involve. Theists have not demonstrated that secular mystical experiences differ in nature or that the phenomenology of the experiences (rather than the differences in postexperiential reports) differs in nature for naturalists and nonnaturalists (see chapter 2). Theists may assert that there is a difference between mystical experiences when natural triggers and a transcendent reality is involved, but that it is a difference that science in principle cannot detect. But naturalists would leave matters with only what science can detect.

Thus, secular mysticism offers another front against the alleged cross-cultural "common core" argument for the validity of mystical claims—i.e., that the cross-cultural presence of mystical experiences means they must be cognitive.[20] As noted above, to naturalists our common neurophysiology is what explains the apparent similarity of the phenomenology of mystical experiences across cultures and eras, not a common cognition of alleged nonnatural realities. That mystical experiences *feel* insightful does not mean that they are—the sense of profundity results only from the stimulation by drugs or meditation of areas of the brain connected to a sense of importance. Alternatively, naturalists can offer arguments that the experiences are indeed insights that may transform a person, but they are only insights into the natural realm and natural mind (see Letheby 2017, 2021). Any "mystical wisdom" is limited to a profound sense of reality and a connection to other persons and to the rest of the natural realm, not any more concrete doctrines or values.

In this way, secular mysticism points to the issue of mystical experiences themselves versus the understanding provided by the experiencer after the experience. No doubt most experiencers today see a transcendent religious significance in these experiences, but a naturalist explanation has become a viable cultural option for understanding these experiences, and this amplifies the philosophical issue of what exactly one actually realizes in a mystical experience. As things stand, we cannot tell, based on the experiences alone, if theists experience God or have the same mystical experiences as nontheists but only interpret them post facto to be experiences of God.

This in turn leads to the matter of what constitutes mystical *knowledge* (see R. Jones 2016: 71–120). What role do the experiences play and what role do the doctrines of a mystic's religion play in what is taken to be "mystical knowledge"? What do mystics actually learn only from the experiences themselves? Even if only relatively few experiencers today explicitly endorse the metaphysics of naturalism, many implicitly assume that there is no awareness or knowledge of nonnatural realities involved in these experiences since for them only the secular effects are of importance. If secularists can easily come away from these experiences without a sense of insight into nonnatural realities, that some mystical experiences must involve some transcendent reality becomes more uncertain than in the past, when the only options were that a transcendent reality of some type was experienced or that the brain was malfunctioning. Nonnaturalists will have to come up with arguments for why naturalists are mistaken that are not based on the experiences themselves. This highlights not only the question of what mystics actually know but also the broader question of the role of experiences and beliefs in any claim to empirical knowledge.

The Question of the Role of Beliefs in Mystical Experiences

The last issue also highlights the constructivist issue: do cultural influences penetrate some or all types of mystical experiences or only the postexperiential reports? Naturalists can readily agree that beliefs or other cultural influences permeate the experiences: that religious beliefs about transcendent realities affect the experiences themselves does not mean that nonnatural realities are involved but only that experiencers' beliefs affect the content of these natural experiences. But naturalists need not require a cultural influence on mystical experiences—such experiences could still be only a culture-neutral matter of the natural mind. Nevertheless, naturalists may well accept that our experiences of ourselves and the world are profoundly contingent and constructed (e.g., Letheby 2021: 219). And it should be noted that naturalists are as much subject to cultural influences as nonnaturalists, even when the influences are purely secular. Thus, if culture shapes mystical experiences, secular mystical experiences are as open to shaping as nonnaturalist ones. So, does secular mysticism offer any new light on the constructivist issue?

Constructivists assert that the conceptual construction of mystical experience themselves by cultural influences—i.e., religious and other cultural beliefs, expectations, and so forth—penetrate mystical experiences and not merely the postexperiential understanding given by mystics.[21] Thus, there is no way to separate mystical experiences completely from their interpretations, since our conceptual apparatus shapes our experiences. Constructivism's epistemic premise is that all human experience is necessarily structured by elements of culture, in particular by language—the mind never transcends language in any cognition. Thus, mystical experiences "are inescapably shaped by prior linguistic influences such that the lived experience conforms to a preexistent pattern that has been learned, then intended, and then actualized in the experiential reality of the mystic" (Katz 1992: 5). There is no direct (i.e., unmediated) experiences of any reality (Katz 1978: 26). Soft constructivism is the view that there are no mystical experiences without at least some concepts provided by one's culture that filter and structure any experiential input but that the experiential input still plays a role in mystical knowledge. Hard constructivists hold that a mystic's specific cultural background completely determines the nature and alleged cognitive content of all mystical experiences, not merely shapes or influences an independent experiential element. In fact, according to Stephen Katz, mystics' socioreligious milieu "*overdetermines*" the cognitive content of mystical experiences (1978: 46). Both soft and hard constructivist arguments have been mobilized against the possibility of pure consciousness events. Nonconstructivists assert that some or all mystical experiences are in fact free of cultural influences.

One's beliefs can later alter one's opinion of what happened in a mystical experience. Martin Buber gives an account (quoted in chapter 5) of his felt sense of "undivided unity" that he initially interpreted to be unity with the Godhead, but his later "responsible understanding" was that he actually experienced only the unity of his soul (1947: 24). The latter understanding was dictated by his theistic background in which the gulf between God and creature is unbridgeable. But this change in understanding did not affect his sense of the character of the experience itself, in which he felt an "undivided unity." The same can occur with secularists. John Horgan gives the account of a psychedelic-enabled experience he had in which he was convinced he was approaching "absolute reality, the source of all things, God" and that he "*knew*" that there is no death." But then the "ground of being was yanked" from under him, and he "*knew* that life is ephemeral; death and nothingness are the only abiding certainties" and that "there is no ground of being, no omnipotent God to catch us" (2003: 13–14; emphasis in the original).

These later changes in interpretation complicate the constructivist issue: it is not clear how the prior cultural understanding affected the experiences themselves. Mystical experiences among the secular will be different to the extent that cultural concepts are components of the experiences, but they would be as constructed as those of traditional religious experiencers—the structuring would only be secular cultural elements, and the experiences would be the same general nature. However, it is not easy to see how to determine whether concepts are experiential components. The principal difficulty in resolving the issue is that all we ever have are only mystics' *postexperiential accounts*, which all parties agree are shaped by a mystic's culture—we can never get to the experiences themselves to see if they are constructed or not. Nor can we demonstrate through neuroscanning the brain that the phenomenology of the experiences differs for mystics with different beliefs undergoing the same meditative practices or psychedelic treatment. Secularists can feel overwhelmed and bathed in love without concluding that a nonnatural god is its source rather than the bliss resulting from emptying the mind of all content. In such circumstances, theists cannot demonstrate that mystical experiences taken to be theistic necessarily differ in content from "natural" mystical experiences. The effects of similar meditations after the experience may differ for the spiritual and the nonspiritual (see, e.g., Wachholtz and Pargament 2005), but the issue here is whether the content of the experiences themselves differ.[22]

Secular mysticism might appear to offer a new opportunity of examining the constructivist claim: we can examine experiencers with competing understandings of the significance (nonnaturalist and naturalist) who are present in the same culture at the same time. Experiencers today are also aware of viable competing interpretations of the nature and significance of mystical experiences. But the basic roadblock remains of not having direct access to the phenomenology of these experiences by third persons to determine their content.

Secular Mysticism and the Meaning of Life

The search for the meaning of life is a matter of trying to see why things exist and are the way they are and how we fit in the big picture. Such a search makes even a secular mysticism spiritual. And this raises a fourth philosophical issue for secular mysticism: can the effect of mystical experiences lead to a meaningful and fulfilling life or sense of purpose without some reference to realities that transcend the natural realm? In fact, according to Owen Flanagan (2007; Flanagan and Caruso 2018), the "really hard problem" for naturalists is not the "hard problem" in consciousness studies of why subjectivity is attached to apparently nonconscious physical events in the brain but how to find meaning in a universe void of nonnatural foundations or life after death. How can naturalists overcome a sense of existential anxiety and find meaning in their lives in a disenchanted world? Can there be a meaning when all there is is only the soulless material universe? Don't we need something *transcending* the natural realm to give this realm a meaning? But isn't everything, as Peter Atkins says, "driven by motiveless, purposeless decay" (1994: 23)? Wasn't the physicist Steven Weinberg correct when he said "[t]he more the universe seems comprehensible, the more it also seems pointless" (1977: 154)? Aren't existentialists correct when they say the universe is "absurd"? When we yearn for meaning, isn't all we get, in Albert Camus's words, "the unreasonable silence of the world"? We appear to be a short-lived evolved animal that loses any significance in the vastness of the universe. Individually, we live for a brief blip of time in only one life and then are gone—no aspect of us survives. Collectively, after our planet or galaxy dies, we do not leave even a dent in the universe. It is as if we were never here. Moreover, the standard naturalist view is that we have no meaningful libertarian free will—our actions are determined by material events. Similarly, our consciousness is a powerless epiphenomenon of matter. Morality or any concern for others has no ultimate foundation. During an introvertive mystical experience or a state of pure mindfulness, the issue of meaningfulness does not arise—one is totally absorbed in the moment and so one is not interested in there being a point to things or the meaning of life—but can such experiences contribute to a later understanding of meaning and purpose or otherwise aid in overcoming any existential crisis for naturalists?

It should be realized, however, that the picture need not be so bleak from a naturalist's point of view. By removing the possibility of otherworldly nonnatural realities from the picture, our consciousness is not split between two realms. We can now focus totally on the world and other people and not have our mind distracted by attention to nonexistent nonnatural realities and otherworldly aspirations. Nor need we puzzle over questions related to transcendent realities such as why and how God exists, what his purpose for creation and humanity is, or how he could affect events in the world. Indeed, the natural realm can seem *more real* than it does within a nonnaturalist framework, where it is a product dependent upon a more real nonnatural reality. This allows for a more authentic existence in this life and a greater appreciation of the beauty and mystery of nature. Realizing that we are dependent upon other people and the world for our existence gives them a greater significance than they would have if we were creations of some other reality. As for whether science reveals the universe to be meaningless: science is not designed to find purpose or meaning any more than neuroscience is currently designed to find consciousness, and so science's lack of finding meaning is irrelevant to the question. Freeman Dyson's reply to Weinberg—that no universe with conscious life is pointless (Horgan 2003: 222)—is an option for naturalists. So too, some naturalists have offered reasonable alternatives to the denial of the reality of free will and consciousness. Morality has the only grounding it needs: like us, other people and other sentient parts of the web of existence suffer, and so we should adopt moral values out of a concern for them. Attaching greater significance to our own personal node in the web is a selfishness that does not reflect reality—we are all equal parts of that web. The universe provides conditions for our flourishing (along with causing us suffering). That we are here at all is amazing—small outcroppings of consciousness in a vast material expanse. Life is an unmerited gift. It is a cause for celebration. Even the inevitability of dying and returning whatever is real to the whole that is the universe can be accepted calmly with reverence. Naturalists can react with joy, awe, and gratitude for being alive (Kurtz 2005). Learning, helping others, and contributing to the overall welfare of what is on our planet can provide a meaningful life in light of what is truly real. In sum, a pessimistic reading of naturalism is not required by science or otherwise.

For naturalists, mystical experiences do not give any knowledge that is not attainable by other means, but they do make us more aware of the reality of the universe and our being in it. Traditional mysticism is seen not as a means to align ourselves with reality but only a way to evade it. Nevertheless, mysticism understood within a naturalist framework helps us overcome a false sense of an isolated "self" and makes us feel our connectedness to all that is real—we are all specks of stardust with no separate entity (a "self") to enhance at the expense of others. We can transcend the false sense of "self" without a dimension transcending the natural world being needed. This also opens us up to what is truly real and thus helps us to align with reality as it truly is. Mysticism helps us gain awe and wonder at what is truly real and makes for a more spiritual approach to the world and ourselves.

In fact, without a religious interpretative framework, some mystical experiences may not have positive effects but may lead instead to less well-being (see Byrd, Lear, and Schwenka 2000). Thus, secular mystics and other naturalists will have to work out a naturalist framework in which mystical experiences (including the different types of introvertive ones) are a source of meaning if mystical experiences are not to have a negative psychological effect. A first step is that the mystical experiences can be treated positively as cognitive of natural realities (see Angel 2002, 2004). Any meaning or purpose that would resonate with naturalists must be sought within this world, but it is possible for naturalists to work out a meaning of life within their framework (see R. Jones 2018a: 167–70; Hearn 2021). Thus, a nonnaturalist framework is not required for a sense of meaning. As just discussed, science is not designed to find meaning, and so we cannot expect it to find something it is not designed to find. Thus, another approach will be needed. That some naturalists decide that the lack of meaningfulness in the scientific picture means the cosmos is meaningless shows only that they do not understand or appreciate the limits of science's design.

Finding meaning in the natural cosmos is part of what would make a secular mysticism a mysticism. The loss of a sense of a self in a secular mysticism can lead to a greater sense of being connected to others or to the rest of reality and to a sense of purpose and profound meaning. Theists may object and insist that a transcendent framework of meaning is needed to make life meaningful, but questions of whether any sense of meaning can be objective or ultimate even with transcendent sources remain (R. Jones 2018a: 165–67, 177–78).

Mysticism cannot overcome the basic mystery of why anything exists—in fact, the shock of the unexpected in these experiences may accentuate this mystery. But it can help us greet there being anything at all with amazement and fascination and lessen any dread at being alive. Psychedelic experiences in general may lessen the fear of death (Sweeney et al. 2022). Overall, mystical experiences may transform a person even within a naturalist framework.

The Future of Mysticism?

All in all, secular mysticism appears to be a viable option in today's cultural marketplace. This mysticism is a paradigm of applied mysticism: it takes mystical practices and experiences away from their traditional role in religious traditions of a total transformation of an individual and applies them to help with more limited problems of this-worldly well-being for individuals and for society in general. This shows how the inward power of psychedelic "sacramental drugs" (and meditation) can be used for the welfare of people living in a technological society hostile to mystical revelations (A. Hoffman 1999 [1977]: iv). Beyond applied mysticism, a new secular form of mysticism has also arisen, even if no complete psychedelic religion (as in Aldous Huxley's novel *Island*) has yet emerged. Psychedelics become a "technology" for the "spiritual realization" of an "existential unification of the self with nature" leading to human flourishing (Steinhart 2018) and our search for meaning.

Secular mysticism shows that mysticism need not be tied to belief in transcendent realities, despite its traditional appeal. Mystical experiences in which a sense of a confined, narrow "self" vanishes and we feel connected to reality can be incorporated into a naturalist worldview without great difficulty and can figure in a specifically naturalized spirituality. The experiences themselves do not conflict with what is deemed a "scientific worldview." Nothing about mystical experiences is irrational by naturalist standards once they are understood within the naturalist framework. Both meditation and psychedelic drugs may be utilized. This adds a specific experiential dimension to a naturalist spirituality. And when mystical experiences are incorporated into a naturalist's way of life, the resulting secular spirituality is indeed a mysticism. As noted above, naturalists may be reticent to employ the term "mysticism," but the term is appropriate in a naturalized spiritual context incorporating these experiences and practices, and there are no better current labels. Naturalists need not use the term "entheogen" to denote psychedelics even if their mysticism is a new category of "religiosity."

Such a naturalization of mystical experience will be a challenge to traditional religions by offering a viable alternative spirituality. Nonnaturalists may object to any naturalization or this-worldly secularization of these experiences. They will claim that naturalists misunderstand what is actually occurring in mystical experiences. Naturalists will reverse the charge. And it does appear that introvertive mystical experiences are not necessarily tied to nonnatural realities but can be disentangled from nonnaturalist metaphysics. Any cognition in those experiences may be limited to the nature of the natural world or the human mind.

It is interesting to note that many in mainstream Abrahamic religions today would be as happy to jettison all talk of mysticism as most naturalists are. In the modern era, mainstream Abrahamic theisms have exhibited hostility to mysticism and psychedelics, but this obviously does not reflect the entire history of each of these religions—that the Abrahamic traditions each have rich mystical traditions does not need documenting here (see R. Jones 2024: chapters 4–6). There is also long history of the religious use of entheogens in religion beginning in our prehistory (e.g., Winkelman 2019; Muraresku 2020). Controversial claims of their use in biblical and postbiblical Judaism (e.g., Shanon 2008) and Christianity (e.g., Merkur 2001) are also worth noting. Today a few Christian churches make psychedelics part of their ceremonies (e.g., the Santo Daime churches in Brazil [Barnard 2014]), and some advocates of psychedelics are trying to make them part of more mainstream religious ceremonies (e.g., Forte 1997; Roberts 2012, 2020).

But these currently are outliers. In the modern West, there has been a steep decline in traditional mysticism within the Abrahamic religions (see R. Jones 2024: chapter 10). Individual members may practice mindfulness or other forms of meditation outside the institutions, but few accept the rigors of traditional mysticism. Catholicism has been more welcoming to mysticism than Protestantism, but a generation ago the Trappist monk Thomas Merton complained that there were few or no real contemplatives even in many Catholic contemplative monasteries because rigid conformity to rules prevented it (2003: 78, 123–30). According to the Benedictine monk Willigis Jager, there has been no place for mysticism in Christian theology for two hundred years (2006: xix). He could not find contemplative teachers in his order and had to get permission to study with Zen Buddhist teachers. In contrast, the most prominent Catholic theologian in the second half of the twentieth century, Karl Rahner, predicted that "the Christian of the future will be a mystic [i.e., one who has experienced God] or not be a Christian at all": in Western society today, institutional support for Christianity has lessened, and so Christianity will have to be grounded in individuals who have had immediate experiences of God (1984: 22).[23] David Hay says of our culture: "[W]hen meditation and contemplative prayer are ignored or disparaged, a large part of our natural human competence is being denied, and, with it, dimensions of the self that make both religion and ethics a possibility, and the human community a reality" (1994: 150).

Many object to the watered-down mindfulness practices adapted from modern forms of Buddhism that are now employed in secular settings such as psychotherapy, dismissing it as "Buddhism-Lite" or "McMindfulness" (see Joiner 2017; Purser 2019). Now "second-generation" mindfulness programs have attempted to restore the original cultural context of mindfulness practices within a Buddhist way of life leading toward a transformative enlightenment (see Kirmayer 2015; Samuel 2015; Van Gordon 2020; Zheng 2022). However, perhaps in an era of pluralism and decline in the participation in religious institutions, the immediate future of mysticism lies in a secular form: the value of mystical experiences will be seen only in their demonstrable ability to provide quick fixes to this-worldly problems, not in any of the alleged nonnatural cognitions fostered by classical mysticism. Any sense of meaning will be confined to the natural realm. This mysticism will reflect today's valuation of the individual. Mystical experiences will no doubt continue to occur as always, but the focus for many will be on the secular effects of the experiences themselves and not on explanations of them in transcendent terms or practicing a way of life geared toward aligning one's life with reality understood to include transcendent realities. In the study of mysticism, any connection of mysticism to transcendent realities can no longer simply be presumed. That is, as mysticism continues to evolve, full mystical ways of life and traditional mystical training will continue to decline. The terms "mysticism" and "mystical experience" may be replaced as old-fashioned and having too many transcendent connotations, even as the phenomena covered by those terms remains common.[24] Neuroscientific explanations will become more and more accepted as sufficient explanations of the experiences. That is, in the short term secular mysticism may well keep gaining support. What the long-term future of mysticism—what shape it takes and whether traditional mysticism retakes a prominent place within the religious traditions—will be probably depends on what the future of religion will be.

But secular mysticism should not be seen as a totally negative phenomenon. Naturalists can accept neurophysiological benefits that mystical experiences might engender, and they can also argue that mystical experiences may help us overcome any sense of isolation from the rest of the natural world and from other people by helping us realize that we are thoroughly embedded in the world and connected to each other. They may even accept that these experiences offer some insights into the nature of the mind or the world, or at least give us a more experiential sense of our state in the world. Secular mysticism may even enhance a sense of mystery at the heart of reality, even if reality is confined to the natural world.

Chapter 9

Quantum Mysticism

Science Meets Mysticism in the New Age

The New Age movement as it has developed over the last few decades involves a spirituality that draws on Western and Eastern religious and esoteric traditions, psychology, holistic health programs, and other sources (see Lewis and Melton 1992). Many New Agers are enthusiastic about science and seek support for their holistic claims on mind, body, and spirit and on the unity of the world in consciousness research and natural science—in particular, quantum physics. The New Age claims about the relation of mysticism and science will be the focus here.[1]

Buddhism was first portrayed as scientific by Western apologists in the mid–nineteenth century. Soon Western–influenced neo-Vedantists were doing the same for Hinduism. In the first half of the last century, some major physicists showed interest in mysticism (Wilber 2000 [1984]).[2] With a few exceptions, the issue of the relation of mysticism and science languished quietly until being revived in the 1960s and took off in the mid-1970s, when Fritjof Capra (2010 [1975]) and Gary Zukav (2001 [1977]) published books that are still popular today. The former's *The Tao of Physics* is considered "one of the canonical books of the New Age movement" (Brooke and Cantor 1998: 80) and "the epitome of New Age science in the eyes of the public" (Hanegraaff 1998: 74). Works on how mystical ideas may have influenced physics have also appeared (Kaiser 2011; R. Jones 2015 [2010]: chapter 4).[3]

However, works on the relation of mysticism and science have remained largely confined to New Age writers. A few recent scientists have shown interest in mysticism, but probably more scientists today would agree with Stephen Hawking, who, in responding to his colleague Brian Josephson's interest in Asian mysticism, said that the idea of mystical influence on science is "pure rubbish," adding: "The universe of Eastern mysticism is an illusion. A physicist who attempts to link it with his own work has abandoned physics" (quoted in Boslough 1985: 12).[4]

But there are social reasons for seeking harmony here. On the one hand, by the 1970s the reputation of science was declining in popular culture because of its increasing ties to high-tech industries and the military. Capra explicitly asserted that his book aimed "at improving the image of science by showing that there is an essential harmony between the spirit of Eastern wisdom and Western science" (2010 [1975]: 31). The sociological Sal Restivo (1978, 1982) has extensively discussed the role of the alleged convergence in rehabilitating science's image at the time. On the other hand, seeing mysticism and science converging is a desideratum in New Age thought: it would give the imprimatur of science to New Age spirituality, and it also removes one general popular reason to reject mysticism—the notion that mysticism necessarily conflicts with science. But the New Age claim is not merely that science and mysticism are compatible or that scientific findings support mystical claims. Rather, a staple of New Age thought is that today science and Asian mystical claims are actually merging. That is, after hundreds of years of strenuous work, modern scientists are finally discovering what mystics have known for thousands of years. It is as if scientists, after struggling up the mountain of empirical knowledge, find mystics meditating at the top.

In the eyes of New Agers, the old "dualistic" and "reductive" science arising from Newtonian physics is being replaced, and today relativity, particle physics, and biology are becoming one with the doctrines of Buddhism or of an abstract "Eastern mysticism." The popular alternative-medicine practitioner Deepak Chopra tells us that scientists have "wound up with nothing less than a mystic's universe" (2012: ix). Others tell us that the Buddha made claims about subatomic levels of structures that are only now finally being confirmed by scientists. Buddhists have "uncovered at least the basic principles of subatomic physics through their meditation practices" (Nisker 1998: 18) and modern physics "echoes" the investigations of Buddhism (Ricard and Thuan 2001: 10). The mystic and the physicist reach the "same conclusion" about the "unity" of things, one starting from exploring the inner realm of consciousness and the other from exploring the external world (Capra 2017: 16). Mystics experience directly the same "truth" that scientists discover intellectually. In the end, mystics and scientists are saying the same thing, just in "different languages" (Capra 2010 [1975]: 8; Mansfield 2008: 88, 141, 162). Seen this way, post-Newtonian science becomes a way to gain mystical knowledge and enlightenment.

The Vagueness of the New Age Claims

Many people no doubt are attracted to the idea that science and spirituality say the same thing or that there is a harmonious oneness to reality that scientists find externally and mystics find internally. But establishing that is not a simple matter. The reasoning of those who see parallels between mysticism and science—the "parallelists" (Restivo 1978)—seems to be this: parallelists compare statements from scientific and mystical texts, and "if the rhetorical, imagery, and metaphoric content of statements on physics and mysticism is similar, the conceptual content must be similar, and the experience of reality must also be similar among physicists and mystics" (Restivo 1978: 151). Thus, the claims of scientists and mystics must be substantively the same or at least on the way to converging.

Unfortunately, the New Age enthusiasm for the convergence of science and mysticism is not well grounded. Mysticism and science could converge in two ways: mystical claims about the nature of the world could converge with scientific theories, or mystical experiences as a particular way of knowing reality could converge with the "scientific method" as a way of knowing reality.[5] But one persistent problem is that parallelists do not clarify what precisely they are claiming. They throw together an amalgam of different ideas: science and mysticism "share the same insight" or have "common ground"; they are "harmonious" or "consistent"; scientific claims "mirror" mystical claims; scientific claims are "implicit" in mystical insights; each endeavor has "implications" for the other; the two have a "synergy"; mysticism "anticipates" or "resonates with" scientific claims; science "validates," "verifies," or "confirms" mystical claims or vice versa; there is a "fusion" or "integration" occurring between the two; or the "confluence" of science and mysticism will produce something new. Moreover, the alleged relations are advanced without precise definitions or specifications of how exactly, for example, science can verify a mystical metaphysical claim.

The most commonly used terms are "parallels," "converges," "complements," and "confirms." But parallelists use these concepts without realizing that they are quite different: if mystical claims parallel scientific claims, then the claims are fulfilling analogous roles in different conceptual systems, but their substantive content is different, so they cannot converge; if the claims are converging, they are not separate complements; if the claims are complements, they are not confirming each other; indeed, if science and mysticism are complements, they cannot directly influence or affect each other but are separate endeavors that give some knowledge that the other omits; one endeavor cannot both complement and reveal the other's truths at the same time; if there is a fusion or integration, then the claim is not about current theories in science and mysticism being the same but a call to produce something new. Nevertheless, parallelists throw these terms around haphazardly, sometimes in the same sentence (e.g., Ricard and Thuan 2001: 276).

Capra sees science as "fully confirming" the oneness that is the "key characteristic" of spiritual experiences (2017: 17). But parallelists miss an ambiguity in the terms "unity" and "oneness." These terms may refer to (1) an introvertive unified state of consciousness free of any differentiations (an introvertive state of "pure" consciousness), (2) the oneness of the beingness of the natural realm, (3) an extrovertive state seeing the integration and interconnection of all the phenomena in the world, or (4) a partless source of the natural realm. An introvertive *partless oneness*, as in Advaita Vedanta's transcendent consciousness, has nothing to do with a *connection of the parts of the phenomenal world* in Buddhism, but parallelists cite mystics discussing the former as support for the latter. Parallelists also tend to treat all mystical experiences as the same in nature rather than distinguishing fundamentally different types (see R. Jones 2021a: chapter 2), and they see the only import of all these experiences as showing *the interconnection of things*. This does not distinguish the "empty" state of consciousness from the different metaphysical understandings of what was actually experienced in that state and mistakenly reduces the different understandings to only one set of beliefs.

Parallelists make much of the problems that practitioners in the two different endeavors have with language when encountering phenomena outside the everyday realm of experience. Apparent paradoxes appear in both endeavors. Nevertheless, parallelists cannot make any substantive convergence out of these problems. Merely because both scientists and mystics have problems expressing what they encounter does not mean that they must be encountering the *same thing*. Both mystics and scientists must extend language through metaphors when encountering what is outside the everyday realm, but this is not a very profound commonality, especially since philosophers and linguists now point out that all our thought is permeated with metaphors. All the use of metaphors means is that mystical and scientific thought is human thought encountering something new. It tells us nothing more about what they are talking about. Nor does it give any reason to suggest that scientists and mystics are encountering the same nonordinary reality—simply because discussing God and the quantum realm presents problems does not mean that God is the quantum realm. Similarly, mysticism and science may share some abstract vocabulary, but the terms in the actual contexts of their systems of thought show that their referents diverge. More argument is needed to make that equation.

Do Science and Mysticism Have the Same Subject Matter?

The epistemic differences between mysticism and science may not be as great as is usually supposed, but the difference in their subject matter and objectives forecloses any substantive convergences, even when their terminology seems to converge in the abstract.[6] But New Age claims on the convergence of mysticism and science are in fact groundless because mysticism and science deal with different dimensions of reality: the structures of nature versus its sure "beingness."

Parallelists usually go no further into the nature of science than noting that science involves empirical observations and then claiming that Newtonian science is reductive.[7] Only one point about science must be emphasized here: basic science is about how things in nature work—i.e., identifying the hidden structures in nature responsible for the lawful changes in phenomena that we observe and offering both explanations of phenomena in terms of these underlying causes and also theories of those structures' nature that ultimately depend on observations checkable by others. Realists and antirealists disagree on whether we can gain any genuine knowledge of those alleged causal structures that we cannot experience. But all agree that scientific knowledge will be tentative and open to revision.

Mystical experiences, in contrast, occur in altered states of consciousness (ASC) that focus on *the "beingness" of the natural world* in extrovertive experiences or *its source* (consciousness or a transcendent reality) in introvertive experiences.[8] Introvertive experiences allegedly are of the transcendent partless source of the being in the experiencer or in the entire world. Extrovertive mindfulness focuses attention on the impermanence and connectedness of the macro-objects we experience in the everyday world, and mindfulness claims remain in that realm. These experiences allegedly expose something constant and uniform about all of the natural realm regardless of any particular state of affairs, while science focuses on the latter and their changes. The focus is not on all mystical traditions but on Buddhism (and to a lesser extent Daoism) because its extrovertive mysticism emphasizes the connection and impermanence of the parts of the phenomenal world. The experienced sense of oneness in the state of "pure consciousness" is given difference metaphysical understandings in different mystical traditions. There is no one generic "mystical" set of beliefs but a great diversity among the world mystical traditions, including within Hinduism (see R. Jones 2024). Traditions that emphasize introvertive mystical experiences do not discuss the impermanence and connectedness of phenomena the way that Buddhism and other extrovertive traditions do—that certainly is not the "essence" of all mysticism.

Parallelists emphasize Buddhism on the impermanence and conditionality of phenomena. The phenomena of the quantum realm are also seen by scientists as impermanent and conditioned. The claims are indeed parallel to that extent. But the Buddhist claims remain about the surface world. It is not as if Buddhists were aware of quantum events and were making claims about them. Some New Agers do contend that we can be directly aware of the quantum realm (e.g., Wendt 2105; also see Kripal 2019: 122–26, 162), but nothing in the Buddhist texts even indirectly indicates that the Buddha was talking about features of the submicroscopic world or that he experienced such phenomena even if awareness of that world were possible. He made no predictions about what would be found nor otherwise showed any interest in a subatomic realm. (It will be noted below that some early Buddhists advanced a view of unbreakable atoms, contrary to current quantum physics.) Like other extrovertive mystics, Buddhists claim to apprehend something common to all of the experienced world—the sheer "is-ness" of things in the phenomenal world—by lessening the grip that our mental conceptions normally have on our perceptions. The basic extrovertive mystical ontological claims are about everyday realities that can be directly experienced, not the quantum realm.

Scientists, in contrast, work through the mediation of our concepts to find *structures underlying the changes* we experience in the everyday world. This diverts attention away from what Buddhists consider important: the scientific focus is on how things work; the Buddhist focus is on the impermanence and conditionality of observed phenomena. In fact, for their purposes scientists can treat the phenomena of the everyday world as distinct from each other and static, unlike the Buddhist claim. Thus, quantum physics does not lead to the mystical claims.

Indeed, to do their job, scientists focus precisely on the *differentiations among phenomena* that mystics bypass. To determine how things work, scientists must distinguish objects and see how they interact with one another, and differentiations among phenomena are necessary for that. Physicists are interested only in what is measurable by the interaction of objects. This includes fields and the smaller and smaller bits of matter that are now being theorized. Even the mass of an object is measured only by the interaction of objects. And since beingness is common to all particulars, it cannot be studied scientifically: beingness is uniform for all phenomena, and thus it cannot be poked and prodded to see how it interacts with something else. Hence, no hypotheses about the nature of beingness can be scientifically tested in any way. Thus, beingness is not a different scientific level that scientists simply cannot reach externally. Rather, it is an aspect of reality that is free of the differentiations necessary to practice science.

This leads to a major difference in the *experiences* deemed central: scientists rely on ordinary sense experience for most cases, while mystics cultivate altered states of consciousness. Scientific experiences remain ordinary, everyday type observations, even when scientists are studying extraordinary parts of the world through experimentation or technology-enhanced observation; mystics' experiences are extraordinary even when they are looking at the ordinary. Scientists at best study ASCs only through ordinary experiences examining brain states.

In such circumstances, it is hard to argue that mystics are making claims about the underlying features of nature that scientists are revealing regarding the causes of things or that scientists are approaching the same aspect of reality as mystics are. Rather, mystics realize a dimension of reality that is missed in scientific knowledge and vice versa. Scientists and mystics each see something different about reality, and their subjects are irrelevant to each other. Thus, their claims do not cross, let alone converge, at any point. Both endeavors are interested in what is "fundamentally real" but in different aspects of it—they are not merely reaching the same substantive claims through different routes. Mystical experiences do not give us any scientific knowledge of reality, and no science gives us any mystical knowledge.

But New Age parallelists see only that both mystics and scientists are approaching reality and are out to gain knowledge; thus, they assume without further analysis that mystics and scientists are engaged in gaining the same type of knowledge through different techniques. Parallelists do not consider that there may be fundamentally different aspects of what is real that must be approached through different functions of the mind and that this would foreclose any substantive convergence of knowledge claims. This parallelist failure extends even to physicists making comparisons to Asian thought (e.g., Mansfield 1976, 1989, 2008).

The Tension between Mysticism and Science

To New Age advocates, the experiential nature of mysticism makes mystics more like scientists than practitioners of other forms of religiosity. However, they overlook how classical mystics' religious objectives affect their endeavor. For example, the point of the Buddha's teaching is to end the pervasive dissatisfaction, frustration, and suffering entailed by merely being alive (*duhkha*). Buddhism is not an applied mysticism of a "science of the mind" in any sense connected to natural science (contra Cabezón 2003: 49–50). Buddhism's central objective is not to acquire disinterested knowledge about how something works; rather it is to transform the person to end suffering. To substitute a disinterested focus on how the parts of nature work—including even the mental states involved in ending suffering—in order to learn more about the universe distorts the fundamental soteriological nature of Buddhism entirely. Today "neo-Buddhists," including the Dalai Lama, find scientific discoveries in physics, cosmology, and biology fascinating, but they must admit that such discoveries in the final analysis are irrelevant to their central quest. As the respected Theravada Buddhist scholar Walpola Rahula has said, while some parallels and similarities between Buddhism and modern science may be intellectually interesting, they are "peripheral and do not touch the essential part, the center, the core, the heart of Buddhism" (quoted in Verhoeven 2003: 45).

A scientific interest in nature's structures is not a path to a mystical enlightenment: identifying and explaining the structures of reality only increase attention to the differentiations in the world and will never lead to the calming of the mind by emptying it of differentiated content that leads to an experience of beingness. Science directs attention in the opposite direction from mysticism. The Buddha condemned astronomy/astrology as a wrong means of livelihood because it was unrelated to the religious concern (*Digha Nikaya* I.12.). The Buddha even forbade monks from practicing medicine, which would help others, since it interfered with their quest to end their own suffering (*Digha Nikaya* I.12, I. 67–69). To use the Buddhist analogy: if we are shot with a poison-tipped arrow, we do not ask who made the arrow or what the arrow is made of (or any other scientific question related to the arrow)—we just want a cure for the poison (*Majjhima Nikaya* I.63). So too, what is vital here and now is finding a way to the deathless state, not wasting time on scientific questions about the construction of the universe. The means to doing so is to end a false sense of permanence in the world and in the mental life, with its accompanying ungrounded emotions, not to learn the scientific mechanisms at work causing this sense, let alone all the other mechanisms in the world. The Buddha would no doubt leave all scientific questions unanswered (including those involving the brain) since they are irrelevant to the soteriological problem of suffering, just as he did with questions about the age and size of the universe (*Digha Nikaya* I.13, III.137; *Majjhima Nikaya* I.427; *Anguttara Nikaya* II.80). Overall, Buddhism has been hostile to science throughout its history (Lopez 2008: 216).

All classical mystical traditions have such religious goals and not interests in natural causes. Daoism in classical China is a good example of the rejection of the discursive type of knowledge of which science is the paradigm: the Daoist interest in nature remained contemplative and did not lead to a scientific interest in how things in nature work (see R. Jones 1993: chapter 6). We cannot simply equate any interest in nature with a scientific interest in understanding the hidden causal order behind things that explains how things work. Daoists were interested in flowing with patterns inherent in nature through nonassertive action (*wei wuwei*), not in any scientific findings or explanations of the efficient causes of those patterns. In the Daoist "forgetting" state of mind (*xu*), our mind is no longer guided by our own mentally conceived divisions of nature but responds spontaneously to what is presented without any preconceptions. Anything free of conceptions cannot guide scientific observations or theorizing since scientific observations and experiments involve predictions and theorizing based in our conceptions. This is not to deny that even enlightened mystics have internalized some concepts, knowledge, and an implicit worldview. In Zhuangzi's example of Ding the cook carving an ox (*Zhuangzi* 2), Ding had an objective and he achieved it. But he did not achieve it by studying anatomy: his mind naturally followed the true nature of things once he stopped letting any conceptual knowledge interfere with the flow of the Dao.

Overall, science increases the number of conceptual differentiations in our mind by its analyzing, selecting, measuring, and theorizing. It utilizes the analytical function of the mind and increases attention to the differentiations within the phenomenal world and thus diverts attention away from what mystics consider the only approach for aligning our lives with reality (calming the mind by freeing it of a sense of self and conceptual differentiations). For mystical experiences to occur, one needs to empty the mind of the very stuff that is central to science. The aim is to achieve a knowledge inaccessible to the analytical mind that is central to science.[9]

Thus, science and mysticism pull in opposite directions, and most practitioners of either endeavor may very well dismiss the other as a waste of valuable time and energy. This picture is complicated by the fact that mysticism involves more than just cultivating mystical experiences; it also involves attempts to understand the significance of these experiences and to lay out the general nature of a person, the world, and transcendent realities in order to live in accord with the way reality truly is (as defined by each particular mystic's own tradition). But this divergence of interests and subject matters in science and mysticism means that it is impossible to say that science and mysticism "converge" or that science "confirms" the specifically mystical claims of any tradition or vice versa.

The Difference in Contexts

In short, science and mysticism substantially diverge in their core subjects and interests. Nevertheless, most New Age parallelists see the same or similar terms being used in mysticism and in discussions of science but miss the differences in context and thus believe that mystics and scientists are discussing the same thing—i.e., extrovertive mystics are experiencing a holism to reality in an ASC that scientists are now finding through their experiments. That scientists and mystics are discussing completely different aspects of what is fundamentally real, not approaching the same aspects of reality through different means, is totally missed. The problem with parallelism is exemplified by an image in *The Tao of Physics* (2010 [1975]: 128–29). Capra puts a page of mathematics next to a page of an Indian text written in classical Devanagari script: if we squint, they do look the same and we can talk about the commonality of their short straight and curved lines; but if we actually examine them closely, we see that they have nothing in common.

For example, parallelists misconstrue the "search for unity" by failing to distinguish the unity of being in mysticism from the unity of structures in the sciences. Any scientific unity unifies apparently different structures (e.g., unifying magnetism and electricity), while the oneness of being has no parts to unite (contra Lorimer 1999). Mysticism is neutral on the question of whether physicists can reduce the apparent levels of structures to only one fundamental level of physical structure, or whether, as antireductionists assert, nonphysicists are also discovering equally fundamental levels of structuring. Nothing in Buddhism, Advaita Vedanta, or any classical mystical tradition East or West suggests any interest in attempting to unify the structures at work in the world. Mystics do not seek a more comprehensive unification than scientists or pursue a Grand Unified Theory (contra Weber 1986). Any Theory of Everything in physics would be simply irrelevant to the mystics' concerns since it would remain a matter of structures. Nothing on this subject is disclosed in mystical experiences. Perhaps if more scholars used *"identity of being"* when discussing such mystical systems as Advaita Vedanta and not *"unity"* (which suggests a unification of connected parts), fewer parallelists would be misled: there are no "real" parts to be connected in mystical "oneness."

The important point here is that extrovertive mysticism remains exclusively on the level that can be directly experienced—nothing in the writings of any classical mystics suggests that our sense experience extends to the submicroscopic world in an ASC. New Age writers commonly argue that the sense of connectedness that mystics have is caused by quantum-level interconnections and that mystics sense the cause. But a far simpler explanation is that mystics have "knowledge by participation" in the beingness of the everyday level or the mind through an altered state of consciousness. There is no reason to believe that mystics experience the underlying *causes* of everyday phenomena any more than we do when we experience solidity in the everyday world. Nothing in the writings of the great Asian spiritual masters claims or even suggests that mystics became aware of the quantum realm or experience subatomic structures or anything other than the mind or the everyday level of phenomena in the external world. Nothing in their writings remotely suggests that they were "quite adept" at seeing into matter and space-time, or that through meditation mystics realize that energy comes in discrete packets (quanta) (contra Nisker 2002: viii, ix). Contrary to what Capra says (2010 [1975]: 171–72), mystics in higher states of consciousness do not have "a strong intuition for the 'space-time' character of reality" or any other postulated scientific explanatory structure.[10] So too, Buddhist theorists do categorize mental structures, but only in the context of how to end suffering, not out of a disinterested desire to discover all the structures of the mind.

Indeed, the connection of space and time would be surprising news to Buddhists: nothing in Buddhist teachings would predict that time is connected to space. In fact, Theravada Buddhists exempt space, but not time, from being "conditioned" (*samskrita*) (*Anguttara Nikaya* I.286). This makes space as independent and absolute as is possible within their metaphysics and precludes any encompassing phenomenal holism. Nor did Nagarjuna connect space with time in his analysis of time (*Mula-madhyamaka-karikas* 19).[11] Nor is Ervin Laszlo's (2004) science-influenced idea of an "Akashic field" that records all information "rediscovering the true meaning of the ancient Vedas." It comes from modern theosophy and is a clear instance of imposing a new doctrine on the Indic notion. In classical Indic culture, space (*akasha*) is a substance pervading the world and thus is not "empty space," but it does not record any information. Nor it is not the source of anything else or in any sense the fundamental reality—it is not a "field" connecting everything with everything else nor out of which entities appear. Rather, space in Vedic thought is one of the five elements of the world (along with earth, water, fire, and air). It provides expanse but is not the ground of the other elements or of anything else—it is independent of all other elements and uninfluenced by them. That is also how Nagarjuna treats it.

Nor is there any reason to believe that the "empty" introvertive depth-mystical experience is an experience of "the four-dimensional space-time continuum" of relativity theory or a "ground manifold state" out of which quantum phenomena emerge and are reabsorbed: it is still "pure" in being free of differentiations. But according to physicists the "space-time manifold" is a structured aspect of reality, and thus it is no more "pure beingness" free of all structures than anything in the natural world. In Buddhist terms, being is "formless" while science can deal only with the differentiated "forms."

Like mysticism in general, Buddhism has no interest in the analysis of underlying structural layers of physical organization or in identifying the lowest structural level of physical realities. Buddhism has no scientific view of the nature of matter (Zajonc 2004: 5), and there is no such thing as a "Buddhist physics" (contra Wolf 1996: 169). Buddhism has never given a physical analysis of matter (contra Ricard and Thuan 2001: 107). The concept in Buddhism usually translated as "matter" is "form" (*rupa*), which is one of dozens and dozens of "factors of experience" (*dharmas*) in the Abhidharma analyses of experience. And even then "form" relates only to *our experience* and not to "matter in itself"—it is about the form of things that we directly experience and not any possible substance behind them. By naming things, we give what is actually real a form based on our perceptions—hence, the common phrase for the physical world: "name and form" (*nama-rupa*). Identifying a new subatomic level in an analysis of matter will not lead to discerning the *dharmas*, which are experiential in nature—if anything, the scientific analysis of matter only increases the danger of discriminations for the unenlightened by introducing a new layer of possible objects and creating new distinctions.

So too, mysticism and science may share a general ideal methodology: careful observation, rational analysis, open-mindedness, and having background beliefs (e.g., Wallace 2003: 1–29). But in actual practice, the differences in objectives between cultivating mystical experiences versus scientific observation and explanation cause very different implementations of any general principles and epistemic values. In the end, the only commonality may be features that any enterprise would have that seeks knowledge of reality and encounters things we would not expect from our ordinary experience in the everyday world. Mystics and scientists value types of experiences (conception-free experiences versus concept-driven observations) and conceptualizations (becoming free of conceptualizations versus coming up with better conceptualizations of how nature works) very differently, and this precludes any deeper convergence in "method."

In sum, scientists and mystics are doing basically different things. The difference is not only that different states of consciousness are involved. Rather, mystics do not directly experience the same "truth" that scientists arrive at tentatively or approximately through the route of theory and experiment. Nor do mystics reach a new structural reality that scientists fail to reach. Each endeavor, if each is in fact cognitive, pursues the depth of a dimension of reality but not the same dimension. The content of science and mysticism will always remain distinct. Thus, their theories and ideas can never converge into one new set of theories replacing those in either science or mysticism. Nor, since their content will always remain distinct, can one endeavor incorporate the other or be reducible to it. So too, meditators may permit neuroscientists to scan their brains while they meditate in order to gather data on their brain activity, but no further "collaborative effort" (Zajonc 2004: 7) is possible, let alone a "synthesis," "fusion," or "conceptual unification" of the two endeavors. Nor can either endeavor discredit or confirm the other. Mystics' claims about the impermanence and interconnectedness of the experienced everyday realm in no way "validate" or "verify" scientific theories of any underlying structures, nor conversely can scientific claims about structure verify mystical claims about beingness or its source (contra Nisker 2002: vii–viii).[12]

The "Emptiness" of Reality

As an example of the difference, consider the ideas of the emptiness in Buddhism and science. Much attention is being paid to the Madhyamaka tradition's concept of emptiness (*shunyata*). The Dalai Lama sees an "unmistakable resonance" between Nagarjuna's notion of emptiness and the new physics (Gyatso 2005: 50). Physicists speak of the emptiness of phenomena on the subatomic level, and Buddhists speak of the emptiness of phenomena, so New Age parallelists conclude that physicists and Buddhists are actually discussing the same thing.

However, the Buddhist concern is exclusively about the lack of any permanent entities in *what we experience in the everyday realm*—all the phenomena that we actually encounter are empty of anything that would give something the "inherent self-existence" (*svabhava*) that would permanently separate one thing from another as distinct and self-existing realities. This lack of self-existence has nothing whatsoever to do with special or general relativity in physics—there is no "striking convergence" or "direct resonance" (contra Jinpa 2010: 873). Nor does the general Buddhism notion of impermanence (*anitya*) have anything to do with the equivalence of matter and energy in Einstein's $E=mc^2$ (contra Jinpa 2010: 873): something could be in a permanent state of matter for all that equation tells us. The lack of "self-existence" has nothing to do with any alleged interaction of space, time, and matter (contra Finkelstein 2003: 383). Nor did the Prajnaparamita or Madhyamaka literature state anything about that scientific issue but only the experiential realm. Thus, Buddhist ideas on the impermanence of the experienced realm cannot even be considered "anticipations" of that issue.

Nor does Buddhism emptiness have anything to do with scientific notions of physical emptiness: it is the metaphysical absence of any power of self-existence, not anything about the absence of material in some space. Buddhist emptiness is not connected to the emptiness of solid matter on the quantum level (e.g., Zohar and Marshall 1993) or, on the other end of the scale, with the vast emptiness in space (Lam 2008; see R. Jones 2015 [2010]: 101–2). The physicist Victor Mansfield thinks particle physics and Madhyamaka Buddhism have "many deep links" and "remarkable and detailed connections" (Mansfield 2008: 6). But the two do not converge on the substance of their claims: the scientific notion of "emptiness" comes from the idea that there are no solid particles in a subatomic sea of energy—only agitations in a field of energy—but the mystics' claim stands or falls on the complete impermanence and interconnectedness of what we actually experience in the everyday world.[13] Any "convergence" is on such an abstract level that the earlier notion cannot be seen as "influencing" or "anticipating" the latter—the two notions cannot be seen as coming from the same insight. Such "uncanny parallels" may be "poetically meaningful" (Raman 2012: 156), but in no way substantive. Just because impermanence on the quantum level is consistent with Buddhism, it does not mean that quantum physics verifies or even supports its claim about the everyday world.[14] Buddhists may be interested to learn that impermanent and conditionality goes all the way down, but they did not have to wait twenty-five hundred years to have their claims about the everyday world be confirmed or disconfirmed by physicists. Indeed, quantum physics does not confirm anything about the everyday level of the world one way or the other.

Nor did the Buddha twenty-five hundred years ago in any way set out the hypothesis that elementary particles are not solid or independent (contra Ricard 2003: 274). Nowhere in the early canon does he ever say anything remotely about atomic particles or anything smaller. In fact, the early Abhidharma Buddhists who came later posited discrete, indivisible, and undestroyable minute particles of matter (*paramanus*) not open to sense experience.[15] Yet these Buddhists affirmed the impermanence of all things in our experiential realm—such atomic particles simply do not affect the impermanence that Buddhists are interested in. Thus, if physicists find permanent bits of matter on the quantum level, it would not refute a mindfulness tradition like Buddhism because it does not affect the impermanence of the "constructed" things of the everyday world that we actually experience.

Nor did Nagarjuna have any concept of a cosmic "Void." Nagarjuna's emptiness is not the "quantum vacuum" out of which things arise (contra Ramanna 1999: 163).[16] It is not a reality that is the source of anything. The term simply denotes the true state of everything in the phenomenal world—i.e., the absence of anything that would make a phenomenon permanent, independent, and self-existent (*svabhava*). The state of emptiness itself is not a self-existent reality; it too is empty of any inherent self-existence. It is not an inherently existing continuum out of which we carve conventional entities; each phenomenon is empty, and the totality of parts is also empty of self-existence. But parallelists routinely reify emptiness into a cosmic "Void" or "Absolute" that is an underlying source of phenomena. However, according to Nagarjuna, anyone who reifies the mere absence of anything that could give self-existence into a reality of any kind is *incurable* (*asadhyan*) (*Mula-madhyamaka-karikas* 13.8; see R. Jones 2022 [2015]: 137–42).

New Agers' ideas on holism are also misleading. Mystical knowledge of *beingness* on the extrovertive level need not be holistic—extrovertive mystics need not see reality as a differentiated whole even if the impermanent parts are connected. Certainly, Nagarjuna's metaphysics of emptiness does not go beyond the impermanence, connection, and conditionality of phenomena (R. Jones 2022 [2015]: 136–43). Nor need mystics have a sense of strong holism in which the whole creates or shapes the parts. Beingness or a source on the transcendent level may be experienced introvertively as totally partless, not as a whole with differentiated parts. So too with the external world: one can focus on beingness without embracing the idea that the natural world involves an encompassing holism. The Buddhist *Avatamsaka Sutra* has the famous illustration of Indra's net of jewels to illustrate the mutual interpenetration of all phenomena: all the jewels in the net are arranged in such a manner that each one reflects all the others. Some Chinese Buddhist schools used this illustration to represents how all the empty factors of the phenomenal world (the *dharmas*) enter one another (see R. Jones 2024: 326–27). This illustration is popular with parallelists. But the doctrine of interpenetration was not accepted by all Buddhist schools and cannot be taken as representing all Buddhism on impermanence, connectedness, and conditionality, let alone representing all mysticism. Moreover, a holism need not mean the parts are impermanent and changing: the fixed and rigid interlocking pieces of a jigsaw puzzle form a whole, but the parts are still discrete and unchanging. In fact, a deterministic Newtonian world is as integrated and holistic as anything in the new physics. However, the interaction of impermanent parts on the quantum level also need not be treated as requiring a holism.

Consciousness and the Phenomenal Realm

Another recurring problem in New Age works involves comparisons of consciousness and Advaita Vedanta's Brahman/Atman. For example, the physicist Amit Goswami's cosmopsychism treats consciousness as the ground of being and also gives consciousness a role in physics (2012: 95–100; also see Goswami 1997). However, there is nothing in classical Advaita's doctrines of

Brahman about consciousness affecting, or interacting with, an object—in fact, all that is real is only Brahman, and thus there is nothing for Brahman to interact with. Brahman does not even cause the entire material realm, since what is conscious cannot cause what is unconscious (Shankara's *Brahma-sutra-bhashya* II.1.4–6). In Advaita, Brahman is never portrayed as any type of causal agent in the phenomenal world; thus, to make it the cause of the wave-function collapse in quantum physics is to change its nature. Rather, Brahman is permanent and unchanging. Brahman is not observable (e.g., Shankara, *Brahma-sutra-bhashya* 1.1.1, 1.1.4, and 2.1.6). It cannot be related to what is not real—the realm of illusion (*maya*). Even if Brahman were the undifferentiated reality for all phenomena, it cannot explain why one phenomenal state of affairs is the case rather than another; thus, it could not function as a scientific explanation. It is not that mystics go further than physicists in observation (contra Capra 2010 [1975]: 331)—what mystics are claiming about what is experienced in introvertive mystical experiences that are free of all differentiated content is fundamentally different from any alleged interaction of the observer and observed in particle physics.[17] Most importantly, in Advaita, Brahman is a consciousness transcending the world and the world is a baseless illusion. This means that parallelists misinterpret Brahman's nature when they take it to be the phenomenal world and that science confirms the identity of Brahman and the ontological essence (*atman*) within us (e.g., Capra 2017: 16–17).

In mindfulness mysticism too, there is nothing about a subject's consciousness affecting objects: we "create" objects by imposing artificial conceptual boundaries onto what is really there in the world—in Buddhism, creating the world of "name and form" out of what is really there (*yathabhutam*, *tattva*, *tathata*)—not by somehow physically affecting what is actually there. That is, we create illusory "entities" in the phenomenal world by erroneously separating off parts of the flux of reality with our analytical mind; the "illusion" is a matter of the conceptualizations of our everyday perceptions and beliefs and has nothing to do with the idea that consciousness is a possible causal factor in events. Nor is there a "holistic consciousness" encompassing everything objective and subjective here.

The Quantum Realm

The quantum realm has become very important for technology today. Quantum computers may usher in a revolution in computing. But in the hands of New Agers, the science of quantum mechanics has been abused. The

New Age claim is that quantum physics proves that "the universe is being created in a dream of a single spiritual entity" (Wolf 1996: 343–44).

Indeed, "quantum" has become the parallelists' favorite word. We now have "quantum yoga" at the interface of matter and energy, and the "quantum shaman" path to "quantum consciousness." Deepak Chopra touts "quantum healing." A remark by Chopra is typical: "The quantum field is just another label for the field of pure consciousness and potentiality" (quoted in Rothman and Sudarshan 1998: 184). The reasoning is simple: everything has a material base, and quantum realities are the basis of physical organization; thus, everything is actually only a quantum reality. All things are just excited states of the underlying "quantum vacuum," and human beings thus are just ripples on the quantum vacuum's sea of potentiality (Zohar and Marshal 1993: 274). Everything arises from a "consciousness field." Human beings are "walking wave functions" (Wendt 2015: 37; but see Kydd 2022). Thus, there is a quantum basis to the mind (Zohar and Marshall 1993: 68–77, 82–85), and therefore there is a quantum basis to all things mystical and psychic. The movie *What the BLEEP Do We Know!?* centers on quantum mysticism. Goswami and Chopra are two of the featured authorities. Goswami sums up its central theme succinctly: "I create my own reality"—we literally make the external reality through our thoughts and will (Arntz, Chase, and Vicente 2005: 125–38). For Goswami and Chopra, consciousness generates reality, and to create a better reality for ourselves we need to correct our consciousness, since our consciousness infects the quantum field (Arntz, Chase, and Vicente 2005: 113–51, 81). Even some people in the popular mysticism movement are embarrassed by this (see Huston 2004).

Ironically, even while disparaging reductionism, parallelists engage in a reductionism of their own: they treat the lowest levels of physical interactions as the only type of action that is real. But merely because everything has a level of quantum activity, it does not follow that that is all we are. Parallelists bash "reductive science" and yet argue that how events occur on those lowest levels must be the model for how we must treat reality on the everyday level (Zajonc 2004: chapter 3). Thereby, biological levels are reduced to quantum effects. Ken Wilber summarizes (and then criticizes) the parallelists' reductionism: "Since all things are ultimately made of subatomic particles, and since subatomic particles are mutually interrelated and holistic, then all things are holistically one, just like mysticism says" (2000 [1984]: 27). For parallelists, Heisenberg's Uncertainty Principle (concerning our inability to measure the exact momentum and exact location of particles at the same time) means that we cannot have certain knowledge about anything on the everyday level of the world. So too, the "wave/particle paradox" in quantum science means that nothing on any level has fixed properties and we must speak paradoxically about everything in the everyday world.

What initially drew the parallelists' attention to the possibility of the convergence of science and mysticism was the fact that our everyday notions do not apply to subatomic events. But the reverse implication of this is somehow forgotten: any theories developed specifically for the subatomic level will *not apply to the everyday world for the same reason.* Thus, in the macroscopic world, planets do not jump orbits like electrons, a baseball thrown at a wall cannot be in two places at once, and so forth.[18] Heisenberg did not point out that the very act of measurement interferes with what one was attempting to measure in all situations (contra Verhoeven 2001: 86): on the tiny quantum scales, measurement ("observation") by injecting light interferes with what is there: there is no scientific basis to date to generalize anything like this to all scales of reality and to all types of measurements—observations on the everyday level do not appear to affect observed objects "in any tangible or significant way" (Raman 2012: 158). No quantum theories lead to Alan Wallace's conclusion that the mind "is necessarily at the heart of every assertion of reality" (Wallace and Hodel 2008: 129). Nor does any role the mind might play in observing quantum events have anything to do with uncertainty in the future course of human affairs (contra Raman 2012: 158–59). Rather, quantum mechanics and relativity reduce to Newtonian physics when velocities involved are much less than the speed of light and the distances are greater than in quantum experiments. It may be that the interaction of a mass of particles washes out quantum effects, but for whatever reason "quantum logic" does not apply to the everyday level of reality.

Thus, establishing any theory or holistic metaphysics on the everyday level cannot be deduced from quantum level theories or relativity: we cannot jump from the fact that everything has a material base to privileging the lowest level of physical organization as the sum of reality—i.e., that the quantum-level structures alone are real and are solely responsible for everyday phenomena. This denies the emergence of genuinely new types of phenomena in the world and layers of types of interactions. Thus, for parallelists there is no emergence of any new, genuinely real levels of causation or any genuine multiplicity of levels to nature's structures and organization. There is only one level of causation and structuring—the lowest level of physical organization dictates how we must see the world. But the only way for this to work is by a reductionist interpretation of all higher-level properties (e.g., life and consciousness)—something parallelists do not accept. Yet they do not see the blatant contradiction here.[19]

But whatever physicists find about the subatomic level, the fact remains that physical forces still produce, for example, solidity on the everyday level—chairs still support us and do not fall through the floor, no matter what post-Newtonian physics says about the "emptiness" of the subatomic level of the world. The standard New Age claim that quantum physics proves there is no solidity in the world is simply wrong. Solidity may be limited to only the everyday level of the world, but regardless of what physicists discover about its causes, it is not an illusion but just as real and nonnegotiable as properties on other levels. Chairs and tables are impermanent, as Buddhists emphasize, but they have a longer-lasting duration than do subatomic particles. The level effect must be taken into consideration to see reality properly, and to understand the Buddhist claim of impermanence and emptiness. The fact that everyday objects are all composed of subatomic particles is irrelevant.

Thus, particle physics is not "forcing" us to see all the world differently (contra Capra 2010 [1975]: 18, 138). Billiard balls still behave like billiard balls, despite what is happening on their subatomic levels. We can measure the speed and location of a train at the same time as exactly as we want. So too, atoms are causal units on their own level of interactions, so physicists and chemists can still properly treat them as entities (contra Capra 2010 [1975]: 68–69). Bell's entanglement theorem may apply to quantum particles, but such entanglement does not occur with the people and objects we encounter every day in the phenomenal world. Scientists can legitimately treat everyday objects as distinct from each other. So too, conditionality and the general impermanence of everyday phenomena were not unjustified until Bell came along. Nothing in science itself justifies making the colossal jump from subatomic physics to an all-encompassing holism for all aspects of all phenomena of reality, regardless of the levels of organization involved. Quantum mechanics does not prove that consciousness is part of reality (contra Capra 2017: 17). So too, nothing in quantum physics requires the denial of genuinely new levels of causation emerging or that the everyday level of phenomena has properties that quantum events do not. Indeed, if there turns out to be no causation on the quantum level, this means only that causation is a level effect on other levels of organization.[20]

In sum, quantum "emptiness" and other properties have nothing to do the macrocosmic properties as seen in mysticism. By ripping the scientific and mystical claims from their contexts within different theories within very different frameworks, we can reach an abstract commonality concerning impermanence and dependence but not any concrete or substantive convergence or verification of theories in science and mysticism. That the scientific theories and mystical beliefs are themselves parts of holistic gestalts—their actual meanings can only be seen in context—is missed by parallelists. (This is somewhat surprising since parallelists emphasize holism in other contexts.) The gestalts often are quite complex, and when the decontexualized claims are returned to their contexts, quantum physicists and mystics are easily seen to be talking about different things.

Also notice that the world of the new physics remains as "objective" as under the old physics despite what parallelists think. Consistently getting the same experimental results means that physicists are hitting structures that exist independently of our minds: they are irrevocably real aspects of the world—i.e., something that we simply cannot get around, whatever we think. There may be severe limits to our knowledge of quantum structures. Empiricists in philosophy of science may be correct that we cannot know something without experiences of it, but they readily concede that something in the objective world is responsible for the reproducible changes we observe. And the actions of the unseen realities remain as rigorous as with Newtonian particles: physicists have replaced the precise Newtonian language of particle trajectories with the precise quantum language of wave functions (Weinberg 1996). Predictions are now a matter of percentages, but very precise and consistent percentages. The objects in the everyday world may be impermanent and thus "illusions" in that sense, but the structures operating in the "illusions" are still objective. Most importantly for the issue at hand, there is nothing "mystical" about the new scientific picture: the parallelists' reductionism misses the fact that mystical experiences deal with the impermanence of the everyday world and the possible source of being, not with anything about scientific structures.

Methodological Distortions

Many of the parallelists' claims are embarrassingly bad. For example, Chopra tells us that the atom has no physical properties and that matter is "literally nothing," even though "empty" space-time has structured field properties and hence is not actually nothing (2012: x).[21] Zukav provides a paradigm of New Age reasoning. He notes that light has no properties independent of our observation and then continues: "To say that something has no properties is the same as saying that it does not exist. The next step in this logic is inescapable. Without us, light does not exist" (2001 [1977]: 105). It is one thing to realize that light has no particle-like or wave-like properties independent of our act of observation; it is another thing altogether to conclude that it therefore has no properties at all and does not exist. Our experimental observation may affect what is there and produce the observable properties, but it is absurd to say that nothing was there to begin with or that we created some physical reality that did not exist before human beings or other observers came along. Nor are the properties of light arbitrary: physicists always get the same properties by the same experimental procedures, so some structures in light must be fixed even if we cannot observe them directly. (If scientists used the term "measurement" more than "observation," perhaps fewer New Agers would believe that our consciousness is part of the measuring event.)

Typical of New Age advocates' reasoning is the conclusion that if *A* in mysticism cannot be visualized and *B* in science cannot be visualized, then *A* and *B* must have something significant in common or in fact must be the same thing, without any analysis of the underlying content of the claims or any discussions of the problems in comparing two different endeavors (see R. Jones 1986: chapters 8–9).[22] The comparisons are of isolated statements with little background on the contexts that would make their meaning clear. Thomas McFarlane's *Einstein and Buddha: The Parallel Sayings* (2002) is the extreme in this regard: he quotes only isolated statements with nothing to give them any context whatsoever. The translations may be by nonspecialists who are trying to make the texts sound compatible with Western thought. By this method, anyone can find the wording in bits of translations from mystical texts that resemble something from scientific writings, and New Age writers conclude without further research that the passage must be referring to the same scientific subject. However, if we look at the full contexts, inevitably we see that the wording clearly does not refer to anything in mystical texts we would consider "scientific." Nothing is established by that method: the unit of meaning is not such isolated short snippets. Rather, we have to consider a total system of thought to see what words mean to the persons using them.

A related problem is translating terms from other cultures to fit a predetermined position. For example, the Buddhist term "*dharmata*" means simply "the nature of things," but in the hands of parallelists it becomes "laws of nature," and Buddhism is thus magically shown to be scientific—the

Buddha was no longer talking about the impermanence and conditionality of phenomena but was aware of scientific laws of nature. Indeed, parallelists distort mysticism from the beginning of their comparisons.[23] Whenever we attempt to understand anything new, we all have previous beliefs that influence us, and when we compare science and mysticism, there is a very real danger of misreading one endeavor in light of our prior commitment to the other. If parallelists rely on Westernized versions of Asian schools for their understanding of mysticism that have been influenced by Western culture, including science (e.g., the works of D. T. Suzuki), the comparisons may well end up being circular. The danger is that we will ultimately see mystical ideas in the scientific ideas or vice versa and not on their own terms. That is, our understanding of one endeavor may be "contaminated" by our understanding of the other endeavor (Restivo 1983: 24), and thus the comparisons will not be of the genuine article.

Comparisons to science also are always comparisons to the theories of the day, and there is thus the danger that convergences parallelists see will disappear in the next generation. But the consequence is not seen: if a mystical claim is the same as a particular scientific claim, then if the science changes, the mystical claim must be rejected too. It is also good to remember that books written on Buddhism and science in the late nineteenth and early twentieth centuries in America and Europe portrayed the Buddha as a good Newtonian. In the 1960s, when interest in the topic of Buddhism and science revived, the Buddha had become an Einsteinian. Capra illustrates the problem well. In the 1970s, Capra championed his teacher Geoffrey Chew's S-matrix theory in particle physics in which there are no fundamental entities or laws of nature. However, the S-matrix's competitor—the particle approach of quarks, leptons, and bosons—won out on scientific grounds: the S-matrix theory did not lead to new predictions, while the particle approach did. Nevertheless, Capra still adheres to the S-matrix theory, while other physicists have made advances in the particle approach under the consensus Standard Model. But incredibly, Capra sees nothing that has developed in physics in the intervening decades as invalidating anything he wrote (Capra 2010 [1975]: 9). To physicists, he is simply in denial (e.g., Woit 2006: 152).

As Victor Mansfield said, since physical theories are intrinsically impermanent and temporary, it is a guarantee of obsolescence to bind Buddhism or any philosophical view too tightly to a physical theory (2008: 6–7). Today, the inconsistency of quantum theory and relativity leads many physicists to believe that their current theories are not final but only approximations. So too, the element of randomness and the general statistical nature of quantum physics suggest to many particle physicists that their science has not yet captured the true structures at work on that level. That "dark" matter and energy—which may constitute 95 percent of the mass of our universe—has only recently been discovered also gives one pause: perhaps other major features of the cosmos are yet to be found. Thus, any attempt at a Theory of Everything today may be premature. So too, today's alleged parallels to mystical claims may prove to be only temporary.

However, if claims from assorted mystical traditions can be attached to whatever the currently accepted theory in particle physics happens to be or whatever is found in the future, then there must be very little substance to the alleged convergence—only very general features of reality converge in the two enterprises. Capra now sees only a more abstract parallel between science and Buddhism: both enterprises espouse a uniformity to nature ("unity"), impermanence, and conditionality in general. These themes he believes will only be reinforced in the future (2010 [1975]: 338). In sum, he sees only general themes converging in a fundamental worldview—he no longer sees specific theories as converging, resonating, or confirming each other.

Beyond contamination, distortions of the basic nature of mysticism also frequently occur. Andrea Diem and James Lewis only slightly exaggerate when they say that Capra in his New Age classic *The Tao of Physics* "misinterprets Asian religions and cultures on almost every page" (1992: 49). There is always a great danger of circular reasoning here: cleansing a mystical tradition of anything that might conflict with current scientific claims as simply "nonessential" cultural accretions (e.g., Buddhism's "flat earth" cosmology, or the astrology and paranormal powers that are part of many mystical ways of life), and then miraculously finding that the tradition was scientific all along.[24] Letting science set what is deemed "essential" to the mystical tradition in the first place results in a blatant circularity. Highlighting selective aspects of a tradition is certainly legitimate, but parallelists tend to reduce a spiritual tradition to only those aspects and to view even the selected aspects through the lens of science, thereby making mystical concepts into scientific concepts when such concepts are not scientific in content or purpose. Parallelists distort mystical doctrines to fit science, and then those doctrines become "anticipations" of specific physical and biological theories. For example, parallelists interpret the Chinese notion of the Dao along the lines of modern field theory in physics and then see science as confirmation of the Chinese anticipation. Not surprisingly, no one saw the "anticipations" until after the scientific changes—the "anticipations" did not guide scientific thinking. But after the scientific innovations, mystical doctrines are reinterpreted to make them sound scientific, even if this changes the nature of the mystical claims. More generally, simply because an ancient tradition and modern science have a general agreement on metaphysical implications does not mean the former "anticipated" the latter in any meaningful sense (Halbfass 1988: 401).

Equally important, parallelists lump all Asian mystical traditions together as if they were in fact only one system of beliefs shared by all. Indeed, many New Agers start by speaking of Buddhism and then generalize to all Asian mysticism and then generalize to all mysticism in general (e.g., Capra 2010 [1975]) without any qualifications, as if all mysticism is really the same. The fundamental differences in doctrines, however, preclude there being an abstract "Eastern mysticism." Parallelists play down or ignore entirely the fact that Advaita's depth-mystical doctrines are very different from those of Daoism and the mindfulness doctrines of the different Buddhist traditions. Even within Hindu mysticism, there is no one "mystical worldview"—e.g., Advaita contrasts with theistic forms of Vedanta and with Samkhya-Yoga's dualism of matter and multiple selves. Theistic forms of Vedanta are ignored completely. So too, the parallelists' approach distorts Advaita by making its claims related to the natural realm its central ontic topic in order to connect it to the idea that change is central to reality (e.g., Capra 2010 [1975]: 194), even though Advaitins take what is changing to be unreal and illusory (*maya*) and emphasize the unchanging reality of Brahman as central—Shankara would dismiss the quantum level changes as "illusions" as readily as he dismissed the everyday level changes. Nor does Advaita metaphysics speak of interdependent parts or inseparable parts of a cosmic whole (contra Capra 2010 [1975]: 130): Brahman is partless and unchanging, and it is the only reality.

The concept of "*maya*" in the Upanishads does not mean that all existence is denied to the phenomenal realm—it is *dependent* on Brahman/Atman, and its deceptive nature as appearing to be *independently real* is the "illusion." The classic example is that in a clay pot the clay is real and its modification as a pot is the illusion: "By a single lump of clay everything made of clay becomes known—the transformation of form is merely a verbal handle, a name, while the reality is only clay" (*Chandogya Upanishad* 6.1.4). So, for all phenomena, their being supplied by Brahman is real, and the appearance that objects exist independently of Brahman is the illusion. Shankara went further: only the transcendent consciousness (Brahman/

Atman) is real, and the phenomenal realm is only a dream, although he had no explanation for why it should even appear. Later Advaitins struggled with the issue. The important thing here is that early Advaitins did not claim that the phenomenal world consisted of a whole of interconnected phenomena. When they wrote of causation, it was a matter of the relation of phenomena to the source, not the interaction of phenomena. Nor did they have any interest in explaining any of the world's phenomena beyond pointing out their "illusory" nature when compared to what alone is actually real—a transcendent consciousness.

Overall, parallelists read all Asian mysticism through a prism of scientific knowledge. Mystical concepts are seen in scientific terms without regard to their original context. This distorts or screens out the original intent and meaning of these teachings and substitutes alien ideas in their place. But only in this way can they find particle physics and modern cosmology in ancient texts—everything from the virtual particles of the quantum field to the Big Bang to relativity to multiple universes.[25] Conversely, in a case of applied mysticism, New Agers let mysticism dictate what is the best understanding in quantum physics, and relativity can be just as distortive. For example, the "quantum consciousness" interpretation of quantum mechanics and Eugene Wigner's theory of a role for consciousness in quantum events are more popular among parallelists than among physicists.[26] Nevertheless, it is a New Agers' hope that compatibility with a theory in a mystical tradition will become a criterion for the acceptability of theory physics. If so, then mysticism will be guiding science.

Ironically, Capra himself has become disenchanted with "Eastern mysticism" and has shifted his focus to Christian mysticism (Capra and David Steindl-Rast 1991) because he found that "many Eastern spiritual teachers . . . [are] unable to understand some crucial aspects of the new paradigm that is now emerging in the West" (2010: 341). Why this should be so would be hard for him to explain since he believes the "new paradigm" is simply the expression of the "essence" of all Asian mystical traditions. How can these teachers not understand themselves? He does not consider the possibility that he might be distorting Asian teachings by seeing them through the prism of modern science. (Capra has since turned his attention to extending the parallels he sees to other sciences such as ecology. At least with ecology the interconnections ("unity" or "oneness") of things is on the everyday level of the world that is also the level in which extrovertive mysticism operates. This may be the basis for him saying the parallels are on a "much firmer ground" today than in 1975 [2010 [1975]: 9].)

Was the Buddha a Scientist?

The filtering problem can occur in another way: the emphasis in mysticism on *experience* as the source of knowledge when seen through the lens of modernity becomes a *scientific method*. For example, Buddhist claims in the New Age view become a matter of tentatively advanced, empirically tested hypotheses. Meditative exercises become scientific experiments on the mind, not means to transform oneself for a religious goal. The basic point that the Buddha exhorted his followers to rely on their own experiences and to examine phenomena dispassionately (*Majjhima Nikaya* I.265) means that the Buddha must have been a scientist—not that he was trying to get them to follow the path to end their suffering themselves.

However, there is nothing "scientific" in the Buddhist aim or purpose.[27] In the *Kalama Sutta*, villagers expressed their confusion to the Buddha about the conflicting religious doctrines they had heard. He exhorted them not to rely on reports, hearsay, the authority of religious texts, mere logic, mere influence, appearances, seeming possibilities, speculative opinions, or teachers' ideas, but to know for themselves what is efficacious and what is not (*Anguttara Nikaya* I.189). But he was not exhorting them to conduct mental experiments over a range of inner states and see what happens: the villagers were told in advance what would work—the prescribed Buddhist path to ending cravings and attachments and thereby ending rebirth and thus permanently ending our existential suffering. And the Buddha already knew what the villagers would find: it was set forth before any mental exercises were undertaken, unlike in science, where scientists do not know beforehand what their experiments will disclose when they test predictions. The villagers' subsequent experiences cannot even be considered attempts to duplicate an experiment in order to confirm or disconfirm an earlier finding since the Buddha is accepted as enlightened and any lack of enlightenment on the part of the villagers would not be seen as disconfirmation of his doctrines but a failure on their part—and if the claim of enlightenment is not seen as falsifiable, it is hard to see it as a scientific claim. (Why these confirmed experiences are not "verification" of Buddhist theory is discussed below.) The Sanskrit scholar Wilhelm Halbfass (1988: 393–94) summed this up nicely:

> Following the experiential path of the Buddha does not mean to continue a process of open-ended experimentation and inquiry. There is no "empiricist" openness for future additions

or corrections: there is nothing to be added to the discoveries of the Buddha and other "omniscient" founders of soteriological traditions. . . . There is no programmatic and systematic accumulation of "psychological" data or observations, no pursuit of fact-finding in the realm of consciousness. . . . [T]here is no more "inner experimentation" in these traditions, than there is experimentation related to the "outer" sphere of nature.

Buddhism is prescriptive in a way science is not. Pinit Ratanakul may say "Buddhism has a free and open spirit of enquiry and encourages the search for truth in an objective way" (2002: 116), but this is deceptive: it is not fresh research, since the Buddha was only prescribing the path to the end of suffering that was already established. In the *Kalama Sutta*, the Buddha is merely saying that by following the path the villagers will then know for themselves because they will have experienced the end of suffering themselves. We have to distort Buddhism to see this as in any way "anticipating the skeptical empiricism of the modern scientific method" (Verhoeven 2001: 90). Discovering something for yourself through experience that you did not know before does not necessarily make you a scientist—sometimes it is only a matter of correctly following a path that others laid out for you. In short, we cannot equate everything based on experience with a "scientific method." Moreover, the Buddha's exhortation did not prevent Buddhist schools over time from accepting the Buddha's testimony (*shabda*) as a means of valid knowledge, as epitomized in schools valuing the *Lotus Sutra* centrally. The Dalai Lama realizes that accepting such authority for settling matters separates Buddhism from science (Gyatso 2005: 28–29). New Agers may dismiss this as something to be ignored.

In sum, Buddhist meditation is less an open-ended inquiry than a method of discovering for oneself the truths authorized by the tradition. As with classical mystics in all religious traditions, mysticism was seen as a way to regain the knowledge enshrined in their religion's fundamental sacred texts—it is a matter of *recovering something already known and complete*, not exploring the mind to gain *new knowledge or otherwise to advance knowledge* (Halbfass 1988: 393–94). This clearly distinguishes mysticism from science as knowledge-giving enterprises. Nevertheless, in the parallelists' eyes, the Buddha is a scientist. But even in a protoscientific sense, let alone a modern sense of natural science, this claim is simply wrong. The Buddha did not have a scientist's interest in understanding how nature works; rather he had only one interest: just as the one flavor of saltiness permeates the entire ocean, so too the Buddha's teaching has only one flavor—how to permanently end the suffering inherent in being alive by ending perpetual rebirth (*Majjhima Nikaya* I.22). The Buddha cannot even be seen as "a scientist of the inner world" of consciousness since he was not interested in establishing a scientific understanding of consciousness. Merely creating a taxonomy of mental states relevant to ending suffering (as Buddhist Abhidharmists did) does not make a meditative tradition scientific in method or intent. The Buddha did not use the "scientific method" to test various hypotheses to create a scientific picture of the inner world. His method does involve experiential investigation of inner mental states, but the objective is not to learn more about the mind. The Buddhist analogy of the man struck by a poisoned arrow mentioned above again applies.

Calling meditation a "contemplative inquiry into the nature of consciousness" (Wallace and Hodel 2008) is at best misleading: the Buddha did not seek to describe whatever he found during his quest to end suffering in order to contribute to a scientific study of the psyche. Buddhists following the prescribed path to end suffering have not developed, as Alan Wallace thinks, a "science of consciousness" by "collecting data by observing mental processes and experimenting" (1989: 29–101). And putting the word "experiments" in quotation marks when discussing meditation (Wallace and Hodel 2008: 142) does not make the meditators' observation of their mental states, as they attempt to calm their mind, into scientific experiments. Buddhists are not "experimenting" or "testing scientific hypotheses" in any scientific sense at all. The Buddha's claims are not "hypotheses" presented for confirmation or disconfirmation as scientists test tentative new ideas (contra Wallace and Hodel 2008: 145). Simply because unenlightened Buddhists have not yet experientially realized their prescribed goal of enlightenment themselves does not mean they are "testing hypotheses scientifically" by their meditative practices and behavior in any sense. And that others have achieved this goal does not mean that the Buddha was offering a "scientific hypothesis" that he and others had "verified" (contra Wallace 2003: 8–9). Having to follow a prescribed path to a goal yourself does not make the path in any sense a scientific hypothesis to be tested. Moreover, to think that the Buddha was setting out a "hypothesis" about subatomic particles (Ricard 2003: 274), which cannot be experienced by mindfulness, only compounds the error.

The New Age position is clearly twisting the Buddha's teaching and practice by viewing it through the perspective of science. Buddhists have indeed developed "rigorous methods for refining attention," but not to explore the nature of consciousness scientifically. Learning meditation is more like learning a musical instrument than scientific research: it is a matter of practice and correcting errors. At the very most, the Buddha can be likened not to a basic research scientist, who is out to find how nature works, but rather to a technician, who used trial and error to learn what worked for a practical goal he already had in mind and then began showing others how to follow the path and use the techniques to achieve what he had discovered.

Meditation, Mystical Experiences, and the Scientific Empirical Method

Mindfulness and scientific observation both involve disinterested observation, but this is not grounds to conclude that even only to that extent Buddhism is "a science of the mind" (contra Gyatso 2003: 101–2). Seeing the relevant inner states as if from a third-person point of view, free of one's beliefs and preferences, and cultivating a general attitude of impartiality and objectivity do not make mindfulness a scientific study of the mind. The Buddhist quest to end suffering is not scientific "research" guided by empirical findings (Gyatso 2003: 102). Another interest is needed for meditation to be science: understanding the processes at work and explaining them. Indeed, the impartiality of mindfulness would actually *interfere* with scientific observation by disconnecting observation from making any phenomenon a priority: in a mindful state, there are no predictions, preset categories of objects, or other conceptual guidance as is needed to conduct a scientific observation. There is a "bare attention" to what is presented to our senses, without attention to anything in particular and with no accompanying intellectual expectations or reactions. Scientific observations that test hypotheses arising from data require responses to predictions created by questions about particular phenomena and thus are necessarily driven by concepts—such directed observations are not the free-floating observations of whatever occurs, as in mindfulness meditation.

Concentrative meditation may help scientists calm their mind and focus their attention. Meditation should also be unbiased and thus objective in that sense. So too, being unbiased is highly valued desideratum in scientific research. However, we cannot use "objectivity" in this sense to claim that meditation is objective in the specifically scientific sense of being presentable to others to experience (contra Wallace and Hodel 2008: 143–44). Nor can we use this sense of "objectivity" to mean "empiricism" (contra Wallace and Hodel 2008: 144–47). The conflict of knowledge claims from different mystical traditions about the same topic (e.g., the nature of the experiencer) makes it hard to see mystical experiences as confirming or disconfirming any claim in a straightforward empiricist manner. Moreover, even whether meditation might at least establish a universally agreed-upon phenomenology of mental states is questionable since meditators of different traditions see the states in terms of different typologies—e.g., the Samkhya versus Buddhist delineation of the constituents of the mind and whether there is a self.

Nor does "empiricism" mean simply "experiential" (contra Wallace and Hodel 2008: 146). Empiricism is a philosophical position that involves more than simply having experiences—it is an epistemic matter of the limits of what we can know. In empiricism, in contrast to rationalism, knowledge is limited to what we can directly experience. In calling for a "return to empiricism," Wallace has no problem utilizing the Yogachara Buddhist concept of the *alayavijnana*—a "substrate consciousness" that precedes life and continues beyond death in which karmic seeds take root and develop; it is the ultimate ground state of consciousness, existing prior to all conceptual dichotomies, including subject/object and mind/matter (Wallace 2006: 33–36). However, it is hard to see how we could know by any experience that this substrate existed prior to all life. How could any experiences prove that there is a reality that existed prior to the dichotomy of "mind" and "matter," or that consciousness has no beginning but has existed since the beginning of the universe, or that consciousness will never end? Thus, it is hard to see the "substrate consciousness" as the result of empiricism. Rather, this appears to be a bit of Buddhist *theorizing*: it is an attempt to answer the problem of how karmic effects can take place in future rebirths when everything under Buddhist metaphysics is momentary. Moreover, most Buddhists do not accept such a posit.

Nor can we simply jump from the fact that mysticism and science are both *experiential* to the conclusion that they therefore make the same type of claims and are both "*empirical*" in the scientific sense of making claims checkable by scientific methods (contra, e.g., Capra 2017: 16). Nor is it at all clear how contemplation can present any information that would shed light on the relationship of the nonphysical mind to the physical body (contra Wallace and Hodel 2008: 147)—whether mystical experiences are products of the brain alone, as naturalists claim, or involve something more, they would still have the same phenomenology (as discussed in chapters 1 and 2).

In short, not everything experiential is scientific. The need for the "direct experience of spiritual truths" makes mysticism experiential, but it does not necessarily make it scientific. Nevertheless, New Age advocates consider meditation "essentially scientific" in method (e.g., Wilber 2006: ix). To Ken Wilber, "contemplative science" is no different from natural science except in its subject matter (Wilber 2006: ix–xii). But again, while meditation is certainly experiential, this does not make it the concept-guided observation of the empirical method of natural scientific knowing. Nor can we speak of Buddhist metaphysics as "a verifiable system of knowledge" (Ricard 2003: 274) when other traditions with knowledge claims that conflict with Buddhist claims about the nature of the mind are "verified" by the same type of experiences. Later practitioners at most could confirm that the general meditative techniques laid out by the Buddha worked to end a sense of self or to calm the mind, but such meditation does not confirm the theory of the mental life and rebirth advanced by Buddhists that is disputed by other mystics.

Complementarity

At the end of the epilogue to *The Tao of Physics*, Fritjof Capra does state the correct relation between science and mysticism in one respect: mysticism and science are distinct approaches to reality involving different functions of the mind. The world is one reality, but it has multiple aspects, dimensions, and levels, and physicists and mystics deal with different aspects (2010 [1975]: 339). "Neither is comprehended in the other, nor can either be reduced to the other, but both of them are necessary, supplementing one another for a fuller understanding of the world. . . . Science does not need mysticism and mysticism does not need science; but man needs both" (Capra 2010 [1975]: 306–7). Nevertheless, in the actual body of his work, he still insists that we need "a dynamic interplay" between science and mysticism. He still advances unsupportable claims of "convergence" and "confirmation" (Capra 2010 [1975]: 114, 161, 223)—and he does so even in the epilogue just quoted (Capra 2010 [1975]: 305). Unfortunately, the same tendency toward inconsistency on the supposed relation between science and mysticism is the norm among New Age parallelists.[28]

Consider "complementarity"—the idea that science and mysticism are different, but together they give us a more complete knowledge of reality. In a typical New Age image, science is the epitome of the aggressive *yang* approach to reality, and mysticism the epitome of the receptive *yin* approach, and together they form a unity to our knowledge, as we balance *qi*, which is merely another name for the quantum energy field. Many see mysticism as a function of the right hemisphere of the brain, and science the left, so only by utilizing what comes through each hemisphere do we have "the full-brain approach" (e.g., Nisker 2002: vii).[29]

José Cabezón elaborates the complementarity position: science deals with the exterior world, matter, and the hardware of the brain, while Buddhism deals with the interior world and the mind; science is rationalist, quantitative, and conventional, while Buddhism is experiential, qualitative, and contemplative (2003: 50). But he realizes there are limitations: Buddhist analyses show a concern with the nature of the external world, and science too can study aspects of mind (Cabezón 2003: 58). That is, mysticism and science do not separate neatly into different compartments. It is not as if mysticism is about the "inner world" of consciousness, while science is about the "outer world" of material objects: mystics work on consciousness, but they are interested in the beingness of all reality, including the beingness of the "outer world." Seeing science as "outer empiricism" and mysticism as "inner empiricism" (Weber 1986: 7) has the same problem. So too, it is also hard to see natural science as "rationalist" as opposed to "experiential." Perhaps Cabezón is highlighting the centrality of thought in scientific theorizing and testing. There are also limitations on compartmentalizing all elements of mystical ways of life from science because mystical ways of life have beliefs about the nature of reality and utilize reason on the path and in the enlightened life (see R. Jones 2015 [2010]: 156–77).

The idea of complementarity at least affirms that science and mysticism involve irreducible differences and that choosing only one gives only a one-sided view of reality and misses something real. However, parallelists still see a similarity between science and mysticism in content or method or both, but if the claims or methods converge, it is hard to see how we can speak of "complements." If the methods or general claims are the same, it is hard to speak of "complementarity" at all.

Moreover, the most popular way to reconcile mysticism and science as complements is to claim that mystics are dealing with the "depth" of reality and scientists with the "surface" of the *same dimension of reality* (Wilber 1998; Capra 2010 [1975]). That is, mystics and scientists are using different approaches to reality, but they apprehend the same thing, not fundamentally different dimensions of reality (substance and structure): mystics simply turn observation inward and find a deeper level of the same truth about structures that scientists reach observing external phenomena. Since science and mysticism both lead to the same basic knowledge, we have only to choose the route that is more suitable to our disposition.

However, parallelists do not see the consequence of this position: either mystics are producing a more thorough account of what scientists are studying—i.e., they get to the root of the same subject matter and therefore are doing a more thorough job than are scientists—or scientists are examining the same subject matter as are mystics but with more precision. Either way, one endeavor is superseded: either mysticism's thoroughness renders science unnecessary, or science's precision replaces mysticism's looser approach. Thus, this New Age position becomes the basis for rejecting either mysticism or science altogether.[30]

So too, since science and mysticism achieve the same knowledge through different routes, there is in fact no reason to bother with the strenuous way of life that serious mysticism requires—all we have to do is read a few popular accounts of contemporary physics or cosmology and we will have the same knowledge that enlightened mystics have and hence will be enlightened without altering our state of consciousness. All that matters is learning a post-Newtonian way of looking at the world—namely, "shifting the paradigm" to the "new worldview," not experiencing the beingness of reality free of all conceptual divisions and a sense of "self" through mystical experiences, and for this, merely accepting the knowledge claims in our ordinary state of consciousness is enough. Conversely, scientists need not go through the expense and trouble of conducting elaborate experiments to learn about structures; mystics have already "intuited" what physicists would learn and in fact have achieved the same knowledge with even more thoroughness through their experiences. Mystics already know what scientists will discover on the quantum level of organization in the future, so there is no need to conduct any more experiments. Physicists are only filling in the details of the holism that mystics experience in ASCs, but they are not discovering anything fundamentally new. What physicists are finding may be of technological value, but it will no longer change our basic view of things. So shut down the CERN supercollider and all research labs—all that scientists need to do is meditate to see the oneness of reality more thoroughly, or even just adopt the general ideas of the new worldview.

Reconciling Different Endeavors

In sum, if scientists and mystics are studying the same thing when it comes to the fundamental nature of reality and one group is doing the job more thoroughly, one of the endeavors is no longer needed. However, it is being asserted here that scientists and mystics are studying different aspects of reality—how things work versus beingness or its source—that result in completely different types of knowledge claims. And if both endeavors do in fact produce knowledge, then both endeavors are needed for a fuller knowledge of reality. It is not as if all we have to do is push further in science and we will end up mystically enlightened, or push further in mysticism and we will end up with a Theory of Everything for physics. Of course, science and mysticism can be said to have a "common pursuit of truth," or are "united in the one endeavor of discovering knowledge and truth about reality," or "seek the reality behind appearances," but such statements only place both endeavors in a more abstract category of being knowledge-seeking endeavors since they are not pursing the same knowledge and do not have the same purpose.

Ken Wilber points out that the physicists from the first half of the twentieth century whom parallelists cite would reject the claim that physics proves or supports Capra's and Zukav's view (2000 [1984]: ix). Rather, those physicists believed that science and mysticism are both needed for a complete view of reality and that neither endeavor is reducible to or derived from the other (Zukav's 2000 [1984]: ix). Few prominent scientists today endorse any form of parallelism. Nor has there been much literature on the issue of mysticism and science since the 1980s, although there have been advances in science that New Agers would no doubt exploit (see Clarke 2005; Lorimer 2017). Capra himself now believes that the parallel between science and mysticism reduces only the general claims of order, impermanence, and conditionality (2010 [1975]: 338).[31] No one would contest such general ontological features of the natural world as common to science and Buddhism despite their differences in interests and goals. Indeed, Newtonian science could affirm those general claims for the everyday level of phenomena, which is the level of phenomena of interest to Buddhism. As long as New Agers do not go further than such general principles to claim convergence in specific scientific theories and more concrete mystical doctrines, parallelism would be acceptable, if not particularly insightful.

But New Age claims of more detailed convergence do not pan out—beingness and structures are the warp and woof of reality that must be approached differently. New Age advocates can accept that mysticism and science are different endeavors with different goals, but they still insist that their claims converge (e.g., Capra 2017: 16) or that everything mysterious in the world is support for mysticism. But if the two endeavors are dealing with fundamentally different aspects of reality—mysticism concerns what is "formless" about reality, and science what is "formed"—their basic claims cannot intersect at all. Each approach would be equal and supply something the other misses—they are "complements" or "supplements" in that sense. If so, mystical and scientific claims will obviously always be "harmonious," "compatible," and "consistent" on basic matters since they logically could not converge or conflict or support each other even in principle. If this is so, it would make reconciling mystical metaphysics and science relatively simple as two ways of knowing reality as long as introvertive mystical claims are confined to claims about transcendent realities or an ontological ground of the world (see R. Jones 2015 [2010]: chapter 16). Each endeavor would then supply knowledge of reality that the other misses, and neither supersedes the other. But the only "collaborative" efforts here would be through the examination of mystics and meditators to see if their previously unexamined states of consciousness add to the spectrum of states and experiences in a way that helps scientists to understand how the brain works. Taxonomies of such states in classical mystical traditions might also give neuroscientists some new ideas.

Working out such a general philosophy of reality would be a case of applied mysticism. That is, there is not generic "mystical worldview," but the metaphysics of a particular mystical tradition would be adapted outside of a mystical quest into an analytic metaphysical framework that absorbs the current body of scientific theories and findings within an encompassing view of the cosmos. This does not make mysticism scientific in nature or science mystical in nature. The metaphysics of the chosen mystical way of life would be removed from its context of pursuing a mystical goal and used instead in another context to construct a worldview incorporating both mystical claims and science. Such a worldview would not be seen in a nondual mystical state of consciousness but worked out in a dualistic state of mind. In effect, mystical concepts would become treated as inherently dualistic. Thus, the role of ASC experiences in mysticism would be lost—the world would be seen from a dualistic state of consciousness. The nature of mystical experiences would be understood in light of the encompassing worldview, but having a mystical experience is no longer needed: we only have to adopt the new worldview to know what all mystics know—we don't have to experience them directly in altered states of consciousness as New Agers claim mystics have done. Such a metaphysics may affect scientific theories by changing the worldview in which the theories must ultimately rest, but this does not make scientists mystics or vice versa. Nevertheless, such a philosophical enterprise would see science through a New Age prism and strip mystical traditions of anything unscientific—each endeavor could then be conducted within the new worldview. For example, that New Agers favor a role of consciousness as fundamental leads them to favor Wigner's theory of a role of consciousness in quantum mechanics as the best theory. This shows the risk of applying mystical doctrines directly to science. It may also limit the acceptance of science more broadly. For example, the Dalai Lama is interested in current science, but there are limits to what he will accept: he states that he would not accept any scientific theory that sees consciousness as evolving from matter or denies karma and rebirth (Gyatso 2005: 109–15; Gyatso and Goleman 2003; also see R. Jones 2011: 108–10). There is a danger that religious beliefs may even become broader "control beliefs" in science (see R. Jones 2011: chapter 3).

Alternatively, reconciling science and mystical spirituality could be sought without distorting their nature. Both mysticism and science in principle may be transformed by studying the other endeavor, but New Agers have so far ended up only distorting the nature of each in trying to make them "converge."

Chapter 10

Applying Mysticism to Social Action Today

A good way to end this book is on one point that requires attention today in any discussion of applied mysticism: social action to improve worldly conditions for all—i.e., the application of mysticism to problems in the world on a societal scale to help others with their secular needs. For this, the focus of a mystic's actions is not primarily the salvation of others but their worldly needs—in fact, focusing on others' salvation might actually limit or interfere with the mystic's social action. Merely because an inner altered states of consciousness (ASC) experience is central to mysticism does not totally "privatize" it: there is still always more to any mystical development or way of life, and this includes interactions with other people. Classical mystics may well have a moral concern for those other people, although contrary to what most Christians appear to think not all mystics have been moral (see R. Jones 2004, 2024: 392–95). (Writers on mysticism and morality tend to treat all mysticisms as the same and as advocating a "perennial philosophy" rather than look at the specifics of different mystical traditions.[1]) For mystics who adopt a moral stance, moral action is part of the cultivation on the path, and action without losing their detachment or equanimity is an expression of the enlightened way of life. But one major difficulty for seeing how to apply mysticism on a societal scale today is the general lack of social action or advocating changes on the societal level in classical mystical record. (Exceptions will be noted below.) And if anything, the historical record is skewed in favor of finding social activism: we know only of mystics who had some impact on society through teaching, works, or writings; those mystics who did not leave such a trace were either not interested in social reform or were not effective.

One preliminary point before proceeding: there is an ambiguity with the word "social" that leads to confusion about whether mystics are "social" or not: mystics' actions toward others are, of course, "social" in the sense of being interpersonal and in the sense that mystics live and act within a society and thus their presence affects their society, but they may not be "social" in the stronger sense of focusing on corporate action or affecting society-wide structures. It is only action in the latter sense—i.e., *group action or societal-level reform*—that will be considered "social" here, not all interactions between people.[2] That is, the term "social action" will refer only to actions revealing an interest in reforming structures in society as a whole or cooperating in groups to help others in their worldly needs, in a way that affects many people in a society, not just the people whom mystics directly encounter. It is that type of action that is noticeably lacking in the majority of classical mystics' actions and writings. In fact, social action may be a modern idea. The issue of applied mysticism can come up in the context of helping people individually with worldly aid, as with the medieval Dominican teacher/preacher Meister Eckhart valuing giving a cup of soup to the sick over remaining in the highest mystical experience (2009: 496; also see R. Jones 2004: 379–435), but only the possibility of applying mysticism on a broader scale will be considered here.

The Individualistic Orientation of Classical Mysticism

Classical mysticism in all major cultures was oriented toward the development of individuals. This is not to say that mystics were all asocial hermits fleeing the world or only selfishly concerned with their own salvation. Rather, the sense of connectedness to others arising from mystical experiences and the other-regarding concern that moral mystics adopt was expressed most often in face-to-face interactions, such as teaching a person or a small group or ministering to the material needs only of the people they encounter. There may be stages on the path or periods in the enlightened state in which mystics withdraw from any interactions for meditative or other exercises, but the moral mystics return to the world. However, even when this-worldly help is offered, still there is little group activity or interest in transforming social institutions or society as a whole. Even among monastics or other mystical groups, there are few group actions for projects to help others or to transform social institutions outside their own—early and medieval Christian monasteries were very much collections of individuals silently working out their own salvation separately even when participating in group mystical practices.³ Indeed, the very term "monastic" comes from the Greek word for "one."

Why are acts of individual help valued over institutional action? After all, other strands of religiosity are socially active.⁴ Why from a mystic's point of view could others not also be helped by fixing society? Couldn't some types of reorganizing social structures materially help others or even make social conditions more conducive to enlightenment? Why cannot mystics' impartial love of all people be manifested in societal-level actions? Is there something in mystical experiences or in mystical value systems or belief claims that devalues or screens out group action or social structures and instead focuses attention solely on individual interactions? Or is the lack of interest in reforming social, economic, and political institutions simply a reflection of cultural values and beliefs in premodern societies?

The principal reason classical mystics have little interest in social action appears to be that their experiences produce an overwhelming sense that another dimension to reality is more real than our world and thus our true well-being lies in that dimension, not in any worldly well-being. Early Buddhists did not discuss what lies beyond death for the enlightened, but getting out of the realm of suffering by ending rebirths was the goal. Moreover, the only way to realize this is individually by an inner experience—no worldly good or group achievement is part of the process. Our problems of living will be solved only by an individual's inner transformation oriented around a transcendent reality or goal, not by changing matters on a societal scale. To put it starkly, in classical mystical traditions what transcends the world renders this-worldly matters not worthy of our attention. It is not that mystics are concerned with nature rather than society—rather, their only worldly interest is with the *beingness* of all things, not with the differentiations within the world. The objective was not to transform the world but to transform an individual's inner relation to all things worldly. A mystical inner calm in response to whatever occurs would naturally lead to an indifference to conditions in the world—whatever exists is fine as it is. Neither the depth-mystical experience nor mindfulness changes anything except our perspective; nothing within the world needs to be changed but only seen properly. For Advaita Vedanta, worldly work would be like trying to improve the conditions in a dream: any desire to change the "dream" realm is based on distinctions of persons and objects, and the enlightened see that all such distinctions are an illusion since there is only one reality. Andrew Fort (1998: 172–81) argues convincingly that Western-style social work cannot be grounded in Advaita metaphysics. Even in moral mystical traditions such as Mahayana Buddhism and Christianity, the fundamental mystical problem is related to the fact *that* we exist, not to *what* we are socially. Thus, taking social concerns seriously—even to help others—only reveals our lack of knowledge of what is fundamentally real. Moral mystics may supply some worldly aid to the people whom they encounter, but the greatest aid would be to help others to see their true situation or otherwise to help them achieve their own inner transformation.

It is often noted that mystics need not flee society since the existential suffering they confront is just as real in a cave or a forest. But the flip side is not often noted: there is also no point in reordering society, since that would not address the mystical problem either. Mystical freedom is unrelated to what structures are in place in a society. Mystics remain emotionally detached, undisturbed by any social conditions, and thus they are not inclined to do anything about them. Needless to say, if they have the joy and inner peace that all beings are good or that everything is all right as it already is (since everything is a product of a morally good or benign transcendent reality), they will have little impetus to change anything. In the enlightened state, they are letting things be, responding to what is in front of them without imposing personal beliefs or desires. This would foreclose any interest in what is not immediately present.

The best help one can give to those not on the mystical path may be material aid, but their true welfare would be addressed by mystical teaching. Each person must walk the path to enlightenment him- or herself. Other-regardingness in this situation is best manifested in helping the person in front of us—whether it is giving them a cup of soup or religious teachings. Thus, compassion remains individualistic, not work on a societal scale. Even political acts such as the monk killing the Tibetan king in the ninth century CE for his persecution of Buddhists are motivated only by concern for the immediate recipients (here, concern for the welfare in future lives of the king and his potential future victims).[5] The actions of the Bodhisattva Vimalakirti (R. Thurman 1976) with his skillful means (*upaya-kaushalya*) for helping others in his community through personal encounters become more representative of moral mystical action than those of Laozi's sage-rulers.

A certain minimal physical health is, of course, needed to maintain a mystical quest; so mystics may be concerned with the physical conditions for maintaining the body and also with the sociopsychological conditions supporting them on the path. But the general lack of social protest suggests that mystics found that each classical society provided the material, social, and psychological conditions needed for the mystical quest. Mystics, that is, could find the personal freedom, material support from the populace for their simple ways of life, and the psychological dignity needed to pursue their quest without changing society. Conditions in societies could in principle be so harsh that human life is not sustainable, let alone a quest of a relatively small number of people for enlightenment. But each classical society had a place in its social order for mystics and provided the minimal physical and psychological security they needed for the quest. To mystics that is all that could possibly matter in our realm, and so no reform of social structure was needed. This does not mean that they envisioned a society in which every member was a monk or beggar and where there would be no householders generating and distributing material goods. It only means that the conditions for such householders were not a subject of their concern.

Face-to-face interpersonal action is adaptable to virtually any political circumstances. Thus, these mystics did not try to reform the politics of their culture. Nor did they explicitly endorse the status quo. Nor were they anarchists or utopians who envisioned a perfect society (Laozi being an exception). Nor were they simply waiting until social ills got so bad that societies would implode and a more mystic-friendly society would emerge. All such stances would be as political as trying to reform a society. These issues were simply screened out of their concerns. Classical mystics could accept their society as they accept its language—as something at hand that they did not need to alter or abolish. Mystics can operate with emotional detachment and even-mindedness regardless of the social structures in their culture. The phenomena of our realm merely have to be seen correctly. Social structures that seem unjust to us (e.g., social status being fixed by birth) are irrelevant to our real suffering. The *Bhagavad-gita* sees the enlightened state in terms of fulfilling a social role to maintain society, but it does not foresee, let alone advocate, any social reform. Arjuna found enlightenment within his social system in conforming to his social role as defined the various *dharma* rules, not in reforming the system in order to help others. The idea of social restructuring could not occur in the *Bhagavad-gita*'s mystical approach—a king who was not fulfilling his dharmic duties might be removed, but the institution would not be abolished. Focusing attention on reforming society would misdirect our energy.[6]

Social reform means wanting to alter the sensory realm, but for classical mystics everything phenomenal remains the same—only our knowledge and dispositions for action through an inner transformation need correcting. No amount of this-worldly fulfillment or comfort can bring about that change, and thus social reform is irrelevant. Of course, a possible consequence of the mystical inner transformation of everyone within society is that the roots of social problems may well end, but that effect is not the focus of concern. Jiddu Krishnamurti was a modern mystic who was appalled by the social conditions in India, but he responded in the traditional mystical fashion: for him, social reform could not answer the fundamental problem but could only scratch its surface—until the nature of man was changed radically, all other change was useless and irrelevant (Lutyens 1983: 42). Outward conditions merely reflect our inner states. For example, to end war we would have to end the war within us (anger, hatred, lust for power) (Lutyens 1983: 40–53, 56–57). Until that happens, we will be dealing only with symptoms and not the causes of disorder, and thus war will not end. Thus, the only change of real value is an inner one of our dispositions and other aspects of consciousness.

That application of mysticism to matters of peace exposes a problem: not all classical mystics engaged in any type of social action. Helping individuals attain inner peace may be their only goal. In Peter Gan's words, "An experience of profound unity among all things in the universe helps to form within the heart of the experiencing subject a sense of connectedness with all beings, and hence serves to strengthen the bond of solidarity between the self and others" (2019: 8). But such empathy may lead only to face-to-face moral actions related to others' religious salvation rather than social action, although it can also lead to applying mysticism to aid an entire society with a worldly goal. For those mystics interested in world peace, all people attaining inner peace is the only way to attain a permanent outer peace—in the words of the psychiatrist Peter Breggin, "Inner peace and world peace are, at root, one and the same" (quoted in Gan 2019: 5). Mystical practices, even if strenuous, can then contribute to such peace building by generating an inner tranquility and a sense of the unity of all beings (e.g., Curle 1972).

Moreover, engaging in social action with others would involve mystics working with the unenlightened who by definition have an unenlightened view of reality. That may lead to difficulties for both the mystics and the unenlightened. In addition, devotion to social causes can *interfere* with a mystical way of life: Gan quotes Dostoevsky from *The Brothers Karamazov* having a character say "I am amazed at myself: the more I love mankind in general, the less I love people in particular, that is individually as separate persons. . . . [T]he more I hate people individually, the more ardent becomes my love for humanity as a whole" (2019: 9). The classical mystics' reaction seems be that they would not let their focus on the individuals standing in front of them be distracted by working on social reform to help with worldly problems. Krishnamurti expressed the problem of teaching large groups: he said that even in India there was not a single person who had listened to him and had taken him seriously enough to actually undergo an inner change.

In sum, under classical mystics' view, we would need to change human beings individually along mystical lines to change society collectively, not vice versa. The classical mystical stance on "social reform" is to reform the inner life of individuals. Only by the inner reform of all individuals will society change for the better. But the important point is that mystics are interested in the inner transformation of persons—even any cumulative social effects on our world is not the goal and is ultimately unimportant. Any social change is neither necessary nor sufficient to bring about what is really needed, and hence is not a concern. Any "collective liberation" concerns the individuals, not a worldly transformation of society. Again, this does not mean that all mystics are selfishly concerned with only themselves and cannot be bothered with other people's problems, but it does mean that even moral classical mystics are typically not out to make social changes. When a radical inner transformation is required to end suffering, aiding one person at a time in his or her own transformation may be the best that can be done.

It should also be noted that the mystical experiences enabled today by psychedelics appear to increase our sense of selflessness and our cognitive and emotional empathy and may lead to a positive feedback loop involving empathy and prosocial and pro-environmental behavior, but they do not necessarily lead to any changes in *behavior* at all (see Bhatt and Weissman 2024: 1–3). The social setting when the drug is ingested affects whether action result and whether the individual's actions are liberal or conservative (Roseman et al. 2022). Some argue that the sense of intimate connectedness to nature resulting from ego-dissolution that occurs in some psychedelic-enabled experiences in the woods will motivate the users to take pro-environmental actions. But while psychedelics may lead to a greater sense of a connection to nature (Lyons and Carhart-Harris 2018; Kettner et al. 2019; Irvine et al. 2023), the sense of connectedness does not necessarily lead to *action*: there may be no change in one's action at all or only ending one's own individual damaging actions—the experiences may not motivate people to engage in *social or political activities* that would bring about change. In addition, the drugs do not necessarily produce liberal or progressive changes or actions for someone not previously so inclined.

In fact, psychedelics have been touted by authoritarian right-wing groups, including neo-Nazis today (Pace and Devenot 2021). It appears that the suggestibility caused by psychedelics leads to *amplifying* whatever values one already has (Pace and Devenot 2021). Meditation is also often associated with the political left (e.g., Rowe 2016), but if a meditator construes the self as an independent reality, mindfulness leads to a *decrease* in prosocial behavior (Poulin et al. 2021).

Mystics' Social Actions

The lack of social action is not to deny that the presence of mystics in a society may have an effect on societal realities. The Buddhist monk's assassination of a Tibetan king would be an instance of an action having a political effect. More generally, mystical religiosity may affect the values of a society, either short- or long-term, and thereby affect the economic and social structures of the larger community. Nor is this to deny that certain social conditions may be needed for mystical religiosity to flourish—mysticism is a social phenomenon and thus needs social support (teachers, students, patrons) as much as any other. But the mystical values and goals preclude granting full value to this realm, and this brings up the issue of whether classical mystics can accept group actions on the collective societal level.

The individualistic inward orientation of mystical enlightenment, however, does not preclude social action in principle: mystics can treat the world and other people as real enough to warrant helping them, even if the mystic is seeing his or her own salvation in other-worldly terms.[7] Laozi's concern for reordering government is a prominent instance of a mystical orientation to social action. Even Plotinus, the epitome of a mystic advocating "the flight of the alone to the Alone," did not withdraw from society: he was a teacher and spiritual advisor on directing one's awareness toward the One, a caretaker for many orphans, the educator of young boys and girls, and an arbitrator of disputes (Porphyry, *Life of Plotinus*, chapters 7 and 9). He asked the Roman emperor to restore a ruined city for philosophers to rule by Plato's laws—"Platonopolis." (But it would have been more like a monastery than a model for general social reform.) He discouraged his students from political involvement (Porphyry, *Life of Plotinus*, chapter 7). His objective was to live with detachment—an emotional isolation of the higher soul from the body. He said that only in cases of *extreme social distress*—e.g., war, famine, extreme injustice—should a sage engage in any actions other than contemplation (see *Enneads* VI.8.5).

The general lack of social action cuts across cultural lines, but cultural beliefs and values do affect the propensity for social action. That is, "mysticism" is not simply having a "mystical experience"—it is itself a social institution, and the beliefs and values adopted in different mysticisms depend upon more than simply having a mystical experience. For example, in India the beliefs in *karma* and rebirth screen out the idea of social reform: everyone has gotten the physical and social circumstances in this life that they deserve from their own actions in their past lives, and no one can help them out of existential suffering but themselves. *Karma* is nature's justice at work, and thus we do not need to try to remedy or correct anything ourselves.[8] There is no need to reorganize society in any way—indeed, redistributing wealth or any other reform of social conditions would be *interfering* with karmic justice and may prolong people's chains of rebirth. At best, it is merely changing the field in which *karma* operates and thus is of little importance. Social projects to help others with worldly problems certainly would not flourish in such an atmosphere. The Indian belief in rebirth would also extend the circle of concern beyond human beings to all forms of sentient life. The Indian belief in the cycle of world ages also blunts any call for progress in the social realm: we live in the dark age (*kali-yuga*), and nothing we can do will stop the further decline of the world. There is no hope for social improvement—the world-age will continue to decline until a new cycle begins. Thus, all that can be done is an individual effort for improvement of one's own karmic fate. (This is not to deny that Hindus as a whole have shown moral concern for human beings and animals.)

The Buddha gave some social teachings (R. Jones 2004: 158–60), and Buddhists (especially the Mahayana in China and Japan) engaged in some social work such as building roads and administering medical care (R. Jones 2004: 204–7). The societal-scale activity could have both a soteriological and a secular objective. But when the great Tibetan master Milarepa was asked if monks could perform works that were in a small way beneficial to others, he answered: "If there be not the least self-interest attached to such duties, it is permissible. But such detachment is indeed rare; and works performed for the good of others seldom succeed, if not wholly freed from self-interest. . . . It is as if a man hopelessly drowning were to try to save another man in the same predicament." He recommended instead resolving to attain Buddhahood for the good of all living beings—i.e., attaining the best position to help others with their true needs. Before that, the monks do not know the true nature of reality and thus may in fact be inadvertently hurting both themselves and those they are trying to help. And, even if the others are materially helped, they may be spiritually hurt—they may become comfortable enough in the realm of suffering not to seek *nirvana*. They may also end up attaching too much significance to what is only one life in a huge chain of rebirths. Both the helper and the helped may become attached to the impermanent and no one may really be helped at all. Thus, getting enlightened first is the best way to help others as well as oneself. The enlightened then focus only on helping others toward the soteriological goal of liberation from rebirth. Thus, when faced with an epidemic, an enlightened Bodhisattva thinks only "What is called 'sickness' is not an element of reality (*dharma*), nor is there any element of reality for sickness to oppress," and then thinks about creating a Buddha-field (Pure Land) free of sickness that has the perfect conditions for people to attain enlightenment and thus end their suffering permanently (*Ashtasahasrika-Prajnaparamita* 364–65). That is the greatest good for the greatest number in Buddhist mysticism, not increasing worldly happiness.

Laozi, reflecting his Chinese cultural interests, took society seriously. He advocated forming a simpler society (*Daodejing* 80; also see Versluis 2011). He also had a political program (R. Jones 2004: 239–43, 2024: 312–15), and later Daoists, perhaps influenced by Buddhism, engaged in social work. Much of the *Daodejing* is devoted to governing and waging war. Thus, one would expect that those in Chinese history who were influenced by this work would be more likely to protest political and social problems. And later religious Daoists did indeed do that. Buddhism, in contrast, proved itself very adaptable to different sociopolitical conditions, which one would expect if mysticism heavily influenced it. As Daisetz T. Suzuki noted of Zen, Buddhism can be wedded to anarchism, fascism, communism, democracy, or any political or economic dogmatism (1970: 63).[9] Gary Synder notes the individualistic nature of Buddhism as a practical system of meditation and admits that "[i]nstitutional Buddhism has been conspicuously ready to accept or ignore the inequalities and tyrannies of whatever political system it found itself under" (in Eppesteiner 1988: 82–83). In the twentieth century, Buddhists supported socialism in Burma, capitalism and a monarchy in Thailand, and communism in China and Laos (Harvey 2000: 118). From the Buddhist point of view, no system is intrinsically better than another, nor is there a need to abolish all of them. Buddhism can also accommodate differing economic and social settings. Inner liberation and not any transformation of the external world is what matters.

The Abrahamic traditions treat this world as real (although dependent upon a transcendent god for its existence) and people as subjects of moral concern. Thus, Western theists are more likely to focus on material aid as well as soteriological aid and hence to have more social reformers than are Asian traditions such as Advaita that dismiss this realm as valueless or unreal. Once Christianity entered the mainstream of Roman culture, it moved from an in-group ethic to add political and society-wide dimensions to its way of life.[10] The ideal for the enlightened mystical life combines "contemplation" and "action" into what Jan van Ruusbroec called the "comprehensive life": an active enlightened life is in effect contemplation in action (see R. Jones 2004: 272–75).[11] And some early and medieval mystics in Christianity did show a social interest, even if most confined their interest in easing others' suffering to face-to-face interactions (Rakoczy 2006; Schroeder 2009; R. Jones 2004: 282–85).[12] The disparity of the wealthy and the poor in society was a concern of such early mystics as Saint Basil of Caesarea and Saint John Chrysostom in the fourth century (Chrysostom 1981; Schroeder 2009). Saint John of the Cross designed and helped build an aqueduct that is still in use today. Saint Catherine of Siena remains in Siena to help plague victims. In modern times, the Quaker pacifist and labor organizer A. J. Muste's activism in the twentieth century was inspired by Christian mysticism. The Quaker mystic and scholar Rufus Jones (2001) also looked to the history of Christian "affirmative mysticism" to support his social activism. Later in the twentieth century, Dorothy Day (Ellsberg 2005) and Thomas Merton (1998; Apel 2003) were prominent examples of mystically inspired advocates of social reform and proponents of peace and disarmament. Today mysticism is not a major topic in Christian theology, but two notable exceptions who were socially active and wrote on connecting mysticism and social action are Howard Thurman (1961; Boeke 2015; L. Smith 1991; Pollard 1992) and Dorothee Soelle (2001; Oliver 2006). Desmond Tutu's activism also has a Christian mystical grounding (Battle 2021). Some mystically inspired theologians advocate social action (e.g., Fox 1991). Liberation theology sometimes has a mystical dimension (e.g., Raggio 2023). Some thinkers see an inherent connection of Christian mysticism and action—as the French poet Charles Peguy put it in 1909, "Everything begins in mysticism and ends in politics." A more tempered position is that contemplation is truncated without action, and action is ungrounded without contemplation (Commins 2105: 11).

Judaism has always had a strong emphasis on community and the Jewish people as a whole, but when the Kabbalists and Hasidim came along, the picture changed: the orientation went from the people of Israel "cleaving to God" (*devekut*) as a whole to individuals cleaving to God in mystical experiences; these mystical groups still valued the community, but they did not engage in secular social reform and instead tried to reform the society by transforming individuals through mystical practices (see R. Jones 2024: 97–105). The Hasidim emphasize personal religious redemption rather than the redemption of the nation or cosmos as a whole. They deemphasize repairing the world (*tikkun*), the process by which the Jewish people collect the scattered sparks of divine light in the world by keeping God's commandments and praying. However, today most Kabbalists are more interested in "repairing" the natural world through social ethics. There is also the notion of a "national salvation"—i.e., every Jew will be rewarded, when the redemption of the nation of Israel is reached, by sharing in the collective salvation and not just by a personal reward from God (Dan 1996: 101–2). Also, the ideal for a Hasidic mystic is to help his community individually: when a mystic reaches the highest goal, the orthodox view is for the "righteous individuals" (the Zaddik) to "step down a little" from the highest form of communion with God in order to be nearer to their community (Scholem 1967: 18–20). Abraham Herschel is an example of a Jewish leader in the twentieth century who tried to combine social action and mysticism.

Mystics may also have an effect on those in their religious tradition who are not interested in mysticism but are interested in social reform. Mystics as exemplars of their tradition may inspire nonmystics to a more impartial or selfless application of their own mystical and nonmystical ideas, such as social reform.[13] In addition, mystics still on the path to enlightenment may see value in social reform since they still have unenlightened beliefs. (Again, there is the danger in any social reform that the unenlightened will simply be imposing their self-will under the guise of aid for others.) Moreover, others within a tradition who have had isolated mystical experiences may also believe greater social reform is worth pursuing. There would, however, be limits to how much mystics' lives of voluntary simplicity could be a model for reforming society as a whole—one could not expect, for example, monastic poverty to be expanded to the abolition of the idea of private property in a society, to say nothing of celibacy. Social reforms within a religious group may also have a limited impact on a society in general. For example, Buddhists, Sikhs, and the devotional Bhakti theists of medieval India in theory rejected caste distinctions within their religious groups, but this had little impact on their society at large.[14]

The focus of mystics' attention is on the individual, but it might be argued that general conditions in our realm could be altered to make the path to enlightenment easier for a greater number of people; thus, rather than direct attention toward helping a few with their inner transformation, mystics arguably should try the type of help in which a large number of people are each helped a little in their material conditions. If, for example, poverty and war were ended, greed and hatred might be reduced and more people would make greater progress on their path to enlightenment. Or, since individual self-interest is at the center of capitalism, installing socialism might weaken self-centeredness. Or, if we believed a long series of rebirths await us all, we might want to improve the conditions of everyone—e.g., Whites in America might be inclined to improve race relations because they would realize that they or loved ones may be reborn as Blacks, or we all may be more concerned with the environment if we expected to be reborn on this planet.

Mystics can engage in social work and influence the social works by others. But again, social work also presents another danger: mystics may get caught up in our realm. They may lose contact with the transcendent dimension in thinking that reforming this realm will help bring about enlightenment. There is also the problem of knowing what would be best for a large number of people or how to help some while not hurting others—by definition, the unenlightened will not have the correct view of reality and thus not know how best to help. In addition, what would count as helping would also depend on one's factual beliefs and thus may vary from tradition to tradition—e.g., Buddhists are more likely than Christians to set up hospitals for birds and animals. Economic prosperity would allow more people to spend more time on their spiritual life, but Buddhist teachers have pointed out the danger of making people so comfortable that they, like the gods in the heavens, will not be inclined to seek enlightenment. And there is no reason to believe that most people would become interested in pursuing a mystical way of life; most would focus instead on new types of material well-being that would only further solidify the hold of this realm. Mysticism was a more influential strand of religiosity when social and economic conditions were worse probably because its aim is to escape this world. It is no coincidence that a high point of mysticism in Europe was at the time of the Black Death and the Hundred Years' War. When conditions improved, people focused more on improving their conditions in this world.

Thus, social help may not do much mystical good and may do damage by making us too comfortable. For mystics, it is only a matter of dealing with the symptoms of suffering and not the root causes (personal desires and the lack of knowledge of the fundamental nature of reality). But again, the more basic problem is that mystics would have to take seriously a realm that they do not take to be fully real or valuable. To mystics, it is better to devote our energies to the inner transformation needed to become enlightened, whatever the social conditions.

The Problem with Politics

Such indifference to social reform would obviously have the *conservative effect* of reenforcing the social status quo, thereby helping the ruling classes, even if that is not the mystics' intent. Politics deals with maintaining or changing the broad social structures of a society, and mystics, despite their individualistic orientation, may be aware of the difference between the way their society is and a way that would be more conducive for others to gain enlightenment. But to bring about societal-level change in this manner, mystics would have to combine forces with the unenlightened who do not see reality as it truly is and this would be problematic.

Moreover, the inherent deception, ruthlessness, and general Machiavellian nature of politics throughout history presents a major problem for mystics who insist on honesty in all forms (see Scharfstein 1995). Enlightened mystics, in dealing only with the person in front of them and not thinking about others, would also be inclined to see things in terms of black and white, not shades of grey. Their precepts for inner change are those such as "Do not kill," not "Kill as few as is reasonably possible to achieve your objective." The enlightened would also have trouble making political compromises with the unenlightened when they believe the unenlightened are living in a world of delusion—trying to compromise with characters in a "dream" or take their unenlightened interests seriously would not occur to those who are certain that they are awake.

Another problem is that the social order involves laws restricting our behavior that are not freely adopted by all. Laws will at most bring about a change in behavior by enforcing an ethical code through civil authorities, but this probably will not do much toward altering a person's inner disposition. Adopting ethical precepts for one's own behavior is the first step on the mystical path toward changing dispositions and beliefs, but requiring others not so inclined to act a certain way will not change their inner disposition; they will simply minimally comply or will look for ways around the regulation. In short, we cannot transform a person from the outside. Laws cannot require that we act out of humility or love, no matter how they constrain our actions. Laws against racist practices in America and untouchability in India are examples of the problem.

From a classical mystical perspective, laws involve a type of *coercion* rather than *persuasion* by teaching, actions, or example. From this perspective, laws are acts by a group of people telling *other people* what they can or cannot do. It is not like mystics freely adopting a code of conduct for themselves without imposing it on others. From the mystical point of view, laws are a form of violence: they impose one's views on others and force others to conform by threats of punishment. In sum, the unenlightened may conform their actions to the laws for reasons totally unrelated to mystical selflessness, and thus the laws would have no effect at all on their mystical development. Mystical precepts are forms of advice for oneself on what we ourselves should do, not laws telling other people what they can or cannot do. The mystics' response to a dilemma such as whether to have an abortion is that we empty ourselves of all sense of self and the answer will appear (as directed by our beliefs and values), not the imposition of laws.

Laws also introduce a problem of third-person interests that does not arise on a path of mystical self-cultivation. What should we do if we see another person being attacked? The precept "turn the other cheek" addresses what we should do when *we* are attacked—some religious people would willingly die rather than fight back—but the precept does not tell us what to do if we see *someone else* being attacked. Similarly, expanding "love your enemies" into a law or national foreign policy requires third-person considerations not given in face-to-face interactions. This means that governing produces a new level of concerns in the realm of nescience that would move mystics further away from their concern.

The history of Christianity shows another persistent problem. Christianity has been the legitimating force for many totalitarian regimes. Christian scriptures have also been used to justify all sorts of social practices that were later judged to be unjust. In fact, its scriptures have been used to justify *both sides* in social disputes: capitalism and socialism, slavery and abolition, polygamy and monogamy, both sides in wars, and so on (see Scharfstein 1995).

Today we can add civil rights, capital punishment, nuclear disarmament, LGBTQ+ issues, and all issues in medical ethics. In such circumstances, it is hard to find one abiding "social ethic" in Christianity (Troeltsch 1931, 1991). Thus, some social values must come from sources other than basic religious beliefs. Religious leaders may just rationalize their self-interested actions by claiming "God is on their side." Why mystics would want to take sides on any sociopolitical issue present in their culture at that moment is not clear, especially if they reject the entire social realm as not an ultimate reality, and they are as concerned with the existential suffering of the oppressors as much as with the oppressed. In particular, the modern form of tribalism—nationalism—must seem to classical mystics to be an artificial creation that has no basis in reality. It is a form of self-love that can only strengthen attachments by fixing an idol in the mind that interferes with seeing reality as it truly is.

All of this leads to the conclusion that any political reform will not solve the fundamental problem of life as mystics see it. Not only is this realm not finally real, social engineering by means of laws will not address our most fundamental suffering. Rearranging the structures of our social world only directs attention away from where it should be—on the transcendent goal. Any social reform without an inner spiritual reform is valueless and makes social reform an end in itself and thus an attachment. As the saying goes, mystics may have first to step into the mud (of the realm of nescience) to help pull someone out of the mud, but this is best limited to helping individuals one at a time, not to getting mired in the additional level of political action. In sociopolitical reform, one must think in more abstract terms of long-range goals, weigh the welfare of different groups, and make other judgments based on utilitarian or other considerations—all in contrast to acting immediately and spontaneously, as with mystical action.

In short, politics introduces a level of problems alien to classical mysticism. It is not that the realm of morality is cut off from the realm of politics: each involves interpersonal actions, and all interpersonal actions may well have political consequences. So too, political beliefs (such as the divine right of kings) may be part of the background framework of beliefs internalized by mystics out of which they act. But moral mystics in the past have primarily focused only on the immediate interaction at hand and thus restricted their considerations to face-to-face encounters regardless of the political situation. Today mystics interested in social reform may prefer to work on projects unrelated to political change, although large-scale social changes always end up having a political dimension.

Examples of Mysticism and Social Issues

Virtues that involve the societal level illustrate the problems just discussed. Consider social justice. To most mystics, justice is a matter of the next life (through remedies from God or *karma*), not social justice within this realm. Granted, a radical impartiality governs mystics' actions, and thus to the extent such impartiality is equated with "social justice" there is no problem. But once impartiality is extended beyond individual face-to-face actions, problems arise.

First, mystics would have no interest in such items as equality before the law for the disenfranchised, the just distribution of material goods, or equal opportunity for worldly success since nothing on the societal level addresses the fundamental misalignment with reality that we all suffer. From a mystical point of view, any redistribution of wealth or other adjustments without changing the dispositions of the people will leave the world basically as it is—it is simply rearranging the deck chairs on the *Titanic*. Meister Eckhart's mystically driven reaction to the conditions of his time would be typical of mystics' responses (R. Jones 2004: 283–85): for him, the "Kingdom of God" is not in this world, and being an "aristocrat" or being "just" was a matter of one's *inner self* and not of one's *social status*—no civil revolt or reform was needed or advocated.

Second, mystics would not typically treat their ethics as a matter of social ethics—e.g., substituting social justice for individual acts of compassion to those in need. Social action would move individuals further from the necessary inner transformation if they focus exclusively on the social actions. Certainly, as noted above, anything that would interfere with caring for the person in front of them or distract from that would be the opposite of the mystics' approach to action.

Third, the suffering of concern to mystics applies to everyone—the oppressors need as much help as the oppressed, and rearranging portions of our world would not help either party with their real problem. The Buddha counseled the rich as well as the poor without arguing for change in the social conditions. He intervened on the battlefield but expressed concern only for the people involved, not for the politics of the conflict. In general, mystics are tolerant of all, not judging anyone but accepting them as they are. This may lead to acts that we would consider unjust, such as letting a murderer go rather than letting others kill or even arrest him (as with the Buddhist Aryadeva's murder), since their unenlightened reactions would only protract their own suffering and further the cycle of violence.

In sum, one would not expect to find concepts related to "social justice" in classical religious traditions heavily influenced by mysticism. And indeed, the major Asian traditions did not have any such concepts. The concepts are modern and Western, and the fight for justice is found in Abrahamic religions but not often in their mystics' writings.

Another example is that rather applying mystical inner peace to the political level and making abolishing war a central concern, religious groups have instead legitimized it by developing the idea of "just wars." Augustine, who was mystically minded, developed the classic defense. Noting that the Old Testament has God repeatedly waging wars, he concluded that wars are a means of judgment commanded by God—indeed, to Augustine wars against heretics were acts of love (*caritas*). He tried to reconcile Jesus' more pacifist statements by interiorizing the ideas of loving one's neighbor and not resisting evil—i.e., applying them only to *attitudes*, not *acts*, thereby enabling Christian soldiers to practice them while killing.[15] (For private action, he required absolute nonviolence in personal relationships, even denying the right to self-defense.) Thus, as with the *Bhagavad-gita*, inner peace need not be reflected in outer peace. Thomas Aquinas, a less mystically minded thinker, also distinguished the private person and the state, claiming that Jesus' remark "Those who live by the sword shall die by the sword" did not apply to official public acts. Thus, the military was accepted as a legitimate vocation in Christianity.[16]

Thus, a "religion of love" adopted the "just war" concept. In fact, some Buddhists also advanced that idea when the existence of the Buddhist teaching was threatened (R. Jones 2004: 156–57; see also Jerryson and Juergensmeyer 2010). Even Jainas permit wars as an exception to their extreme principle of absolute nonviolence (*ahimsa*). And not all mystics are nonviolent or oppose war. Laozi accepted the inevitability of wars and fighting defensively (*Daodejing* 30, 31, 68, 69). The *Bhagavad-gita* makes *dharma*-required wars an integral part of its way of life. The rules of war were devised by others in the *dharma* texts. (Many Hindus ended up restricting *ahimsa*, like Augustine on love, to personal, not governmental, actions.) Bernard of Clairvaux supported the Crusades. In Islam, Sufis internalized the concept of "holy war": the greater jihad (*mujahada*) was overcoming a sense of self (the lower soul). But Sufis did not reject external warfare (the "lesser *jihad*"), and some Sufis were warriors who utilized the concept of a greater jihad to prepare participating in external battles (Neale 2017: 57–73).[17]

That the nonmystical would adopt the "just war" concept is not surprising—the nonmystical are out to maintain their institution and society.

However, that mystics or those heavily influenced by them would be instrumental in the adoption such policies is surprising. The usual mystical response concerns what the individual soldier should do. The Quaker George Fox's advice is typical: if a soldier's conscience does not bother him, he is not ready to give up the sword. It is not the mystical point of view to think in political terms of which wars are or are not justified or how much violence should be used to counter other violence—even whether force should be used to protect the innocent is a third-person issue not central to mystical ways of life. In the *Bhagavad-gita*, whether the war was justified is not Arjuna's concern but Krishna's; Arjuna's dilemma was not over those matters but was solely over whether to fulfill his personal duty (*dharma*) or not. More generally, mystics probably would not consider which side might be more in the right in a given conflict, since wars involve hatred on a huge scale. The effect again would be conservative—not to oppose their rulers' choice. Of course, religious authorities routinely declare wars to be "just" (Vietnam being an exception), since the religious authorities are those accepted by the civil authorities. But mystics may instead see war as an opportunity for compassionate action on both sides. However, Christians heavily influenced by mystics have ended up being quite fanatical in their violence.[18]

Another example is the issue of human rights, i.e., rights we all have simply by reason of our being human. The concept of "human rights" is a modern Western one, arising from the modern idea of each individual as being entitled to respect and dignity. It is often pointed out that classical cultures, both Western (including Greece) and Eastern, have no concept remotely connected to such rights.[19] The idea is foreign to the *Bhagavad-gita*, even with its concept of class duties for a functioning society, and to the *Daodejing*. It is not that these traditions favor society over the individual but that the entire issue of rights as human beings does not arise. The traditions, including their mystical strands, are not framed in terms of individuals' rights within this world. If people in general in premodern cultures did not think in these terms, then it is not surprising that their mystics with their individualistic orientation and transcendent goals did not either. More importantly, nothing in the idea of mystical selflessness would lead one to suspect that human rights would be relevant. Indeed, demanding rights would be an instance of unenlightened self-assertiveness and thus run counter to mysticism. The mystical freedom of enlightenment is not easily relatable to our freedoms in society. Thus, any focus on the social rights of individuals or communities misdirects our energies.

Thus, the general lack of protest of social and political conditions—again, there are exceptions—is not surprising. But social "progress" is another nonmystical modern idea. Classical mystics gave greater weight to mystical enlightenment. To them, our ultimate happiness lies outside of history. These examples also show the difficulty of translating mystical precepts for individuals focusing on personal inner transformation into any policies for an entire society for worldly well-being.

Modern Mystics

The conclusion for classical mystics, as John Hick concluded (1989: 304–5, 338), is that the moral mystics express their compassion mainly in individual acts of charity, leaving untouched the structural evils of society. One explanation is, as Hick notes, a universal blindness to such social issues shared by all people prior to the modern social consciousness (Hick 1989: 338). The economic and political institutions already in place in a society were accepted as ordained by God or as fixed as the laws of nature; they were unquestioned, and the issue of reform thus would not arise. It would be anachronistic to look for doctrines of human rights or political or economic liberation when political power and responsibility were beyond the horizon of all except those at the top of the social hierarchy (Hick 1989: 305).

Thus, classical mystics could not be expected to see a social remedy that others in their culture could see. But to say that mystics knew they could not change social structures and so turned inward (Hick 1989: 178) assumes that they thought social change would have been relevant if only they could have brought it about. It is being argued here that that is wrong: mystics deem a personal inner transformation necessary to end our fundamental suffering and to attain enlightenment, and the individualistic approach is the best way to help others. That individualistic approach is not an afterthought simply because mystics did not see how to transform society to induce inner transformations—social changes may be good to end worldly types of suffering but not for the type of change that we need to attain the mystical goals.

But the change in modern times in social perspective and the society-wide or global scope of work can affect mysticism. After all, mysticism, like all cultural phenomena, can evolve through interaction with other elements of culture. Technological advancements now allow us to provide aid not only for the people we happen to encounter directly: modern communications can make us intimately aware of the suffering throughout the world, and modern transportation makes it possible to deliver aid to the other side of the world. Thus, today we can see people globally in a way not possible before and in a way that brings social structures and more types of group action into the picture.

Such changes would help expedite worldly aid on a much larger scale. But help could still remain instances of applying mysticism toward worldly aid, not helping others toward a soteriological goal. Could that change mystics' attitude toward mystical personal aid? Well, there are figures in the modern world—from the Dalai Lama to the Ayatollah Khomeini—who are mystics and yet politically active. The field may be expanded to include people from Dag Hammarskjöld to the fundamentalist Jews in Israel who are asserting their political presence. Some are shifting attention to bringing secular worldly aid. In India, neo-Vedantins, claiming an Advaita heritage, have introduced socially active missions that help the lower castes, the poor, and the ailing. As Vivekananda put it, we should "worship Shiva in the poor, the sick, and the feeble." By their own admission, neo-Vedantins have been heavily influenced by Western and Christian ideas. Ramakrishna, a product of a Westernized Indian middle class, is another instance. Discussing the value of medical work, he says: "Hospitals, dispensaries, and all such things are unreal. God alone is real. . . . Why should we forget him and destroy ourselves in too many activities? After realizing him, one may, through his grace, become his instruments in building many hospitals and dispensaries."[20] And people in the West who now take up meditation without adopting a full mystical way of life often become more involved with others (see Kipnis 1994).[21] But there are also modern mystics who take a more traditional approach to inner change and rejecting sociopolitical reform as a means of helping others (e.g., Krishnamurti).

Three things should be noted about this change today. First, meditation, mindfulness, and psychedelics are often tied to socially progressive positions today (see, e.g., Nour, Evans, and Carhart-Harris 2017; Du Plessis and Just 2021: 4–5, 6–8). Mystical practices have been employed by advocates for social and racial justice, environmental protection, and other social changes that cannot be fixed by individual actions alone. There were mindfulness meditation sessions at the Occupy Wall Street events (Du Plessis and Just 2021: 6). However, mysticism is not necessarily tied to such social and political positions: some authoritarian right-wing groups, including neo-Nazis today, have employed psychedelics (Pace and Devenot 2021). Progressives also complain that mindfulness meditation has been ripped from its original setting within religious traditions (where moral values may be fostered) and made a handmaid of the status quo rather than social reform: the cure to our suffering lies within—we need only to change our outlook to find happiness, not change the social institutions that cause suffering for ourselves and others. In effect, mindfulness has been coopted by neoliberal capitalism to maintain society as it is by directing our attention inwardly and individualistically to relieve stress, anxiety, and so forth in order to function in everyday life and not challenge social structures (see Purser 2019).

Thus, mystical and other psychedelic experiences themselves appear to be morally and politically neutral. A mystic's basic values and ethics will come from cultural sources. This leads to the second point: mystics are influenced by factors other than their mystical experiences. Mystical experiences may be the most powerful or important experiences, but they are not the only factors in determining the beliefs and values of a way of life. A mystical experience may result in the mystics selflessly applying those values that they adopt. The belief that the world is a real forum in which people's true lot (from the mystic's point of view) can be improved and the value of social reform do not come from mystical experiences but from beliefs and values coming from other sources. Thus, any modern evolution of mysticism incorporating social well-being as a value will have to come from cultural sources outside of meditation and mystical experiences themselves.

Third, the lack of social action in classical mysticism is more than just the product of premodern social beliefs—there remains the tension between the mystic's call for the personal development of inner stillness and the prophetic call of social reform to change the world. Mystical selflessness and each individual's experience of the ground of reality still remain central to a mystical way of life, and they are not fostered through social reform. Despite Western society today being ingrained with the three Buddhist marks of all phenomena—everything is impermanent, no eternal self is experienced, and everything is ultimately unsatisfying (*dukkha*)—that mystics of all traditions may feel that only helping one person at a time is worth the effort. Thus, one can still expect few social reformers among mystics even today.

Mahatma Gandhi

For an example of a modern mystic who attempted to apply mysticism to societal-scale situations, consider Mohandas Gandhi, the "great soul" (*maha-atma*).²² He tried to show how the New Testament's "love your neighbor" and "turn the other check" could be applied on a society-wide scale, not just practiced by a few on a mystical path. Gandhi was a Hindu, but the influences for his social actions were not primarily Hindu. He accepted Advaita metaphysics (although he was a theist) as a basis for the claim that all life is one, but influence on him on social matters from Hindu sources was minimal. He defended most of the traditional religious Hindu system, including inherited class distinctions, but his stress on the equality of all people caused him to reject "untouchability." He learned from his mother about the devotional love of the Bhakti devotional tradition. As a young man in England, he read the *Bhagavad-gita*, but later he gave it a symbolic interpretation, interiorizing the war as an allegory of the inner struggle that we all go through, and the text remained important to him for the rest of his life. His major non-Hindu influences were Jaina and Buddhist on nonviolence (*ahimsa*); the Sermon on the Mount; such modern figures as Henry David Thoreau on civil disobedience; Leo Tolstoy, and John Ruskin. However, he was not very impressed with the Christians he encountered, and after he saw how Christians treated people of color in South Africa, he never considered becoming a Christian. Indeed, the personal and collective humiliations of Indians in British South Africa convinced him of the need for political action.

But Gandhi was a mystic, and traditional mysticism was behind his actions. For him, God was ultimate reality, and all his efforts were directed toward attaining his release (*moksha*) through "reducing himself to zero." That he saw his work as mystical in nature can be seen in his answer when asked why he was helping some poor villagers: "I am here to serve no one else but myself, to find my own self-realisation through the service of these village-folks" (Chander 1947: 375). (The Christian Mother Teresa said essentially the same thing about her work among the poor of Calcutta.) Gandhi added: "My national service is part of my training for freeing my soul from the bondage of flesh. Thus considered, my service may be regarded as purely selfish" (Chander 1947: 375). That is, he was out to enlighten himself but through a focus on the help that would result for others. After the birth of his third child, Gandhi adopted a life of renunciation and self-restraint in all matters (*brahmacharya*). This included celibacy as a shield against temptation, but it also involved control of all the senses in thought, word, and deed. This personal self-rule (*svaraj*) was necessary to truly practice nonviolence. Indeed, his entire inner discipline was to prepare himself for the service of others—he had to purify himself continuously if he was to attempt to help others to purify. Thus, a highly ascetic form of mysticism was the religious basis for his political activity. He reinterpreted the Indian concept of austerity (*tapas*) to mean self-suffering, even joyfully suffering death, for the sake of others. Fasting and intense prayer preceded his acts of civil disobedience, and he maintained his disciplines during them. Self-purification could be attained only through doing one's duty without any attachment to the fruits of one's actions, as with the *Bhagavad-gita*'s *karma-yoga*. But his devotion to God (Reality) was manifested in political and economic activity—his way to God was through social action for others.

The importance of nonviolence (*ahimsa*) to Gandhi's social efforts cannot be overemphasized. But it was not just a tool to attain political ends—it was a fundamental principle of reality. Gandhi, however, was never as radical as enlightened in applying this principle as Jainas, who argue that we cannot be completely free of killing in our personal or social lives here on earth no matter what we do. He accepted exceptions to nonviolence (e.g., killing a suffering calf to end its suffering)—most significantly, if one is forced to choose between violence and cowardice in the defense of the innocent or forced to do something that would degrade one's dignity or self-respect, one must choose violence. But on the scale of a society as a whole and on the level of group action, nonviolence is absolute. (Thus, Gandhi *inverted* what Augustine did with Christian love.) Any war of self-defense is rejected. A country should not resist invasion but accept annihilation rather than fight. Even violence as a means to a legitimate end is rejected absolutely: one's attitude is what has to be changed, and this would not occur if even a little violence were acceptable.

However, for Gandhi nonviolence is not merely the passive avoidance of harm but an active means to political change (1961). His nonviolence is filled with the positive action of compassion toward his enemies in all of his thoughts, words, and deeds. It is not passive submission to a tyrant's will but suffering with the aim of an inner conversion of one's enemies. This was central to his experiments in "grasping Reality/Truth" (*satya-graha*). Inwardly, this means discipline and selfless devotion to duty. The idea is to attain an even-mindedness to friend and foe alike and to all that happens. Outwardly, this means acts of total, nonviolent noncooperation. Gandhi's own acts included boycotts (including English courts and schools), strikes, nonpayment of taxes, the march to the sea to make salt, imprisonment, abandoning Western medicine and technology, abandoning English clothing (hence spinning cotton), abandoning the English language, and general self-sufficiency. *Satyagraha* is not surrender, capitulation, or cowardice. It is a weapon only of the strong and the brave—one must be willing to lay down one's life, to stand quietly before cannons and be willing to be blown to bits.

The theory behind *satyagraha* is that Reality/Truth (*satya*) is a power that can accomplish things—it is literally the "power of truth" to move the hearts of others. The objective is to help the oppressor as much as the victim, and the power of reality will work an inner change within an oppressor. But this can be done only by converting people, and that cannot be achieved by external coercion: violence begets only violence. Instead, an inner transformation of the aggressor is needed. Anything less would only be suppressing violence temporally. Thus, one should give material goods to thieves—eventually they will have a change of heart and give up their ways. (Gandhi's advice to Jews in World War II was to accept their fate nonviolently in order to convert the Nazis.) The oppressor is bound to turn away from evil if enough victims continue to suffer long enough. To accomplish this, however, the *satyagrahin* needs an infinite capacity for suffering and patience. His or her intention must remain pure: one never acts for one's own gain but only for others. But given a just cause, the capacity for endless suffering, and the total avoidance of violence, Gandhi was confident that victory was inevitable in the long run. (Gandhi did, however, have doubts about many of his followers. He realized that an unarmed army of trained *satyagrahins* would be needed to effect social change, but he had to call off some actions because of their violence.) But he was sure this way was grounded in reality (*satya*). Indeed, according to Gandhi a belief in God was needed to be a *satyagrahin*, since it is God (Reality) who would bring the victory—the *satyagrahin*'s role was only to suffer patiently. For his part, Gandhi said he was willing to suffer for the sake of others for a thousand years.

This mystical foundation became more prominent in his later years. He believed no positive change would be permanent unless he acted for pure motives and changed the hearts and minds of others. But his uncompromising stance ended up limiting his political impact. In South Africa, he helped Indians gain more self-respect, but there were no political changes. In India, he did accomplish some changes, but more through embarrassing the British than through the inner transformation he sought. His lack of a role in the final settlement that granted India independence reveals the problem. He had been instrumental in the Indian National Congress gaining power, but he left the organization when Jawaharlal Nehru agreed to fight for England in World War II in exchange for India's independence after the war. For Gandhi, nonviolence was not merely an expedient means to an end but a fundamental principle, and he would not compromise it—he wanted to found a religious community, not a political party. His stance in the end led to him having no role in the political solution creating India and Pakistan. Indeed, this outcome probably would have occurred in the same way and at the same time if Gandhi had never existed. He was out to transform both Indians and the British, not exchange one unenlightened government for another. In short, he was trying to lead an entire country to *moksha*. He did want to free India from modernity and return to a self-sufficiency on a village scale, but his ultimate goal was to change persons—self-rule (*svaraj*) on a personal scale (personal self-control, self-respect, and nonviolence), not just self-rule for India. Only that, he believed, would bring about a permanent positive change.[23]

However, Gandhi realized that his influence was waning rapidly by the end of his life—he said shortly before his death, "Everyone is eager to garland my photos, but nobody wants to follow my advice." His fasting to quell the intense rioting after the announcement of the independence plan partitioning the subcontinent into two countries was ignored—and his violent death at the hands of Hindu fundamentalists who opposed the division of the subcontinent only accented his lack of success. He had some disciples (notably the land reformer Vinoba Bhave) and has influenced some people outside of India working for secular change (notably the nonviolent resistance of Martin Luther King, Jr.). However, in India he had little lasting social influence, as the continuing violence between religious groups indicates.

Gandhi may have shown the limitations of social change through mysticism: if social actions did not work in the relatively liberal British India, they probably would have limited effect elsewhere. In addition, he may have shown the indispensability of a charismatic leader in any attempt of mystical social action. It also must be admitted that the combination of influences that created a new nonviolent form of social action introduced something new to mysticism. It does not reflect classical Hinduism—indeed, Hindus accused Gandhi of distorting their tradition with his social concern (Bowker 1970: 234–36). It is a product of the modern era, both in its social focus and in its use of multiple Western and Eastern sources.

However, none of that changes the fact that Gandhi's mysticism had a strong social component. His yoga was one of service to others, not just inner contemplation; it was not merely a form of "contemplation in action" but "contemplation in social action." This keeps his yoga from fitting neatly into categories of either "this-worldly" or "otherworldly" since there was a focus on this-worldly action as the means to a transcendent goal. But this yoga was clearly moral, although Gandhi was also doing it for his own salvation: he was concerned with helping both the victims of oppression and also the oppressors by changing their hearts and minds. His "experiments with Truth/Reality" may not have proven that nonviolence is in fact a fundamental law of human existence or that suffering can melt the heart of aggressors, but the mysticism of it all is undeniable—the spiritual component of personal liberation coincided with a secular component of helping others achieve a worldly end.

Thus, Gandhi was engaged in a mystical way of life both for himself and to help others to enter the mystical life. This aspect is not applied mysticism, but Gandhi also realized that most of his followers engaged in his political campaigns were not engaged in changing their inner life but wanted only to change the political and social conditions of India. This aspect had the effect of converting his mystical quest into one having only worldly effects for most people. Thus, his action straddled both the mystical life and applied mysticism.

Socially Engaged Buddhism

Many Buddhists in the twentieth century became much more active with Western-type social projects in many Theravada and Mahayana Asian countries, although most Buddhists remained more traditional. There was a shift from the transcendent goal of ending rebirths to helping society with worldly aims. There also was some shift from traditional forms of almsgiving to monks and nuns to supporting schools, hospitals, and other public projects. Some Buddhists worked out a "Buddhist economics" in the form of socialism and other ways to combat poverty, pollution, and other social ills. Some monks and laity became more politically active—e.g., those in Soka Gakkai in Japan and some Zen monks of Vietnam in the 1960s who carried on its monks' traditional opposition to foreign invaders (sometimes immolating themselves to bring attention to their country's suffering, although many fellow Zen Buddhists objected). But Zen leaders also supported Japanese militarism, and Zen monks trained Japanese soldiers for World War II in Zen temples (see Victoria 1997)—indeed, some Zen leaders in Japan made World War II a "holy war" for Zen.[24] A monk in

Sri Lanka assassinated a politician in 1956, and monks now participate in the politics (and the religious violence) of that island nation. The Buddhist "just war" doctrine returned in the Thai fight against communists.[25]

However, many Western-oriented Buddhists have acknowledged the social and political indifference of traditional Buddhism. Buddhists have traditionally adopted the existing social and political structures of whatever society they entered. Buddhism, like religions everywhere, was used to legitimate the classes in power. But some thinkers such as Thich Nhat Hanh (1993, 2008) and Ken Jones (1989, 2003) have proposed adapting social structures to make it easier for all persons to achieve the traditional Buddhist goal of individuals achieving enlightenment to end their existential suffering (*dukkha*). But in a case of applied mysticism, other modern thinkers are now rejecting this traditional view and are attempting to create a "socially engaged Buddhism" to achieve more secular ends (see Sivaraksa 1992; Queen and King 1996; Queen 2000, 2013; Ambedkar 2016; Strain 2024).[26]

These thinkers are attempting to develop a form of Buddhism that will address Western interests in freedom, social justice and equality, democracy, wealth and poverty, human rights, and the environment. For instance, Christopher Ives (1992) has given a complete rereading of Zen Buddhism along these lines.[27] Some advocates of the new socially engaged Buddhism argue that it is "latent" in the Buddhist tradition but has been "inhibited in premodern Asian settings" (Kraft 1988: xiii). But other thinkers acknowledge that this was not the traditional goal of Buddhism (see K. Jones 2003: 213–14). Socially engaged Buddhists readily concede both that they are not addressing the problem the Buddha addressed and that social reform will not bring about mystical enlightenment. They admit they are doing something else. There is a fundamental reorientation away from enlightenment to worldly matters that reflects their Western background more than Buddhism. Switching the focus from enlightenment to the improvement of social conditions—"from a transmundane (*lokuttara*) to a mundane (*lokiya*) definition of liberation" (Queen and King 1996: 11)—is not merely to deal with issues previously unaddressed by Buddhists but radically to reorient Buddhism. They emphasize the Buddha's few discourses addressed to the laity's worldly needs and a few historical instances of social activism in Buddhist history. But Christopher Queen concedes that the spirit and substance of anything like a socially engaged Buddhism first manifested itself only in the nineteenth century in Sri Lanka (Queen and King 1996: 20). This was after Western influence, in particular Christianity—indeed, this form of Sri Lankan Buddhism is called "Protestant Buddhism" (see

Gombrich 1988: 172–97). It is sometimes touted as a new Buddhist path (*yana*) (Queen 2013: 524).

Indeed, finding any doctrinal support for this enterprise is difficult. Claiming that Westerners after more than two millennia have discovered the "essence" of Buddhism free of all cultural accretions in a few passages from the Pali canon (some of questionable authenticity) is absurd. This distorts Buddhism more than the typical Western exposition of Buddhism as a religion of only a few religious virtuosi or as scientific. First, Buddhists have never been "disengaged" from society: the monks, nuns, and laity all interact with others—it was simply a different type of engagement with a different goal than what these thinkers want. The Buddha and the Bodhisattvas are exemplars of moral conduct toward others, although Buddhism is an "individual transcendentalism" (R. Thurman 1983, 1992). Second, as discussed above, it is not a simple matter to derive answers for social problems from the face-to-face, individualistic approach. Institutional issues were not merely unaddressed by traditional Buddhists, no answers to them are entailed by its individualistic approach. They are a new set of issues, and the individualistic approach has no straightforward bearing on them. Earlier Buddhists (with a very few exceptions) did not address the latter because these problems were irrelevant to our fundamental existential suffering. Such suffering cannot be remedied by social and political action but only by escaping the chain of rebirths. Political indifference was a straightforward consequence of this mystical religiosity.

Most importantly, socially engaged Buddhism is not about changing social and political conditions so that a large number of people can overcome at least a little of their self-centeredness, greed, hatred, anger, or aggression. These thinkers are not trying to make social conditions more conducive to mystical enlightenment for a greater number of people but are making the social world an end in itself. Indeed, the socially engaged Buddhists have completely abandoned the traditional transcendent orientation of ending rebirths in favor of reforming the world toward social freedom for all and the improvement of social well-being. They differ from most modern social reformers in that they accept the idea that changing social structures without changing people's *inner attitudes* will not produce a permanent improvement (Kraft 1992: 12; Ives 1992: 134–35). But they are no longer interested in any transcendent dimension. *Nirvana* is not different from this world of rebirths (*samsara*), so all we should do is make this world better. This approach omits the entire thrust of Buddhism's soteriological goal of getting out of the realm of suffering. Buddhists were not out to save the world, or at best to save it by ending it through the inner transformation of each individual. The Buddha was not tempted to be a world monarch (*cakka-vatti*), since the world held nothing of value.

In sum, adapting Buddhist precepts to a societal scale while retaining the soteriological goal of ending individuals' rebirth is one thing, but in a case of applied mysticism, secular socially engaged Buddhists are creating something new by giving "new readings to ancient Dharma"—something modern and Western in foundation and outlook. It is applying the compassion of Mahayana Buddhist mysticism to worldly problems for worldly ends, and that is a radical break with Buddhism's traditional purpose. Taking Buddhism out of its soteriological context of attaining a transcendent goal changes its character. This new approach no doubt has a Buddhist influence, but the switch in aims "from a highly personal and other-worldly notion of liberation to a social, economic, this-worldly liberation" (Queen and King 1996: 10) is so radical that whether it can be called "Buddhism" in any meaningful sense is open to debate.

Reinventing Mysticism

Gandhi's social action did retain the individualistic approach from classical mysticism: individual persons remained central, whether they were a victim or an oppressor; changing the social conditions was necessary and required group action, but Gandhi's ultimate objective was to change souls, not just to create new social and political structures. He also stressed that each participant in a mass *satyagraha* action must maintain his or her own individual responsibility and not relinquish his or her will to the group. He hoped that the social actions would very much be by an aggregate of individuals working out their own salvation individually and not involving one unified selfless unit in motion. In fact, one point that follows from the above discussions is that classical mystics are individualistic in the sense of emphasizing personal interactions over group actions. Mystics can work within society and still see society as merely an aggregate of individuals to interact with. In short, society is reduced to a collection of individuals—a "nonsociety" of people. Even socially engaged Buddhism theorists admit that traditionally Buddhists see society as "no more than the aggregate of the individuals composing it" (e.g., K. Jones 1989: 202). So too for many advocates of meditation today (e.g., Goleman and Davidson 2018: 290–91). Inwardly transforming the attitudes of individuals through meditation or mystical training may make persons calmer and feel connected to the rest of society and the world, and this will result in changes in their actions. For example, it will lessen material desires and may well generate empathy and compassionate actions toward others.[28] These inner changes in individual persons, advocates believe, will have a cumulative effect on a society-wide scale.

It is only natural that mysticism, with its focus on personal inner experiences, should be individualistic in nature. It is also an instance of what William Inge called "the hardness of all ancient ethics" (Rist 1967: 153, 260)—that no one can do anything for anyone else.[29] Everyone must travel the mystical path themselves and do their own mystical cultivation. Everyone must have their own experiences and are responsible only for themselves. Any "social realities" would not fit in this picture—it is a matter only of individuals and transcendent realities. Community is not the way to connect to such realities. This does not mean that there are no mystical groups practicing together or that mystical experiences cannot occur in a group setting, nor is it to deny that there is a social dimension to full mystical ways of life. But it does mean that the center of mystical ways of life is each person ultimately working out his or her own soteriological goal individually.

Thus, one can see why classical mystics typically did not participate in social reform. The problem is more than just the premodern belief that the realm of change cannot be improved: mystics are focused on the eternal and are not concerned with the temporal things of this world. Inner reform is central and cannot be replaced by outer social reform. It is not so much that society cannot be repaired as that it is not worth bothering with it at all. No amount of social or technological change will correct the problems of living that mystics find central. In addition, we cannot easily derive social answers from the mystical solutions—societal-level answers cannot be deduced from individualistic precepts. Mystical freedom—freedom from attachments—simply does not relate to social and economic freedoms. Mystical concepts of "right" and "wrong" cannot be translated in any simple and straightforward manner into social concepts of justice or equality. Mystical selflessness is not an impetus to changing social conditions. External forms of reform attempt to manipulate and dominate and thus cannot be effective in producing an inner change. Liberals see human beings as changeable by changing social structures; thus, solutions to our problems lie on the social level. Mystics see the opposite: only through an inward change can any lasting outward changes be brought about, and, they would add, with the inward change the outward changes are no longer needed. Thus, devoting energy to restructuring social institutions is a waste of time. Accepting society as it is thus is the norm for these mystics.

Again, this does not mean all mystics are selfishly focused only on their own lives—many mystics have been great workers. It means only that their help is primarily limited to beings immediately in front of them and that providing them help on the mystical path is most important. To the nonreligious, the mystics' idea that the final cure to all human ills lies outside this world may look unfounded or incredibly unrealistic, but mystics have not set out to cure social ills but to help individuals, and for this only a radical inward change is worth devoting energy to.

In principle, mystics can apply their experiences and ideas for worldly ends: mystical experiences do not entail other-regardingness, but that can be opted for, and similarly advocating social reform for secular ends can be opted for to help individuals. But for social action to be adopted into the mystical life, mystics must adopt the belief-claim that our realm is more than just the stage on which we individually develop our spiritual career. Without such a realism, social problems are at most just opportunities for the soteriological development of oneself and others. The sociological cause for such a new belief may be that in modern times we now believe that social and natural conditions can be improved and thus that some worldly suffering of many people can be alleviated by group action.

However, the mystical inward individualistic focus still makes the idea of societal-level reform very hard to advocate today. The type of action that is appropriate for the mystical quest is still individual teaching and advising, and the social scale they see as useful for this is at best their immediate community. Switching to larger-scale action or societal-level reform would change the dynamics dramatically. Moreover, it is safe to assume that physical and social conditions were much harsher in premodern societies than they are today, and yet mystics in those times did not believe the conditions had to be changed. If the mystical quest did not appear to classical mystics to be incompatible with the social conditions then, why would they want social change today? Any further improvement would be irrelevant from their point of view and may make people too comfortable to focus on anything but material satisfaction.

All of this shows the challenge for any applied mysticism in repackaging traditional mysticism with its transcendent soteriological goals and individualistic orientation into a social force to improve worldly conditions for secular ends today.

Notes

Preface

1. A mystical sense of selflessness need not lead to a moral concern for others (R. Jones 2016: chap. 9; Millière et al. 2017; see R. Jones 2004 on the different relationships of mysticism and morality). The immoral conduct of some New Age gurus (R. Jones 2024: chap. 10) is a type of applied mysticism that illustrates the danger of claiming "instant enlightenment" through having an isolated mystical experience outside the context of training in a mystical tradition.

2. Mystical experiences and other altered states of consciousness have aided science in the past by supplying ideas that have been worked into scientific hypotheses (see R. Jones 2015 [2010]: chap. 4; Gandy et al. 2022; also see Wilber 2000; Kaiser 2011).

Chapter 1

1. Neuroscientists are not necessarily *reductive* in studying the brain activity during mystical experiences rather than all of the nervous system or other aspects of the body. It may be that the entire nervous system and indeed other parts of the body are involved in consciousness—we are embodied beings, and experiencing may be integrated into the full body. But neuroscientists can focus on what their technology illuminates without denying any of that: they are revealing part of the story that can be studied in its own right even if it turns out that the neurological study of the brain is not the complete account of the bodily grounding of these experiences. That many neurologists who study mystical experiences accept that "set and setting" (discussed below) shape the experiences also shows that at least some see the experiences as not merely a mechanical product of the brain.

2. Some mystical training techniques utilize *reasoning*, but these have not been the subject of scientific study. Whether scans of such everyday activity would

differ from nonmystics' same activity is an issue. A similar situation may arise for meditative techniques involving visualizations.

3. What members of a control group are doing during a brain scan would affect the baseline for recognizing differences that meditation may cause—e.g., are the members of the control group engaged in some cognitive activity such as reading, or are they simply relaxing?

4. It should also be noted that there is a great danger of *bias* in this field: many researchers are out either to discredit mystical claims or to validate them (see chapter 5). Most researchers also meditate themselves (Schmidt and Walach 2014: 2).

5. However, Papanicolaou does suggest that more detailed work may change the situation in the future (2021: 125).

6. Normally our brain activity does not change more than 5 to 10 percent during the day when we are awake, but when participants engage in mystical activities, that change may be more than 20 percent (Newberg and Waldman 2016: 87). The significance of this is not yet clear.

7. The loss of a sense of an individual empirical ego is central to mystical experiences, and comparisons have been made to theories such as Daniel Dennett's that the "self" is only an artifice generated by the brain (e.g., Lancaster 1993; Simpson 2014; Johnstone et al. 2016; Hood 2017).

8. The Newberg-d'Aquili study actually showed an initial increase in activity in the frontal regions followed by "significant decreases" in activity there as the "intensity" of the meditation increased (Newberg and Waldman 2016: 156).

9. One recurring issue is whether mystical experiences occurring in a lab are the *same in nature or character* as those occurring outside a lab. Does a laboratory setting affect the subjective side of the experience since "set and setting" (see the next chapter) matter for altered states of consciousness? Even if some genuine mystical experiences do occur in the lab, is the full phenomenology of all mystical experiences of the same type duplicated? Might even a low electric current of an fMRI scan affect the subtle neural current in the brain?

10. "State of unity" is ambiguous: it can refer to the *unified state of consciousness* when all differentiated content is absent or it can refer to the unity or a connection with some other *reality* (either through a sense of identity or "absorption" or "communion" of separate realities).

11. "Altered states of consciousness" involve a qualitative shift in the stabilized pattern of mental functioning from our baseline state (Tart 1969: 1). Common ASCs are dreaming, daydreaming, and being drunk. There is no reason to suspect in advance of study that there is only one ASC for all mystical experiences. But it may be that all ASCs are associated with activity in the same area of the brain (e.g., perhaps a decrease in prefrontal cortex activity) or have either some mystical attributes (e.g., some degree of a sense of oneness with phenomena or ego-dissolution) or some visionary attributes.

12. An underlying problem is that cognitive scientists today cannot decide what *consciousness* is—views run the gamut from consciousness being the primary (or indeed only) reality to it being an irreducible fundamental property of matter to it not existing at all. In a conference titled "Toward a Science of Consciousness" in Tucson, Arizona, in 1994 (see Hameroff et al. 1996), attendees' views on anomalous phenomena (which included mystical experiences) apparently were divided in thirds: one-third thought that anomalous phenomena did not really occur, one-third thought that they occurred but could be explained at least in principle in physical terms, and one-third thought that not only did the phenomena occur but that consciousness was the primary reality (Baruss and Mossbridge 2016: 28). Those who want to reject both a dualism of mind and body and that consciousness can be explained in physical terms as an emergent phenomenon see the only logical alternatives to be a panpsychism in which all matter has conscious or protoconscious properties, or to treat consciousness as a fundamental reality perhaps more fundamental than matter (cosmopsychism). Nor is dualism dead today: phenomena such as near-death experiences and periods of lucidity near death in Alzheimer patients with degenerative brain conditions lead some in the field to conclude that the brain does not generate consciousness but is a filter or even an inhibitor of a transcendent consciousness.

13. For the prospects of a genuine "science of consciousness," see Hameroff et al. 1996; Chalmers 2004.

14. Whether all states of "enlightenment"—i.e., enduring states of consciousness in which all sense of a phenomenal "self" has evaporated (rather than sporadic experiences of selflessness)—are neurologically the same would be an issue. Experienced meditators carry their changes in neural activity from mystical experiences into their waking life outside of meditation in the lab, and the changes can become lasting traits of an enlightened life. But one problem with determining long-term effects of meditation is that many subjects who are studied by neuroscientists may well be self-selected participants who are members of particular religious traditions, and thus it is difficult to determine if any changes in values or ways of living are the results of meditation or of their religious beliefs and their prior or continuing nonmystical training. Do the lasting effects result from new brain-conditioning or merely from a memory of the mystical experience added to the mystic's cultural beliefs?

15. There would be only one possible state here (if it is truly empty) and so no possible inverse multiple realization issue.

16. Newberg and d'Aquili's explanatory theory is that pure consciousness is an "Absolute Unitary Being" that is anterior to either subject or object (Newberg and d'Aquili 1999: 188, 201). They postulate that this transcendent beingness is real, based on it seeming to the experiencer "vividly and convincingly real" and even "more real" than the world perceived through ordinary consciousness after the experience is over when the experiencer has returned to our baseline dualistic consciousness. They also believe that they saw "evidence of a neurological process

that has evolved to allow us humans to transcend material existence and acknowledge and connect with a deeper, more spiritual part of ourselves perceived of as an absolute, universal reality that connects us to all that is" (Newberg et al. 2002: 9). But they realize that *none of their patients claimed this* and that this is only their *explanatory/metaphysical theory* and a separate claim and different in nature from claiming that the experiences are genuine neurological events. And it must be noted that an empty pure consciousness event is open to different theoretical explanations: it may be an experience of a theistic god, a nontheistic transcendent absolute (such as Advaita Vedanta's Brahman), an isolated transcendent self (as in the Jaina and Hindu Samkhya traditions), the bare beingness of the universe, or only a naturally generated monitoring activity of our background consciousness that precedes conceptualization and intention and does not divide the field of experience into subject and object. Or the mind may be simply spinning its gears by being "on" but having no input to work with; such a malfunction could not be the basis for any insight into the nature of reality. No such theory can be derived from, or justified by, the phenomenology of an empty consciousness alone. Neuroscience would be irrelevant to such understanding since the science involves only the workings grounding the mystical experiences themselves in the body. But this does not mean that neuroscientists must deny such understandings.

17. Whether there have been scans of such consciousness events *while they are happening* is open to question. If a participant signals the researcher when he or she is having a "pure consciousness event," then he or she is not having one: there is still a dualism of experiencer and experience and still differentiated content in the participant's mind. Some scans are of participants only remembering their experiences (e.g., Beauregard and O'Leary 2007). That may tell us something about the neurology of remembering but nothing about the neurology underlying mystical experiences even if the meditation has a holdover effect on other ASCs.

18. There is a metaphysical caveat here: if eliminationism concerning the mind is correct, then studying the brain is studying the only reality involved in experiences.

Chapter 2

1. Since mystical experience cannot be *forced* by any actions or triggers, all mystical experiences are "spontaneous" and "unexpected" in one sense. But the label "*spontaneous*" will be reserved here for mystical experiences that are not sought but occur out of the blue to persons with no meditative or other spiritual preparation or expectation and without ingesting psychedelics. (Spontaneous mystical experiences would still be subject to the same conditioning as sought or cultivated ones.) Scientists must explain what triggers such unexpected experiences and determine if the neurological base is the same as for drug-enabled experiences occurring in the lab. On triggers, see chap. 4.

2. The effects of psilocybin and a classic hallucinogen (dextromethorphan) have been compared and found to have differences in the experiences occasioned and in their effects (Carbonaro et al. 2018; Barrett et al. 2018).

3. This definition in terms of ASCs reflects the new scientific interest in mystical experiences, but no definition of "mystical experience" is dictated by science unless all ASCs have the same neurological states grounding them, which currently appears not to be the case. Thus, scholars have to decide what range of ASCs to include in their definition and what range to exclude. A designated range is not arbitrary if there is a legitimate reason for it—here, emptying the mind of a sense of self and conceptualizations is central to any definition of "mystical experience" for studying classical religions, and "mysticism" in terms of practices and ways of living for aligning one's life with reality is equally central. But scholars will probably never reach a consensus on the issue. All a scholar can do is specify his or her usage to indicate what phenomena are being included.

4. The distinction of two classes of mystical experiences—extrovertive and introvertive—is empirically supported by differences in their neurophysiological effects (Hood 2001: 32–47; Dunn, Hartigan, and Mikulas 1999). There are also different types of experiences within each class, and how the brain functions during the different experiences may well differ. If the neural bases associated with different types of mystical experiences differ, there is no reason in advance of study to presume that the effect of psychedelics on the brain would enable only one generic "mystical experience." Thus, if, for example, some drug can stimulate some part of the brain and enable introvertive mystical experiences with differentiated content to occur, this does not mean that that drug can enable mindfulness or that the same areas of the brain become more active (or less active) in both types of experiences.

5. Today there are people who have mystical experiences but see no significance in them oriented about transcendent realities (see chap. 8). Thus, "mystical" and "religious" must be distinguished. This will be discussed below under attribution theory.

6. One problem is that our experiential vocabulary has arisen from ordinary dualistic experiences—experiencers in any culture have no ready terminology for nondual experiences from the culture's general vocabulary. Thus, it is difficult to determine from experiencers' language whether an experience is a *vision* or a *nonvisual mystical experience* when they speak of "seeing," "encountering," or a "vision."

7. Psychedelic substances may have evolved as a defense mechanism for plants since they are toxic to most animals, but hominids evolved in a way to utilize them (Winkelman 2014: 343–44). There also is evidence that animals searched out intoxicants (Siegel 1989).

8. In the nineteenth century, psychoactive drugs (if not psychedelics) were utilized to explore the mind. "Psychonauts" included Samuel Taylor Coleridge, the chemist Humphrey Davy, and Sigmund Freud (Jay 2023). No doubt some mystical experiences were touched off.

9. Leary later gave a physicalist interpretation of drug-enabled mystical experiences: in the drug experiences one returns consciousness to the genetic code, DNA (2001). Mystical experiences take us "beyond the senses into the world of cellular awareness" (Leary 1968: 114; also see Narby 1998). Under this theory, the gods whom people tend to project exist only in their own psyches.

10. But it should be noted that in the 1950s and 1960s the CIA funded research on the potential of psychedelics for applications such as mind control (see O'Neill and Piepenbring 2019). Charles Manson participated in one program. R. Gordon Wasson's initial expedition to Mexico to study "sacred mushrooms" was (unbeknownst to him) funded by the CIA.

11. But Huxley's novel *Brave New World* should also be noted: there a psychedelic ("Soma") was used to help maintain a dystopian society by keeping the people happy and complacent.

12. In the 1960s, some communes, such as Stephen Gaskin's "The Farm" in Tennessee, used psychedelics as sacraments. But most of these communes did not last long—psychedelic experiences do not, as many thought, lead to a sense of community.

13. Bruce Eisner, a recent follower of Huxley, found that the quasipsychedelic drug ecstasy (MDMA) led patients to a profound sense of "unconditional love" and to a state of empathy in which they, others, and the world all seemed basically good (1989). Ecstasy is the partygoer's drug of choice at "raves." The setting of such affairs and the mental set of those participating apparently are not conducive to mystical experiences. Instead, other types of psychedelic experiences may occur. MDMA has also been found to have negative effects: serious impairment to memory, sleep, cognition, problem-solving, emotional balance, and social intelligence (Newberg and Waldman 2016: 77).

14. There is now ayahuasca tourism in the Amazon basin. Because of the role of the mental set in psychedelic experiences, it is doubtful that the Western tourists' experiences are the same as those the indigenous people have. For example, the Amazon people use ayahuasca as a medicine in shamanic rituals that invoke spirits in order to cure people of diseases caused by curses and so on, and they do not have many mystical experiences. The negative effect of commercialism on indigenous cultures has become a concern today.

15. "Subconscious" should be distinguished from a transpersonal "Mind at Large." The former contains personal elements and perhaps universal elements such as Jungian archetypes, but the latter (if it exists) would transcend any human mind. An "expanded consciousness" thus would not delve into a personal subconscious.

16. The criteria used by Pahnke (1966), Ralph Hood for his M-Scale, and the Johns Hopkins' MEQ scale are based on Walter Stace's features of a mystical experience (1960: chap. 2). There are seven elements: unity (introvertively as a pure awareness or a merging with ultimate reality, and extrovertively as the unity of all things or sense of "all is one"); transcendence of time and space (both a sense of timelessness and that concepts of space and time do not apply to transcendent

realities); ineffability (the inability to describe in words both the experience and what is experienced); paradoxicality (related to ineffability); a sense of sacredness or awe; a noetic quality (a sense of knowing what is ultimately real); and a deeply felt positive mood (joy, peace, and love). There is pushback from some Chrisitan theologians because love is not a separate category, and a selfless "union" rather than a "communion" with God in which the self remains distinct in some way appears more central (Cole-Turner 2024). They suspect that experiences of a sense of being loved or the presence of God may be being suppressed. They also object that the focus is on mystical experiences and states of consciousness rather the encompassing mystical way of life. While mystical ways of life do involve a development that involves much more than cultivating isolated mystical experiences (see R. Jones 2021a: 3–8) and theologians may wish to consider all that way of life as a "religious experience," the neuroscientists' interest is in the workings of the brain and the nature of consciousness, and for that interest focusing on mystical experiences is certainly a legitimate topic.

17. On the possible chemical effect of psychedelics on the brain, see Nichols and Chemel 2006; Winkelman 2013; Carhart-Harris et al. 2014; Barrett and Griffiths 2018: 415–21. See Kwan et al. 2022 and Erritzoe 2024 for overviews. Other areas of the body might also be affected (see Kargbo 2023). Psychedelics also affect the gastrointestinal tract, and the "gut-brain axis" is now gaining attention in psychedelic studies (Hashimoto 2024).

18. Ego-dissolution is the opposite of "ego-inflation" often associated with cocaine (Nour et al. 2016: 1). The latter sees the universe absorbed into the self, not the absence of a self.

19. Even *not* having a positive effect or mystical experience in a drug program may lead to very negative results if the participants were expecting spectacular results (see Borrell 2024).

20. Sometimes the participants felt like they were in a dream, the afterlife, purgatory, a movie, a computer game, or a fake reality (Evans et al. 2023: 15). How this might relate to, say, an Advaita sense that this world is a "dream" is an interesting question.

21. After the experience has faded, experiencers may also feel depressed or frustrated that they cannot get it back (Taylor and Egeto-Szabo 2017: 56). Whether the desire to recapture the experience (Taylor and Egeto-Szabo 2017: 55) is a matter of reentering the state of consciousness simply for the pleasure of the experience or for feeling in a state of insight again is not always clear.

22. Another risk arises from even positive experiences: the changes in a person's values, character, and behavior may lead to marriages and friendships breaking up.

23. Ralph Hood (2013: 301) found that persons rate prayer-occasioned mystical experiences as more legitimate or "real" than drug-enabled ones, more so to the extent that the persons are religiously dogmatic. Among persons reporting mystical experiences, he also found that the more "spiritual" report psychedelics as a trigger, whereas the more "religious" do not.

24. That conducive set and setting induce more mystical experiences does not mean that the psychedelic-enabled experiences may not be cognitive—it only means that some sets and settings are more conducive to the insight-experiences. For similar reasons, that some lead to fewer mystical experiences does not mean that they cannot be insights.

25. Newberg found that if one had a foundation of mindfulness and the ability to remain deeply relaxed when one enters and exits ASCs, one can more quickly alter one's consciousness and is less likely to have bad experiences; he thus advises relaxing before and after ingesting psychedelics (Newberg and Waldman 2016: 210).

26. Another problem is that scientists cannot administer psychotropic drugs to people without their consent because of the danger of very negative effects (see Villiger 2024). Thus, even those who are not interested in spiritual experiences are aware of the nature of the study, and this may dispose them toward having such experiences. It may dispose even those who are given a placebo. Doctors who are advocates of entheogens or drug therapies and skeptical doctors can also unintentionally skew the results of drug studies one way or the other.

27. Psilocybin appears more effective in inducing mystical experiences than the relatively low doses of LSD used in therapy sessions (Liechti, Dolder, and Schmid 2017). Higher dosages enable a higher percentage of mystical experiences in a predictable fashion. One study noted that even a relatively high dose of LSD was not as effective in inducing mystical experiences as psilocybin. That psilocybin and LSD have different pharmacodynamic effects on the brain is one possible explanation, but researchers have wondered whether the difference in effects was only a matter of dosage or of differences in set (especially expectancy) or setting or both; (Griffiths et al. 2018: 67; Johnson et al. 2019: 46–47). But it appears that there is no evidence of qualitative differences in ASCs that were induced by equally strong doses of mescaline, LSD, and psilocybin (Ley et al. 2023).

28. Because a trigger cannot always produce an ASC experience virtually every time, no terms related directly or indirectly to *causation* are appropriate. For example, "produce," "catalyze," "stimulate," "trigger," and "induce" all carry connotations of causation. Speaking of the "origins" in the brain may be heard as meaning the experiences are only brain-generated. But there is no term in English that captures what the drugs do. "Enable," "occasion," and "facilitate" are used here to convey the idea that psychedelics are one way to set up necessary conditions in the brain for mystical experiences to occur but are not sufficient to produce those experiences. So too, the terms are intended here to be neutral, between the possibility that mystical experiences are merely brain-generated subjective experiences and that they are genuine insights into the nature of reality. The word "trigger" is used to mean drug-induced neural conditions that may or may not occasion mystical experiences.

29. As discussed in chapter 6, this variety of states of consciousness connected to one state of brain conditions produced by the drug presents the inverse of the

"multiple realization" problem—i.e., more than one state of consciousness is associated with the same brain state.

30. "Genuine" has two senses in discussions of mystical experiences that are not usually distinguished clearly: establishing that mystical experiences are *unique experiences* distinct from other types of experiences, versus establishing that the experiences *convey a genuine insight* into reality. Here "genuine" will be used only in the first sense.

31. Pantheism equates God with the natural realm. It should be distinguished from "panentheism," which sees God as a transcendent entity that encompasses and permeates the universe.

32. Scientists do not usually even discuss whether God or another transcendent reality may cause introvertive or extrovertive mystical experiences that are distinguishable in content from drug-enabled ones—it is not an issue of scientific interest.

33. The expectancy bias and confirmation bias discussed in chapter 5 complicates the issue of whether psychedelic-enabled mystical experiences are the same as any initiated by transcendent realities (if that in fact is what occurs).

34. Theists can invoke the concept of "grace" to explain why psychedelics and other triggers cannot force ASC experiences 100 percent of the time: God chooses to whom to give experiences and what kind of experiences to give. But then they would have to admit that such mystical experiences are in fact genuine despite the natural triggers involved.

35. In one study comparing the experiences of psilocybin users and nonusers (Cummins and Lyke 2013), researchers found that the "peak experiences" of psilocybin users showed much higher occurrences of mystical experiences ("oceanic boundlessness") and visual distortions ("visionary restructuralization") than among the peak experiences of those who never used the drug—this was so even when the psilocybin users were *not using* the drug at the time of these experiences. This suggests that the peak experiences of psilocybin users involved greater alterations of consciousness than the state of consciousness during the peak experiences of those who had never used it. It also raises the issue of whether the psilocybin had a longer lasting effect on the users' brains. More studies on the phenomenology of the experiences of subjects who have had *both* drug-enabled and nondrug mystical experiences may be valuable.

36. Due to a declining interest in religious experiences in religious studies, many within the field (and also some outside the field) now group mystical experiences in with all other religious and spiritual experiences under the general label "RSMEs" (religious, spiritual, and mystical experiences) as if all are the same in nature and have the same neural bases or effects in psychotherapy—thus, what can be said of one type of experience applies equally to all types. Different types of mystical experiences need not be distinguished in their nature and effects. The difference in phenomenology of mystical experiences of nonduality and loss of a

sense of an experiencing self from visions or a sense of the presence of transcendent beings is irrelevant. In this approach, the distinctiveness of various types of mystical experiences and states is lost, as are differences in different mediation practices. The differences in scientific findings concerning brain activity become irrelevant, and the psychological effects of the different experiences is assumed to be the same. The psychological effects of the different experiences are apparently assumed to be the same, but there is evidence that a loss of a sense of self can lead to positive changes in our sense of well-being, but visual or auditory experiences do not (Kangaslampi 2023: 23).

37. Attribution theory should be distinguished from constructivism. For constructivists, cultural phenomena structure genuine mystical experiences. For advocates of attribution theory, "mystical experiences" are actually only ordinary states of mind seen mystically—it is the *interpretation* of an ordinary experience that makes it "mystical."

38. Objections have also been raised concerning Proudfoot's use of the psychological data (Barnard 1992; Spilka and MacIntosh 1995).

39. If mystical experiences are caused only by the brain, this does not absolutely rule out their being cognitive, but it would be good grounds to disqualify mystical cognitive claims.

40. Long-lasting effects on one's character are more likely the result of the immediate impact of the psychedelic experience on one's already existing mental set of beliefs and values than any lingering *chemical effects* of the drugs on the brain. That would also explain why some positive effects increased over time. A person's practices also figure in.

41. Checkable empirical matters may be distinguished from broader matters of the metaphysical nature of the phenomenal realm and ego. But the "noetic" quality of a sense of *knowing* in these "Aha moments" is more a matter of a psychological sense of *certainty* than necessarily cognitive *truth*. Experiencers often have a sense that they have found the secret of the meaning of life during the experience only to realize that that was not so after the experience was over—the experiences feel "real" even when they are not cognitive. For example, Arthur Koestler said of the "instant mysticism" of a psilocybin experience: "[T]here is no wisdom there. I solved the secret of the universe last night, but this morning I forgot what it was" (quoted in Shipley 2015: 78). He also recounted a story from his friend George Orwell: every night that a friend smoked opium he heard a single phrase that contained the whole secret of the universe, but he always forgot it in the morning; however, one night he managed to write it down: "The banana is big, but its skin is even bigger" (Koestler 1968: 210–11).

42. Merely being in a drug-enabled ASC does not mean that a person must be compassionate or can perform only moral actions. The English word "berserk" comes from the Norse word for the Viking "Berserkers" who ingested psychedelic drugs before going on their rampages.

43. In contrast, our baseline consciousness has evolved for our survival, but this does not mean that it is the absolute arbiter in all cognitive matters. There is no obvious reason to assume that the default mode of consciousness must be the only cognitive state even if we try to check mystical claims in the baseline state of consciousness. Perhaps, as the philosopher C. D. Broad said, we may have to be a little cracked to see some things about reality.

44. For example, that disease can radically impair our thinking does not show that the mind is merely the brain or is generated by it. Dualists can respond that the changes in the brain merely damage our reception of the mind, like damage to a radio interferes with it receiving radio signals. Treating the mind as separate and as a cause would require a change in the prevailing materialistic framework in neuroscience today.

45. Smith believed that in his psychedelic experiences he had experienced only the penultimate level, not "the infinite, the Absolute" (2005: 227). But some depth-mystical experiences are also enabled by psychedelics. Aldous Huxley also said: "I am not so foolish as to equate what happens under the influence of mescalin or of any other drug, prepared or in the future preparable, with the realization of the end and ultimate purpose of human life: Enlightenment, the Beatific Vision" (1954: 73).

Chapter 3

1. One issue is whether such a consciousness would be a core consciousness that is present in all states of consciousness or is a separate state of consciousness. The prevailing position in mystical studies seems to be that it is layer of consciousness integrated into all states, although the issue is not often noticed.

2. The Cartesian dualism of mind and body does not seem to fit our everyday mental life: the body seems to be active or part of even most thinking, and emotions do not seem confined to the brain but seem to affect more of the body. But pure consciousness does not seem attached to the experiencer.

3. Some scientists assert that it is generally accepted that we construct the world and our sense of "self" from our perceptions and nonconscious mental processes, but that meditation *inhibits this process* (Goleman and Davidson 2018: 148–49, 153–55). Meditation upon a specific image or concept (e.g., a deity or compassion) would provide content that could be structured.

4. Even if meditation is an unconstructed state of consciousness, any subsequent "enlightened" state of consciousness will be structured by the mystic's cultural beliefs, although the mystic's relation to the structured content will change—the structuring will be seen as reflecting the cultural perspective imposed on natural phenomena as they really are.

5. Mindfulness can be described as an "awareness that arises through paying attention, on purpose, in the present moment, non-judgmentally" (Kabat-Zinn 2005:

4). A state of mindfulness may be structureless (and hence "pure awareness") or it may be structured, as with Buddhist mindfulness involving applying its metaphysics of selflessness and impermanence to perception.

6. Such a state of enlightenment is not a state of "pure" consciousness; still it would involve structuring—if the enlightened can communicate, they make distinctions and have concepts operating in their mind. Thus, the state would be an extrovertive state of consciousness but with structured perceptions and thinking that are dependent upon the conceptual categories of a mystic's culture: cultural conceptions of what is real in the world and ways of thinking would not be taken as reflecting the way the world truly is but only as useful tools for navigating the world and leading others to enlightenment. But the enduring selfless state of consciousness can be lost. Maintaining the enlightened state requires work—even the Buddha continued to meditate after his enlightenment experience.

7. The seventeenth-century German mystic/theosophist Jakob Boehme also thought consciousness arises only through an object to be conscious of—i.e., through "opposition." Our self-consciousness arises only through encountering something other than ourselves. This also includes God's consciousness and self-consciousness: God's consciousness arose only with something other to be aware of (creation). For Boehme, this makes creation real.

8. One early Buddhist school—the Pudgalavadins—did posit a self arising from the aggregates like fire arising from wood. It is not the same nor different from the aggregates, like fire is to wood. This self is impermanent, but it is reborn and enters nirvana.

9. What exactly is meant by a "loss of a sense of 'self'" in psychedelic and meditative experiences is a matter of debate in neuroscience (see Millière 2017).

10. In Buddhism, such a pure consciousness contrasts with ordinary dualistic consciousness. The latter is taken as carving (nonexistent) objects out of the field of phenomenal experience that become objects of desire.

11. Advaitins (and Samkhya-Yogins) distinguish the mind (*manas*) with its particular functions from a transcendent featureless, unmoving consciousness (*chitta*, *chit*) that is independent of the mind. For Samkhya-Yogins the mind is actually *material*, unlike the transcendent centers of pure consciousness (*purushas*).

12. Advaitins do no explain how the "unreal" individual centers of consciousness originally emerged from Brahman and reemerge after an experiential oneness with Brahman.

13. In the modern world, one option that some philosophers and psychologists have advanced is the idea of a transcendent selfless consciousness. In the first half of the twentieth century, F. W. H. Myers, William James, Henri Bergson, C. D. Broad, and Aldous Huxley advocated a "reducing valve" theory of the brain: the brain normally limits the input it receives from a transcendent "Mind at Large" to only what we need to survive, but mystical experiences loosen the valve. That is, mystical experiences and psychedelics decrease the blocking or filtering functions of the brain, deactivating the default mode network or whatever, thereby letting in more of a transpersonal

or transcendent consciousness into our conscious mind. That is, there needs to be something in the brain that enables us to become aware of the consciousness that transcends the body, but the brain or anything related to the body is not the source of consciousness—the brain is merely a receiver of consciousness. Today such a Mind at Large can be given either a transcendent or a naturalist understanding.

14. A classic example is the cosmological argument for God's existence: since we cannot imagine an infinite chain of causes existing in the past flowing forward, it then is "logically necessary" that a first cause must exist, even if this means adopting the absurd idea of a "self-created" cause and admitting that we do not understand that concept either. One could just as easily argue that self-creation is absurd, so we should accept an infinite chain of causes—at least we see finite chains of causes in the natural world.

Chapter 4

1. Not all drugs that disrupt our ordinary states of consciousness enable mystical experiences and other psychedelic experiences. Scientists will have to be explain that. The explanation probably will involve the particular receptors that psychedelics activate.

2. In certain studies involving online respondents, psychedelics were not a major trigger. Instead, psychological turmoil, contact with nature, and spiritual practices such as meditation were the three most prominent triggers; 7 percent had no discernible trigger (Taylor and Egeto-Szabo 2017).

3. The usual alternatives to the label "trigger" also relate directly or indirectly to causation. For example, "produce," "catalyze," "stimulate," "trigger," and "induce" all carry connotations of causation. Speaking of "originating" in the brain may be heard as meaning the experiences are only brain-generated. But there is no English term that captures what the drugs do. "Enable," "occasion," and "facilitate" are used here to convey the idea that psychedelics are one way to set up necessary conditions in the brain for mystical experiences to occur but are not sufficient to produce those experiences. So too, the terms are intended here to be neutral between the possibilities that mystical experiences are merely brain-generated subjective experiences or are genuine insights into the nature of reality.

4. To permit an ASC experience, a person's beliefs need not be tied to a particular religious tradition—any religious or nonreligious beliefs will do. Even beliefs that should close off an experiencer to the very possibility of having mystical experiences (e.g., a reductive materialism) does preclude its holders from having mystical experiences.

Chapter 5

1. Shankara states that this appeal to revealed authority (*shruti*) is necessary since philosophers constantly contradict each other (*Brahma-sutra-bhashya* 2.1.11).

In this passage, Shankara acknowledges the objection that this is itself an instance of reasoning, but he still asserts that the Vedas, being eternal, provide the necessary true knowledge. The standard of knowledge in Indian philosophy is certainty, and for Vedantins only revealed texts provide that.

2. Buber's example also shows the difficulty of determining the phenomenological features of an experience or what was actually experienced when the experiencers use canned cultural descriptions such as "union with God." Any account of a mystical experience from the experiencer may be heavy with highly ramified theological terminology from the experiencer's own culture, and such culturally determined expressions may not reflect the experience itself but the experiencer's postexperiential understanding. And whether highly ramified conceptualization penetrates the experiences themselves is an issue. The answer to that issue does not negate the possibility of a level of low-ramified conceptualization impinging upon the experiences.

3. But Smith added that he knew people, including positivists, for whom the experiences "just exploded their view of reality and gave them a totally different worldview to live in" (2005: 235). He does not say if they adopted perennial philosophy or another worldview.

Chapter 6

1. At present, the possibility of multiple neural pathways to the same types of mystical experiences cannot be ruled out. Such multiple realization would further complicate the picture, but this possibility will not be discussed here.

2. There is no reason to suspect that there is only one ASC for all mystical experiences or for all ASC experiences. But it may be that ASCs result from activity in the same area of the brain (e.g., perhaps a decrease in prefrontal cortex activity). So too, they all may have either some mystical attributes (e.g., sense of oneness with the phenomena around the experiencer) or some visionary attributes even though they remain distinct.

3. Psilocybin appears more effective in inducing mystical experiences than the relatively low doses of LSD used in therapy sessions (Liechti, Dolder, and Schmid 2017). That psilocybin and LSD have different pharmacodynamic effects on the brain is one possible explanation. But researchers have wondered whether the difference in effects was only a matter of dosage or differences in set or setting or both (Griffiths et al. 2018: 67; Johnson et al. 2019: 46–47).

4. The electrical neurotransmitter activity measured in electroencephalograms (EEG) and the magnetic fields produced by electrochemical currents occurring in the brain during meditation measured in magnetoencephalograms (MEG) are currently are more fine-grained than the other measurement procedures.

5. Even if each experience has a unique base in brain activity, physicalists would still have to explain how such diverse experiences (extrovertive and introvertive,

with differentiated content and a unified consciousness without such content) can occur. Such diversity is not like a simple switch in one's perception of a Gestalt figure.

Chapter 7

1. Some within this fledgling field question the quality of the science (see Noorani and Martell 2021; van Elk and Fried 2023). (Research on mindfulness meditation has also come under similar criticism [Chiesa and Serretti 2010].) Most of the studies involve relatively few participating subjects and lack of gender, ethnic, racial, educational, and socioeconomic diversity (Ko et al. 2022). Double-blind experiments are difficult: the intense effects of psychedelics make blinding the participant and researcher from whether the participant had taken the drug or a placebo difficult to maintain and renders trials susceptible to expectation bias (Aday, Carhart-Harris, and Wooley 2023: 533). But more rigorous procedures are being proposed (e.g., Aday et al. 2021) that would tighten up the research.

2. Negative experiences that are enabled by psychedelic drugs (and also by meditation) are much less often reported than positive experience and are usually downplayed in scientific reports (see chaps. 1–2). In particular, ego–dissolution can cause anxiety and dread to the unprepared subject. Even when the context is limited to therapy, many participants experience anxiety, and this could have a very negative effect. Such negative experiences usually do not last past the drug session (Griffiths et al. 2006; Griffiths et al. 2008) but are still seen as one reason to develop nonpsychedelic analogs.

3. The fact that some experiences may be correlated with specific brain states does not mean that the brain states *caused* the experiences—correlation does not imply causation in one direction or the other (see chap. 1). So too, correlating changes in brain states with mystical experiences does not explain either the brain activity or the felt content of experiences but only adds one more thing that needs explaining.

4. The use of "trip killer" drugs to cut short negative experiences has proven to be problematic (Yates and Melon 2024).

5. The role of the therapist in a course of treatments is also part of the nonchemical subjective side of therapy, but it is the experiential component that is at issue here.

6. Tests are also going on to determine if MDMA used in conjunction with psilocybin or LSD lessens the negative experiences while leaving the therapeutic positive ones (including mystical ones) unaffected (Zeifman et al. 2023).

7. If one-to-one correlations of mystical experiences and psychedelic triggers were established, such correlations would not prove psychedelic-enabled experiences are active causes rather than powerless side effects but only that they appear together (see chap. 4). However, there appears to be no one-to-one relation of different triggers and different types of experiences: based on the phenomenological accounts

of experimental subjects, different psychedelics, meditation, and other natural (and perhaps nonnatural) triggers produce some experiences that are experientially indistinguishable. The same trigger may produce different experiences, and the same experiences may come from different triggers. It is not as if different triggers "enter" the experiences and produce experiences unique to that trigger. Inverse multiple realization (discussed in the last chapter) is also possible.

8. Those researchers who want to dismiss the psychedelic-enabled experiences as part of an effective therapy would see no reason to be concerned with the set and setting—the drug's pharmacological effect would not depend on the subject's subjective response.

9. Two further problems are that nonpsychedelic drugs (e.g., alcohol) also can disrupt the default mode network without producing psychedelic experiences, and that psychedelics apparently cause wider network changes than merely disrupting the baseline mental state (Johnson 2021: 579).

10. Spontaneous mystical experiences have not received the attention in scientific circles that they should. The differences between those and psychedelic-enabled mystical experiences are not well described (James et al. 2020). Of course, it is harder to study spontaneous mystical experiences because researchers by definition cannot control when they occur. Spontaneous ASC experiences may result from triggers (e.g., the fatigue of long-distance running) that have the effect on the brain that psychedelics have, but that would have to be established empirically. The basic issue of whether experiences are responsible for the altered brain configurations or vice versa also arises.

11. The "noetic" quality should be seen as more a matter of a psychological and emotional sense of *absolute certainty* than of *cognitive truth*.

12. "Ineffability" is central to modern philosophical characterizations of mysticism. However, it should be noted that when classical mystics used related terms, they usually meant only that the reality allegedly experienced is *more than can be described*, not that it is *completely indescribable*, and that terms designating ordinary phenomena can be applied only *metaphorically* (see R. Jones 2016: 204–8, 2024: 384–85). The term emphasizes the otherness of the experiences and the reality allegedly experienced, but people who have had mystical experiences can characterize the felt phenomenology of the experiences themselves in some terms (see Yaden et al. 2016) and adopt descriptions from their religious traditions.

13. Some in the religious field (e.g., Sotillos 2024) argue that a "desacralized" secular psychedelic therapy does not duplicate the role entheogens played in traditional societies and may not reach the depths of the mind that the religious believe exist or address the mental health problems arising in the void left by the loss of the sense of a transcendent reality. But the therapist's applied mysticism is for limited problems, not religious practice.

14. Interestingly, these studies show that these experiences also increase a sense of *fatalism*—that every event is determined and thus beyond our control. This

may be related to the common reaction that mystical experiences are *happening to the experiencers* rather than coming from them—the experiencers do not seem to own the experience.

15. There now are also "religious naturalists" who reinterpret monotheistic language into naturalist terms—e.g., "God" becomes only the laws of nature (see Crosby and Stone 2020). Such naturalists highlight awe and wonder at the majesty of nature, but mystical and psychedelic-enabled experiences do not appear to play a major role in this religiosity.

16. Whether indigenous mystical and shamanic practices should be incorporated into psychotherapy is a matter of disagreement (see Yaden et al. 2022: 2).

Chapter 8

1. In the earlier history of Christianity, the term "secular" was used for anything *worldly*, in contrast to *"religious."* For example, in the Middle Ages only monks and nuns were considered "religious." So today some Christians use "secular mysticism" to mean a way to *experience God through worldly phenomena*—taking "nature mysticism" as leading to "cosmic consciousness" and then to direct mystical experiences of God. But here "secular mysticism" will refer to a mysticism that entails the denial of a god or other nonnatural realities, life after death, or related traditional religious claims. Thus, mystical experiences in this context are seen as involving no nonnatural realities and not leading to experiences of such alleged realities.

2. For a typology of mystical experiences, see R. Jones 2021a: chap. 2. In their aversion to the very term "mysticism," many who value mindfulness do not want to consider it "mystical" (e.g., Varela, Thompson, and Rosch 2016: 23), but this can be done only if one limits "mystical experience" to introvertive experiences.

3. David Hay believes there is a "astonishing surge" in reports of religious or spiritual experiences (1994: 3), but this may be accounted for simply by the fact that the Internet allows more mystical experiences to be reported than in the past.

4. Other psychedelic experiences can also have an influence. Simone de Beauvoir claimed that her husband, Jean Paul Satre, formed his idea of "existential nausea" under the influence of a horrific mescaline experience (Moen 2022: 171).

5. On the reduction of mystical experiences, see R. Jones 2000: chap. 8.

6. Scholars and public intellectuals almost uniformly perceive scientists as carriers of a "secularist impulse" (Ecklund and Long 2011: 254), but the majority of scientists at the top research universities consider themselves *spiritual* even if they do not believe in a god (Ecklund and Long 2011: 254–55). The spiritual scientists did not compartmentalize their lives (secular in the lab and spiritual outside); rather, most saw science as "meaning-making" (Ecklund and Long 2011: 260). For many, "spirituality" was defined in terms of awe and transcendence in relationship to the natural world (Ecklund and Long 2011: 265). For a significant minority,

their spirituality was also led to engaged, other-directed actions and caring for the world (Ecklund and Long 2011: 267–70). Thus, science does not necessarily lead to secularization (Ecklund and Long 2011: 271).

7. This reflects postmodern academic religious studies in which mystical experiences—indeed, all religious experiences—have fallen out of favor (see McDaniel 2018; R. Jones 2021a: 210–13). In the United States, psychedelic drug use among adolescents, young adults, and adults of all ages has also dramatically decreased from recent highs a few decades ago, let alone the much higher use in the 1970s (SAMHSA 2023: 18–19).

8. The limitations on scientific findings actually refuting transcendent belief claims are discussed in chapters 1 and 2. But in a secular atmosphere, more and more people may simply come to ignore the transcendent option and rest content with natural explanations.

9. For discussions of the significance and limitations of neuroscience and psychedelic drugs for philosophy of mysticism, see chap. 2; R. Jones 2016: chap. 4; and Letheby 2021: chap. 5.

10. Not everyone who takes a psychedelic or meditates becomes a mystic. But whether even having a mystical experience makes a person a "*mystic*" is a matter of choosing a definition. However, if a person has one or more mystical experiences but the experiences do not affect that person's subsequent life, it is hard to consider that person a "mystic" in any meaningful sense. In contrast, if an experience does profoundly affect all of one's inner life (beliefs, attitudes, emotions) and actions, at least the word "spiritual" should apply, especially if the term "mystic" is reserved for a person practicing full-time in a mystical way of life or aspiring to a mystical goal. But if a naturalist attains an enduring state of selflessness, that person should be classified as "enlightened" even though he or she understands the experience in naturalist terms.

11. For a study of the historical roots of modern secularized mysticism, see Hunt 2003.

12. Meditation with a spiritual component may also produce different effects on the mind than a secular approach and may produce experiences with more mystical characteristics (Wachholtz and Pargament 2005). Whether meditation in secular contexts has no more than a placebo effect when it comes to psychophysiological benefits is also a matter of debate. Whether the mystical experiences of theists and nontheists are the same in nature is another issue. So too, long-term meditators may be more religious, but is it the result of meditative experiences or other personal factors? Are the religious simply more likely to continue with meditation?

13. Such bad experiences are usually short-lived and can even lead to positive effects (Schlag et al. 2022: 5).

14. New Age spirituality has both nonnaturalist and naturalist forms. Since Fritjof Capra's *The Tao of Physics* (2010 [1975]), the alleged convergence of science and mysticism within an encompassing naturalist or nonnaturalist worldview has gained popularity. But the knowledge of both mysticism and science of the advocates of this position is open to question (see chap. 9; R. Jones 2010, 2021a: 129–46).

15. Philosophers have also dealt with this issue. See, e.g., Dworkin 2013; Gutting 2013; and Nagel 2009.

16. Buddhist meditation went from originally viewing the world and oneself as foul in order to end desires and rebirth to becoming in Western hands a way to reaffirm a sense of individual selves and to appreciate being in this world—it went from trying to dismantle the sense of an isolated self to strengthening it in some practices. For a history of how Buddhist meditation was modernized and Westernized into secular forms of mindfulness with worldly goals, see McMahan 2023.

17. Naturalism can also lead to distorting an experiencer's understanding of mystics' teachings. See the example of Mark Waldman mentioned in chapter 5.

18. "Spontaneous" mystical experiences—i.e., those not sought, cultivated, or expected—do not prove that some nonnatural reality initiated them: purely natural mechanisms may still be all that is at work. These experiences occur, but we cannot control their occurrence, just as we cannot control many other aspects of our mental life.

19. The noetic quality is often prominent in mystical experiences, but as noted in previous chapters, it is more a matter of psychological sense of *certainty* than *objective truth*.

20. For a discussion of the common core claims for alleged common experiential elements or alleged common belief elements, see R. Jones 2016: 288–93, 2021b.

21. See Katz 1978, 1983; for nonconstructivism, see Forman 1990, 1999. For evaluations, see Stoeber 1992; R. Jones 2016: 52–69; and R. Jones 2020a.

22. Even if psychedelics or meditation disables a sense of self and cultural beliefs, postexperiential effects will depend on such factors as prior beliefs, how seriously participants in an experiment take meditation, prior experiences, how experienced the participants are in meditation, and what a person wants from an experience. One issue mentioned earlier is: are subsequent benefits the result of the experience or of continuing in the participant's prior religious way of life? Do mystical experiences in the end contribute no more than a shock that shakes up experiencers, sometimes leading them to change their beliefs or way of life?

23. Rahner also believed that mystics are the paradigms of being truly human. The rest of us are falling short by blocking the mystical potential latent in each of us.

24. In the twentieth century, the terms were rejected even by many persons who are classifiable as "mystics." Jiddu Krishnamurti disliked the term. Maharishi Mahesh Yogi of TM fame did not label himself a "mystic" and did not classify TM practices as "mystical."

Chapter 9

1. For more on New Age mysticism, see R. Jones 2015 [2010], 2024: 352–61.

2. Why didn't the "mystical outlook" of some early twentieth-century physicists survive into the second half of the twentieth century? Perhaps because

the cultural context of those physicists was German; after World War II, Anglo-American interpretative frameworks took over that did not have a mystical interest (see Marin 2009).

3. Many scientists may have been inspired to become scientists because of experiences when young of awe and wonder when gazing at the night sky, insects, or something else in nature that at least approached nature mystical experiences, but this does not mean mysticism influenced their scientific work as adults. However, ASC experiences such as dreams and those induced by psychedelics may give scientists ideas (Gandy et al. 2022) that can be worked into scientific hypotheses and tested. Such experiences may also enhance our general creativity by disrupting our accustomed ways of thinking, which may help scientists. As Max Planck said, scientists need "a vivid, intuitive imagination, for new ideas are not generated by deduction, but by an artistically creative imagination" (1949: 109).

4. New Agers' writings on mysticism and science focus on Asian mystical traditions. But Western mystical traditions could also be tried (e.g., Malin 2001 on Neoplationist emanationism; Canova 2022). That there is no one "mystical worldview" is discussed below.

5. As mystical traditions developed, some quite elaborate metaphysics were produced that covered more aspects of reality. But such treatises go beyond the basic mystical interest. Mysticism can interact with scientific theories through these encompassing philosophical (metaphysical) claims about the basic nature of reality in each mystical tradition that are less connected to mystical experiences. Such potential interaction will not be discussed here.

6. For more on New Age distortions, see R. Jones 2015 [2010], 2016: chap. 8. Of course, New Agers are not alone in this. Carl Jung did the same in his writings on Asian thought (see R. Jones 1986: 169–83), as did Joseph Needham on Daoism and science (R. Jones 1986: 127–46).

7. However, no scientific analysis is necessarily reductive. See R. Jones 2013: chap. 3.

8. A broader definition of "mysticism" than the one employed here that covers other types of experiences may produce other types of interaction with science, but New Age advocates typically focus on the claims in Buddhism, Hinduism, and Daoism connected to the experiences central to a narrow definition of "mysticism." Thus, the definition is warranted here.

9. As noted in chapter 1, integrating first-person experience into a science of the mind has been purposed but faces difficulties.

10. Capra had a nature-mystical experience on a beach in which he "saw" (his quotation marks) that the sand, rocks, and water were made of "vibrating molecules and atoms which interacted with one another by creating and destroying other particles" and "saw" the cascades of energy (cosmic rays) coming down from outer space and "heard" the rhythm of the "cosmic dance"—all were in the dance of Shiva (2017: 15–16). One issue is whether he "saw" molecules, atoms, and cosmic

rays in any sense, rather than simply saw the rocks, sand, and water vibrating while in an ASC and applied his knowledge of physics to conclude that he "saw" their atomic state. He puts "saw" and "heard" in quotation marks, suggesting they are not meant literally. Physics may have become vivid to him in that moment, but that does not mean that that he was actually aware of submicroscopic particles.

11. In mystical experiences in general, time often does not seem to exist. If we are looking for a parallel, this has more in common with Einstein's theory of time not being a real component of reality—it is something our brain cooked up to organize our experiences.

12. As Andrew Papanicolaou points out, the new physics is not evidence that supports or proves mysticism, but it does remove the "veneer of bizarreness and extravagance" of the mystics' claims (2021: 114; also see 112–13). Physicists have no problem working with the logically inconsistent claims of relativity and quantum mechanics (although they hope for a Theory of Everything that will resolve the conflict). They also work with picturing invisible, colorless subatomic particles. Papanicolaou believes that the new physics renders mystical claims "no more and no less reasonable than any other hypothesis, to be assessed on the basis of evidence" (Papanicolaou 2021: 112–13). Of course, naturalists and traditional mystics would disagree on what the "evidence" is. But when scientists are making claims that are weirder than those made by mystics, this does remove a common objection to mysticism.

13. Some parallelists see "energy" as "immaterial" or as matter "dematerialized," and thus jump from "immaterial energy" to "spirit." But energy is in effect equivalent to matter as "$E=mc^2$" made famous—there is nothing "spiritual" about it. So too with "fields"—they may seem "immaterial," but they are still as physical as matter and not any closer to "spirit."

14. Nature's laws and forces (e.g., gravity) may be eternal or permanent in some sense, but if so, this permanence does not affect the Buddhist picture of reality any more than does the permanence of the law of karma—the Buddhist view concerns the impermanence of the things that we experience in the world of interacting laws, not the nature of the laws governing the impermanent phenomena. Whatever scientists discover about the permanence of laws, the world we actually experience still appears impermanent and constantly changing, and this is the focus of Buddhist mindfulness.

15. New Agers will see these atoms (along with Greek atomism) as an "anticipation" or "harbinger" of modern atomism, if not quantum physics. At least Greek atomism was studied in modern times. These particles are impermanent, existing only for a moment, and thus share that feature with modern views of quantum phenomena, but they do not break down into smaller units when they disappear—they vanish totally. Medieval Abhidharmists did posit small bundles (*kalapas*) as the smallest indivisible unit of matter and claimed that they were open to experience in meditative concentration (*samadhi*). The Buddha did not make that claim.

16. Zohar and Marshall equate the quantum vacuum from physics not only with the Buddhist "Void" but with all other religious concepts of a source of the natural world: God, Meister Eckhart's Godhead, and Being, and the quantum vacuum are all names for the same thing since they are all names of the source of our being (1993: 240, 275). Leaving aside the issue of whether the different religious concepts are interchangeable, this is an instance of treating realities that are traditionally presented as *transcending the natural universe* (i.e., transcending the realm of reality open to sense experience and to scientific investigation) as in fact parts of the natural realm.

17. Advaitins adopted the classical Indian theory of sense-perception: the mind goes out and "grasps" a sense object (i.e., takes its form) and brings the form back to consciousness. But there is nothing in this theory about perception creating a material object or affecting what is perceived. For Advaita, all that is actually involved is an inactive consciousness.

18. Quantum particles are in fact *particles*—discrete entities that exhibit wave-like properties (as well as particle properties) *only in groups* (Stenger 2012: 154). They can be treated individually, and when that is done, they do not exhibit any holistic properties. The "wave function" is a mathematical formalism indicating the *probabilities* of where a particle may be—it does not mean that particles are waves.

19. Science per se is *not* a form of reductionism—reductionism remains a form of metaphysics (see R. Jones 2000). It should also be noted that emergence is not an *explanation* of an event but only a *description*: we put hydrogen and oxygen together in a certain way and something with unexpected properties appears—water. But calling water merely "an emergent property" does not explain how or why the new phenomenon and its properties appear. Labeling the phenomenon "an emergent property" is not a final explanation of the phenomenon in the sense that we no longer need to explain the nature of the phenomenon or how it is related to the base conditions. Emergence as an explanation is no better than saying that when we rub Aladdin's Lamp and a genie emerges it means that the genie, although nothing like the lamp, must be the product of the metal lamp and the process of rubbing simply because "that's what happens," and so the genie is explained. So too with the complexity of neurons and consciousness: the brain state does not explain how or why the new phenomenon of consciousness could appear—it shows only the state of the brain when consciousness and its properties do appear. It does not mean that consciousness is material in nature in any way or merely a product of the brain. It may be only that the base conditions for something nonmaterial to become "attached" to the brain have been identified.

20. Quantum decoherence and whether it introduces something new into the nature of reality will not be discussed here.

21. New Agers might like a claim from Stephen Hawking: the universe arose from "nothing" by means of scientific laws (Hawking and Mlodinow 2010; Krauss 2012), although he pushes aside the question of where the laws came from or why

something exists that obeys such laws (see R. Jones 2018a: 51–52). Those under the thrall of materialism think anything that is not *material* in nature is not real and so is "*nothing.*"

22. So too, if *x* in science is inexpressible, and *y* in mysticism is inexpressible, we have no way to compare them and certainly cannot conclude that *x* and *y* must be the same thing.

23. For New Age distortions of *science*, see R. Jones 2015 [2010]: 124–27. Most scientists reviewing the works of Capra and Zukav generally do not have problems with their presentation of physics. Rather, it is the implications that Capra and Zukav see that, for example, Leon Lederman finds "bizarre" (1993: 190–91).

24. This distortion began early in the West: when Buddhism and Vedanta were introduced to America in the nineteenth century, both were presented as fundamentally scientific.

25. Parallelists have yet to see the early Advaitin Gaudapada's Advaita theory of the phenomenal realm as the "vibration of consciousness" (*chitta-spandita*), later adopted by some Kashmiri Shaivites (see Dyczkowski 1987), as an anticipation of string theory.

26. Federico Faggin's "quantum consciousness" theory in which matter arises out of an underlying consciousness may have been inspired by Neoplatonist theories of the One—the focus of study of his father, the scholar Giuseppe Faggin, was Plotinus.

27. Indeed, a strong case can be made that the Buddha was not interested in "reality as it truly is" but was interested only in ending people's existential suffering. He would have dismissed questions of the true nature of reality unanswered as he dismissed the questions of the age and size of the universe noted above. He only prescribed a point of view to end suffering, not a metaphysical ontology of what is real. That is, his teachings are a prescription to end suffering rather than a description of how the world really exists apart from the point of view needed to end suffering. In effect, he says, "I don't care what the world is like in itself, but if you look at the things in the world, including yourself, as inherently dissatisfying, impermanent, and conditioned, this will lead to ending your desires and attachments, and this will end your existential suffering." Only later did philosophers such as the Abhidharmists and Nagarjuna work out ontologies to ground the prescribed perspective.

28. Not too much can be read into Niels Bohr adopting the Chinese yin-yang symbol into his coat of arms. Certainly, that he adopted a popular and colorful symbol of complementarity does not mean that he saw physics as mystical in nature.

29. However, today research in neurology focuses more on how the two hemispheres interact and work together and does not compartmentalize matters so neatly.

30. Many who reject mysticism agree. If there is only one type of knowledge of reality, then mysticism and science either converge or conflict. Thus, the claims that (1) there is only one type of knowledge of the world, that (2) science is our best way of providing such knowledge, and that (3) mystics are attempting to provide scientific information through improper means—means that produce claims

that conflict with science—lead to the conclusions that science and mysticism are inherently in conflict and that mysticism should be rejected (see, e.g., Stenger 2012). But if mysticism and science provide fundamentally different types of knowledge of different aspects of reality, this conclusion does not follow.

31. It should be noted that we do not need quantum physics to show our connectedness with all of life and the rest of the natural world: the fact that we are all stardust—material from some early supernova—and that we have evolved with the rest of life on this planet and are shaped by its natural forces is enough to establish our interconnection with all of the natural universe. Indeed, we are integrated into the planet and solar system. This may be why Capra has turned to studying biological systems.

Chapter 10

1. Also, contrary to popular opinion, the metaphysics of "oneness" actually precludes morality (see R. Jones 2016: 305–8), but an interconnected wholeness permits morality but does not require it (R. Jones 2016: 308–11). "Nonduality" may refer to either concept and leads to confusion.

2. Possible paranormal powers add a new wrinkle: if meditating mystics radiate compassion, love, or otherwise affect people in general, that would be a type of social action (since it affects everyone and not just the people they personally encounter)—acts of an individual having a social effect. Bodhisattvas' creation of Buddha-fields, which have ideal conditions for practitioners to attain Buddhahood, can also be seen as a type of social action to help people in their religious advancement toward enlightenment.

3. Many traditions have communal practices, but the individuality of the goal is still central, although the social dimension is being emphasized today (see, e.g., Yang 2017).

4. It appears that the unaffiliated "spiritual" people in America are as politically active as the "religious" (Kucinskas and Stewart 2022). For many Americans who feel alienated from conventional religion, spirituality may serve as an alternative path to political engagement (Kucinskas and Stewart 2022: 23). Spirituality also may lead to charity and other social engagement (Oh and Sarkisian 2012; Berghuijs et al. 2013; King, Duffy, and Steensland 2024; Meintel 2024).

5. But it should be noted that this action reflected Mahayana Buddhist beliefs and values: the monk assassinated the king for *the king's own good*. That is, the king was karmically harming himself by persecuting Buddhists—his actions would lead him to bad future rebirths leading away from enlightenment. And the monk who did the "killing" was karmically *rewarded* with a rebirth in a heaven for his selfless act of risking karmic damage to himself to help another, since no real "person" was killed.

6. Theistic mystics, as with the *Bhagavad-gita*, may accept the social order of their society as ordained by God. This would obviously have a conservative effect: there would be no impetus to reject what God has instituted. At best, theists of the classical period would see a right to remove a king who is violating the system but not to question "the divine right of kings" in general. Only under the influence of secular modern culture has this changed.

7. Max Weber thought that the idea of "this-worldly mysticism" was an oxymoron because of mystics' individualistic orientation and other-worldly personal goals, but some have used his term for harnessing mystical experiences for the service of practical social reform and world peace (Alexander 2000: 269; also see Summers-Effler and Kwak 2015).

8. In all the major Indian traditions, such karmic individualism also prevails (Jhingran 1989: 140–41). Some traditions tried to temper the harshness of this with "merit transfer" and "group *karma*," but the inherent individualism of the basic doctrine was always the prevailing belief.

9. Suzuki qualified the remark by adding that Buddhism is animated with a certain *revolutionary spirit* that comes to the fore when things become deadlocked (Suzuki 1970: 63).

10. Since Christianity's early days, there have always been Christians who have separated themselves from the world (i.e., withdrawn from society at large) rather than try to engage it. Once Christianity became the official religion of Rome, such aspirations for the general population changed. After that, even joining the army became acceptable for Christians.

11. The story of Martha and Mary in Luke 38–42 is often cited for valuing the "contemplative life" (Mary) over the "active life" (Martha). But in his sermons Meister Eckhart portrayed the active Martha as spiritually more mature (2009: 77–90) because he saw her life as integrating contemplation with action, while the contemplative Mary was still on the path.

12. Also see Woods 1996; Ruffing 2001. New Age thinkers also see "quantum mysticism" leading to social action (e.g., Goswami 2011; Zohar and Marshall 1993; Wendt 2015).

13. It should not require mention that in even the most mystical of traditions not all members are mystically inclined—people with worldly goals will always influence the tradition.

14. World rejection and a lack of social concern can occur in the devotional strand of religiosity in general. J. C. Ghosh writes of Vaishnavism in Bengal in the seventeenth and eighteenth centuries: "For two centuries the Bengali people sang, danced, and passed out in ecstatic trance while the world around them remained sunk in ignorance and misery."

15. In general, Augustine interiorized Christian love as an *inner attitude* regardless of the act. Thus, love was separated from law. (This leads to the paradox of "loving one's enemies" even while killing them.) External actions could then

be judged by civil authorities in terms of justice and laws regardless of the actor's inner Christian attitude.

16. Evelyn Underhill (1915) touched on applied mysticism in writing a book on "practical mysticism" as England prepared to enter World War I. She advanced a combination of mystical detachment and military service, thereby permitting participation in the war. But she also believed that the aims of mysticism are "wholly transcendental": mysticism "is in no way concerned with adding to, exploring, re-arranging, or improving anything in the visible universe" (1911: 81).

17. Sufis had various relations with rulers in the past—some supported them, some criticized them, and many were indifferent (Anjum 2006).

18. See Greeley 1974 on Thomas Müntzer and John Bockelson of Leyden. Mystics themselves who turn to social actions may become fervent radicals in social situations with their sense of certainty of what is real and what is the only way to realize it.

19. It would be a mistake to conclude that because Buddhists do not believe in selves that therefore they would reject individual rights—i.e., asserting human rights would mean they believe in a self. The metaphysics of the nature of the self does not preclude being moral (see R. Jones 2004: 192–93), and the same applies here. In fact, the Buddhist no-self (*anatta*) doctrine may be grounds to become socially active: it dismantles the sense of being an isolated reality and inculcates a sense of being connected to and conditioned by others and the world around us. Thus, a moral concern may well develop. But that is not what happened for monks and nuns in the Theravada tradition; however, it did happen in Mahayana Buddhism (see R. Jones 2004: chaps. 8–9).

20. Quoted in Parrinder 1976: 41. Why God would want us to build "unreal" things is not clear, but this shows the problem of mixing Advaita metaphysics and Western social ethics. Trying to see social reform as present in classical Indian thought is to distort it through modern and Western glasses.

21. Whether Kipnis means actual "social reform" rather than merely "personal interaction" with others when he refers to "social action" is not clear. The sensitivity, cooperation, and caring he mentions in connection with the yoga students can be more easily manifested in face-to-face interactions.

22. Gandhi disliked the title "Mahatma" because he thought only those who were socially effective truly deserved it.

23. Gandhi was interested in reforming Indian society in many areas (including education and sanitation) and in introducing a sense of community. He was not interested in gifts to the poor but in creating jobs and a viable small-scale economy. However, Gandhi's economics may not have been practical on a national scale. The quip made during his life was that it cost a fortune to keep him in a loincloth.

24. The Mahayana has a long history of militant monks. Such texts as the *Mahaparinirvana Sutra* state that monks can kill to protect the Buddha's doctrine and that kings can go to war to protect his subjects. This has led to monasteries

of monks warring with each other (over who has the correct interpretation of the doctrine) and aiding their government. Needless to say, this is moving the justification for killing more and more outside of the mystical context of helping the person with whom a Bodhisattva is interacting along the path to enlightenment, but the aim remained religious rather than applied mysticism for secular help.

25. One Buddhist monk concluded (although many others disagreed) that it was not demeritorious to kill communists by arguing that such killing did not constitute murder "because whoever destroys the nation, the religion, the monarchy, such bestial types are not complete persons. Thus, we must intend not to kill people but to kill the Devil (Mara); this is the duty of all Thai" (quoted in Ives 1992: 142).

26. The term comes from the Vietnamese Zen monk Thich Nhat Hanh (1967). Matthew Fox (1980a, 1980b) has similarly attempted to use Meister Eckhart's works (taken out of their mystical context) to make a modern "socially-engaged Christian mysticism" for the betterment of the world's secular conditions.

27. Also see Aitken 1984. Ives recognizes Zen's traditional conservative stance toward social structures (1992: 66), but it is not, as he claims, just the result of a division of intellectual labor leaving social matters to Confucianism (Ives 1992: 101). The focus on individuals' spiritual development and enlightenment (which Ives acknowledges) makes social matters irrelevant to classical mystics, even if the full religious way of life for the general Zen Buddhists included a Confucian-influenced social dimension.

28. As for psychedelics, psilocybin may enhance emotional (if not cognitive) empathy, but it may not enhance moral decision making (Pokorny et al. 2017). As noted in chapter 7, some advocates of psychedelics see them as a source for social change.

29. Inge was discussing Plotinus in the context of the ancient Greek and Roman ethos. Plotinus's ethics was even more self-centered and otherworldly than most classical Greek ethical thought (Dillon 1996: 319–20; see also Rist 1976).

References

Abhyananda, Swami. 2012. *History of Mysticism: The Unchanging Testament*. Olympia, WA: Atma Books.
Acevedo, Elias C., Scott Uhler, Kaitlyn P. White, and Laith Al-Shawaf. 2024. "What Predicts Beneficial Outcomes in Psychedelic Use? A Quantitative Content Analysis of Psychedelic Health Outcomes." *Journal of Psychoactive Drugs*, 10 (February): 1–10. https://doi.org/10.1080/02791072.2024.2314729.
Aday, Jacob, et al. 2020. "Long-Term Effects of Psychedelic Drugs: A Systematic Review." *Neuroscience & Biobehavioral Review* 113 (June): 179–89.
Aday, Jacob, et al. 2021. "Great Expectations: Recommendations for Improving the Methodological Rigor of Psychedelic Clinical Trials." *Psychopharmacology* 239:1989–2010.
Aday, Jacob S., Robin L. Carhart-Harris, and Joshua D. Woolley. 2023. "Emerging Challenges for Psychedelic Therapy." *JAMA Psychiatry* 80 (6): 533–34.
Aday, Jacob S., et al. 2024. "Psychedelic-Assisted Psychotherapy: Where Is the Psychotherapy Research?" *Psychopharmacology* 241 (August): 1517–26. https://doi.org/10.1007/s00213-024-06620-x.
Ahlskog, Raphael. 2017. "Moral Enhancement Should Target Self-Interest and Cognitive Capacity." *Neuroethics* 10:363–73.
Aitken, Robert. 1984. *The Mind of Clover: Essays in Zen Buddhist Ethics*. San Francisco, CA: North Point Press.
Alexander, Jeffrey C. 2000. "This-Worldly Mysticism: Inner Peace and World Transformation in the Work and Life of Charles 'Skip' Alexander." *Journal of Adult Development* 7 (4): 269–74.
Ambedkar, B. R. 2016. *Annihilation of Caste: The Annotated Critical Edition*. London: Verso Books.
Andersen Kristoffer A., et al. 2021. "Therapeutic Effects of Classic Serotonergic Psychedelics: A Systematic Review of Modern-Era Clinical Studies." *Acta Psychiatrica Scandinavica* 143 (2): 101–18. https://doi.org/10.1111/acps.13249.
Andresen, Jensine. 2000. "Meditation Meets Behaviourial Medicine: The Story of Experimental Research on Meditation." *Journal of Consciousness Studies* 7:17–73.

Angel, Leonard. 2002. "Mystical Naturalism." *Religious Studies* 38 (September): 317–38.

———. 2004. "Universal Self Consciousness Mysticism and the Physical Completeness Principle." *International Journal for Philosophy of Religion* 55 (1): 1–29.

Anjum, Tanvir. 2006. "Sufism in History and Its Relationship with Power." *Islamic Studies* 45 (2): 221–68.

Apel, William. 2003. "Mystic as Prophet: The Deep Freedom of Thomas Merton and Howard Thurman." *Thomas Merton Association* 16:172–87.

Arce, José M. Rodríguez, and Michael J. Winkelman. 2021. "Psychedelics, Sociality, and Human Evolution." *Frontiers in Psychology* 12: article 729425. https://doi.org/10.3389/fpsyg.2021.729425.

Arntz, William, Betsy Chase, and Mark Vicente. 2005. *What the BLEEP Do We Know? Discovering the Endless Possibilities for Altering Your Everyday World.* Deerfield Beach, FL: Health Communications.

Atkins, Peter William. 1994. *Creation Revisited: The Origin of Space, Time, and the Universe.* New York: Penguin Books.

Austin, James H. 1998. *Zen and the Brain: Toward an Understanding of Meditation and Consciousness.* Cambridge, MA: MIT Press.

Ayer, Alfred J. 1973. *The Central Questions of Philosophy.* London: Weidenfeld.

———. 1990. "The Undiscovered Country" and "Postscript to a Postmortem." In *The Meaning of Life*, 197–208. New York: Charles Scribner's Sons.

Azari, Nina P. 2006. "Neuroimaging Studies of Religious Experience: A Critical Review." In *Where God and Science Meet: How Brain and Evolutionary Studies Alter Our Understanding of Religion*, vol. 3, *The Psychology of Religious Experience*, ed. Patrick McNamara, 33–54. Westport, CT: Greenwood Press.

Badiner, Allan, and Alex Grey, eds. 2015. *Zig Zag Zen: Buddhism and Psychedelics.* 2nd ed. Santa Fe, NM: Synergetic Press.

Ballesteros, Virginia. 2019. "Applied Mysticism: A Drug-Enabled Visionary Experience against Moral Blindness." *Zygon* 54 (September): 731–55.

Barnard, G. William. 1992. "Explaining the Unexplainable: Wayne Proudfoot's *Religious Experience*." *Journal of the American Academy of Religion* 60 (2): 231–57.

———. 2014. "Entheogens in a Religious Context: The Case of the Santo Daime Tradition." *Zygon* 49 (3): 666–85.

Barrett, Frederick S., and Roland R. Griffiths. 2018. "Classic Hallucinogens and Mystical Experiences: Phenomenology and Neural Correlates." In *Behavioral Neurobiology of Psychedelic Drugs*, ed. Adam L. Halberstadt, Franz X. Vollenweider, and David E. Nichols, 393–430. New York: Springer.

Barrett, Frederick S., et al. 2018. "Double-Blind Comparison of the Two Hallucinogens Psilocybin and Dextromethorphan: Effects on Cognition." *Psychopharmacology* 235 (10): 2915–27.

Baruss, Imants, and Julia Mossbridge. 2016. *Transcendent Mind: Rethinking the Science of Consciousness.* Washington, DC: American Psychological Association.

Batchelor, Stephen. 2015. *After Buddhism: Rethinking the Dharma for a Secular Age*. New Haven, CT: Yale University Press.
Battle, Michael. 2021. *Desmond Tutu: A Spiritual Biography of South Africa's Confessor*. Louisville, KY: Westminster John Knox Press.
Bayne, Tim, and Olivia Carter. 2018. "Dimensions of Consciousness and the Psychedelic State." *Neuroscience of Consciousness* 4 (1): 1–8.
Beans, Carolyn. 2024. "If Psychedelics Heal, How Do They Do It?" *Proceedings of the National Academy of Sciences of the United States of America* 121 (2): e2321906121. https://doi.org/10.1073/pnas.2321906121.
Beauregard, Mario, and Denyse O'Leary. 2007. *The Spiritual Brain: A Neuroscientist's Case for the Existence of the Soul*. New York: HarperCollins.
Benson, Herbert, and Miriam Z. Klipper. 2000 [1975]. *The Relaxation Response*. New York: HarperCollins.
Berger, Peter L. 2014. *The Many Altars of Modernity: Toward a Paradigm for Religion in a Pluralistic Age*. Boston, MA: De Gruyter.
Berghuijs, Joantine, Cok Bakker, and Jos Pieper. 2013. "New Spirituality and Social Engagement." *Journal for the Scientific Study of Religion* 52 (4): 775–92.
Berkovich-Ohana, Aviva, et al. 2024. "Pattern Theory of Selflessness: How Meditation May Transform the Self-Pattern." *Mindfulness* 15:2114–40. https://doi.org/10.1007/s12671-024-02418-2.
Bermudez, Jose. 2015. "Nonconceptual Mental Content." *Stanford (Online) Encyclopedia of Philosophy*. https://plato.stanford.edu/entries/content-nonconceptual/.
Bermudez, Jose, and Arnon Cahen. 2020. "Nonconceptual Mental Content." In *The Stanford Encyclopedia of Philosophy*, ed. Edward N. Zalta (summer 2020 ed.). https://plato.stanford.edu/archIves/spr2024/entries/content-nonconceptual/.
Bernhardt, Stephen. 1990. "Are Pure Consciousness Events Mediated?" In *The Problem of Pure Consciousness: Mysticism and Philosophy*, ed. Robert K. C. Forman, 220–36. New York: Oxford University Press.
Beswerchij, Andrew, and Dominic Sisti. 2022. "From Underground to Mainstream: Establishing a Medical Lexicon for Psychedelic Therapy." *Frontiers in Psychiatry* 13. https://doi.org/10.3389/fpsyt.2022.870507.
Bhatt, Kush V. and Cory R. Weissman. 2024. "The Effect of Psilocybin on Empathy and Prosocial Behavior: A Proposed Mechanism for Enduring Antidepressant Effects." *NPJ Mental Health Research* 3 (1). https://doi.org/10.1038/s44184-023-00053-8.
Binns, Peter. 1995. "Commentary on 'Contentless Consciousness.'" *Philosophy, Psychiatry and Psychology* 2:61–63.
Blackmore, Susan. 2009. *Ten Zen Questions*. Oxford: Oneworld.
Boeke, Richard. 2015. *Mysticism and Social Action: Lawrence Lecture and Discussions with Dr Howard Thurman*. London: IARF.
Boly, Melanie, Marcello Massimini, Naotsugu Tsuchiya, Bradley R. Postle, Christof Koch, and Giulio Tononi. 2017. "Are the Neural Correlates of Consciousness

in the Front or in the Back of the Cerebral Cortex? Clinical and Neuroimaging Evidence." *Journal of Neuroscience* 37:9603–13.

Borrell, Brendan. 2024. "The Psychedelic Evangelist." *New York Times*, March 26, D1. https://www.nytimes.com/20.

Boslough, John. 1985. *Stephen Hawking's Universe*. New York: Quill.

Bowker, John. 1970. *Problems of Suffering in Religions of the World*. New York: Cambridge University Press.

———. 1973. *The Sense of God: Sociological, Anthropological, and Psychological Approaches to the Origin of the Sense of God*. Oxford: Oxford University Press.

Bradford, David T. 2013. "Emotion in Mystical Experience." *Religion, Brain & Behavior* 3 (2): 103–18.

Breeksema, Joost J., and Michiel van Elk. 2021. "Working with Weirdness: A Response to 'Moving Past Mysticism in Psychedelic Science.'" *ACS Pharmacology & Translational Science* 4 (July): 1471–74.

Bremler, Rebecka, et al. 2023. "Case Analysis of Long-Term Negative Psychological Responses to Psychedelics." *Scientific Reports* 13 (15998, September 25): n.p.

Brooke, John, and Geoffrey Cantor. 1998. *Reconstructing Nature*. Edinburgh: T & T Clark.

Buber, Martin. 1947. *Between Man and Man*. Translated by Maurice Friedman. New York: Routledge & Kegan.

Buric, Ivana, et al. 2017. "What Is the Molecular Signature of Mind-Body Interventions? A Systematic Review of Gene Expressions Changes Induced by Meditation and Related Practices." *Frontiers in Immunology* 8 (June 16): 1–17.

Butler, Matt, Luke Jelen, and James Rucker. 2022. "Expectancy in Placebo-Controlled Trials of Psychedelics: If So, So What?" *Psychopharmacology* 339:3047–55.

Byrd, Kevin R., Delbert Lear, and Stacy Schwenka. 2000. "Mysticism as a Predictor of Subjective Well-Being." *International Journal for the Psychology of Religion* 10 (4): 259–69.

Cabezón, José Ignacio. 2003. "Buddhism and Science: On the Nature of the Dialogue." In *Buddhism and Science: Breaking New Ground*, ed. B. Alan Wallace, 35–68. New York: Columbia University Press.

Cahn, B. Rael, and John Polich. 1999. "Meditation States and Traits: EEG, ERP, and Neuroimaging Studies." *Psychological Bulletin* 132:180–211.

Canova, Peter. 2022. *Quantum Spirituality: Science, Gnostic Mysticism, and Connecting with Source Consciousness*. Rochester, VT: Bear & Company.

Cao, Dongmei, et al. 2022. "Structure-Based Discovery of Nonhallucinogenic Psychedelic Analogs." *Science* 375 (January 28): 403–11.

Capra, Fritjof. 2010 [1975]. *The Tao of Physics: An Exploration of the Parallels between Modern Physics and Eastern Mysticism*. 5th ed. Boston, MA: Shambhala Press.

———. 2017. "Mystics and Scientists in the Twenty-First Century: Science and Spirituality Revisited." *Network Review* 1:15–17.

Capra, Fritjof, and David Steindl-Rast. 1991. *Belonging to the Universe: Explorations of Science and Spirituality*. New York: HarperCollins.

Carbonaro, Teresa M., Ethan Hurwitz, Matthew W. Johnson, and Roland R. Griffiths. 2018. "Double-Blind Comparison of the Two Hallucinogens Psilocybin and Dextromethorphan: Similarities in Subjective Experiences." *Psychopharmacology* 235 (2): 521–34.

Carhart-Harris, Robin L. 2023. "Translational Challenges in Psychedelic Medicine." *New England Journal of Medicine* 388 (February): 476–77.

Carhart-Harris, Robin L., et al. 2012. "Neural Correlates of the Psychedelic State as Determined by fMRI Studies with Psilocybin." *Proceedings of the National Academy of Sciences* 109:2138–43.

Carhart-Harris, Robin L., et al. 2014. "The Entropic Brain: A Theory of Conscious States Informed by Neuroimaging Research with Psychedelic Drugs." *Frontiers in Human Neuroscience* 8 (February 3). https://doi.org/10.3389/fnhum.2014.00020.

Carhart-Harris, Robin L., et al. 2015. "LSD Enhances Suggestibility in Healthy Volunteers." *Psychopharmacology* 232 (4): 785–94.

Carhart-Harris, Robin L., Mendel Kaelen, David J. Nutt. 2014. "How do Hallucinogens Work on the Brain?" *The Psychologist* 27 (9): 662–65.

Carhart-Harris, Robin L., et al. 2016. "The Paradoxical Psychological Effects of Lysergic Acid Diethylamide (LSD)." *Psychological Medicine* 46:1379–90.

Carhart-Harris, Robin L., et al. 2018. "Psychedelics and the Essential Importance of Context." *Journal of Psychopharmacology* 32 (7): 725–31.

Carhart-Harris, Robin L., and Karl J. Friston. 2019. "REBUS and the Anarchic Brain: Toward a Unified Model of the Brain Action of Psychedelics" *Pharmacological Reviews* 71 (July): 316–44.

Carrette, Jeremy, and Richard King. 2005. *Selling Spirituality: The Silent Takeover of Religion*. New York: Routledge.

Cavanna, Frederico, et al. 2022. "Microdosing with Psilocybin Mushrooms: A Double-Blind Placebo-Controlled Study." *Translational Psychiatry* 12 (August 2): 307–15.

Chalmers, David. 1995. "Facing Up to the Problem of Consciousness." *Journal of Consciousness Studies* 2:200–19.

———. 2004. "How Can We Construct a Science of Consciousness?" In Michael S. Gazzaniga, ed. *The Cognitive Neurosciences*, 1111–19. 3rd ed. Cambridge, MA: MIT Press.

Chander, Jag Parvesh, ed. 1947. *Teachings of Mahatma Gandhi*. Lahore, India: Indian Printing Works.

Chari, Anita. 2016. "The Political Potential of Mindful Embodiment." *New Political Science* 38 (2): 226–40.

Cheung, Katherine and David B Yaden. 2024. "Commentary: On the Need for Metaphysics in Psychedelic Therapy and Research." *Frontiers in Psychology* 14 (January 5): article 1341566. https://doi.org/10.3389/fpsyg.2023.1341566.

Chiesa, Alberto, and Alessandro Serretti. 2010. "A Systematic Review of Neurobiological and Clinical Features of Mindfulness Meditations." *Psychological Medicine* 40 (8 August): 1239–52.
Chomsky, Noam. 2006. *The Architecture of Language*. New York: Oxford University Press.
Chopra, Deepak. 2012. Foreword to Ervin Laszlo and Kingsley L. Dennis, eds., *The New Science and Spirituality Reader*. Rochester, VT: Inner Traditions.
Chrysostom, St. John. 1981. *On Wealth and Poverty*. Translated by Catharine P. Roth. Yonkers, NY: St. Vladimir's Seminary Press.
Clark, A. 2013. "Whatever Next?" Predictive Brains, Situated Agents and the Future of Cognitive Science." *Behavioral Brain Science* 36:181–204.
Clarke, Chris, ed. 2005. *Ways of Knowing: Science and Mysticism Today*. Charlottesville, VA: Imprint Academic.
Clausen, Shawn S., Cindy C. Crawford, and John A. Ives. 2014. "Does Neuroimaging Provide Evidence of Meditation-Mediated Neuroplasticity?" In Stefan Schmidt and Harald Walach, ed. *Meditation: Neuroscientific Approaches and Philosophical Implications*, 115–35. New York: Springer.
Cole-Turner, Ron. 2014. "Entheogens, Mysticism, and Neuroscience." *Zygon* 49 (3): 642–51.
———. 2024. "Psychedelic Mysticism and Christian Spirituality: From Science to Love. *Religions* 15:537–47. https://doi.org/10/3990/rel15050537.
Commins, Gary. 2015. *If Only They Could See: Mystical Vision and Social Transformation*. Eugene, OR: Wipf and Stock.
Costines, Cyril, Tilmann Lhündrup Borghardi, and Marc Wittman. 2021. "The Phenomenology of 'Pure' Consciousness as Reported by an Experienced Meditator of the Tibetan Buddhist Karma Kagyu Tradition. Analysis of Interview Content Concerning Different Meditative States." *Philosophies* 6 (50): 1–22.
Crane, Tim. 2003. "The Intentional Structure of Consciousness." In *Consciousness: New Philosophical Perspectives*, ed. Quentin Smith and Aleksandar Jokic, 33–56. New York: Oxford University Press.
Cristofori, Irene, et al. 2016. "Neural Correlates of Mystical Experience." *Neuropsychologia* 80:212–20.
Crosby, Donald A. 2008. *The Thou of Nature: Religious Naturalism and Reverence for Sentient Life*. Albany: State University of New York Press.
Crosby, Donald A., and Jerome A. Stone, eds. 2020. *Routledge Handbook of Religious Naturalism*. New York: Routledge.
Csikszentmihalyi, Mihaly. 1990. *Flow: The Psychology of Optimal Experience*. New York: Harper Perennial.
Cummins, Christina, and Jennifer Lyke. 2013. "Peak Experiencers of Psilocybin Users and Non-Users." *Journal of Psychoactive Drugs* 45 (2): 189–94.
Curle, Adam. 1972. *Mystics and Militants: A Study of Awareness, Identity, and Social Action*. London: Tavistock.

Damasio, Antonio R. 2018. *The Strange Order of Things: Life, Feeling, and the Making of Cultures*. New York: Viking.

Dan, Joseph. 1996. *Jewish Mysticism and Jewish Ethics*. Northvale, NJ: Jason Aronson.

D'Aquili, Eugene G., and Andrew B. Newberg. 1999. *The Mystical Mind: Probing the Biology of Religious Experience*. Minneapolis, MN: Fortress.

Davanger, Svend. 2013. "The Natural Science of Meditation: A 'Black Box' Perspective?" In Halvor Eifring, ed., *Meditation in Judaism, Christianity and Islam: Cultural Histories*, 227–36. New York: Bloomsbury.

Davis, Alan K., et al. 2020. "Survey of Entity Encounter Experiences Occasioned by Inhaled N,N-dimethyltryptamine: Phenomenology, Interpretation, and Enduring Effects." *Journal of Psychopharmacology* 34 (9): 1008–20.

Davis, Alan K., et al. 2021. "Effects of Psilocybin-Assisted Therapy on Major Depressive Disorder: A Randomized Clinical Trial." *JAMA Psychiatry* 78 (5): 481–89.

De Caro, Mario, and David Macarthur, eds. 2004. *Naturalism in Question*. Cambridge, MA: Harvard University Press.

Dennett, Daniel C. 1991. *Consciousness Explained*. New York: Little, Brown.

Devereux, Paul. 1997. *The Long Trip: A Prehistory of Psychedelia*. New York: Penguin Books.

Devinsky, Orrin, and George C. Lai. 2008. "Spirituality and Religion in Epilepsy." *Epilepsy & Behavior* 12 (4): 636–43.

Diem, Andrea Grace, and James R. Lewis. 1992. "Imagining India: The Influence of Hinduism on the New Age Movement." In *Perspectives on the New Age*, ed. James R. Lewis and J. Gordon Melton, 48–58. Albany: State University of New York Press.

Dillon, John M. 1996. "An Ethic for the Late Antique Sage." In *The Cambridge Companion to Plotinus*, ed. Lloyd P. Gerson, 315–35. New York: Cambridge University Press.

Doblin, Rick. 1991. "Pahnke's 'Good Friday Experiment': A Long-Term Follow-Up and Methodological Critique." *Journal of Transpersonal Psychology* 23 (1): 1–28.

Doss, Manoj, et al. 2021. "Psilocybin Therapy Increases Cognitive and Neural Flexibility in Patients with Major Depressive Disorder." *Translational Psychiatry* 11 (November 8): 574–83.

Du Plessis, Erik Mygind, and Sine Nørholm Just. 2021 "Mindfulness—It's Not What You Think: Toward Critical Reconciliation with Progressive Self-Development Practices." *Organization* 29 (1): 1–13.

Dupuis, David, and Samuel Veissière. 2022. "Culture, Context, and Ethics in the Therapeutic use of Hallucinogens: Psychedelics as Active Superplacebos?" *Transcultural Psychiatry* 59 (October): 571–78. https://doi.org/10.1177/13634615221131465.

Dunn, Bruce R., Judith A. Hartigan, and William L. Mikulas. 1999. "Concentration and Mindfulness: Unique Forms of Consciousness." *Applied Psychophysiology and Biofeedback* 24 (3): 147–65.

Dworkin, Ronald. 2013. *Religion without God*. Cambridge, MA: Harvard University Press.

Dyczkowski, Mark S. G. 1987. *The Doctrine of Vibration: An Analysis of the Doctrines and Practices of Kashmir Shaivism*. Albany: State University of New York Press.

Earleywine, Mitch, Fiona Low, and Joseph De Leojdeleo. 2021. "A Semantic Scale Network Analysis of the Revised Mystical Experiences Questionnaire: A Call for Collaboration." *Journal of Psychedelic Studies* 5 (November 16): 1–10.

Eckhart, Meister. 2009. *The Complete Mystical Works of Meister Eckhart*. Edited and translated by Maurice O'C. Walshe. Revised by Bernard McGinn. New York: Crossroad.

Ecklund, Elaine Howard, and Elizabeth Long. 2011. "Scientists and Spirituality." *Sociology of Religion* 72 (3): 253–74.

Eifring, Halvor, ed. 2016. *Asian Traditions of Meditation*. Honolulu: University of Hawai'i Press.

Eisner, Bruce. 1989. *Ecstasy: The MDMA Story*. Berkeley, CA: Ronin.

Ellens, J. Harold, ed. 2015. *Seeking the Sacred with Psychoactive Substances: Chemical Paths to Spirituality and to God*, vol. 2. Santa Barbara, CA: Praeger.

Ellsberg, Robert, ed. 2005. *Dorothy Day: Selected Writings*. Maryknoll, NY: Orbis Books.

Eppesteiner, Fred, ed. 1988. *The Path of Compassion: Writings on Socially Engaged Buddhism*. Berkeley, CA: Parallax Press.

Erritzoe, David, et al. 2024. "Exploring Mechanisms of Psychedelic Action Using Neuroimaging." *Nature Mental Health* 2 (2): 141–53.

Esch, Tobias. 2014. "The Neurobiology of Meditation and Mindfulness." In *Meditation: Neuroscientific Approaches and Philosophical Implications*, ed. Stefan Schmidt and Harald Walach, 153–73. New York: Springer.

Evans, Donald. 1989. "Can Philosophers Limit What Mystics Can Do? A Critique of Steven Katz." *Religious Studies* 25:53–60.

Evans, Jules, et al. 2023. "Extended Difficulties Following the Use of Psychedelic Drugs: A Mixed Methods Study." *PloS One* (October 24): 1–24.

Evens, Ricarda, et al. 2023. "The Psychedelic Afterglow Phenomenon: A Systematic Review of Subacute Effects of Classic Serotonergic Psychedelics." *Therapeutic Advances in Psychopharmacology* 13 (May 29). https://doi.org/10.1177/20451253231172254.

Fingelkurts, Alexander A., and Andrew A. Fingelkurts. 2009. "Is Our Brain Hardwired to Produce God, or Is Our Brain Hardwired to Perceive God? A Systematic Review on the Role of the Brain in Mediating Religious Experience." *Cognitive Processing* 10:293–326.

Fink, Sasha Benjamin. 2020. "Look Who's Talking! Varieties of Ego-Dissolution without Paradox." *Philosophy and the Mind Sciences* 1 (1): 1–36.

Finkelstein, David Ritz. 2003. "Emptiness and Relativity." In *Buddhism and Science: Breaking New Ground*, ed. B. Alan Wallace, 365–86. New York: Columbia University Press.

Flanagan, Owen. 2007. *The Really Hard Problem: Meaning in a Material World*. Cambridge, MA: MIT Press.

Flanagan, Owen, and George Graham. 2017. "Truth and Sanity: Positive Illusions, Spiritual Delusions, and Metaphysical Hallucinations." In *Extraordinary Science and Psychiatry: Responses to the Crisis in Mental Health Research*, ed. Jeffrey Poland and Serife Tekin, 293–313. Cambridge, MA: MIT Press.

Flanagan, Owen, and Gregg D. Caruso. 2018. "Neuroexistentialism: Third Wave Existentialism." In *Neuroexistentialism: Meaning, Morals, and Purpose in the Age of Neuroscience*, ed. Gregg D. Caruso and Owen Flanagan, 1–22. New York: Oxford University Press.

Forman, Robert K. C., ed. 1990. *The Problem of Pure Consciousness: Mysticism and Philosophy*. New York: Oxford University Press.

———. 1993. "Mystical Knowledge by Identity." *Journal of the American Academy of Religion* 61 (4): 705–38.

———, ed. 1998. *The Innate Capacity: Mysticism, Psychology, and Philosophy*. New York: Oxford University Press.

———. 1999. *Mysticism, Mind, Consciousness*. Albany: State University of New York Press.

———. 2011. *Enlightenment Ain't What It's Cracked Up to Be*. Washington, DC: O-Books.

Formoso, Kirsti. 2023. "Factor Analysis of the MEQ43 Suggests Non-psychedelic Mystical Experiences are Different from Psychedelic Mystical Experiences." *Consciousness, Spirituality & Transpersonal Psychology* 4 (November): 28–45. https://doi.org/10.53074/cstp.2023.63.

Fort, Andrew O. 1998. *Jivanmukti in Transformation: Embodied Liberation in Advaita and Neo-Vedanta*. Albany: State University of New York Press.

Forte, Robert. 1997. *Entheogens and the Future of Religion*. San Francisco, CA: Council on Spiritual Practices.

Fox, Kieran et al. 2016. "Functional Neuroanatomy of Meditation: A Review and Meta-Analysis of 78 Functional Neuroimaging Investigations." *Neuroscience and Biobehavioral Review* 65 (June): 208–28. https://doi.org/10.1016/j.neubiorev.2016.03.021.

Fox, Matthew. 1980a. *Breakthrough: Meister Eckhart's Creation Spirituality, in New Translation*. Garden City, NY: Doubleday.

———. 1980b. "Meister Eckhart and Karl Marx: The Mystic as Political Theologian." In *Understanding Mysticism*, ed. Richard Woods, 541–63. Garden City, NY: Image Books.

———. 1991. *Creation Spirituality: Liberating Gifts for the Peoples of the Earth*. San Francisco, CA: Harper.

Fuentes, Juan José, et al. 2020. "Therapeutic Use of LSD in Psychiatry: A Systematic Review of Randomized-Controlled Clinical Trials." *Frontiers in Psychiatry* (January 21): 1–14.

Gamma, Alex, and Thomas Metzinger. 2021. "The Minimal Phenomenal Experience Questionnaire (MPE-92M): Towards a Phenomenological Profile of 'Pure Awareness' Experiences in Meditators." *Plos One* (July 14): 1–39.

Gan, Peter. 2019. "Can Mystical Peace Contribute to Global Peace?" *Peace and Conflict Studies* 26 (2): article 3, 1–24.

Gandhi, Mohandas. 1961. *Non-Violent Resistance (Satyagraha)*. New York: Schocken Books.

Gandy, Sam. 2022. "Predictors and Potentiators of Psychedelic-Occasioned Mystical Experiences." *Journal of Psychedelic Studies* 6 (1): 31–47.

Gandy, Sam, et al. 2022. "Psychedelics as Potential Catalysts of Scientific Creativity and Insight." *Drug Science, Policy and Law* 8:1–16.

Garb, Bradley A. and Mitchell Earleywine. 2022. "Mystical Experiences Without Mysticism: An Argument for Mystical Fictionalism in Psychedelics." *Journal of Psychedelic Studies* 6 (1). https://doi.org/10.1556/2054.2022.00207

Geertz, Armin W. 2009. "When Cognitive Scientists Become Religious, Science Is in Trouble: On Neurotheology from a Philosophy of Science Perspective." *Religion* 39:319–24.

Gennaro, Rocco J. 2008. "Are There Pure Conscious Events?" In *Mysticism Revisited*, ed. Chandana Chakrabarti and Gordon Haist, 100–20. Newcastle, UK: Cambridge Scholar.

Gill, Shivjot, and John Clammer. 2019. "Multidimensional Mysticism." In *Practical Spirituality and Human Development: Transformations in Religions and Societies*, ed. Ananta Kumar Giri, 17–37. New York: Springer.

Gilovich, Thomas. 1993. *How We Know What Isn't So: The Fallibility of Human Reason in Everyday Life*. New York: The Free Press.

Gladziejewski, Pawel. 2023. "From Altered States to Metaphysics: The Epistemic Status of Psychedelic-induced Metaphysical Beliefs." *Review of Philosophical Psychology* 10:1–23. https://doi.org/10.1007/s13164-023-00709-6.

Glausser, Wayne. 2021. "Psychedelic Drugs and Atheism: Debunking the Myths." *Religions* 12 (8): 614–21.

Goldberg, David W. 2009. "D'Aquili and Newberg's Neurotheology: A Hermeneutical Problem with Their Neurological Solution." *Religion* 39: 325–30.

Golden, Tasha L., et al. 2022. "Effects of Setting on Psychedelic Experiences, Therapies, and Outcomes: A Rapid Scoping Review of the Literature." *Current Topics in Behavioral Neurosciences* 56:35–70. https://doi.org/10.1007/7854_2021_298.

Goleman, Daniel, and Richard J. Davidson. 2018. *Altered Traits: Science Reveals How Mediation Changes Your Mind, Brain, and Body*. New York: Avery.

Goleman, Daniel, and Robert A. F. Thurman, eds. 1991. *MindScience: An East-West Dialogue*. Boston, MA: Wisdom.

Gombrich, Richard F. 1988. *Theravada Buddhism: A Social History from Ancient Benares to Modern Colombo*. New York: Routledge and Kegan Paul.

Goodenough, Ursula. 1998. *The Sacred Depths of Nature*. New York: Oxford University Press.

Goodman, Neil. 2002. "The Serotonergic System and Mysticism: Could LSD and the Nondrug-Induced Mystical Experiences Share Common Neural Mechanisms?" *Journal of Psychoactive Drugs* 34 (July–September): 263–72.

Goodwin, Guy M., et al. 2024. "Must Psilocybin Always 'Assist Psychotherapy'?" *American Journal of Psychiatry* 181 (1): 20–25.

Goswami, Amit. 2011. *How Quantum Activism Can Save Civilization: A Few People Can Change Human Evolution*. Charlottesville, VA: Hampton Roads.

———. 2012. "The Real Secret of How We Create Our Own Reality." In *The New Science and Spirituality Reader*, ed. Ervin Laszlo and Kingsley L. Dennis, 95–100. Rochester, VT: Inner Traditions.

Goswami, Amit, with Maggie Goswami. 1997. *Science and Spirituality: A Quantum Integration*. New Delhi: History of Indian Science Project, Philosophy and Culture.

Gray, Mel, and Terence Lovat. 2008. "Practical Mysticism, Habermas, and Social Work Praxis." *Journal of Social Work* 8 (2): 149–62.

Greeley, Andrew M. 1974. "Ecstatic Politics." In *Ecstasy: A Way of Knowing*, 98–111 Englewood Cliffs, NJ: Prentice-Hall.

Greif, Adam, and Martin Šurkala. 2020. "Compassionate Use of Psychedelics." *Medicine, Health Care and Philosophy* 23 (May 28): 485–96.

Greyson, Bruce, et al. 2015. "Mystical Experiences Associated with Seizures." *Religion, Brain & Behavior* 5 (3): 182–96.

Griffiths, Roland R., et al. 2006. "Psilocybin Can Occasion Mystical-Type Experiences Having Substantial and Sustained Personal Meaning and Spiritual Significance." *Psychopharmacology* 187 (3): 268–83.

Griffiths, Roland R., et al. 2008. "Mystical-Type Experiences Occasioned by Psilocybin Mediate the Attribution of Personal Meaning and Spiritual Significance 14 Months Later." *Journal of Psychopharmacology* 22 (3): 621–32.

Griffiths, Roland R., et al. 2011. "Psilocybin Occasioned Mystical-Type Experiences: Immediate and Persisting Dose-Related Effects." *Psychopharmacology* 218 (4): 649–65.

Griffiths, Roland R., et al. 2016. "Psilocybin Produces Substantial and Sustained Decreases in Depression and Anxiety in Patients with Life-Threatening Cancer: A Randomized Double-Blind Trial." *Journal Psychopharmacology* 30 (12): 1181–97.

Griffiths, Roland R., et al. 2018. "Psilocybin-Occasioned Mystical-Type Experience in Combination with Meditation and Other Spiritual Practices Produces Enduring Positive Changes in Psychological Functioning and in Trait Measures of Prosocial Attitudes and Behaviors." *Journal of Psychopharmacology* 32 (1): 49–69.

Griffiths, Thomas L., Charles Kemp, and Joshua B. Tenenbaum. 2008. "Bayesian Models of Cognition." In *Cambridge Handbook of Computational Psychology*, ed. Ron Sun, 59–100. Cambridge, MA: Cambridge University Press.

Grof, Stanislav. 2009. *LSD: Doorway to the Numinous: The Groundbreaking Psychedelic Research into Realms of the Human Unconscious.* 4th ed. Rochester, VT: Park Street Press.

Guerra-Doce, Elisa. 2015. "Psychoactive Substances in Prehistoric Times: Examining the Archaeological Evidence." *Time and Mind* 8 (1): 91–112.

Gunnlaugson, Olen, et al. eds. 2014. *Contemplative Learning and Inquiry across Disciplines* Albany: SUNY Press.

Gutting, Gary. 2013. "Religious Agnosticism." *Midwest Studies in Philosophy* 37 (1): 51–67.

Gyatso, Tenzin (His Holiness the XIVth Dalai Lama). 2003. "Understanding and Transforming the Mind." In *Buddhism and Science: Breaking New Ground*, ed. B. Alan Wallace, 91–106. New York: Columbia University Press.

———. 2005. *The Universe in a Single Atom: The Convergence of Science and Spirituality.* New York: Morgan Road Books.

Gyatso, Tenzin, and Daniel Goleman. 2003. "On the Luminosity of Being." *New Scientist* 178:42–43.

Hajicek-Dobberstein, S. 1995. "Soma, Siddhas and Alchemical Enlightenment: Psychedelic Mushrooms in Buddhist Tradition." *Journal of Ethnopharmacology* 48 (2): 99–118.

Halberstadt, Adam, and Mark Geyer. 2015. "Do Psychedelics Expand the Mind by Reducing Brain Activity?" *Scientific American Global*, web publication, June 12.

Halbfass, Wilhelm. 1988. *India and Europe: An Essay in Understanding.* Albany: State University of New York Press.

Halpern, John H., Arturo G. Lerner, and Torsten Passie. 2018. "A Review of Hallucinogen Persisting Perception Disorder (HPPD) and an Exploratory Study of Subjects Claiming Symptoms of HPPD." In *Behavioral Neurobiology of Psychedelic Drugs*, ed. Adam L. Halberstadt, Franz X. Vollenweider, and David E. Nichols, 333–60. New York: Springer.

Hameroff, Stuart, Alfred W. Kaszniak, and Alwyn C. Scott, eds. 1996. *Toward a Science of Consciousness: The First Tucson Discussions and Debates.* Cambridge, MA: MIT Press.

Han, Shihui, et al. 2008. "Neural Consequences of Religious Belief on Self-Referential Processing." *Social Neuroscience* 3 (1): 1–15.

Hanegraaff, Wouter J. 1998. *New Age Religion and Western Culture: Esotericism in the Mirror of Secular Thought.* Albany: State University of New York Press.

Hardy, Alister. 1983. *The Spiritual Nature of Man.* Oxford: Clarendon Press.

Harris, Sam. 2014. *Waking Up: A Guide to Spirituality without Religion.* New York: Simon & Schuster.

Hartogsohn, Ido. 2016. "Set and Setting, Psychedelics and the Placebo Effect: An Extra-Pharmacological Perspective on Psychopharmacology." *Journal of Psychopharmacology* 30 (12): 1259–67.

Harvey, Peter. 2000. *An Introduction to Buddhist Ethics.* New York: Cambridge University Press.

Hashimoto, Kenji. 2024. "Are 'Mystical Experiences' Essential for Antidepressant Actions of Ketamine and the Classic Psychedelics?" *European Archives of Psychiatry and Clinical Neuroscience*. Published online February 27.

Hauskeller, Christine, and Peter Sjöstedt-Hughes, eds. 2022. *Philosophy and Psychedelics: Frameworks for Exceptional Experience*. London: Bloomsbury Academic.

Hawking, Stephen W., and Leonard Mlodinow. 2010. *The Grand Design*. New York: Bantam Books.

Hay, David. 1994. "The Biology of God: What Is the Current Status of Hardy's Hypothesis?" *International Journal for the Psychology of Religion* 4 (1): 1–23.

Hearn, Benjamin. 2021. "Psychedelics, Mystical Experiences, and Meaning Making: A Renegotiation Process with the Challenges of Existence." *Journal of Humanistic Counseling* 60 (October): 180–96.

Heller, Rick. 2015. *Secular Meditation: 32 Practices for Cultivating Inner Peace, Compassion, and Joy*. Novato, CA: New World Library.

Hergovich, Andreas, Rienhard Schott, and Christoph Burger. 2010. "Biased Evaluation of Abstracts Depending on Topic and Conclusion: Further Evidence of a Confirmation Bias within Scientific Psychology." *Current Psychology* 29 (August 29): 188–209.

Hick, John. 1989. *An Interpretation of Religion: Human Responses to the Transcendent*. New Haven, CT: Yale University Press.

Hinterberger, Thilo. 2014. "I Am I from Moment to Moment: Methods and Results of Grasping Intersubjective and Intertemporal Neurophysiological Differences during Meditation States." In *Meditation: Neuroscientific Approaches and Philosophical Implications*, ed. Stefan Schmidt and Harald Walach, 95–113. New York: Springer.

Hoffman, Albert. 1999 [1977]. "Preface." In *Moksha: Classic Writings on Psychedelics and the Visionary Experience*, ed. Michael Horowitz and Cynthia Palmer, xiii–xiv. Rochester, VT: Park Street Press.

Hoffman, Sarah. 2022. "Positive Affect and Letheby's Naturalization of Psychedelic Therapy." *PhiMiSc: Philosophy and the Mind Sciences* 3. https://doi.org/10.33735/phimisci.2022.9285.

Holas, Pawel, and Justyna Kamińska. 2023. "Mindfulness Meditation and Psychedelics: Potential Synergies and Commonalities." *Pharmacological Reports* (November). https://doi.org/10.1007/s43440-023-00551-8.

Holzel, Britta, et al. 2011. "Mindfulness Practice Leads to Increases in Regional Brain Gray Matter." *Psychiatry Research* 191:36–43.

Hood, Ralph W., Jr. 1997. "The Empirical Study of Mysticism." In *The Psychology of Religion: Theoretical Approaches*, ed. Bernard Spilka and Daniel N. McIntosh, 222–32. Boulder, CO: Westview Press.

———. 2001. *Dimensions of Mystical Experiences: Empirical Studies and Psychological Links*. Amsterdam: Rodopi.

———. 2002. "The Mystical Self: Lost and Found." *International Journal for the Psychology of Religion* 12 (1): 1–14.

———. 2005. "Mystical, Spiritual, and Religious Experiences." In *Handbook of the Psychology of Religion and Spirituality*, ed. Raymond F. Paloutzian and Crystal L. Park, 348–64. New York: Guilford Press.

———. 2006. "The Common Core Thesis in the Study of Mysticism." In *Where God and Science Meet: How Brain and Evolutionary Studies Alter Our Understanding of Religion: The Psychology of Religious Experience*, ed. Patrick McNamara, 3:119–38. Westport, CT: Greenwood Press.

———. 2013. "Theory and Methods in the Psychological Study of Mysticism." *International Journal for the Psychology of Religion* 23 (4): 294–306.

———. 2014. "Chemically Assisted Mysticism and the Question of Veridicality." In *Seeking the Sacred with Psychoactive Substances: Chemical Paths to Spirituality and God*, vol. 1, *History and Practices*, ed. J. H. Ellens, 395–410. Santa Barbara, CA: Praeger.

———. 2016. "The Common Core Thesis in the Study of Mysticism." *Oxford (Online) Research Encyclopedia*. https://doi.org/10.1093/acrefore/9780199340378.013.241.

———. 2017. "Self-Loss in Indigenous and Cross-Cultural Psychologies: Beyond Dichotomies?" *Research in the Social Scientific Study of Religion* 28 (1): 112–32.

Hood, Ralph W., Jr., and G. N. Byrom. 2010. "Mysticism, Madness, and Mental Health." In *The Healing Power of Spirituality: How Faith Helps Humans Thrive*, ed. J. Harold Ellens, 3:171–91. Santa Barbara, CA: Praeger.

Horgan, John. 2003. *Rational Mysticism: Dispatches from the Border between Science and Spirituality*. Boston: Houghton Mifflin.

Horrobin, David F. 1990. "The Philosophical Basis of Peer Review and the Suppression of Innovation." *Journal of the American Medical Association* 263 (10): 1438–41.

Hummel, Leonard. 2014. "By Its Fruits? Mystical and Visionary States of Consciousness Occasioned by Entheogens." *Zygon* 49 (3): 685–95.

Hunt, Harry T. 2003. *Lives In Spirit: Precursors and Dilemmas of a Secular Western Mysticism*. Albany: State University of New York Press.

Huston, Tom. 2004. "Taking the Quantum Leap . . . Too Far?" *What Is Enlightenment?* 27 (October–December): 1–5.

Huxley, Aldous. 1944. *The Perennial Philosophy*. New York: Harper & Row.

———. 1954. *The Doors of Perception*. New York: Harper & Row.

———. 1955. *Heaven and Hell*. New York: Harper & Row.

———. 1958. *Drugs that Shape Men's Minds*. Philadelphia, PA: Curtis.

———. 1999 [1977]. *Moksha: Writings on Psychedelics and the Visionary Experience (1931–1963)*. Edited by Michael Horowitz and Cynthia Palmer. Los Angeles: J. P. Tarcher.

Ives, Christopher. 1992. *Zen Awakening and Society*. Honolulu: University of Hawaii Press.

Jager, Willigis. 2006. *Mysticism for Modern Times: Conversations with Willigis Jäger*. Edited by Christoph Quarch. Translated by Paul Shepherd. Liguori, MO: Liguori/Triumph.

James, Edward, Thomas L. Robertshaw, Matthew Hoskin, and Ben Sessa. 2020. "Psilocybin Occasioned Mystical-Type Experiences." *Human Psychopharmacology: Clinical & Experimental* 35 (5): e2742. https://doi.org/10.1002/hup.2742.

James, William. 1958 [1902]. *The Varieties of Religious Experience*. New York: New American Library.

Jay, Mike, 2023. *Psychonauts: Drugs and the Making of the Modern Mind*. New Haven, CT: Yale University Press.

Jerryson, Michael, and Mark Juergensmeyer, eds. 2010. *Buddhist Warfare*. New York: Oxford University Press.

Jhingran, Saral. 1989. *Aspects of Hindu Morality*. Delhi: Motilal Banarsidass.

Jinpa, Thupten. 2010. "Buddhism and Science: How Far Can the Dialogue Proceed?" *Zygon* 45 (4): 871–82.

Johnson, Matthew W. 2021. "Consciousness, Religion, and Gurus: Pitfalls of Psychedelic Medicine." *ACS Pharmacology & Translational Science* 4 (April): 578–81.

———. 2022. "Introduction: Psychedelic Science Needs Philosophy." *PhiMiSci: Philosophy and the Mind Sciences* 3 (3): 1–6.

Johnson, Matthew W., Peter S. Hendricks, Frederick S. Barrett, and Roland R. Griffiths. 2019. "Classic Psychedelics: An Integrative Review of Epidemiology, Therapeutics, Mystical Experience, and Brain Network Function." *Pharmacology & Therapeutics* 197 (May): 83–102.

Johnstone, Brick, Daniel Cohen, Kelly Konopacki, and Christopher Ghan. 2016. "Selflessness as a Foundation of Spiritual Transcendence: Perspectives from the Neurosciences and Religious Studies." *International Journal for the Psychology of Religion* 26:287–303.

Joiner, Thomas. 2017. *Mindlessness: The Corruption of Mindfulness in a Culture of Narcissism*. New York: Oxford University Press.

Jones, Ken. 1989. *The Social Face of Buddhism: An Approach to Political and Social Activism*. London: Wisdom.

———. 2003. *The New Social Face of Buddhism: An Alternative Perspective*. Boston, MA: Wisdom Books.

Jones, Richard H. 1986. *Science and Mysticism: A Comparative Study of Western Natural Science, Theravada Buddhism, and Advaita Vedanta*. Lewisburg, PA: Bucknell University Press.

———. 2000. *Reductionism: Analysis and the Fullness of Reality*. Lewisburg: Bucknell University Press.

———. 2004. *Mysticism and Morality: A New Look at Old Questions*. Lanham, MD: Lexington Books.

———. 2011. *For the Glory of God: The Role of Christianity in the Rise and Development of Modern Science*, vol. 1, *The Dependency Thesis and Control Beliefs*. Lanham, MD: University. Press of America.

———. 2013. *Analysis and the Fullness of Reality: An Introduction to Reductionism & Emergence*. New York: Jackson Square Books / Createspace.

———, trans. 2014. *Early Indian Philosophy*. New York: Jackson Square Books.
———. 2015 [2010]. *Piercing the Veil: Comparing Science and Mysticism as Ways of Knowing Reality*. Rev. ed. New York: Jackson Square Books/Createspace.
———. 2016. *Philosophy of Mysticism: Raids on the Ineffable*. Albany: State University of New York Press.
———. 2018a. *Mystery 101: Introduction to the Big Questions and the Limits of Human Knowledge*. Albany: State University of New York Press.
———. 2018b. "Limitations on the Neuroscientific Study of Mystical Experiences." *Zygon* 53 (December): 992–1017.
———. 2019. "Limitations on the Scientific Study of Drug-Enabled Mystical Experiences." *Zygon* 54 (September): 756–92.
———. 2020a. "On Constructivism in the Philosophy of Mysticism." *Journal of Religion* 100 (1, January): 1–41.
———. 2020b. "Transcendent Knowledge-Claims and the Scientific Study of Mystical Experiences." In *Mysticism: Twenty-First Century Approaches and Perspectives*, ed. Alex S. Kohav, 247–70. Lanham, MD: Lexington Books.
———. 2021a. *An Introduction to the Study of Mysticism*. Albany: State University of New York Press.
———. 2021b. "Perennial Philosophy and the History of Mysticism." *Sophia* 60 (2, June): 1–20.
———, trans. 2022 [2015]. *Nagarjuna: Buddhism's Most Important Philosopher*. Rev. and expanded ed. New York: Jackson Square Books/Createspace.
———. 2022. "Secular Mysticism." *Religions* 13 (7, July): 650–77.
———. 2024. *A History of Mysticism*. Albany: State University of New York Press.
Jones, Richard H., and Jerome Gellman. 2022. "Mysticism." *Stanford Encyclopedia of Philosophy (Online)*. https://plato.stanford.edu/entries/mysticism/
Jones, Rufus M. 2001. *Essential Writings*. Selected by Kerry Walters. Maryknoll, NY: Orbis Books.
Josipovic, Zoran. 2019. "Nondual Awareness: Consciousness-as-Such as Nonrepresentational Reflexivity." *Progress in Brain Research* 344:273–98.
Josipovic, Zoran, and Vladimir Miskovic. 2020. "Nondual Awareness and Minimal Phenomenal Experience." *Frontiers in Psychology* 11 (August): article 2087.
Jylkkä, Jussi. 2021. "Reconciling Mystical Experiences with Naturalistic Psychedelic Science: A Reply to Sanders and Zijlmans." *ACS Pharmacology & Translational Science* 4 (July): 1468–70.
Kabat-Zinn, Jon. 2005. *Wherever You Go, There You Are: Mindfulness Meditation in Everyday Life*. New York: Hachette Books.
Kaelen, Mendel, et al. 2018. "The Hidden Therapist: Evidence for a Central Role of Music in Psychedelic Therapy." *Psychopharmacology* 235 (2): 505–19.
Kaiser, David. 2011. *How the Hippies Saved Physics: Science, Counterculture, and the Quantum Revival*. New York: W. W. Norton.

Kałużna, Ada, et al. 2022. "Being No One, Being One: The Role of Ego-Dissolution and Connectedness in the Therapeutic Effects of Psychedelic Experience." *Journal of Psychedelic Studies* 6 (2): 111–36.

Kang, Do-Hyung, et al. 2013. "The Effect of Meditation on Brain Structure: Cortical Thickness Mapping and Diffusion Tensor Imaging." *Social Cognition and Affective Neuroscience* 8:27–33.

Kangaslampi, Samuel. 2023. "Association between Mystical-type Experiences under Psychedelics and Improvements in Well-Being or Mental Health—A Comprehensive Review of the Evidence." *Journal of Psychedelic Studies* 7 (1): 18–28. https://doi.org/10.1556/2054.2023.00243.

Kaplan, A. L., et al. 2022. "Bespoke Library Docking for 5-HT2A Receptor Agonists with Antidepressant Activity." *Nature* 610:582–91.

Kargbo, Robert B. 2023. "Microbiome: The Next Frontier in Psychedelic Renaissance." *Journal of Xenobiotics* 13 (3): 386–401. https://doi.org/10.3390/jox13030025.

Katz, Steven T., ed. 1978. *Mysticism and Philosophical Analysis.* New York: Oxford University Press.

———, ed. 1983. *Mysticism and Religious Traditions.* New York: Oxford University Press.

———. 1988. "On Mysticism." *Journal of the American Academy of Religion* 56 (4): 751–57.

———, ed. 1992. *Mysticism and Language.* New York: Oxford University Press.

———, ed. 2013. *Comparative Mysticism: An Anthology of Original Sources.* New York: Oxford University Press.

———. 2014. "Analyzing Mystical Experience." Address given to Conference on Contemporary Philosophy of Religion in Teheran, Iran, January 14, 2014.

Kelly, Edward F., and Michael Grosso. 2007. "Mystical Experience." In *Irreducible Mind: Toward a Psychology for the 21st Century,* by Edward F. Kelly et al., 495–575. Lanham, MD: Rowman & Littlefield.

Kettner, Hannes. 2021. "Psychedelic Communitas: Intersubjective Experience during Psychedelic Group Sessions Predicts Enduring Changes in Psychological Wellbeing and Social Connectedness." *Frontiers in Pharmacology* 12 (March 25). https://doi.org/10.3389/fphar.2021.623985.

Kettner, Hannes, et al. 2019. "From Egoism to Ecoism: Psychedelics Increase Nature Relatedness in a State-Mediated and Context-Dependent Manner." *International Journal of Environmental Research and Public Health* 16 (no 24): 5147. https://doi.org/10.3390/ijerph16245147.

King, David P., Barbara J. Duffy, and Brian Steensland. 2024. "The Role of Spiritual Practices in the Multidimensional Impact of Religion and Spirituality on Giving and Volunteering." *Nonprofit and Voluntary Sector Quarterly* (January 23). https://api.semanticscholar.org/CorpusID:267235655.

Kipnis, Andrew B. 1994. "Yogic Meditation and Social Responsibility." *Buddhist-Christian Studies* 14:111–25.

Kirmayer, Laurence J. 2015. "Mindfulness in Cultural Context." *Transcultural Psychiatry* 52 (4): 447–69.

Ko, Kwonmok, Gemma Knight, James J. Rucker, and Anthony J. Cleare. 2022. "Psychedelics, Mystical Experience, and Therapeutic Efficacy: A Systematic Review." *Frontiers in Psychiatry* 13 (July): article 917199.

Koch, Christof, Marcello Massimini, Melanie Boly, and Guilio Tononi. 2016. "Neural Correlates of Consciousness: Progress and Problems." *Nature Reviews Neuroscience* 17:307–21.

Koehler, Jonathan J. 1993. "The Influence of Prior Beliefs on Scientific Judgments of Evidence Quality." *Organizational Behavior and Human Decision Processes* 56 (1): 28–55.

Koestler, Arthur. 1968. "Return Trip to Nirvana." In *Drinkers of Infinity: Essays, 1955–1967*, 201–12. London: Hutchinson.

Komarovski, Yaroslav. 2015. *Tibetan Buddhism and Mystical Experience* (New York: Oxford University Press.

Komjathy, Louis. 2018. *Introducing Contemplative Studies*. New York: Wiley-Blackwell.

Kornfield, Jack. 2001. *After the Ecstasy the Laundry: How the Heart Grows Wise on the Spiritual Path*. New York: Bantam.

Kraft, Kenneth. 1988. "Introduction." In *The Path of Compassion: Writings on Socially Engaged Buddhism*, ed. Fred Eppsteiner, ix–xv. Berkeley, CA: Parallax Press.

———, ed. 1992. *Inner Peace, World Peace: Essays on Buddhism and Nonviolence*. Albany: State University of New York Press, 1992.

Krauss, Lawrence M. 2012. *A Universe from Nothing: Why There Is Something Rather Than Nothing*. New York: Free Press.

Kripal, Jeffrey J. 2019. *The Flip: Epiphanies of Mind and the Future of Knowledge*. New York: Bellevue Literary Press.

Kucinskas, Jaime, and Evan Stewart. 2022. "Selfish or Substituting Spirituality? Clarifying the Relationship between Spiritual Practice and Political Engagement." *American Sociological Review* 87 (4): 584–617.

Kurtz, Paul. 2005. *Affirmations: Joyful and Creative Exuberance*. Rev. ed. Buffalo: Prometheus Books.

Kwan, Alex C., David E. Olson, Katrin H. Preller, and Bryan L. Roth. 2022. "The Neural Basis of Psychedelic Action." *Nature Neuroscience* 25 (11): 1407–15.

Kydd, Andrew H. 2022. "Our Place in the Universe: Andrew Wendt and Quantum Mechanics." *International Theory* 14 (1): 130–45.

Lam, Harry Chi-sing. 2008. *The Zen in Modern Cosmology*. Hackensack, NJ: World Scientific.

Lancaster, Brian L. 1993. "Self or No-Self? Converging Perspectives from Neuropsychology and Mysticism." *Zygon* 28 (September): 507–26.

———. 2005. "Mysticism and Cognitive Neuroscience: A Partnership in the Quest for Consciousness." *Conscienscias* 2:247–68.

Langlitz, Nicolas. 2012. *Neuropsychedelia: The Revival of Hallucinogen Research since the Decade of the Brain*. Berkeley: University of California Press.
Lanzetta, Beverly. 2005. *Radical Wisdom: A Feminist Mystical Theology*. Minneapolis, MN: Fortress.
Laszlo, Ervin. 2004. *Science and the Akashic Field*. Rochester. VT: Inner Traditions.
Lazar, Sara W., George Bush, Randy Lyanne Gollub, and Herbert Benson. 2000. "Functional Brain Mapping of the Relaxation Response and Meditation." *NeuroReport* 11:1581–85.
Lazar, Sara W., et al. 2005. "Meditation Experience Is Associated with Increase in Cortical Thickness." *NeuroReport* 16:1893–97.
Leary, Timothy. 1968. *The Politics of Ecstasy*. New York: Putnam.
———. 2001. *Your Brain Is God*. Berkeley, CA: Ronin.
Leary, Timothy, G. H. Litwin, and Ralph Metzner. 1963. "Reactions to Psilocybin Administered in a Supportive Environment." *Journal of Nervous and Mental Disease* 137:561–73.
Leary, Timothy, Ralph Metzner, and Richard Alpert. 1964. *The Psychedelic Experience: A Manual Based on the Tibetan Book of the Dead*. New York: Academic Press.
Lebedev, Alexander V., et al. 2015. "Finding the Self by Losing the Self: Neural Correlates of Ego-Dissolution Under Psilocybin." *Human Brain Mapping* 36:3137–53.
Lederman, Leon, with Dick Teresi. 1993. *The God Particle*. New York: Houghton Mifflin.
Letheby, Chris. 2017. "Naturalizing Psychedelic Spirituality." *Zygon* 52 (September): 623–42.
———. 2021. *Philosophy of Psychedelics*. New York: Oxford University Press.
———. 2022. "Psychedelics, Atheism, and Naturalism: Myth and Reality." *Journal of Consciousness Studies* 29 (nos. 7–8): 69–92.
———. 2024. "How Do Psychedelics Reduce Fear of Death?" *Neuroethics* 17 (27). https://doi.org/10.1007/s12152-024-09564-3.
———. Forthcoming. "Psychedelics: Recent Philosophical Discussions." In *Handbook of the Philosophy of Medicine*, ed. Thomas Schramme and Mary Walker. 2nd ed. New York: Springer (November 2024).
Letheby, Chris, and Jaipreet Mattu. 2021. "Philosophy and Classic Psychedelics: A Review of Some Emerging Themes." *Journal of Psychedelic Studies* 5 (3): 166–75.
Letheby, Chris, Jaipreet Mattu, and Eric Hochstein. 2024. "How to End the Mysticism Wars in Psychedelic Science." In *Palgrave Handbook of Philosophy and Psychoactive Drug Use*, ed. Rob Lovering, 127–54. New York: Palgrave Macmillan.
Lewis, James R., and J. Gordon Melton, eds. 1992. *Perspectives on the New Age*. Albany: State University of New York Press.
Lewis-Williams, David, and David Pearce. 2005. *Inside the Neolithic Mind: Consciousness, Cosmos, and the Realm of the Gods*. London: Thames and Hudson.
Ley, Laura, et al. 2023. "Comparative Acute Effects of Mescaline, Lysergic Acid Diethylamide, and Psilocybin in a Randomized, Double-Blind, Placebo-

Controlled Cross-Over Study in Healthy Participants." *Neuropsychopharmacology* (May 25). https://doi.org/10.1038/s41386-0230-01607-2.

Liechti, Matthias E., Patrick C. Dolder, and Yasmin Schmid. 2017. "Alterations of Consciousness and Mystical-Type Experiences after Acute LSD in Humans." *Psychopharmacology* 234 (nos. 9–10): 1499–510.

Lopez, Donald S., Jr. 2008. *Buddhism and Science: A Guide for the Perplexed*. Chicago, IL: University of Chicago.

Lorimer, David. 1999. "Introduction: From Experiment to Experience." In David Lorimer, ed., *The Spirit of Science: From Experiment to Experience*, 17–29. New York: Continuum.

———. 2017. "40 Years of 'Mystics and Scientists' Conferences: The Continuing Quest for Unity and Integration." *Journal for the Study of Spirituality* 7 (2): 167–73.

Lutyens, Mary. 1983. *Krishnamurti: The Years of Fulfilment*. New York: Farrar, Straus & Giroux.

Lutz, Antoine, John D. Dunne, and Richard J. Davidson. 2007. "Meditation and the Neuroscience of Consciousness: An Introduction." In *The Cambridge Handbook of Consciousness*, ed. Philip David Zelazo, Morris Moscovitch, and Evan Thompson, 499–552. New York: Cambridge University Press.

Lutz, Antoine, et al. 2004. "Long-Term Meditators Self-Induce High-Amplitude Gamma Synchrony during Mental Practice." *Proceedings of the National Academy of Sciences* 101:16369–73.

Lutz, Antoine, Amishi P. Jha, John D. Dunne, and Clifford D. Saron. 2015. "Investigating the Phenomenological Matrix of Mindfulness-Related Practices from a Neurocognitive Perspective." *American Psychologist* 70:632–58.

Lutz, Antoine, and Evan Thompson. 2003. "Neurophenomenology: Integrating Subjective Experience and Brain Dynamics in the Neuroscience of Consciousness." *Journal of Consciousness Studies* 10 (9–10): 31–52.

Lyon, Aidan, and Anya Farennikova. 2022. "Through the Psychedelic Looking Glass." *PhiMiSci: Philosophy and the Mind Sciences* 3. https://doi.org/10.33735/phimisci.2022.9323.

Lyons, Taylor, and Robin L Carhart-Harris. 2018. "Increased Nature Relatedness and Decreased Authoritarian Political Views after Psilocybin for Treatment-resistant Depression." *Journal of Psychopharmacology* 32 (7): 811–19.

Malin, Shimon. 2001. *Nature Loves to Hide: Quantum Physics and the Nature of Reality, A Western Perspective*. New York: Oxford University Press.

Mansfield, Victor N. 1976. Review of *The Tao of Physics* by Fritjof Capra. *Physics Today* 29 (8, August): 56.

———. 1989. "Madhyamika Buddhism and Quantum Mechanics: Beginning a Dialogue." *International Philosophical Quarterly* 29 (September): 371–91.

———. 2008. *Tibetan Buddhism and Modern Physics: Toward a Union of Love and Knowledge*. West Conshohocken, PA: Templeton Foundation Press.

Marin, Juan Miguel. 2009. "'Mysticism' in Quantum Mechanics: The Forgotten Controversy." *European Journal of Physics* 30:807–22.

Marschall, Josephine, et al. 2022. "Psilocybin Microdosing Does Not Affect Emotion-related Symptoms and Processing: A Preregistered Field and Lab-based Study." *Journal of Psychopharmacology* 36 (1): 97–113.

Masters, Robert E. L., and Jean Houston. 1966. *The Varieties of Psychedelic Experience*. New York: Holt, Rinehart and Winston.

McCulloch, Drummond E-Wen, et al. 2022. "Psilocybin-Induced Mystical-Type Experiences are Related to Persisting Positive Effects: A Quantitative and Qualitative Report." *Frontiers in Pharmacology* 13 (March 9): article 841648. https://doi.org/10.3389/fphar.2022.841648.

McDaniel, June. 2018. *Lost Ecstasy: Its Decline and Transformation in Religion*. New York: Palgrave MacMillan.

McFarlane, Thomas J., ed. 2002. *Einstein and Buddha: The Parallel Sayings*. Berkeley, CA: Seastone.

McGinn, Bernard. 1994. *The Foundations of Mysticism: Origins to the Fifth Century*. New York: Crossroads.

———, ed. 2006. *The Essential Writings of Christian Mysticism*. New York: Random House.

McGovern, H. T., Pantelis Leptourgos, Brendan T. Hutchinson, and Philip R. Corlett. 2021. "Do Psychedelics Change Beliefs?" *PsyArXiv* (September 15).

McGovern, H. T. et al. 2023. "The Power of Insight: How Psychedelics May Solicit False Beliefs." *PsyArXiv* (July 3). (Preprint.) https://doi.org/10.31234/osf.io/97gjw.

McKenna, Terence. 1992. *Food of the Gods: The Search for the Original Tree of Knowledge*. New York: Bantam.

McMahan, David L. 2023. *Rethinking Meditation: Buddhist Meditative Practice in Ancient and Modern Worlds*. New York: Oxford University Press.

Meintel, Deirdre. 2024. "Spirituality and Social Engagement." *Social Compass*. https://doi.org/10.1177/00377686231219362.

Merkur, Dan. 2001. *The Psychedelic Sacrament*. Rochester, VT: Park Street Press.

Merton, Thomas. 1998. *Contemplation in a World of Action*. Notre Dame, IN: University of Notre Dame Press.

———. 2003. *The Inner Experience: Notes on Contemplation*. Edited by William H. Shannon. New York: HarperOne.

Metzinger, Thomas. 2004. *Being No One: The Self-Model Theory of Subjectivity*. Cambridge, MA: MIT Press.

———. 2024. *The Elephant and the Blind: The Experience of Pure Consciousness: Philosophy, Science, and 500+ Experiential Reports*. Cambridge, MA: MIT Press.

Millière, Raphaël. 2017. "Looking for the Self: Phenomenology, Neurophysiology and Philosophical Significance of Drug-Induced Ego Dissolution." *Frontiers in Human Neuroscience* 11: article 245. https://doi.org/10.3389/fnhum.2017.00245.

———. 2020. "The Varieties of Selflessness." *PhiMiSci: Philosophy and the Mind Sciences* 1 (1): 1–41.

Millière, Raphaël, et al. 2018. "Psychedelics, Meditation, and Self-Consciousness." *Frontiers in Psychology* 9 (September): 1–29 (article 1475).

Millière, Raphaël, and Thomas Metzinger. 2020. "Radical Disruptions of Self-Consciousness: Editorial Introduction." *Philosophy and the Mind Sciences* 1 (1): 1–13.

Millière, Raphaël, and Albert Newen. 2024. "Selfless Memories." *Erkenntnis* 89:897–918.

Moen, Ole Martin. 2022. "Are Psychedelic Drugs Distorting?" In *Philosophy and Psychedelics: Frameworks for Exceptional Experience*, ed., Christine Hauskeller and Peter Sjöstedt-Hughes London: Bloomsbury Academic.

Mosurinjohn, Sharday, Leor Roseman, and Manesh Girn. 2023. "Psychedelic-Induced Mystical Experiences: An Interdisciplinary Discussion and Critique." *Frontiers in Psychiatry* 14 (April 5): 1–12.

Muraresku, Brian C. 2020. *The Immortality Key: The Secret History of the Religion with No Name*. New York: St. Martin's Press.

Nagel, Thomas. 1986. *The View from Nowhere*. New York: Oxford University Press.

———. 2009. *Secular Philosophy and the Religious Temperament: Essays 2002–2008*. New York: Oxford University Press.

Narby, Jeremy. 1998. *The Cosmic Serpent: DNA and the Origins of Knowledge*. New York: Tarcher.

Nash, Jonathan D., and Andrew Newberg. 2013. "Toward a Unifying Taxonomy and Definition of Meditation." *Frontiers in Psychology* 4 (November): 1–18.

Nayak, Sandeep M., et al. 2023a. "Belief Changes Associated with Psychedelic Use." *Journal of Psychopharmacology* 37 (1): 80–92.

Nayak, Sandeep M., et al. 2023b. "Naturalistic Psilocybin Use Increases Mind Perception but Not Atheist-Believer Status: A Prospective Longitudinal Study." Preprint. (June 9.)

Nayak, Sandeep et al. 2024. "Psychedelic Experiences Increase Mind Perception but do not Change Atheist-Believer Status: A Prospective Longitudinal Study." *Journal of Psychoactive Drugs*. https://doi.org/10.1080/02791072.2024.2346130.

Nayak, Sandeep M., and Matthew W. Johnson. 2021. "Psychedelics and Psychotherapy." *Pharmacopsychiatry* 54 (July): 167–75.

Nayak, Sandeep M., and Roland R. Griffiths. 2022. "A Single Belief-Changing Psychedelic Experience Is Associated with Increased Attribution of Consciousness to Living and Non-living Entities." *Frontiers in Psychology* 13 (March 28). article 852248.

Neale, Harry S. 2017. *Jihad in Premodern Sufi Writings*. New York: Palgrave Macmillan.

Newberg, Andrew B. 2018. *Neurotheology: How Science Can Enlighten Us about Spirituality*. New York: Columbia University Press.

Newberg, Andrew B., and Eugene d'Aguili. 1999. *The Mystical Mind: Probing the Biology of Religious Experience*. Minneapolis, MN: Fortress Press.

Newberg, Andrew B., Eugene d'Aquili, and Vince Rause. 2002. *Why God Won't Go Away: Brain Science & the Biology of Belief.* New York: Ballantine Press.

Newberg, Andrew B., and Bruce Y. Lee. 2005. "The Neuroscientific Study of Religious and Spiritual Phenomena: Or Why God Doesn't Use Biostatistics." *Zygon* 40:469–89.

Newberg, Andrew, and Mark Robert Waldman. 2009. *How God Changes Your Brain: Breakthrough Findings from a Leading Neuroscientist.* New York: Ballantine Books.

———. 2016. *How Enlightenment Changes Your Brain: The New Science of Transformation.* New York: Penguin Random House.

Nhat Hanh, Thich. 1967. *Vietnam: Lotus in a Sea of Fire.* New York: Hill and Wang.

———. 1993. *Love in Action: Writings on Nonviolent Social Change.* Berkeley, CA: Parallax Press.

———. 2008. *Good Citizens: Creating Enlightened Society.* Berkeley, CA: Parallax Press.

Nichols, David E., and Benjamin R. Chemel. 2006. "The Neuropharmacology of Religious Experience: Hallucinogens and the Experience of the Divine." In *Where God and Science Meet: How Brain and Evolutionary Studies Alter Our Understanding of Religion*, ed. Patrick McNamara, 3:1–34. Westport, CT: Greenwood Press.

Nickerson, Raymond S. 1998. "Confirmation Bias: A Ubiquitous Phenomenon in Many Guises." *Review of General Psychology* 2 (2): 175–220.

Nisbett, Richard E., Kaiping Peng, Incheol Choi, and Ara Norenzayan. 2001. "Culture and Systems of Thought: Holistic versus Analytic Cognition." *Psychological Review* 108:291–310.

Nisker, Wes. 1998. *Buddha's Nature: Who We Really Are and Why This Matters* London: Rider.

———. 2002. "Introduction." In *Einstein and Buddha: The Parallel Sayings*, ed. Thomas J. McFarlane, n.p. Berkeley, CA: Seastone.

Noë, Alva, and Evan Thompson. 2004. "Are There Neural Correlates of Consciousness?" *Journal of Consciousness Studies* 11:3–28.

Noorani, Tehseen, and Jonny Martell. 2021. "New Frontiers or a Bursting Bubble? Psychedelic Therapy beyond the Dichotomy." *Frontiers in Psychiatry* 12 (September 10): 727050. https://doi.org/10.3389/fpsyt.2021.727050.

Nour, Matthew M., and Robin L. Carhart-Harris. 2017. "Psychedelics and the Science of Self-Experience." *British Journal of Psychiatry* 210:177–79.

Nour, Matthew M., Lisa Evans, and Robin L. Carhart-Harris. 2017. "Psychedelics, Personality and Political Perspectives." *Journal of Psychoactive Drugs* 49 (3): 182–91.

Nour, Matthew M., et al. 2016. "Ego-Dissolution and Psychedelics: Validation of the Ego-Dissolution Inventory (EDI)." *Frontiers in Human Neuroscience* 10 (June): article 269.

Nygart, Victoria Amalie, et al. 2022. "Antidepressant Effects of a Psychedelic Experience in a Large Prospective Naturalistic Sample." *Journal of Psychopharmacology* 36 (8): 932-42. https://doi.org/ 10.1177/02698811221101061

Oh, Seil, and Natalia Sarkisian. 2012. "Spiritual Individualism or Engaged Spirituality? Social Implications of Holistic Spirituality among Mind-Body-Spirit Practitioners." *Sociology of Religion* 73 (3): 299–322.

Oliver, Dax. 2023. "Negative Mystical Experiences: Why Methods for Determining Mysticality of Psychedelic Experiences Should Not Include Measuring Positivity of Mood." *Journal of Psychedelic Studies* 7 (3): 158–60. https://doi.org/10.1556/2054-2023.00286.

Oliver, Dianne L., ed. 2006. *Dorothee Soelle: Essential Writings*. Maryknoll, NY: Orbis Books.

Olson, David E. 2020. "The Subjective Effects of Psychedelics May Not Be Necessary for Their Therapeutic Effects." *ACS Pharmacology & Translational Science* 4 (December): 563–67.

———. 2022. "Biochemical Mechanisms Underlying Psychedelic-Induced Neuroplasticity." *Biochemistry* 61 (3): 127–36.

Olson, Jay A., et al. 2020. "Tripping on Nothing: Placebo Psychedelics and Contextual Factors." *Psychopharmacology* 237 (5, May): 1371–82.

Ona, Genís, Maja Kohek, and José Carlos Bouso. 2022. "The Illusion of Knowledge in the Emerging Field of Psychedelic Research." *New Ideas in Psychology* 67 (December): 100967.

O'Neill, Tom, with Dan Piepenbring. 2019. *Chaos: Charles Manson, the CIA, and the Secret History of the Sixties*. New York: Little, Brown.

Ornstein, Robert E. 1978. *The Mind Field*. New York: Pocket Books.

Ospina, Maria B., et al. 2007. "Meditation Practices for Health: State of the Research." *U.S. Department of Health and Human Services: AHRQ Publication No. 07-E010*.

Overgaard, Morten. 2017. "The Status and Future of Consciousness Research." *Frontiers in Psychology* 8 (October): 1–5.

Pace, Brian A., and Nese Devenot. 2021. "Right-Wing Psychedelia: Case Studies in Cultural Plasticity and Political Pluripotency." 2021. *Frontiers in Psychology* 12 (December 10): 1–18. article 733185. https://doi.org/10.3389/fpsyg.2021.733185.

Pahnke, Walter N. 1966. "Drugs and Mysticism." *International Journal of Parapsychology* 8 (Spring): 295–414.

Pahnke, Walter N., and William A. Richards. 1966. "Implications of LSD and Experimental Mysticism." *Journal of Religion and Health* 5 (July): 175–208.

Papanicolaou, Andrew C. 2021. *A Scientific Assessment of the Validity of Mystical Experiences: Understanding Altered Psychological and Neurophysiological States*. New York: Routledge.

Parrinder, Geoffrey. 1976. *Mysticism in the World's Religions*. New York: Oxford University Press.

Partridge, Christopher H. 2005. "Cleansing the Doors of Perception: The Contemporary Sacralization of Psychedelics." In *The Re-Enchantment of the West*,

vol. 2, *Alternative Spiritualities, Sacralization, Popular Culture and Occulture*, 82–134. New York: T & T Clark International.
———. 2018. *High Culture: Drugs, Mysticism, and the Pursuit of Transcendence in the Modern World*. New York: Oxford University Press.
Palitsky, Roman, et al. 2023. "Importance of Integrating Spiritual, Existential, Religious, and Theological Components in Psychedelic-Assisted Therapies." *JAMA Psychiatry* 80 (7): 743–49. https://doi.org/10.1001/jamapsychiatry.2023.1554.
Peacocke, Christopher. 1992. *A Study of Concepts*. Cambridge, MA: MIT Press.
———. 2001. "Does Perception Have a Nonconceptual Content?" *Journal of Philosophy* 98:239–64.
Peill, Joseph M. 2022. "Validation of the Psychological Insight Scale: A New Scale to Assess Psychological Insight Following a Psychedelic Experience." *Journal of Psychopharmacology* 36 (1): 31–45.
Penner, Hans. 1983. "The Mystical Illusion." In *Mysticism and Religious Traditions*, ed. Steven T. Katz, 89–116. New York: Oxford University Press.
Perlman, David M., Tim V. Salomons, Richard J. Davidson, and Antoine Lutz. 2010. "Differential Effects on Pain Intensity and Unpleasantness of Two Meditation Practices." *Emotion* 10 (1): 65–71.
Persinger, Michael A. 1987. *Neuropsychological Bases of God Beliefs*. New York: Praeger.
Peters, Frederic H. 1998. "Lucid Consciousness in Traditional Indian Psychology and Contemporary Neuro-Psychology." *Journal of Indian Psychology* 16 (January): 1–25.
———. 2000. "Neurophenomenology." *Method and Theory in the Study of Religion* 12:379–415.
Petitmengin, Claire, ed. 2011. *Ten Years' Viewing from Within: Further Debate*. Bowling Green, OH: Academic Imprint.
Pew Research Center. 2024. "Religious 'Nones' in America: Who They Are and What They Believe." (January 24).
Planck, Max. 1949. *Scientific Autobiography and Other Papers*. Translated by Frank Gaynor. New York: Philosophical Library.
Plesa, Patric, and Rotem Petranker. 2023. "Psychedelics and Neonihilism: Connectedness in a Meaningless World." *Frontiers in Psychology* (August): 1–14. Article 1125780. https://doi.org/10.3389/fpsyg.2023.1125780.
Pokorny, Thomas, et al. 2017. "Effect of Psilocybin on Empathy and Moral Decision-Making." *International Journal of Neuropsychopharmacology* 20 (9): 747–57.
Polger, Thomas W., and Lawrence A. Shapiro. 2016. *The Multiple Realization Book*. New York: Oxford University Press.
Pollan, Michael. 2018. *How to Change Your Mind: What the New Science of Psychedelics Teaches Us about Consciousness, Dying, Addiction, Depression, and Transcendence*. New York: Penguin Press.

Pollard, Alton B. III. 1992. *Mysticism and Social Change: The Social Witness of Howard Thurman*. New York: Peter Lang.
Poulin, Michael J., Lauren M. Ministero, Shira Gabriel, C. Dale Morrison, and Esha Naidu. 2021. "Minding Your Own Business? Mindfulness Decreases Prosocial Behavior for Those with Independent Self-Construals." *Psychological Science* 32 (11): 1699–708.
Preller, Katrin H., and Franz X. Vollenweider. 2018. "Phenomenology, Structure, and Dynamic of Psychedelic States." *Current Topics in Behavioral Neuroscience* 36:221–56.
Proudfoot, Wayne. 1985. *Religious Experience*. Berkeley: University of California Press.
Purser, Ronald. 2019. *McMindfulness: How Mindfulness Became the New Capitalist Spirituality*. London: Repeater Books.
Queen, Christopher S, ed. 2000. *Engaged Buddhism in the West*. Somerville, MA: Wisdom.
———. 2013. "Socially Engaged Buddhism: Emerging Patterns of Theory and Practice." In Steven M. Emmanuel, ed., *A Companion to Buddhist Philosophy*, 524–35. John Wiley & Sons.
Queen, Christopher S., and Sallie B. King, eds. 1996. *Engaged Buddhism: Buddhist Liberation Movements in Asia*. Albany: State University of New York Press.
Radakovic, Chelsea, Ratko Radakovic, Guy Peryer, and Jo-Anne Geere. 2022. "Psychedelics and Mindfulness: A Systematic Review and Meta-Analysis." *Journal of Psychedelic Studies* 6 (2): 137–53.
Raggio, Marcela. 2023. "Ernesto Cardenal: A Latin American Liberation Mystic." *Religions* 14 (5): 655–70. https://doi.org/10.3390/rel14050655.
Rahner, Karl. 1984. *The Practice of Faith: A Handbook of Contemporary Spirituality*. New York: Crossroad.
Rakoczy, Susan. 2006. *Great Mystics and Social Justice: Walking on the Two Feet of Love*. New York: Paulist Press.
Raman, Varadaraja V. 2012. "Quantum Mechanics and Some Hindu Perspectives." In *The Routledge Companion to Religion and Science*, ed. James W. Haag, Gregory R. Peterson, and Michael L. Spezio, 156–68. New York: Routledge.
Ramanna, Raja. 1999. "Divergence and Convergence of Science and Spirituality." In L. L. Mehrotra, ed., *Science, Spirituality and the Future: A Vision for the Twenty-First Century*. New Delhi: Mudrit.
Ratanakul, Pinit. 2002. "Buddhism and Science: Allies or Enemies?" *Zygon* 37 (March): 115–20.
Ratcliffe, Matthew. 2006. "Neurology: A Science of What?" In Patrick McNamara, ed., *Where God and Science Meet: How Brain and Evolutionary Studies Alter Our Understanding of Religion*, vol. 3, *The Psychology of Religious Experience*, 81–104. Westport, CT: Greenwood Press.
Restivo, Sal. 1978. "Parallels and Paradoxes in Modern Physics and Eastern Mysticism: A Critical Reconnaissance." *Social Studies of Science* 8 (1): 143–81.

———. 1982. "Parallels and Paradoxes in Modern Physics and Eastern Mysticism: II: A Sociological Perspective on Parallelism." *Social Studies of Science* 12 (1): 37–71.

———. 1983. *Social Relations of Physics, Mysticism, and Mathematics: Studies in Social Structure, Interests, and Ideas*. Boston, MA: D. Reidel.

Ricard, Matthieu. 2003. "On the Relevance of a Contemplative Science." In *Buddhism and Science: Breaking New Ground*, ed. B. Alan Wallace, 261–79. New York: Columbia University Press.

Ricard, Matthieu, and Trinh Xuan Thuan. 2001. *The Quantum and the Lotus: A Journey to the Frontiers Where Science and Buddhism Meet*. New York: Crown.

Richards, William A. 2014. "Here and Now: Discovering the Sacred with Entheogens." *Zygon* 49 (September): 652–65.

———. 2016. *Sacred Knowledge: Psychedelics and Religious Experiences*. New York: Columbia University Press.

Rist, J. M. 1967. "The Self and Others." In Plotinus: The Road to Reality, 153–68. Cambridge, MA: Cambridge University Press.

———. 1976. "Plotinus and Moral Obligation." In *The Significance of Neoplatonism*, ed. R. Baine Harris, 217–33. Norfolk: International Society for Neoplatonic Studies.

Ritchie, Sarah Lane. 2021. "Panpsychism and Spiritual Flourishing: Constructive Engagement with the New Science of Psychedelics." *Journal of Consciousness Studies* 28 (9): 268–88. https://doi.org/10.53765/20512201.28.9.268.

Roberts, Thomas, ed. 2001. *Psychoactive Sacramentals: Essays on Entheogens and Religion*. San Francisco, CA: Council on Spiritual Practices.

———. 2012. *Spiritual Growth with Entheogens: Psychoactive Sacramentals and Human Transformation*. Rochester, VT: Park Street.

———. 2013. *The Psychedelic Future of the Mind: How Entheogens Are Enhancing Cognition, Boosting Intelligence, and Raising Values*. Rochester, VT: Part Street.

———, ed. 2001. *Psychoactive Sacramentals: Essays on Entheogens and Religion*. San Francisco, CA: Council on Spiritual Practices.

———, ed. 2020. *Psychedelics and Spirituality: The Sacred Use of LSD, Psilocybin, and MDMA for Human Transformation*. Rochester, VT: Park Street.

Roseman, Leor, David J. Nutt, and Robin L. Carhart-Harris. 2018. "Quality of Acute Psychedelic Experience Predicts Therapeutic Efficacy of Psilocybin for Treatment-Resistant Depression." *Frontiers in Pharmacology* 8 (January 17). https://doi.org/10.3389/fphar.2017.00974.

Roseman, Leor, et al. 2022. "Editorial: Psychedelic Sociality: Pharmacological and Extrapharmacological Perspectives." *Frontiers in Pharmacology* 13 (July 22): 979764. https://doi.org/10.3389/fphar.2022.979764.

Roth, Harold D. 2006. "Contemplative Studies: Prospects for a New Field." *Teachers College Record* 108 (9, September): 1187–215.

———. 2014. "A Pedagogy for the New Field of Contemplative Studies." In *Contemplative Learning and Inquiry across Disciplines*, ed. Olen Gunnlaugson et al., 97–118. Albany: SUNY Press.

Rothman, Tony, and George Sudarshan. 1998. *Doubt and Certainty*. Reading, MA: Perseus Books.

Rowe, James K. 2016. "Micropolitics and Collective Liberation: Mind/Body Practice and Left Social Movements." *New Political Science* 38 (2): 206–25.

Ruck, Carl A. P. 2006. *Sacred Mushrooms of the Goddess and Secrets of Eleusis*. Oakland, CA: Ronin.

Ruck, Carl A. P., Jeremy Bigwood, Danny Staples, Jonathan Ott, and R. Gordon Wasson. 1979. "Entheogens." *Journal of Psychedelic Drugs* 11 (1–2): 145–46.

Rudgley, Richard. 1999. *The Lost Civilizations of the Stone Age*. New York: Simon & Schuster.

Ruffell, Simon G.D., et al. 2024. "Participation in an Indigenous Amazonian-Led Ayahuasca Retreat Associated with Increases in Nature Relatedness—A Pilot Study." *Drug Science, Policy and Law* 10 (February 28): 1–10. https://doi.org/10.1177/20503245241235100.

Ruffing, Janet. 2001. *Mysticism and Social Transformation*. Syracuse, NY: Syracuse University Press.

Russell, Bertrand. 1918. *Mysticism and Logic*. London: Longmans, Green.

Sagan, Carl. 1985. *Cosmos*. New York: Ballantine Books.

SAMHSA (Substance Abuse and Mental Health Services Administration). 2023. "Key Substance Use and Mental Health Indicators in the United States: Results from the 2022 National Survey on Drug Use and Health." US Department of Health and Human Services, publication number PEP23-07-01-006.

Samuel, Geoffrey. 2015. "The Contemporary Mindfulness Movement and the Question of Nonself." *Transcultural Psychiatry* 52 (4): 485–500.

Sanders, James W., and Josjan Zijlmans. 2021. "Moving Past Mysticism in Psychedelic Science." *ACS Pharmacology & Translational Science* 4 (3): 1253–55.

Scharfstein, Ben-Ami. 1995. *Amoral Politics: The Persistent Truth of Machiavellism*. Albany: State University of New York Press.

Schjoedt, Uffe. 2009. "The Religious Brain: A General Introduction to the Experimental Neuroscience of Religion." *Method and Theory in the Study of Religion* 21:310–39.

Schlag, Anne K., et al. 2022. "Adverse Effects of Psychedelics: From Anecdotes and Misinformation to Systematic Science." *Journal of Psychopharmacology* 36 (March): 258–72.

Schmidt, Stefan, and Harald Walach, eds. 2014. *Meditation: Neuroscientific Approaches and Philosophical Implications*. New York: Springer.

Scholem, Gershom G. 1967. "Mysticism and Society." *Diogenes* 58 (Summer): 1–24.

Schroeder, C. Paul. 2009. *On Social Justice: St. Basil the Great*. Yonkers, NY: St Vladimir's Seminary Press.

Schutt, William, et al. 2024. "Psychedelic Experiences and Long-term Spiritual Growth: A Systematic Review." *Current Psychology* (July 12). https://doi.org/10.1007/s12144-024-06272-2.

Schwartz, Jeffrey M., and Sharon Begley. 2002. *The Mind and the Brain: Neuroplasticity and the Power of Mental Force.* New York: HarperCollins.

Searle, John R. 1992. *The Rediscovery of Mind.* Cambridge, MA: MIT Press.

Sebastián, Miguel Ángel. 2020. "Perspectival Self-Consciousness and Ego-Dissolution: An Analysis of (Some) Altered States of Consciousness." *Philosophy and the Mind Sciences* 1 (1): 1–27.

Sedlmeier, Peter, et al. 2012. "The Psychological Effects of Meditation: A Meta-Analysis." *Psychological Bulletin* 138:1139–71.

Shanon, Benny. 2008. "Biblical Entheogens: A Speculative Hypothesis." *Time and Mind: Journal of Archeology, Consciousness, and Culture* 1 (1): 51–74.

Shear, Jonathan, ed. 2006. *The Experience of Meditation: Experts Introduce Major Traditions.* New York: Paragon House.

———. 2014. "Meditation as First-Person Methodology: Real Promise—and Problems." In *Meditation: Neuroscientific Approaches and Philosophical Implications*, ed. Stefan Schmidt and Harald Walach, 57–74. New York: Springer.

Shear, Jonathan, and Ron Jevning. 1999. "Pure Consciousness: Scientific Exploration of Meditation Techniques." *Journal of Consciousness Studies* 6:189–209.

Sheldrake, Philip. 2014. *Spirituality: A Guide for the Perplexed.* New York: Bloomsbury.

Shimomura, Tsuyoshi, et al. 2008. "Functional Brain Mapping during Recitation of Buddhist Scriptures and Repetition of the Namu Amida Butsu: A Study in Experienced Japanese Monks." *Turkish Neurosurgery* 18:134–41.

Shinozuka, Kenneth, et al. 2024. "Synergistic, Multi-level Understanding of Psychedelics: Three Systematic Reviews and Meta-analyses of their Pharmacology, Neuroimaging and Phenomenology." *Translational Psychiatry* 14 (1, December 4). https//10.1038/s41398-024-03187-1.

Shipley, Morgan. 2015. *Psychedelic Mysticism: Transforming Consciousness, Religious Experiences, and Voluntary Peasants in Postwar America.* Lanham, MD: Lexington Books.

Shulman, Robert G. 2013. *Brain Imaging: What It Can (and Cannot) Tell Us about Consciousness.* New York: Oxford University Press.

Siegel, Joshua S., et al. 2024. "Psilocybin Desynchronizes the Human Brain." *Nature* 632:131–38 (August 1). https://doi.org/10.1038/s41586-024-07624-5.

Siegel, Ronald K. 1989. *Intoxication: The Universal Drive for Mind-Altering Substances.* Rochester, VT: Park Street Press.

Simpson, William. 2014. "The Mystical Stance: The Experience of Self-Loss and Daniel Dennett's 'Center of Narrative Gravity.'" *Zygon* 49:458–75.

Sivaraksa, Sulak. 1992. *Seeds of Peace: A Buddhist Vision for Renewing Society.* Berkeley, CA: Parallax Press.

Sjöstedt-Hughes, Peter. 2023. "On the Need for Metaphysics in Psychedelic Therapy and Research." *Frontiers in Psychology* 14: article 1128589. https://doi.org/10.3389/fpsyg.2023.1128589.

Skrbina, David. 2017. *Panpsychism in the West*. Rev. ed. Cambridge, MA: MIT Press.

Sloan, Richard P. 2006. *Blind Faith: The Unholy Alliance of Religion and Medicine*. New York: St. Martin's Press.

Smith, Allan L., and Charles T. Tart. 1998. "Cosmic Consciousness Experience and Psychedelic Experiences: A First-Person Comparison." *Journal of Consciousness Studies* 5 (1): 97–107.

Smith, Huston. 1964. "Do Drugs Have Religious Import?" *Journal of Philosophy* 61 (18, October 1): 517–30. (Reprinted in Smith 2000: 15–32.)

———. 2000. *Cleansing the Doors of Perception: The Religious Significance of Entheogenic Plants and Chemicals*. New York: Penguin Putnam.

———. 2005. "Do Drugs Have Religious Import? A Forty Year Follow-Up." In *Higher Wisdom: Eminent Elders Explore the Continuing Impact of Psychedelics*, ed. Roger Walsh and Charles S. Grob, 223–39. Albany: State University of New York Press.

Smith, Luther E., Jr. 1991. *Howard Thurman: The Mystic as Prophet*. Richmond, IN: Friends United Press.

Soelle, Dorothee. 2001. *The Silent Cry: Mysticism and Resistance*. Minneapolis, MN: Fortress Press.

Solomon, Robert C. 2002. *Spirituality for the Skeptic: The Thoughtful Love of Life*. New York: Oxford University Press.

Søndergaard, Anna, et al. 2022. "Lasting Increases in Trait Mindfulness after Psilocybin Correlate Positively with the Mystical-Type Experience in Healthy Individuals." *Frontiers in Psychology* 13. https://doi.org/10.3389/fpsyg.2022.948729.

Sotillos, Samuel Bendeck. 2024. "Entheogens and Sacred Psychology." *Spiritual Studies* 10 (1): 40–68.

Spilka, Bernard, and Daniel N. McIntosh. 1995. "Attribution Theory and Religious Experience." In *The Handbook of Religious Experience*, ed. Ralph W. Hood, Jr., 421–45. Birmingham, AL: Religious Education Press.

Staal, Frits. 1975. *Exploring Mysticism: A Methodological Essay*. Berkeley: University of California Press.

Stace, Walter Terrence. 1960. *Mysticism and Philosophy*. New York: Macmillan.

Steinhart, Eric. 2018. "Practices in Religious Naturalism." In *Routledge Handbook of Religious Naturalism*, ed. Donald Crosby and Jerome Stone, 341–51. New York: Routledge.

Stenger, Victor J. 2009. *Quantum God: Creation, Chaos, and the Search for Cosmic Consciousness*. Amherst, NY: Prometheus Books.

———. 2012. *Gods and the Folly of Faith: The Incompatibility of Science and Religion*. Amherst, NY: Prometheus Books.

Stoeber, Michael F. 1992. "Constructivist Epistemologies of Mysticism: A Critique and a Revision." *Religious Studies* 28 (1): 107–16.
Stone, Jerome A. 2012. "Spirituality for Naturalists." *Zygon* 47 (3): 481–500.
Strain, Charles R. 2024. *Prophetic Wisdom: Engaged Buddhism's Struggle for Social Justice and Complete Liberation*. Albany: SUNY Press.
Strassman, Rick. 2001. *DMT—The Spirit Molecule: A Doctor's Revolutionary Research into the Biology of Near-Death and Mystical Experiences*. Rochester, VT: Park Street Press.
Studerus, Erich, et al. 2012. "Prediction of Psilocybin Response in Healthy Volunteers." *PloS ONE* 7 (2). https://doi.org/10.1371/journal.pone.0030800.
Sullivan, Philip R. 1995. "Contentless Consciousness and Information-Processing Theories of the Mind." *Philosophy, Psychiatry and Psychology* 2:51–59.
Summers-Effler Erika, and Hyunjin Deborah Kwak. 2015. "Weber's Missing Mystics: Inner-Worldly Mystical Practices and the Micro Potential for Social Change." *Theory and Society* 44 (4): 251–82.
Sutherland, Stuart. 2013 [1992]. *Irrationality: The Enemy Within*. London: Pinter & Martin.
Suzuki, Daisetz Teitaro. 1970. *Zen and Japanese Culture*. Princeton, NJ: Princeton University Press.
Sweeney, Mary M., et al. 2022. "Comparison of Psychedelic and Near-Death or Other Non-ordinary Experiences in Changing Attitudes about Death and Dying." *PLoS One* 17 (8, August 24): e0271926.
Swimme, Brian T. 2019. *Hidden Heart of the Cosmos: Humanity and the New Story*. Maryknoll, NY: Orbis Books.
Tagliazucchi, Enzo, et al. 2016. "Increased Global Functional Connectivity Correlates with LSD-Induced Ego Dissolution." *Current Biology* 26:1043–50.
Tang, Yi-Yuan, Britta K. Hölzel, and Michael I. Posner. 2015. "The Neuroscience of Mindfulness Meditation." *Nature Reviews Neuroscience* 16 (March 18): 213–25.
Tang, Yi-Yuan, and Michael I. Posner. 2013. "Editorial: Special Issue on Mindfulness Neuroscience." *Social Cognitive and Affective Neuroscience* 8 (January): 1–3.
Tart, Charles T., ed. 1969. *Altered States of Consciousness: A Book of Readings*. New York: Wiley.
———. 1972. "States of Consciousness and State-Specific Sciences." *Science* 176: 1203–10.
———. 1975. *States of Consciousness*. New York: Dutton.
———. 1994. *Living the Mindful Life: A Handbook for Living in the Present Moment*. Boston, MA: Shambhala.
———. 1998. "Investigating Altered States of Consciousness on Their Own Terms: A Proposal for the Creation of State-Specific Sciences." *Ciencia e Cultura* 50:103–16.
Taves, Ann. 2009. *Religious Experience Reconsidered: A Building-Block Approach to the Study of Religion and Other Special Things*. Princeton, NJ: Princeton University Press.

Taylor, Steve, and Krisztina Egeto-Szabo. 2017. "Exploring Awakening Experiences: A Study of Awakening Experiences in Terms of Their Triggers." *Journal of Transpersonal Psychology* 49 (1): 45–65.

Tennison, Michael N. 2012. "Moral Transhumanism: The Next Step." *Journal of Medicine and Philosophy* 37 (4): 405–16.

Thomas, Owen C. 2000. "Interiority and Christian Spirituality." *Journal of Religion* 80 (1): 41–60.

Thurman, Howard. 1961. *The Inward Journey: Meditations on the Spiritual Quest*. New York: Harper & Brothers.

Thurman, Robert A. F., trans. 1976. *The Holy Teaching of Vimalakirti: A Mahayana Scripture*. University Park: Pennsylvania State University Press.

———. 1983. "Guidelines for Buddhist Social Activism Based on Nagarjuna's *Jewel Garland of Royal Counsels*." *The Eastern Buddhist* 16 (Spring): 19–51.

———. 1992. "The Politics of Enlightenment." *Tricycle: The Buddhist Review* 2 (Fall): 28–33.

Timmermann, Christopher, et al. 2021. "Psychedelics Alter Metaphysical Beliefs." *Scientific Reports* 11 (22166, November 23): 1–13.

Travis, Frederick, and Craig Pearson. 2000. "Pure Consciousness: Distinct Phenomenological and Physiological Correlates of 'Consciousness Itself.'" *International Journal of Neuroscience* 100:77–89.

Troeltsch, Ernst. 1931. *The Social Teaching of the Christian Churches*. London: George Allen & Unwin.

———. 1991. *Religion in History*. Edinburgh: T. & T. Clark.

Underhill, Evelyn. 1911. *Mysticism: A Study in the Nature and Development of Man's Spiritual Consciousness*. New York: E. P. Dutton.

———. 1915. *Practical Mysticism*. New York: E. P. Dutton.

Uttal, William R. 2001. *The New Phrenology: The Limits of Localizing Cognitive Functions in the Brain*. Cambridge, MA: MIT Press.

Vago, David R., and David A. Silbersweig. 2012. "Self-Awareness, Self-Regulation, and Self Transcendence (S-ART): A Framework for Understanding the Neurobiological Mechanisms of Mindfulness." *Frontiers in Human Neuroscience* 6 (296): 1–30.

Valentine, Elizabeth R., and Philip G. Sweet. 1999. "Meditation and Attention: A Comparison of the Effects of Concentrative and Mindfulness Meditation on Sustained Attention." *Mental Health, Religion & Culture* 2 (1): 59–70.

Van Cleve, James. 2012. "Defining and Defending Nonconceptual Contents and States." In *Philosophical Perspectives: Philosophy of Mind* 26, ed. John Hawthorne and Jason Turner, 411–30. New York: Wiley.

van Elk, Michiel, and David Bryce Yaden. 2022. "Pharmacological, Neural, and Psychological Mechanisms Underlying Psychedelics: A Critical Review." *Neuroscience & Biobehavioral* Reviews 140 (September): 104793.

van Elk, Michiel, and Eiko Fried. 2023. "History Repeating: Guidelines to Address Common Problems in Psychedelic Science." *Therapeutic Advances in Psychopharmacology* 14:1–20.

Van Eyghen, Hans. 2023. "Psychedelics and the Entropic Brain beyond the Self." *International Journal for the Psychology of Religion* 33 (4): 1–17.

Van Gordon, William and Edo Shonin. 2020. "Second-Generation Mindfulness-Based Interventions: Toward More Authentic Mindfulness Practice and Teaching." *Mindfulness* 11:1–4. https://doi.org/10.1007/s12671-019-01252-1.

Varela, Francisco J. 1996. "Neurophenomenology: A Methodological Remedy for the Hard Problem." *Journal of Consciousness Studies* 3:330–49.

Varela, Francisco J., and Jonathan Shear, eds. 1999. *The View from Within: First-Person Approaches to the Study of Consciousness*. Bowling Green, OH: Academic Imprint.

Varela, Francisco J., Evan Thompson, and Eleanor Rosch. 2016. *The Embodied Mind: Cognitive Science and Human Experience*. Rev. ed. Cambridge, MA: MIT Press.

Verhoeven, Martin J. 2001. "Buddhism and Science: Probing the Boundaries of Faith and Reason." *Religion East and West* 1 (June): 77–97.

———. 2003. "Western Science, Eastern Spirit: Historical Reflections on the East/West Encounter." *Religion East and West* 3 (June): 46–48.

Versluis, Arthus. 2011. *The Mystical State: Politics, Gnosis, and Emergent Cultures*. Minneapolis, MN: New Cultures Press.

Victoria, Brian. 1997. *Zen at War*. New York: Weatherhill.

Villiger, Daniel. 2024. "Giving Consent to the Ineffable." *Neuroethics* 17 (1): 1–16.

Vos, Cato M. H. de, Natasha L. Mason, and Kim P. C. Kuypers. 2021. "Psychedelics and Neuroplasticity: A Systematic Review Unraveling the Biological Underpinnings of Psychedelics." *Frontiers in Psychiatry* 12 (September): article 724606.

Wachholtz, Amy B., and Kenneth I. Pargament. 2005. "Is Spirituality a Critical Ingredient of Meditation? Comparing the Effects of Spiritual Meditation, Secular Meditation, and Relaxation on Spiritual, Psychological, Cardiac, and Pain Outcomes." *Journal of Behavioral Medicine* 28 (4): 369–84.

Wallace, B. Alan. 1989. *Choosing Reality: A Contemplative View of Physics and the Mind*. Boston, MA: Shambhala New Science Library.

———, ed. 2003. *Buddhism and Science: Breaking New Ground*. New York: Columbia University Press.

———. 2006. "Buddhism and Science." In *Oxford Handbook of Religion and Science*, ed. Philip Clayton and Zachary Simpson, 24–40. New York: Oxford University Press.

———. 2007. *Contemplative Science: Where Buddhism and Neuroscience Converge*. New York: Columbia University Press.

Wallace, B. Alan., and Brian Hodel. 2008. *Embracing Mind: The Common Ground of Science and Spirituality*. Boston, MA: Shambhala.

Walsh, Roger N. 1990. *The Spirit of Shamanism*. Los Angeles, CA: Jeremy P. Tarcher.

Wasson, R. Gordon, et al. 1986. *Persephone's Quest: Entheogens and the Origins of Religion*. New Haven, CT: Yale University Press.

Watts, Alan. 1962. *The Joyous Cosmology: Adventures in the Chemistry of Consciousness*. New York: Pantheon Books.

Watts, Rosalind, et al. 2017. "Patients' Accounts of Increased 'Connectedness' and 'Acceptance' after Psilocybin for Treatment-Resistant Depression." *Journal of Humanistic Psychology* 57 (5): 520–64.

Watts, Rosalind. 2022. "Can Magic Mushrooms Unlock Depression? What I Learned in the Five Years since TEDx Talk." *Medium* (February 28).

Weber, Renée. 1986. *Dialogues with Scientists and Sages: The Search for Unity*. New York: Routledge & Kegan Paul.

Weil, Andrew. 1986. *The Natural Mind: An Investigation of Drugs and the Higher Consciousness*. Boston: Houghton Mifflin.

Weinberg, Steven. 1977. *The First Three Minutes*. New York: Basic Books.

———. 1996. "Sokal's Hoax." *New York Review of Books* 43 (August 8): 11–15.

Weiss, Brandon. 2024. "Unique Psychological Mechanisms Underlying Psilocybin Therapy versus Escitalopram Treatment in the Treatment of Major Depressive Disorder." *International Journal of Mental Health and Addiction*. https://doi.org/10.1007/s11469-024-01253-9.

Wendt, Alexander. 2015. *Quantum Mind and Social Science: Unifying Physical and Social Ontology*. New York: Cambridge University Press.

Wilber, Ken. 1998. *The Marriage of Sense and Soul: Integrating Science and Religion*. New York: Broadway Books.

———, ed. 2000 [1984]. *Quantum Questions: Mystical Writings of the World's Great Physicists*. Rev. ed. Boulder, CO: Shambhala New Science Library.

———. 2006. Foreword to *The Experience of Meditation: Experts Introduce Major Traditions*, ed. Jonathan Sheer. New York: Paragon House.

Wildman, Wesley J. 2011. *Religious and Spiritual Experiences*. New York: Cambridge University Press.

Winkelman, Michael. 1999. "Altered States of Consciousness and Religious Behavior." In *Anthropology of Religion: A Handbook*, ed. Stephen D. Glazier, 393–428. Westport, CT: Greenwood Press.

———. 2010. *Shamanism: A Biological Paradigm of Consciousness and Healing*. 2nd ed. Santa Barbara, CA: Praeger.

———. 2013. "Shamanism and Psychedelics: A Biogenetic Structuralist Paradigm of Ecopsychology." *European Journal of Ecopsychology* 4:90–115.

———. 2014. "Evolutionary Views of Entheogenic Consciousness." In *Seeking the Sacred with Psychoactive Substances: Chemical Paths to Spirituality and to God*, ed. J. Harold Ellens, 1:341–64. Santa Barbara, CA: Praeger.

———. 2017. "The Mechanisms of Psychedelic Visionary Experiences: Hypotheses from Evolutionary Psychology." *Frontiers in Neuroscience* 11:1–17.

———. 2019. "Evidence for Entheogen Use in Prehistory and World Religions." *Journal of Psychedelic Studies* 3 (2): 43–62.
———. 2024. "Shamanism and Psychedelic, Religious, Spiritual, and Mystical Experiences." In *The Oxford Handbook of Psychedelic, Religious, Spiritual, and Mystical Experiences* (online ed.), ed. David Yaden and Michiel van Elk. Oxford: Oxford Academic, May 22, 2024. https://doi.org/10.1093/oxfordhb/9780192844064.013.37.
Winter, Ulf, et al. 2020. "Content-Free Awareness: EEG-fcMRI Correlates of Consciousness *as Such* in an Expert Meditator." *Frontiers in Psychology* 10 (February): 1–11.
Wit, Harriet de, et al. 2022. "Repeated Low Doses of LSD in Healthy Adults: A Placebo-Controlled, Dose–Response Study." *Addiction Biology* (February 10). https://doi.org/10.1111/adb.13143.
Woit, Peter. 2006. *Not Even Wrong: The Failure of String Theory and the Continuing Challenge to Unify the Laws of Physics.* London: Jonathan Cape.
Wolf, Fred Alan. 1996. *The Spiritual Universe: How Quantum Physics Proves the Existence of the Soul.* New York: Simon & Schuster.
Woods, Richard. 1996. "Mysticism and Social Action: The Mystic's Calling, Development and Social Activity." *Journal of Consciousness Studies* 3 (2): 158–71.
Woods, Toby J., Jennifer M. Windt, and Olivia Carter. 2022. "Evidence Synthesis Indicates Contentless Experiences in Meditation Are neither Truly Contentless nor Identical." *Phenomenology and the Cognitive Science.* https://doi.org/10.1007/s11097-022-09811-z.
Wu, Yanhong, Cheng Wang, Xi He, Lihua Mao, and Li Zhang. 2010. "Religious Beliefs Influence Neural Substrates of Self-Reflection in Tibetans." *Social Cognitive and Affective Neuroscience* 5:324–31.
Yaden, David B., et al. 2016. "The Language of Ineffability: Linguistic Analysis of Mystical Experiences." *Psychology of Religion and Spirituality* 8 (3): 244–52.
Yaden, David B., et al. 2017a. "The Noetic Quality: A Multimethod Exploratory Study." *Psychology of Consciousness: Theory, Research, and Practice* 4 (1): 54–62.
Yaden, David B., et al. 2017b. "The Varieties of Self-Transcendent Experience." *Review of General Psychology* 21 (2): 143–60.
Yaden, David B., et al. 2017c. "Of Roots and Fruits: A Comparison of Psychedelic and Nonpsychedelic Mystical Experiences." *Journal of Humanistic Psychology* 57 (4): 338–53.
Yaden, David B., Jonathan Iwry, and Andrew B. Newberg. 2017. "Neuroscience and Religion: Surveying the Field." In *Religion: Mental Religion*, edited by Niki Clements, 277–99. New York: Macmillan.
Yaden, David B., and Roland R. Griffiths. 2021. "The Subjective Effects of Psychedelics Are Necessary for Their Therapeutic Effects." *ACS Pharmacology & Translational Science* 4 (April): 568–72.

Yaden, David B., et al. 2021. "Psychedelics and Consciousness: Distinctions, Demarcations, and Opportunities." *International Journal of Neuropsychopharmacology* 24 (8): 615–23.

Yaden, David B., et al. 2022. "Psychedelics and Psychotherapy: Cognitive-Behavioral Approaches as Default." *Frontiers in Psychology* 13 (May 23): 873279. https://doi.org/10.3389/fpsyg.2022.873279.

Yaden, David B., et al. 2024. "Clinically Relevant Acute Subjective Effects of Psychedelics Beyond Mystical Experience." *Nature Reviews Psychology* 3 (September 3): 606-21. https://doi.org/10.1038/s44159-024-00345-6

Yaden, David B., and Andrew B. Newberg. 2022. *The Varieties of Spiritual Experiences: 21st Century Perspectives*. New York: Oxford University Press.

Yang, Larry. 2017. *Awakening Together: The Spiritual Practice of Inclusivity and Community*. Somerville, MA: Wisdom.

Yates, Gregory, and Emily Melon. 2024. "Trip-Killers: A Concerning Practice Associated with Psychedelic Drug Use." *Emergency Medicine Journal* 41 (2): 112–13. https://doi.org/10.1136/emermed-2023-213377. PMID: 38123961.

Zarrabi-Zadeh, Saeed. 2009. "Practical Mysticism: Its Definition, Parts and Characteristics." *Studies in Spirituality* 19 (December): 1–13.

Zaehner, Robert C. 1957. *Mysticism Sacred and Profane: An Inquiry into Some Varieties of Praenatural Experience*. New York: Oxford University Press.

———. 1972. *Zen, Drugs, and Mysticism*. London: Collins.

Zajonc, Arthur, ed. 2004. *The New Physics and Cosmology: Dialogues with the Dalai Lama*. New York: Oxford University Press.

Zeifman, Richard J., et al. 2023. "Co-use of MDMA with Psilocybin/LSD May Buffer against Challenging Experiences and Enhance Positive Experiences." *Scientific Reports* 13: article 13645. https://doi.org/10.1038/s41598-023-40856-5.

Zeller, Maximiliano. 2024. "Psychedelic Therapies and Belief Change: Are There Risks of Epistemic Harm or Epistemic Injustice?" *Philosophical Psychology* (June 3). DOI:10.1080/09515089.2024.2362284.

Zheng, Yuan et al. 2022. "A New Second-Generation Mindfulness-Based Intervention Focusing on Well-Being: A Randomized Control Trial of Mindfulness-Based Positive Psychology." *Journal of Happiness Studies* 23 (6): 2703–24. https://doi.org/10.1007/s10902-022-00525-2.

Zohar, Danah, and Ian Marshall. 1993. *The Quantum Society: Mind, Physics, and a New Social Vision*. London: Bloomsbury.

Zukav, Gary. 2001 [1977]. *The Dancing Wu Li Masters: An Overview of the New Physics*. New York: HarperCollins.

Index

Abhyananda, Swami, 114–15
Advaita Vedanta, 83–84, 192, 199, 204–205, 213, 229–30, 237, 247, 249, 270nn11–12, 280n17, 281n25, 284n20
Alpert, Richard (Ram Dass), 33
altered states of consciousness (ASC), ix, xv, 3, 25, 47–48, 66, 69, 118, 123, 124, 171, 193, 199, 227, 260n11, 272n2
applied mysticism, x–xiv
Aquinas, Thomas, 244
Aryadeva, 243
Atkins, Peter, 182
attribution theory, 56–59, 268n37
Augustine, 244, 250, 283n15
Ayer, A. J., 16, 162

Ballesteros, Virginia, xiii
Barrett, Frederick, 63–64
Basil of Caesarea, 237
Beauvoir, Simone de, 275n4
Benson, Herbert, 19, 173
Bergson, Henri, 62, 110, 270n13
Bernard of Clairvaux, 84, 244
Bhagavad-gita, 231, 244, 245, 249, 250, 283n6
Bhaktism, 239, 249
Bhave, Vinoba, 252

bias, cognitive, 103–16, 141, 147, 148, 152, 158, 164, 260n4
bias, confirmation, 103–105, 267n33; in mysticism, 106–110; in mystical studies, 110–15
bias, expectancy, 43, 105–106, 267n33
Blackmore, Susan, 173
Bockelson, John, 284n18
Bodhisattvas, 230, 236, 255, 282n2, 285n24
Boehme, Jakob, 270n7
Bohr, Niels, 281n28
Bowker, John, 57
Breeksema, Joost, 136–37, 141–42
Breggin, Peter, 232
Brentano, Franz, 78
Broad, C. D., 62, 269n43, 270n13
Buber, Martin, 107–108, 180
Buddha, 113, 196, 215–18, 243, 270n6, 281n27
Buddhism, 2, 11, 28, 81–82, 83, 113, 114, 123, 194, 196–97, 200–201, 202–205, 210–11, 215–18, 219–20, 230, 235–36, 239, 244, 270n8, 270n10, 277n16, 279n14, 281n27, 282n2, 282n5, 284n19, 284n24, 285n25; engaged Buddhism, 253–56, 285n26; and psychedelics, 32

Camus, Albert, 182
Capra, Fritjof, 189, 190, 192, 198, 211, 212, 214, 220, 223, 276n14, 278n10, 281n23, 282n31
Carhart-Harris, Robin, 37, 43, 58
Castaneda, Carlos, 34
Catherine of Siena, 237
Chalmers, Robert, 18
Chew, Geoffrey, 211
Chomsky, Noam, 24
Chopra, Deepak, 190, 206, 209
Christianity, 11, 34, 79, 84, 113, 121, 186, 239, 241–42, 249, 254, 275n1, 283nn10–11, 283n15; and psychedelics, 33
Chrysostom, John, 237
Coleridge, Samuel Taylor, 263n8
complementarity, 220–22
concentrative meditation, 2, 3, 8, 10, 11, 111, 121, 168, 173, 218, 279n15; *samadhi*, 3, 111, 279n15
consciousness, xiv, 261n12; and the phenomenal realm, 204–205; "Mind at large," 62, 170, 264n15, 270n13; "pure consciousness," 3, 6, 20–24, 69–75, 144, 156, 192, 194, 200, 262n17, 269n5, 270n6; and neuroscience, 23–25, 75–77
constructivism, 12, 20–23, 50, 72–73, 74, 86, 105, 112, 149, 179–81, 268n37
contemplation, 186, 197, 217, 219, 220, 235, 237, 252–53, 283n11; contemplative studies, xi. *Also see* meditation

Dalai Lama, 6, 216, 202, 216, 225, 247
Daoism, xii, xv, 194, 197, 236, 245. *Also see* Laozi and Zhuangzi
D'Aquili, Eugene, 4, 8–10, 81, 121–23, 261n16

Darwin, Charles, 173
Davy, Humphrey, 263n8
Day, Dorothy, 237
Dennett, Daniel, 80, 87, 165, 260n7
depth-mystical experience, 20, 21, 22, 30, 49, 62, 70, 77, 78, 82, 94, 106, 113, 162, 176, 200, 229, 269n45
Diem, Andrea, 212
Doblin, Rick, xii
Dostoevsky, Fyodor, 232
Dyson, Freeman, 183

Eckhart, Meister, xi, 50, 107, 113, 228, 243, 280n16, 283n11
Einstein, Albert, 202, 279n11
Eisner, Bruce, 294n13
Ellens, J. Harold, 45, 95
emptiness (*shunyata*), 202–204
enlightenment, x, 7, 9, 41, 44–45, 66, 76, 94, 113, 114, 215, 227, 228, 229, 231, 234, 236, 237, 244, 250, 261n14, 269n4, 270n6
entheogen, 30, 50, 63, 186
Evans, Donald, 86

Faggin, Federico, 281n26
fatalism, 274n14
Flanagan, Owen, 182
Forman, Robert, 20, 73, 79
Fort, Andrew, 229–30
Fox, George, 245
Fox, Matthew, 285n26
Freud, Sigmund, 144, 263n8

Gan, Peter, 232
Gandhi, Mohandas, 248–53, 256, 284nn22–23
Gaskin, Stephen, 264n12
Gennaro, Rocco, 71
Ghosh, J. C., 283n14
Gilovich, Thomas, 104
Girn, Manesh, 41

Goswami, Amit, 204, 206
Greek mysticism, 32–33, 285n29
Greif, Adam, 152
Griffiths, Roland, 43, 63–64, 106, 134
Grof, Stanislav, 47, 119–20, 137
Grosso, Michael, 9

Hadot, Pierre, 163
Halbfass, Wilhelm, 215–16
Hammarskjöld, Dag, 247
Harner, Michael, 34
Harris, Sam, 173
Hawking, Stephen, 159, 190, 280n21
Hay, David, 186, 275n3
Heffter, Arthur, 35
Herschel, Abraham, 238
Hick, John, 246
Hinduism, 84, 111, 114, 160, 194, 213, 235, 244, 249, 252, 262n16; and psychedelics, 32. *Also see* Advaita Vedanta, Samkhya, and the Yoga school
Hood, Ralph, Jr., 21, 23, 264n16, 265n23
Houston, Jean, 33, 36
Hume, David, 80
Huxley, Aldous, x–xi, 30, 33, 34, 36, 62, 108–109, 185, 264n11, 269n45, 270n13

illusion, mystical, 18, 50, 85, 165, 205, 208, 209, 213–14, 229
ineffability, 80, 144, 265n16, 274n12
Inge, William, 257, 285n29
intentionality, 22, 69, 78, 83, 85, 86, 87, 163; and mystical experiences, 78–81
inverse multiple realization, 13–14, 19, 117–26, 274n7
Islam, 84, 112, 244, 284n17; and psychedelics, 33
Ives, Christopher, 285n27

Jager, Willigis, 186
Jainism, 49, 160, 244, 249, 250, 262n16
James, William, 12, 35–36, 42, 62, 89, 177, 270n13
Johnson, Matthew, 155
Jones, Ken, 254
Jones, Rufus, 237
Josephson, Brian, 190
Judaism, 33, 186, 238
Jylkkä, Jussi, 154

Kabat-Zinn, Jon, 173
karma and justice, 235
Katz, Steven, 20, 21, 72–73, 112, 180
Kelly, Edward, 9
Khomeini, Ayatollah, 247
King, Martin Luther, Jr., 252
Kipnis, Andrew, 284n21
Koestler, Arthur, 61, 268n41
Kornfield, Jack, 34
Krishnamurti, Jiddu, 232, 233, 277n24

Lancaster, Brian, 9–10, 24–25
Laozi, 230, 231, 234, 236, 244. *Also see* Daoism
Laszlo, Ervin, 200
Leary, Timothy, xi, 33, 34, 42, 47, 120, 264n9
Lee, Bruce, 10
Letheby, Chris, 84, 132, 135, 154, 156
Lewis, James, 212
Lightman, Alan, 153, 163
Litwin, G. H., 42

Madhva, 107
Madhyamaka, 202–204
Mansfield, Victor, 202–203, 211
Manson, Charles, 296n10
Marshall, Ian, 280n16

Masters, Robert, 33, 36
materialism. *See* physicalism
McFarlane, Thomas, 210
McGinn, Bernard, xviii, 79
McKenna, Terence, 31, 34
McTaggart, John, 162–63
meditation, x, xi–xii, 1–6, 8–9, 10–13, 15–17, 18–19, 26, 27, 40–41, 45, 73, 75, 92, 119, 121–24, 140, 167–69, 173–75, 186, 216–17, 217–20, 234, 247, 269n3, 276n12, 277n16; two tracks, 2–3; negative effects, 38; and inverse multiple realization, 121–24; and scientific method, 217, 218–20
Merton, Thomas, 186, 237
Metzner. Ralph, 33, 42
Metzinger, Thomas, 81
Milarepa, 235
Millière, Raphaël, 81
mindfulness, xii, xiii, 1–3, 8, 83, 145, 164, 173–74, 205, 218, 269n5; practices today, 186–87, 277n16; and psychedelics, 94, 145; and politics, 234, 247–48
morality, mysticism and, xii, xiii, 62, 167, 173, 227, 229–30, 232, 233, 235, 237, 243, 246, 248, 253, 244, 248, 259n1, 268n42, 282n1, 284n28; and secular mysticism, 172–73; and psychedelics, 285n28
Mosurinjohn, Sharday, 41
Müntzer, Thomas, 284n18
Muste, A. J., 237
Myers, F. W. H., 62, 270n13
mystical experience, ix, 30, 161–62, 263n2, 263n4; extrovertive, ix; introvertive, ix; depth-mystical experience, and neuroscience, 7–8, 8–10, 10–13; spontaneous, 95–96, 262n1, 274n10, 277n18; and the dispute in psychotherapy, 127–58; the term "mystical experience," 145, 146–49; contribution to science, 155–57; potential negative effect on religious belief, 163; and transcendent realities, 177–79
mystical liberation (*moksha, nirvana*), mystical, 168, 233, 236, 249, 249, 252, 253, 254, 255, 256
mystical state of consciousness, ix–x
mysticism, x, 161–62, 278n6; future, 184–87, 276n10; and science, 189–225, 259n2

Nagarjuna, 200, 203–204, 281n27
Nagel, Thomas, 70
naturalism and naturalists, 22, 74, 151–55, 160–66; and spirituality, 166–67, 181–84; mysticism and naturalists' beliefs, 169–75; religious naturalists, 167, 275n15; naturalistic beliefs in psychotherapy, 151–55
Needham, Joseph, 278n6
Nehru, Jawaharlal, 251
Neoplatonism, 27, 197, 113, 160, 178n4, 281n26. *Also see* Plotinus
neo-Nazis, 127, 234, 247
neo-Vedanta, 189, 247
neuroscience, xiv, 4–5, 7, 22; study of experiences, 13–18; and mystical experiences, 18–19, 27–28, 167–69; and philosophy, 25–26; and psychedelics, 36–38
New Age, xi, xii, xv, 34, 159, 189–90, 191, 193, 194, 195, 196, 198, 199, 202, 204, 205–206, 208, 209–10, 212, 213, 214, 215, 216, 217, 220, 222, 223, 224–25, 259n1, 276n14, 277n1, 278n4, 278n6, 278n8, 279n15, 280n21, 281n23, 283n12. *Also see* parallelism

Newberg, Andrew, 4, 7, 8, 10, 13, 81, 121–23, 261n16, 266n25
Nhat Hanh, Thich, 254, 285n26
Nickerson, Raymond, 116
Nietzsche, Friedrich, 162
nonconstructivism, 21–22, 24, 73, 76, 122, 124, 180, 277n21
nonduality (experienced sense and ontological), ix, 3, 21, 50, 70, 75–76, 79, 86, 107, 118, 149, 224, 263n6, 267n36, 282n1

Olson, David, 130, 132, 133
oneness (experienced sense and ontological), 2, 45, 153, 172, 178, 191, 192, 194, 199, 214, 222, 260n11, 270n12, 272n2, 282n1. *Also see* nondualism
Ornstein, Robert, 17
Orwell, George, 268n41
Osmond, Humphrey, 30, 108

Pahnke, Walter, 36, 38, 40, 264n16
pantheism and panentheism, 50, 170, 267n31
Papanicolaou, Andrew, 7, 260n5, 279n12
parallelism, 191–93, 195–96, 198–99, 206, 207–208, 209, 211, 212, 213, 222, 223, 279n13
paranormal phenomena and powers, 161, 212, 282n2
Parfit, Derek, 80
Peguy, Charles, 237
Penner, Hans, 73
perennial philosophy, xvi, xxi–xxiii, 41–42, 108, 110, 112, 114–15, 148, 227, 272n6
Persinger, Michael, 91
philosopher's syndrome, 87

physicalism (materialism), 3, 16, 27, 61, 100, 117–18, 124–25, 135–36, 150, 156, 160, 171, 172, 264n9, 269n44, 271n4, 272n5
placebo, 46, 47–48, 95, 105, 120, 134, 139, 140, 162, 266n26, 276n12
Planck, Max, 278n3
Plotinus, 234–35, 281n26, 285n27
Pollan, Michael, xi, 128, 163
Proudfoot, Wayne, 57, 268n38
psychedelic drugs, 29–68, 90, 94–95; history of religious use, 31–35; negative effects, 38–40, 130–31, 273n2; and mystical experiences, 48–56, 137–41; and the validity of mystical claims, 59–63; and inverse multiple realization, 119–20
psychedelic experiences, not necessarily mystical, 54–55, 248, 264nn13–14; and metaphysical belief, 61, 149–51

quantum mysticism, 189–225
quantum realm, 205–209
Queen, Christopher, 254

Rahner, Karl, 186, 277n23
Rahula, Walpola, 196
Ramakrishna, 247
Ramanuja, 107
Ratanakul, Pinit, 216
reductionism, 14, 15, 27, 172, 190, 193, 206, 208, 209, 259n1, 271n4, 278n7, 280n19
religious studies, 267n36, 276n7
Restivo, Sal, 190
Richards, William, xiii, 45, 50, 94–95, 175
Ritchie, Sarah Lane, 170
Roberts, Thomas Roberts, 65
Roseman, Leor, 41

Ruskin, John, 249
Russell, Bertrand, 153, 162, 174
Ruusbroec, Jan van, 237

Sagan, Carl, 159, 160
Samkhya, 49, 160, 213, 219, 262n16, 270n11
Sartre, Jean Paul, 275n4
satyagraha (Gandhi's "grasping hold of truth/reality"), 250–51, 253, 256
science and mysticism, 189–225; reconciliation, 222–25
scientific study of mysticism. *See* neuroscience
Sebastián, Miguel Ángel, 111
secular mysticism, 159–87, 275n1, 275n6
self, loss of sense of, 2, 3, 9, 15, 50, 66, 71, 80–86, 87, 99, 111, 118, 127, 128, 131, 140, 142–45, 150, 156, 161, 162, 165, 166, 172, 198, 230, 241, 255n1, 265n18, 268n36
Searle, John, 78, 86
set and setting, 33–34, 42–45, 47, 48, 52, 56, 63, 65, 91, 92, 96, 97, 105–106, 120, 123, 139, 147, 151, 260n9, 266n24, 274n8
shamanism, 31–32, 264n14, 275n16
Shankara, 106–107, 205, 213–24, 271n1
Shipley, Morgan, 108–109
Sikhism, 239
Sloan, Richard, 6, 10, 19
Smith, Huston, 29, 34, 38–39, 47, 52, 63, 65–67, 110, 113, 119, 269n45, 272n3
social action, 227–58; individualistic orientation, 228–34, 257–58; mystics' social action, 234–40; politics, 240–42
Stace, Walter, 42, 52, 144, 264n16

Steinhart, Eric, 167
Sufism. *See* Islam
Sullivan, Philip, 22–23, 74
Šurkala, Martin, 152
Suzuki, D. T., 211, 236, 283n9

Tantrism, 32
Tart, Charles, 46, 118
Teresa, Mother Mary, 249
Thoreau, Henry David, 249
Thurman, Howard, 237
Tolstoy, Leo, 249
triggers of mystical experiences, 45–48, 89–101, 266n28, 267n34; natural and transcendent, 96–98
Tutu, Desmond, 237

Underhill, Evelyn, 284n16
Upanishads, 107, 213–14

van Elk, Michiel, 115, 136–37, 141–42
Vaughan, Frances, 112
visions, 1, 30, 31–32, 34, 45, 46, 47–48, 53, 61, 63, 79, 91, 93, 94, 100, 105, 113, 137, 138, 143–44, 157, 168, 260n11, 263n6, 267n35, 268n36
Vivekananda, 247

Waldman, Mark, 114
Wallace, B. Alan, 207, 217, 219
Walsh, Roger, 50, 94
Wasson, R. Gordon, 264n10
Watts, Alan, 33, 39
Watts, Rosalind, 132
Weber, Max, 283n7
Weinberg, Steven, 182, 183
Wendt, Alexander, xiii
Wigner, Wugene, 214
Wilber, Ken, 206, 220, 223

Wildman, Wesley, 167

Yaden, David Bryce, 115, 134–35, 155–56
yoga, 173, 250, 252–53
Yoga school, 49, 160, 213
Yogi, Maharishi Mahesh, 277n24

Zaehner, R. C., 52
Zen Buddhism, 186, 236, 253, 254, 285nn26–27
Zhuangzi, 197
Zohar, Dinah, 280n16
Zukav, Gary, 189, 209–10, 223, 281n23

www.ingramcontent.com/pod-product-compliance
Ingram Content Group UK Ltd.
Pitfield, Milton Keynes, MK11 3LW, UK
UKHW040651090325
456023UK00005B/36